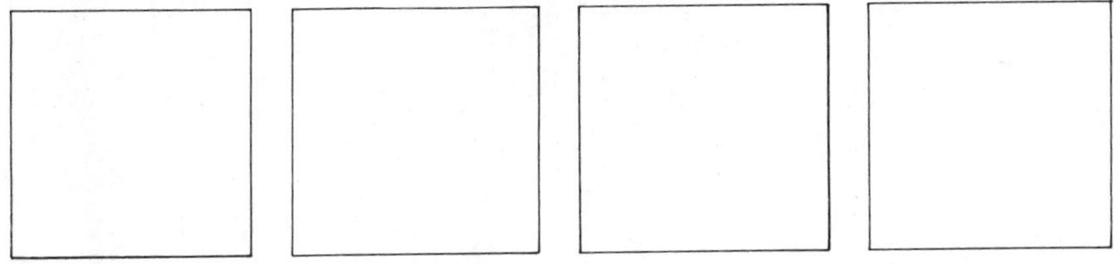

Basic Statistics for Social Research

Second Edition

DEAN J. CHAMPION
Department of Sociology / University of Tennessee

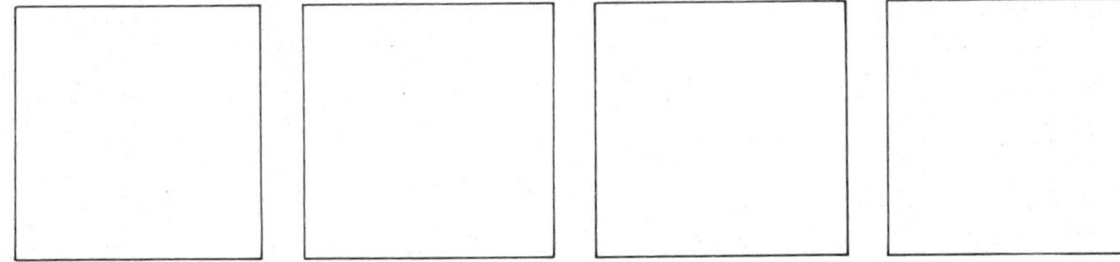

MACMILLAN PUBLISHING CO., INC.
New York

COLLIER MACMILLAN PUBLISHERS
London

TO LYNN

Printed in the United States of America.

Macmillan Publishing Co., Inc.
866 Third Avenue, New York, New York 10022

Collier Macmillan Canada, Ltd.

Library of Congress Cataloging in Publication Data

Champion, Dean J
Basic statistics for social research.

Includes bibliographical references and indexes.
1. Social sciences–Statistical methods.
2. Sociology–Statistical methods. 3. Statistics.
I. Title.
HA29.C5414 1981 300'.72 80-17875
ISBN 0-02-320600-4

Printing: 1 2 3 4 5 6 7 8 Year: 1 2 3 4 5 6 7 8

Preface

A statistics book can be a valuable reference source for both the social researcher and the more-than-casual student of social phenomena. The value of the book will depend upon a number of things. First, the book should be fairly broad in its coverage of statistical tests and techniques. This by no means implies that the text must be encyclopedic in scope. Rather, it is important that the most frequently used tests be included.

Second, the text should be reasonably simple. Formulas and symbolic expressions should be rendered in simple forms to permit the widest possible usage for a variety of readers with different levels of statistical sophistication.

Third, examples should be used that reflect proper applications of the tests discussed. The more realistic the examples, the better. The frequent use of tabular presentations accompanying the examples, together with step-by-step procedures for utilizing the tests, combine to heighten the relevance of the book for those engaged in social research.

Fourth, informative rationales for test selections and preferences should be provided. A person will want to know *why* a particular test is used in one situation but not in another. Also, one may wish to determine which tests are best for certain applications when several tests seem suitable.

The first edition of this book attempted to meet these criteria. The present edition seeks the same objectives; for, in spite of the fact that our social science fields have been growing in popularity and sophistication, there continues to exist the need for a simplified presentation of subject matter, particularly in the area of social statistics. Also, new developments have occurred, stimulated in part by our increasing use of, and reliance upon, computer systems for social data analyses and problem-solving activities. These developments have often been new statistical tests or new and unusual applications of some of the older tests with which we are familiar.

Improvements that have been incorporated into this edition include more-extensive discussions of statistical tests, and their assumptions, weaknesses, and strengths relative to one another. Also, greater stress has been placed on the interpretation of statistical test results in conjunction with one's research.

Another positive feature is the expanded exercise sections at the ends of chapters, which will provide students with a greater opportunity to work problems in preparation for statistics examinations and to increase their ability to work through statistical formulas with confidence.

A more-detailed discussion of the logic of hypothesis testing in social research is included to illustrate more clearly the interplay between statistics and research methodology. It is hoped that this will provide students with a more informed perspective concerning the exact role of statistics in social problem-solving endeavors.

For persons with more professional research interests, this book continues to function as a potential sourcebook and guide. The statistical tables in the appendix are accompanied by step-by-step instructions for using them and interpreting observed values meaningfully. This is also a new feature of the present edition.

It should be noted that statistics are not ends themselves but rather means toward ends. In the traditional view of the research process as a chain of events leading from the definition of a researchable problem to a potential working solution for it, statistics are only one link in the chain. Also, statistics are *never* the most important link, contrary to the thinking of some researchers who try to prove everything with numbers. Statistical tests and measures continue to function *purely as aids* rather than as substitutes for sound theorizing and good thinking. They serve primarily a *supporting role* in our quest for establishing facts about things of interest to us. This theme will be repeated at appropriate places in the book as a reminder to the reader that there are equally and more important activities in the process of social research beside the quantitative manipulation of data.

I am grateful to the Literary Executor of the late Sir Ronald A. Fisher, F.R.S., to Dr. Frank Yates, F.R.S., and to Longman Group Ltd., London, for permission to reprint Tables III, IV, and V from their book *Statistical Tables for Biological, Agricultural and Medical Research* (6th edition, 1974).

D. J. C.
Knoxville, Tennessee

Contents

1

2

NOMINAL TESTS OF SIGNIFICANCE 220

ORDINAL-LEVEL TESTS OF SIGNIFICANCE 258

11

MEASURES OF ASSOCIATION FOR TWO VARIABLES 300

12

k-VARIABLE MEASURES OF ASSOCIATION 362

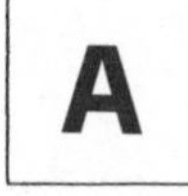

APPENDIX
TABLES 379

An Introduction to Social Statistics

The Food and Drug Administration of the United States frequently acts to limit the distribution and sale of particular products to the general public. The FDA recommendations influence our economy in significant ways, and there are numerous implications of their decisions for our personal health, public policies, and general quality of life. FDA reports and recommendations almost always contain supportive information in the form of statistical findings. Statistical results of one scientific investigation or another are responsible for much FDA decision-making action.

In the political arena, city, state, and federal elections are prefaced by claims and counterclaims by political opponents. An incumbent mayor might state that during the previous 4 years, the city's crime rate decreased by 12 percent. The impression that the mayor is responsible for the reduction might well be challenged by an opponent, who will cite statistics to show that crime in the city actually increased by 20 percent. A dispute follows, in which both candidates' statistical information is closely scrutinized by campaign committee members. The result is often greater confusion among an already confused and somewhat gullible public.

In these two examples, statistics have performed a key role in influencing social policies and consumer's product alternatives, and influencing public voting patterns in political elections. The fact is that statistics are a vital part of our daily lives. In a world that is becoming increasingly technical, mechanical, and socially and psychologically complex, we are turning more and more to statistics and statistical information in our planning and decision-making activities. In order to cope more successfully with contemporary society, it is increasingly necessary for us to have a solid grasp of what statistics are and what they can do. By the same token, it is important to recognize what they *cannot* do.

Statistics can be defined as the general body of methods and procedures used to assemble, describe, and infer something from numerical data. In the context of this book, *numerical data* refer to any information we might collect about people and their characteristics (e.g., race, sex, religion, attitudinal traits and patterns, social class).

Data collected by the FDA might include figures showing the incidence of cancerous tissue among persons consuming products containing suspect chemicals or substances. Data collected by politicians might reflect the number of burglaries, robberies, or rapes in a given city over a designated period of time, or perhaps a city's financial indebtedness.

The examination of these data by persons skilled in data analysis and interpretation will yield statistical information or statistical results that can be presented to others for their consideration and/or action. All of us are consumers of statistical information of one sort or another.[1] Some of us are also generators of statistical information, by doing research or conducting scientific investigations. It makes sense to develop some degree of familiarity with a subject that affects us in so many ways.

This book has been prepared to meet certain needs of persons desiring to learn what statistics are and how they can be used in a variety of ways for decision-making purposes. The intended audience is the student of social science and the beginning social researcher.

The primary assumptions made about your background as a reader are that (1) you can add, subtract, multiply, and divide; and (2) you want to learn about and understand a variety of statistical procedures that will be useful to you in your professional reading and research

[1] A monthly publication familiar to many of us, *The Reader's Digest*, requires a limited amount of statistical literacy if the reader is to derive full value from some of the articles.

work. A table of squares and square roots is available for your use in Table A.1, Appendix A.

Some of the things this book attempts to do are

1. To familiarize the student with the role statistics plays in the overall social research picture.
2. To present an array of descriptive procedures for portraying statistical information in graphic form (this will not be comhensive, although some of the more popular or representative graphic techniques will be described and discussed).
3. To give the reader a variety of tests and procedures that can be useful in data analysis and subsequent hypothesis-testing and decision-making activity.
4. To provide real examples of how these tests can be applied, their major weaknesses and strengths, and crucial assumptions underlying their legitimate application.
5. To create an awareness of qualitative differences in collectible data that will influence, if not determine, the choice of statistical test or procedure a researcher might use in a given instance.
6. To provide the reader with a set of easy-to-use tables to aid in statistical interpretations.
7. To present problems to be solved, to encourage a degree of statistical independence and confidence (answers to all mathematical exercises are found in Appendix B).
8. To give the reader a basic foundation for pursuing more elaborate and advanced statistical methods later.

Among the things this book will *not* do are

1. To present and discuss the theoretical derivation of statistical formulas.
2. To present procedures requiring more than simple arithmetic skills.

It is important to note here that not everyone agrees about how much statistical sophistication one should acquire before attempting to engage in data analysis and interpretation and statistical decision making. Some persons feel that a sound, in-depth understanding of the *theory* underlying statistical tests and their application is vital before embarking on a course of social research. Others feel that it is primarily necessary to have a working familiarity with various tests and procedures, to know how to apply them properly, and perhaps most important, to know when not to apply them. Needless to say, those stressing a theoretical understanding of statistics expose students to complex statistical formulas and emphasize how these formulas are mathematically derived. It is not unusual to expect that students will have elementary and advanced calculus as prerequisites.

Those stressing *application* are sometimes said to have a "cookbook" orientation. Given the fact that many social science students are attracted to social science because they believe it to be less technical and mathematical than subjects such as chemistry or physics, it is not unusual to find entering students in social science programs who have severely limited statistics and mathematics background.

This book is directed to students with limited mathematical experience. It has been intentionally simplified in order to maximize the reader's understanding of what is being done and why. For instance, if 15 different mathematical formulas exist for computing standard deviation (a measure of variability discussed in Chapter 5), the simplest one has been selected to present here.

Also, simplicity has been incorporated into this book's *notation system*, the symbols that stand for various procedures and measures. Unnecessary or superfluous subscripts and other notation have been deleted wherever possible. For instance, if we wanted to write a symbolic expression for summing an array of 10 test scores for a sociology class, we could write this expression as

$$\sum_{i=1}^{N=10} X_i.$$

The subscript i refers to any particular score, such as the first score, the second score, and so on. Under the summation sign, $\sum$, is found "$i = 1$." This instructs you to start summing the scores beginning with the first score, X_1. Above the summation sign is found "$N = 10$," which instructs you to sum all 10 scores (i.e., $X_1 + X_2 + X_3 + X_4 + X_5 + X_6 + X_7 + X_8 + X_9 + X_{10}$). In certain instances a researcher will want to sum the last five scores only, or the first five scores only, or the middle six scores, or some other arrangement. But most of the time in social research work, an investigator will want to sum all the scores, so this notation that instructs us to sum all scores (N) beginning with the first score ($i = 1$) may be conveniently deleted. Although generally used to provide the full, formal symbolic expression, in this text we regard this notation as assumed or understood, and write the expression "sum all of the scores" simply as

$$\sum X_i.$$

This modest change vastly alters our initial impression of the formula. The simpler form makes the notation significantly less "threatening" to students with limited statistics backgrounds. Few persons will disagree that many beginning students are frightened away from statistics courses because of the appearance of certain formulas and the complexity associated with statistical procedures.

Notation systems vary from book to book. It may come as a surprise to some readers to learn that there is no single notation system common to all statistics books. The system used in any book is that preferred by the author, who believes that it expresses statistical information in what he or she regards as a clear and usable format. It is necessary only that the author clearly define every symbol used, and that procedure will be followed in this book.

Finally, it should be understood that although the external appearance of a particular formula may be different from that encountered in other books, the results will always be identical regardless of the form in which the formula has been cast. This is why it is possible for a researcher to select a more familiar or easy-to-use formula for a given test or procedure with no harm to the final outcome.

□ SOME OBJECTS OF INQUIRY IN SOCIAL RESEARCH

Earlier it was noted that social scientists are interested in the collection and analysis of data or information expressed in a quantified form. Psychological and/or social information is frequently collected through interviewing, through the administration of questionnaires, or through observation. This information is transformed into numerical quantities in order to simplify the tabulation and subsequent statistical analysis of the data. The process whereby personal and social information is transformed into numerical values is called *coding.*

Various bits and pieces of information are assigned numerical values. For instance, we might assign a 1 to the category "male" and a 2 to the category "female." A 1 is then said to *stand for* "male" and a 2 is *to stand for* "female." Coding, the assignment of numbers to data collected, makes it possible for us to feed large quantities of data into computer systems and obtain printouts of the information within a matter of seconds. Coding not only saves the researcher a lot of time and energy, but it also makes possible the application of a wide variety of statistical tests and procedures which help to answer questions about the numerical data that have been collected.

Indeed, there are computer programs specifically designed to electronically analyze data that researchers have collected in ways that are consistent with social scientific principles.[2] Many of the tests discussed in later chapters are an integral part of these computer programs which are at the social investigator's disposal.

[2] One of the more popular programs or packages is the SPSS, or Statistical Package for the Social Sciences. See Norman H. Nie, C. H. Hull, J. G. Jenkins, K. Steinbrenner, and D. Bent, *Statistical Package for the Social Sciences*, 2nd ed. (New York: McGraw-Hill Book Company, 1975), for a comprehensive description of this program.

Social scientists are interested in both individual and social variables. *Variables* are defined as quantities that can assume more than one value (e.g., "sex" is a variable because more than one "value" is possible—male and female). Individual or psychological variables might encompass such phenomena as attitudes of all kinds (e.g., anxiety, depression, sociability, sensitivity, aloofness, or prejudice). Age, height, weight, race, ethnic background, and years of education are additional variables that assist us in describing individuals and their characteristics. Such phenomena as social class or socioeconomic status, group solidarity or cohesiveness, group size and social structure, and supervisor–subordinate behaviors are also included within the category of social variables.

Variables may be labeled in different ways. For example, one distinction that can be made is between discrete and continuous variables. *Discrete variables* are those which have a set of fixed values. Sex is a discrete variable (as conventionally treated in social science literature) because the subcategories male and female are fixed. For research purposes, there is no such thing as $\frac{1}{4}$ male or $\frac{1}{2}$ female. Religion, race, and political affiliation are examples of other discrete variables. Catholic, Protestant, and Jewish are three finite religious distinctions that can be made. Democrat, Republican, and American Independent are three finite political subcategories of the variable "political affiliation."

Continuous variables are those which can theoretically assume an unlimited number of values. Such variables as age and income are continuous because they can be infinitely divided. Age can be divided into weeks, months, years, minutes, seconds, microseconds, and so on. Similar subdivisions of income are also possible. It will be seen later that certain statistical tests make assumptions about the variables they are analyzing. These assumptions will be discussed thoroughly in conjunction with each of the statistical tests presented.[3]

Variables may also be distinguished from one another in terms of independent and dependent. *Independent variables* are those which effect or elicit changes in other variables. *Dependent variables* are those whose values change in response to changes in other variables. Consider the following "chain reaction" between variables in the work setting:

supervisory style → job satisfaction → productivity

[3] Some statistical tests require that the variables be continuous, although the actual application of the test is to tables where the data have been rendered into a set of discrete categories. For example, "income" might be subdivided into high, medium, and low—discrete classifications of a continuous variable.

We might argue theoretically that the type of supervision a worker receives will influence the worker's satisfaction with the job, which, in turn, influences the worker's rate of output or productivity. "Supervision" is depicted here as an independent variable contributing to or causing changes in the job satisfaction of workers. "Job satisfaction" in relation to supervision would be a dependent variable. "Productivity" is also a dependent variable in relation to job satisfaction. This relation follows the idea that a happy or contented employee is a more productive employee.

Observe that job satisfaction actually performs a dual role here. It is viewed as both dependent and independent (i.e., job satisfaction is independent in relation to productivity, but job satisfaction is dependent upon or in relation to supervision). Investigators usually designate in advance of their research studies how particular variables will be used and subsequently analyzed statistically. Some researchers want to examine those factors that may influence the job satisfaction of employees. Other researchers might be concerned with examining the implications of changes in job satisfaction for other variables, such as work group cohesion, productivity, job security, and employee morale.

Therefore, the specific focus of a research project will determine which variables are independent and which are dependent. Such distinctions between variables will make a difference regarding how these variables are placed in tables for various kinds of analyses. Chapters 8 through 12 present many variables in a wide assortment of tables designed for particular statistical analyses.

□ WHAT ARE STATISTICAL TECHNIQUES?

Statistical techniques encompass all the methods used to assemble, describe, and infer something from numerical data. Basically, these techniques enable the researcher to do two important things:

1. Describe information collected.
2. Infer something about a particular population based on information taken from a sample drawn from that population.

Descriptive statistical information includes graphic charts and illustrations of various kinds (see Chapter 3). Also included are statistical measures that depict qualitative and quantitative characteristics of samples in terms of their central tendency (see Chapter 4) and dispersion or variability (see Chapter 5).

The descriptive function performed by statistics is sometimes played down by researchers as not being particularly important. In fact, just the opposite is true. The old saying that a picture is worth a thousand words is apt when it pertains to descriptive statistics. Some researchers fail to spend sufficient time looking at the data they have collected and appreciating certain qualitative characteristics of it. The insights we gain from more intensive examinations of the descriptive information we have collected are often helpful in shaping and modifying existing theoretical schemes of social behavior. Also, we might be directed toward considering certain alternative statistical tests for subsequent data analysis in preference to other tests selected before we had looked more closely at the data.

Statistical inference is the name given to the process whereby statistical tests and measures, when applied to samples of persons, permit us to make generalizations about larger populations from which those samples have been drawn. (See Chapter 7 for a more extensive treatment of statistical inference.)

Social researchers seek information about *populations* of persons or *elements.*[4] The characteristics of populations or elements are called *parameters.* One way of obtaining information about the entire population and its parameters or characteristics is to study the population in its entirety. But the cost in time and money would be prohibitive, especially if the population were quite large (e.g., the population of the city of Chicago). Instead of studying entire populations, researchers draw samples of elements from them. A *sample* is defined as any smaller collection of elements taken from a larger population of those elements. Sample characteristics are called *statistics* (this is an additional, separate meaning of the term apart from the meaning "a collection of tests and techniques").

Over the years, researchers have found that an examination of sample statistics (characteristics of samples) will permit the investigator to make inferences about the true value of population parameters (characteristics of populations). This statement holds to the extent that the sample studied bears a close resemblance to or is said to be *representative* of the population from which it was drawn. For instance, if a population consists of 40 percent male, 60 percent female, the sample should resemble this proportionate distribution of sex to a high degree. This is also true of other characteristics deemed to be important, such as the population ethnic composition, religious preference, socioeconomic status, and educational level.

Therefore, if a sample is representative of the population from which it was drawn, then statements that are true of the sample are

[4] The term *element* is used throughout this book to refer to people or things, and it is consistent with accepted or conventional statistical discussions of the composition of populations.

also probably true about the population. Unfortunately, not all samples are representative of the populations from which they are drawn. It is soon discovered that it is possible to select samples from populations in many different ways. Some ways are superior to others, in that the samples subsequently selected are more likely to be representative of their populations. (In Chapter 2, various sampling techniques will be presented which influence favorably the representativeness of the samples that we desire to have in our statistical inferential work.)

For the time being, it is only important to note that *it is not necessary to study entire populations to gather information about them.* Samples taken from populations are satisfactorily used for making inferences about population characteristics or parameters. We may say that sample statistics are our educated guesses or estimates of their population parameter counterparts. A sample "average age" value (a statistic) is our *estimate* of the population average age (parameter). Table 1.1 illustrates the relation and distinction between population parameters and sample statistics.

Throughout the book, sample statistics and population parameters are distinguished by various *statistical symbols.* Sample statistics conventionally are represented by Roman (English alphabet) letters (e.g., X, s, t, etc.). Population parameters are represented by lowercase Greek letters (e.g., μ, σ, α, τ, λ, ω, etc.).

Statistical techniques should not be confused with statistics as sample characteristics. Social researchers usually refer to statistical methods or tests as "statistics," and as a result, it is sometimes not easy for the beginning student to distinguish between the terms and their particular referents. We use such terms as *statistical tests* or *procedures* or *methods* when discussing techniques to assist beginning students in their understanding of subsequent discussions.

Statistical tests and procedures may be regarded as *strategies* to apply in certain problem-solving situations. This book might be viewed as a compilation of strategies designed to answer particular

TABLE 1.1
Distinction Between a Population and a Sample.

Population (100%)	*Sample* (20%)
All Lion's Club members in the United States	Some Lion's Club members in the United States
Some Characteristics of Elements	
The percentage of men over age 50 in the Lion's Clubs in the United States	The percentage of men over age 50 in the sample of Lion's Clubs in the United States

kinds of social research questions or implemented to describe clearly social and/or psychological information that has been collected and coded. It is not a comprehensive compilation, however. An effort has been made to include those kinds of procedures that are most frequently and typically employed in data analysis and decision-making situations in social research.

Certainly, it will be in the researcher's best interest to learn about as many statistical strategies as possible. This will provide a greater degree of flexibility later when choosing between descriptive and inferential statistical procedures. Statistical consultants are equipped with numerous strategies which they can recommend to customers of their consulting services. The better prepared and informed the consultant, usually the better the advice received by the client.[5] The same thing can be said about the student of social science who is planning to conduct social research.

In all discussions of statistical procedures to follow (both descriptive and inferential), only *samples of elements* will be discussed and described. Statistical techniques will be described in terms of how they can be applied to samples, not populations. In short, we are making the assumption that the researcher is going to select a sample from a population and study it. Naturally, questions will arise about what the researcher can do with or say about the sample in relation to the parent population. The tests contained in later chapters are various strategies that can be employed to answer certain research questions raised by the investigator about the sample to be studied.

□ THEORY AND METHODS IN SOCIAL RESEARCH: THE PLACE OF STATISTICS

In any scientific field, including the social sciences, an integral feature of research activity is the construction of theory and sound theoretical schemes. *Theoretical schemes* are arrangements of assumptions and propositions that predict and explain relationships between variables. For instance, suppose that we wanted to study some potential causes of juvenile delinquency by examining a sample of juvenile delinquents from the local community. First, we would construct a theoretical scheme (the purpose being that of relating juvenile delinquency to one or more other variables). The theoretical scheme will perform an important function for us. It will predict and explain *how* juvenile delinquency is conceivably a prod-

[5] Such a strategies orientation might help the reader to better understand the role of statistical tests and techniques in social research problem solving.

uct of some other variable or variables that we believe to be causes of delinquency. If we believe that boys from broken homes (through desertion or divorce) are more likely to be delinquent compared with boys from more stable home environments, then the variable "broken home/stable or unbroken home" becomes a potential explanatory factor or precondition of delinquency.

We are led to examine a sample of boys who are delinquent and to compare them with a sample of nondelinquents. Ideally (according to our theoretical scheme), all the delinquents will come from broken homes, whereas nondelinquents will come from homes not broken by desertion or divorce. In reality, some delinquents will come from broken homes and some will not. Also, some nondelinquents will come from stable homes and some will not. We will place our data collected from delinquents and nondelinquents in some sort of tabular form and analyze it, probably with some of the statistical procedures outlined in later chapters.

Prior to the application of statistical measures, however, we have no support for our idea that delinquency and broken homes are related in some causal way other than the tabular arrangement of the data. We may tentatively conclude that it appears that a relationship exists between broken homes and delinquency. Until some kind of statistical verification is employed, however, we make what are at best subjective judgments about how our data should be interpreted. We may feel that our data support the relation. Of course, other researchers may feel that our data do not support the relation. Using some statistical test or procedure as an objective arbiter will resolve to some degree any conflict of opinion that might arise as to how our data ought to be interpreted and judged.

It is at this point in our data analysis that statistical tests and procedures perform a most vital role. These procedures do not by themselves prove or disprove any theoretical argument we might build. Rather, the application of statistical tests will provide independent evidence that will influence our eventual interpretation of the data and decisions we might make about how our data relate to the theoretical scheme we have devised.

Therefore, statistical tests and techniques function in a supportive role in relation to our theories and tests of them. Statistical tests are *aids, not substitutes*, for good thinking. In fact, statistical tests are a relatively minor part of the overall research process when all its aspects are considered relative to one another. Some persons give such an inordinate amount of attention to statistical tests and their application that they lose sight of more important aspects of the research process and give them little attention. The research process is like a chain; it is no better or stronger than its weakest link. Figure

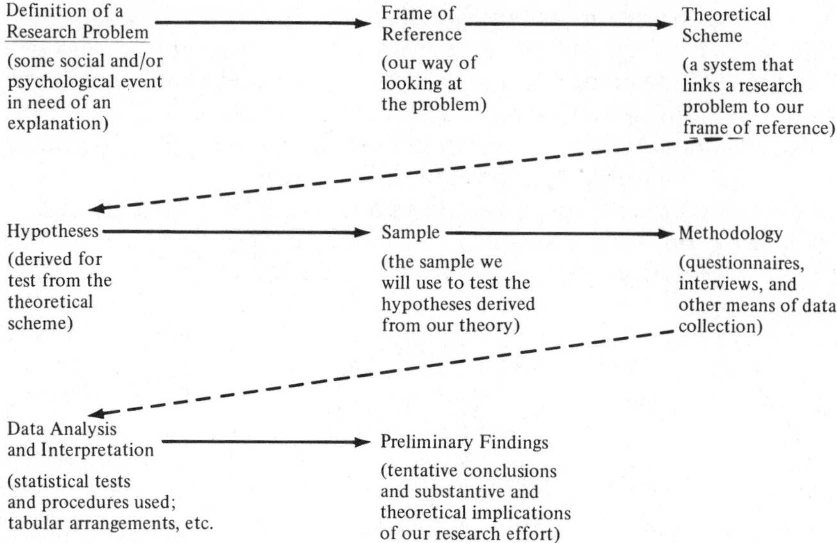

FIGURE 1.1 One Way of Conceptualizing the Research Process. Statistical tests enter the picture at the point of data analysis and interpretation.

1.1 illustrates one way of looking at the research process from the formulation of a research problem to its eventual research resolution.

If we fail to develop a thorough and comprehensive theoretical scheme, to deduce clearly stated hypotheses about relations between variables, or to obtain a representative sample of elements from the population, no amount of statistical test manipulation or application will save our research from mediocrity or from being less meaningful than it would have been had things gone perfectly. Some people have the mistaken belief that if their research looks complex as a result of using extremely complicated and complex-looking statistical tests and procedures, by definition their work will be judged as being important or "significant."

Statistical procedures are not ends in and of themselves. They assist us in our research work in describing what we have found and in making inferences from the data which apply to the larger population. Since persons taking statistics courses tend to focus intensely on this subject as they study it, they run the risk of failing to "see the forest because of the trees." They might fail to appreciate the true role of statistical tests and procedures in the overall research effort. It is for this reason that theory and every other aspect of one's research activity is underscored as being at least as important (if not more so) as the statistical procedures one uses in the analysis of data.

□ THE MODUS OPERANDI OF THE SOCIAL SCIENTIST

The social scientist is interested in learning about people, either in groups or individually. Whether a person's interest is the study of crime and delinquency, family structure and change, population growth and decline, collective behavior associated with mobs and crowds, personality systems, or interpersonal relations in work settings, several persistent questions link all such social inquiry.

1. What are the patterns of social and individual behavior?
2. Can these patterns be charted in such a way that predictions can be made about behaviors observed?
3. What factors will increase our understanding of human behavior?
4. In what ways will such factors contribute to our level of understanding?

Every social scientist enters his or her field (e.g., sociology, psychology, history, political science, etc.) and embarks upon the quest of seeking answers to questions such as those above. Although different social scientists will employ varieties of data-gathering strategies, such as questionnaires, interviews, or analysis of historical information, they all adhere to several basic principles and rules that have been developed over the years. The rules and principles are a part of the scientific method, a particular way of obtaining information about things for the purpose of understanding them.

It is not the task of this book to discuss the scientific method in detail. But it is important to recognize several features of the method that help to explain why statistical tests and procedures are logical aids as we seek information about things. The scientific method specifies that we must seek information *objectively and systematically.* Furthermore, this method stresses that the data we examine be *empirical*, or amenable to our senses in one way or another. Finally, we must relate to the data we collect with emotional detachment or in an affectively neutral manner. These prescriptions for our research behaviors are not intended to breed generations of cold, heartless scientists. On the contrary, they are designed to eliminate from our decision-making behavior certain elements of bias and vested interest.

It would be relatively easy for a drug manufacturer to appoint an unscrupulous team of researchers to turn up findings that would cause the product or drug to be viewed favorably by the medical profession. Unsystematic and subjective interpretations of results of drug experiments will lead to false claims about what the drug is capable of doing for patients. To boost sales of drug products, deliberate distortions of the truth about drug effects might be utilized.

By following a prescription of emotional detachment and objectivity, however, study results are less likely to be misinterpreted or mishandled. The scientific method, therefore, functions as a set of *positive constraints* on our behaviors as scientists. The do's and don't's of the scientific method are calculated to introduce objectivity and clarity into the work we do and the research we report. Statistical tests and procedures go hand in hand with the scientific method.

When we follow closely the rules governing the application of particular tests and procedures to the data we have collected in an objective and systematic manner, our test results are comparable to a second, independent opinion about any decision we might make. The point is that our research activity from the very beginning is *governed by rules.* By the same token, statistical tests have requirements that must be met before they can be properly applied. It is important for us to familiarize ourselves with these rules and requirements and follow them closely if we are to be consistent with the canons of scientific inquiry.

□ SUMMARY

This chapter has attempted to illustrate the importance of studying statistics. Statistics has been defined as the general collection of methods used to assemble, describe, and infer something from numerical data.

It was shown that numerical data have been generated from the process of coding applied to our data collection techniques and information derived from them. These numerical data can be described through the application of particular statistical techniques.

Two important functions of statistical procedures are *description* and *inference.* In the case of statistical inference, samples are taken from populations for further study. Sample characteristics or statistics (a second meaning of the term) are used as the basis for inferences about population characteristics or *parameters.* English alphabet or Roman letters are symbols for sample statistics, and lowercase Greek letters are symbols for population parameters.

All statistical procedures throughout the book utilize sample data rather than population data as examples. This is at least one reason why this book is about "basic statistics" rather than "basic parameters."

Social scientists typically examine a number of variables relevant to their specialty areas (e.g., crime, organizations, family, abnormal psychology, etc.). These variables are critical to the development of the theoretical schemes that researchers construct. Theories are integrated bodies of assumptions and propositions that explain and predict relations between these variables.

In an effort to be objective and systematic in tests of theories and hypotheses derived from them, social researchers follow the scientific method and the rules associated with it. These rules govern how data are initially collected and subsequently analyzed. Accordingly, rules also govern the legitimate application of particular statistical tests selected for certain kinds of data analysis situations. The researcher learns to be cognizant of these rules and to strive to adhere to them.

In Chapter 2 we focus on the kinds of assumptions that must be made whenever statistical tests are to be considered. Also, various kinds of samples and sampling plans will be presented in the context of prerequisites to statistical applications.

SELECTED STUDY TERMS

Notation system
Coding
Discrete variable
Continuous variable
Independent variable
Dependent variable
Statistical technique, test, or measure
Description
Statistical inference
Population
Element
Parameter
Sample
Statistic
Representativeness
Statistical symbols
Theory
Scientific method

EXERCISES

1. What are statistics? What are two meanings of the word *statistics?* Differentiate between them.
2. How does a sample relate to the population? Why is it important for a sample to be representative of the population from which it was drawn? Explain briefly.
3. What is a parameter? What are five parameters of a university or college

student body? What are considered as *estimates* of these population parameters? Discuss briefly and give examples.

4. Is it necessary for researchers to follow a single notation system in their statistical work? Why or why not? Explain. What are the primary functions of notation systems?
5. How do statistical techniques relate to theory? How does theory relate to statistical techniques? Explain in each case the relation between each.
6. List four discrete variables and four continuous variables. Can continuous variables be rendered in some kind of discrete form? Why or why not? Try to create a set of discrete categories for the continuous variables you have listed.
7. Identify the following variables as either discrete or continuous: (a) income, (b) eye color, (c) political affiliation, (d) union membership, (e) supervisory style, (f) work group productivity, and (g) socioeconomic status. In each case, explain briefly why you labeled the variables as you did.
8. Why are statistical tests so compatible with the scientific method? Explain.
9. Below is a list of variables. Write a short paragraph relating each with one another. Next, underline each variable you have used as an independent variable. What is the difference between an independent and a dependent variable? Explain. The variables are (a) labor turnover, (b) supervisory style, (c) employee motivation, (d) work group cohesion or "togetherness," (e) job status, (f) pay, and (g) working hours.
10. What is coding? How is it relevant for the subsequent use of statistical techniques?
11. Where do statistics fit into the overall research process? In your own words, define the critical parts of the research process, identifying that point where statistical tests will typically be found and have the greatest relevance. Explain your choice briefly.

REFERENCES

Black, James A., and Dean J. Champion, *Methods and Issues in Social Research.* New York: John Wiley & Sons, Inc., 1976.

Bonjean, Charles M., Richard J. Hill, and S. Dale McLemore, *Sociological Measurement: An Inventory of Scales and Indices.* San Francisco: The Chandler Publishing Company, 1967.

Devine, Richard P., and Laurence L. Falk, *Social Surveys: A Research Strategy for Social Scientists and Students.* Morristown, N.J.: General Learning Corporation, 1972.

DiRenzo, Gordon J., *Concepts, Theory, and Explanation in the Behavioral Sciences.* New York: Random House, Inc., 1966.

Lastrucci, Carlo L., *The Scientific Approach: Basic Principles of the Scientific Method.* Cambridge, Mass.: Schenkman Publishing Co., Inc., 1963.

Lazarsfeld, Paul F., and Morris Rosenberg, eds., *The Language of Social Research.* New York: The Free Press, 1955.

Miller, Delbert C., *Handbook of Research Design and Social Measurement.* New York: David McKay Co., Inc., 1977.

Phillips, Bernard S., *Social Research, Strategy and Tactics.* New York: Macmillan Publishing Co., Inc., 1971.

Wallace, Walter, *Sociological Theory.* Chicago: Aldine Publishing Company, 1969.

Whitehead, Alfred N., *Science and the Modern World.* New York: The Free Press, 1967.

2

On Meeting the Assumptions

Some of the statistical tests and techniques described and discussed in later chapters were originally devised by statisticians for purposes other than social scientific ones. For instance, several procedures were developed in conjunction with the work of agricultural economists and agrobiologists.

A typical problem might have been to examine differences in crop yield from one plot of land to the next, where each of several different plots of land had been treated with chemicals and soil and plant nutrients of various kinds. The agrobiologist exercised considerable control over the different land plots and the chemicals and soil nutrients that were administered to each of them. In the course of their experimentation, questions were raised by these researchers about the significance of differences in crop yield that might be attributable to different soil nutrients used. Frequently, statistical tests were devised to enable them to answer such questions.

In the course of developing these tests, assumptions were made about the similarity of land plots prior to their chemical treatments and about the measures used to evaluate resulting crop yield. Given the nature of the highly controlled experiments, these investigators experienced little difficulty in meeting the assumptions of their statistical tests used.

Later, in social scientific research, the same statistical tests were selected by investigators to assist them in the analysis of data collected from several groups of persons, where attitudes and opinions about different things varied from one group to the next. The reasoning perhaps was as follows: if this statistical test can be used to tell us whether or not there are variations in crop yield from one land plot to the next, it might also be able to tell us whether there are attitudinal variations from one group of persons to the next. Or the test might be able to tell us whether several different groups of employees in a large company vary in their productivity level as a result of experiencing different kinds of supervision from their supervisors. As can be seen from these illustrations, the application possibilities for this and other statistical tests are virtually unlimited.

There are substantial gaps in our reasoning, however. First, we are not sure that all employee work groups are sufficiently similar to one another prior to our experimentation. Second, our measures of attitudinal phenomena are somewhat imprecise, and often we are not sure that raw scores themselves are true indicators of one's attitudinal position. Compared with the agrobiologist, the social scientist cannot always control the experimental setting and the measures used to an equivalent degree. Questions inevitably arise concerning the *quality* of data one has collected. It is much easier to measure precisely crop yield and amount of soil nutrient administered than it is to measure attitudinal phenomena, group properties, or supervisory style.

Thus it seems fair to ask to what extent the conditions have been met for applying a statistical technique in one field (e.g., sociology, psychology, political science, etc.) when the technique was originally designed for application in another field (e.g., agrobiology, chemistry, biology, etc.).[1]

The proper application of statistical techniques, regardless of whether they are descriptive or inferential or used in tests of hypotheses, is dependent upon the extent to which the researcher adheres to or satisfies certain rules or *assumptions.* Every statistical test has associated with it a set of assumptions governing its legitimate application to data analysis and interpretation. Some procedures have more

[1] Social scientists have developed many statistical tests of their own for application to social phenomena. But as far as "borrowing" a test from another field is concerned, the question remains a legitimate one.

assumptions than others. However, all statistical tests and techniques have several general assumptions that are common to all of them. These assumptions pertain to (1) levels of measurement, (2) sampling procedures, and (3) sample size.

□ LEVELS OF MEASUREMENT

Statistical procedures invariably involve the manipulation of numbers. Depending upon the statistical test or procedure selected for use by the social scientist, certain arithmetic operations are required. It will be recalled from the discussion in Chapter 1 that coding is a process whereby data of any kind are transformed into numerical quantities. The fact that a researcher has "transformed" data into numbers, however, does not automatically mean that all arithmetic operations are now permissible. We must pay attention at all times to what the numbers mean and what they stand for.

A 1 and a 2 applied to the sex categories of "male" and "female" do not mean the same things as a 1 and a 2 applied to "upper class" and "lower class." In the first instance, the 1 and 2 are intended to stand for sex classifications with no implication of "better than" or "more than." We might even use as alternatives the letters A and B instead of 1 and 2 to represent these categories.

In the second instance, the 1 is higher than the 2 when we apply these numbers to different socioeconomic or social-class levels. The point is that *numbers mean different things depending on what they stand for.* And depending on what these numbers mean, our choice of statistical procedures will be affected accordingly. This is because different arithmetic operations are required of each statistical procedure we might use with the numbers we are analyzing. If we fail to achieve a particular *level of measurement* with the data we have collected, then we will obviously be limited in our choice of statistical procedures for the analysis of that data. The levels of measurement of interest to us include (1) nominal, (2) ordinal, (3) interval, and (4) ratio.

The Nominal Level of Measurement

The nominal level of measurement has been referred to by some researchers as the level of *classifiables.*[2] Numbers that are applied to data of the nominal level stand for nothing more than categorical or

[2] See Julian L. Simon, *Basic Research Methods in Social Science: The Art of Empirical Investigation* (New York: Random House, Inc., 1969).

classifiable information. Such variables as political affiliation, sex, race, or religious preference are categorical only. The assignment of a 1 to Democrat, a 2 to Republican, and a 3 to an American Independent does nothing other than differentiate one category from another. We can count the numbers of persons in each category. We can determine proportionate numbers of persons from one category to the next. But we cannot multiply or divide numbers assigned to these nominal designations.

For example, suppose that we observe the following three Social Security numbers:

411-82-1075
233-41-0026
551-24-9907.

If we sum these numbers, we would get 1,196,481,008. If we divide this sum by 3, we would get 398-82-7002.66, which might stand for the average Social Security number. This is completely meaningless because of the fact that Social Security numbers are only categorical themselves and serve merely to differentiate one person from another for income tax and related purposes.

Furthermore, if we assign a 1 to Democrat, a 2 to Republican, and a 3 to Communist, we cannot say that a 1 (Democrat) plus a 2 (Republican) equals a 3 (Communist). A 1 is only different from a 2, and so on. In the case of nominal measurement, numbers are arbitrarily assigned without regard for order among the subclasses or subcategories of the variable under investigation.

The Ordinal Level of Measurement

The ordinal level of measurement contains the classification properties of the nominal scale or level. The ordinal level also implies that numbers assigned to subclasses of any variable may be *rank-ordered* or *gradated* according to some low-to-high arrangement. Table 2.1 shows a national preseason ranking of college football teams arranged according to an ordinal scale or measurement level.

As is always the case with numbers that represent information at the ordinal level, we can say that one team is ranked higher or lower than another. We are not able to say how much higher or how much lower, however. We cannot argue effectively that all teams in Table 2.1 are equally spaced from one another. Oklahoma and Notre Dame may be quite similar in their respective strengths as nationally ranked teams, but there may be considerable difference between Notre Dame and Alabama or between Nebraska and Michigan in terms of their respective skills and strengths. The rankings assigned to these

TABLE 2.1
National Preseason Ranking of Five Football Teams.

Team	*Rank*
Oklahoma	1
Notre Dame	2
Alabama	3
Nebraska	4
Michigan	5

teams merely serve to indicate that one team is better than another, but again, we do not know how much better.

Another example is illustrated by a set of anxiety attitudinal scores arranged along a continuum from low to high as shown in Figure 2.1. Suppose that these scores refer to anxiety levels of a sample of psychoneurotic patients in a mental hospital. An examination of Figure 2.1 will reveal that the numbers are ordinally spaced in relation to one another, but that is all. Notice the large gaps between the scores of 50 and 51 and between 60 and 63. Then note the smaller gaps between the scores of 51 and 60 and between 63 and 80. This underscores the fact that the ordinal level of measurement permits only statements of "greater than" or "less than" but not "how much greater than or less than." We cannot say, for instance, that the person with an anxiety score of 100 is twice as anxious as the person with a score of 50. We can only say that one person is more anxious (but not how much more) than the other.

In the social sciences, almost all attitudinal variables are measured according to ordinal scales. Such variables as socioeconomic status, group cohesiveness, and worker morale are frequently measured according to the ordinal level of measurement as well.

The Interval Level of Measurement

The interval level of measurement contains all of the properties and characteristics of the nominal and ordinal levels of measurement. In addition, we are permitted to make *interval statements* about relations between numbers in terms of how far one number is from an-

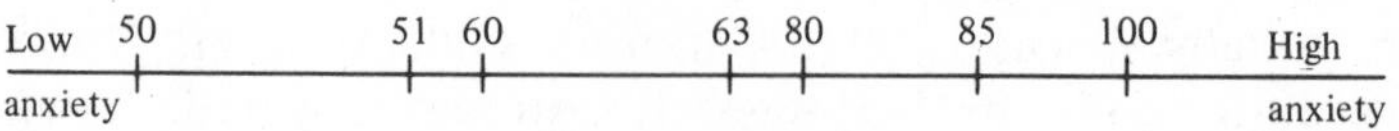

FIGURE 2.1. Continuum of Anxiety Scores for Mental Patients. (A continuum is a straight line representing some characteristic from the lowest to the highest, or highest to lowest degree.)

other. The interval level of measurement provides for *equal spacing* between numbers.

For example, the variable "years of education" conforms to the interval level of measurement. We can say that a person with 4 years of college has exactly 1 year more than a person with 3 years of college. In fact, there is the same distance between a freshman and a sophomore as exists between a sophomore and a junior or between a junior and a senior.

Other variables that reflect interval spacing between subclasses might be age, height, and weight. In each case it can be assumed that equal distances exist between units on a *continuum* of ages, heights, or weights from high to low.

Arithmetic operations of addition, subtraction, multiplication, and division are permissible with data measured according to the interval measurement level. Most statistical tests and techniques have as their *maximum* level of measurement assumption the interval level. Many statistical procedures require only that the data be measured according to an ordinal or a nominal scale, however. Generally, the higher the measurement level (moving from the lowest, nominal, toward the highest, ratio), the greater the number of statistical techniques one can choose from for data analysis purposes. This statement specifies that the researcher can do more with the data collected, inasmuch as a maximum number of statistical test options can be exercised.

The Ratio Level of Measurement

Seldom referred to or used in statistical work is the ratio level of measurement. Few statistical tests or procedures require that the data collected be measured according to the properties of the ratio level. The ratio level of measurement contains all properties and characteristics of the nominal, ordinal, and interval levels. In addition, it has an *absolute zero* associated with it.

Specifying income in terms of dollars and cents makes it possible to measure income according to a ratio scale. There is an absolute zero achieved where a person has no money whatsoever. Furthermore, a person with $10,000 has twice as much as the person with $5000. In fact, ratio statements can be made, such as $10 is to $20 as $50 is to $100.

On very rare occasions, a statistical test may have the assumption of the ratio level of measurement accompanying it. If this is so, the researcher will have to demonstrate that the data conform to such a scale and that the numbers to be manipulated stand for data that are amenable to ratio-level analysis.

TABLE 2.2
Levels of Measurement and Appropriate Statistical Techniques to Use.

If the Investigator Has:	*The Kind of Statistical Techniques That Can Be Used Are:*
Nominal information	Nominal-level techniques
Ordinal information	Ordinal- and nominal-level techniques
Interval information	Interval-, ordinal-, and nominal-level techniques
Ratio information	Ratio-, interval-, ordinal-, and nominal-level techniques

Levels of Measurement and Statistical Techniques

The level of measurement assumption is important because it is directly connected to the arithmetic operations involved in statistical tests and procedures. It is one of several assumptions that must be met and considered in the selection of statistical techniques.

A researcher must first examine the data collected and determine the level of measurement associated with every variable to be examined or analyzed. Once the measurement level has been determined for each variable, a more direct determination of statistical test can be made. The researcher will be in the position of knowing which tests are appropriate as well as which ones are not appropriate for data analysis. Table 2.2 summarizes the relation between measurement level and statistical techniques that the researcher can legitimately apply.

Later chapters are arranged in such a way that the researcher can assume that statistical tests covered in Chapter 8, for example, all require data of the interval level of measurement. Chapter 9 requires that data be of the nominal level; and so on. In each statistical test discussion, the major assumptions, including the level of measurement, will be made explicit.

□ THE RANDOMNESS ASSUMPTION

A second important assumption underlying the appropriate application of all statistical tests without exception is that the researcher first obtain a random sample of elements. A *random sample* is defined as a sample drawn in such a way so that each element has an equal and an independent chance of being included.

An equal chance means that all persons in the population are first given an equal opportunity of being included in the sample to be drawn. If there are 100 persons in the original population, then each person must have $\frac{1}{100}$ of a chance of being included in the subsequent sample. If there are 500 persons in the population, then each person must be given $\frac{1}{500}$ of a chance of being drawn, and so on.

Independence of draw means that the selection of any given person will not affect the chances of the remaining persons being drawn. In short, each time a person is selected from an original population of 500, the remaining persons must still have $\frac{1}{500}$ of a chance of being included. Samples selected in this fashion (i.e., with an equal and independent chance of elements being included) are frequently referred to as probability samples. *Probability samples* are those from which inferences can be made about population parameters. These inferences about population parameters are always couched in a probabilistic context. This means, simply, that the researcher knows (and is able to calculate) the chances that sample statistics are good estimates of their respective population parameters. The average age of a probability sample of University of Maryland students, for instance, is an estimate of the unknown population age of these university students. It is an estimate that can be evaluated in terms of its precision or accuracy. Considerably more will be stated about sample statistics as estimates of population parameters in Chapter 7.

For the present, only probability samples based on one of several *probability sampling plans* will allow the researcher the opportunity of using techniques of statistical inference and statistical tests of significance meaningfully. The use of statistical tests and procedures of statistical inference with samples not drawn randomly or in accordance with probability sampling principles will yield statistical results that cannot be systematically and meaningfully interpreted. Misleading results will almost certainly follow whenever statistical tests are misapplied. The researcher must carefully evaluate the sample obtained and make a decision as to whether or not the sample qualifies as a probability sample. In the discussion to follow, several alternative probability sampling plans will be presented. Also, several nonprobability sampling plans will be discussed.[3]

Probability Sampling Plans

Four sampling plans that fall within the probability sampling rubric are (1) simple random sampling, (2) proportionate stratified random sampling, (3) disproportionate stratified random sampling, and (4) cluster or area sampling.

[3] It should be noted that these discussions are not intended to be comprehensive. Here the primary intent is to provide the reader with some of the general procedures that qualify (as well as those that do not qualify) as probability sampling plans. For a more detailed discussion of the sampling plans presented in this section, see James A. Black and Dean J. Champion, *Methods and Issues in Social Research* (New York: John Wiley & Sons, Inc., 1976), especially Chap. 8; and Delbert C. Miller, *Handbook of Research Design and Social Measurement*, 3rd ed. (New York: David McKay Co., Inc., 1977).

Simple Random Sampling. A population about which one seeks information is designated in advance by the researcher (Winer, 1971). In *simple random sampling*, all elements or nearly all elements are identified by the researcher, and a desired number of them is selected randomly for subsequent study. (The question of how many elements should be drawn will be discussed in the section to follow on "Sample-Size Considerations.")

Random samples of elements may be obtained several ways. There are computer programs available at colleges and universities (if the reader has access to such facilities) that can yield random samples of any size, given a population of a specified size. However, if such facilities are not available, a simple method, called a *table of random numbers*, can be used as an alternative. Such a table is found in Appendix A, Table A.2.

The digits in this table of random numbers were randomly determined by computer. Two unique features of this table are that (1) no digit occurs any more frequently than any other digit (i.e., there are the same number of 1's, and 2's, etc.), and (2) there is no order attached to the occurrence of the digits in the table. In short, the distribution of digits is purely random. A sample selected by using the table of random numbers is, by definition, a random sample.[4]

To use the table of random numbers for drawing a random sample, a researcher must:

1. Enumerate the population, assigning a number to each element within it from 1 to N (the total number of population elements).
2. Determine the desired sample size.

To provide a simple illustration of how this table can be used, suppose that a researcher has a population of 100 elements and desires to draw a random sample of 10 elements from it. All 100 elements are identified and enumerated from 1 to 100.

Next, the researcher enters the table of random numbers at any point and focuses upon the first set of three digits.[5] In Table A.2, let us suppose that the researcher starts by focusing on the first three digits in the upper left-hand corner of the page (the first page of the

[4] The spacing between the groups of digits (five digits per group) is merely to ease the burden on your eyes when examining the table. There is no other significance attached to the spacing. Also, these pages are only a few extracted from the entire set of tables originally created by the Rand Corporation for sampling purposes. To that extent, at least, a few digits *may* occur more or less often compared with the frequency of occurrence of other digits within these few pages.

[5] Three digits are selected because there are three digits in the population size of 100–1 0 0.

table). The first set of three digits encountered is 100. Therefore, the researcher designates the person numbered 100 as the first element to be included in the sample.

Next, we proceed directly down the page with the next set of three digits. These are 375. Since no person in our population is numbered 375, we skip this number and go on to the next set of three, which is 084. This is the person numbered 084 or 84 in the population. This is the second person to be included in our sample.

Continuing down the page, we encounter 990, 128, 660, 310, 852, 635, and so on, until the bottom of the page is reached. If we have not achieved our desired sample size by then, we simply go back to the top of the page and move exactly one digit to the right. We pick up the next set of three digits which will be 009 in this case. This is the person numbered 9 in the population. We proceed down the page with each set of three digits (e.g., 754, 842, 901, 280, 606, 106, and so on) until we reach the bottom of the page. We then go back to the top of the page, move one digit to the right, and begin again with three digits.

Moving through this table as has been suggested by the method above, we will obtain the following 10 elements for inclusion in our sample:

100 84 98 44 5 9 12 33 54 95.

Those persons in our population with these numbers will be selected for our random sample. By definition, our sample will be a random sample.

Stratified Random Sampling. If the researcher wants to select persons with particular attributes such as "year in school," "race," or "sex," a *stratified random sample* will be required. For instance, the investigator may wish to conduct an experiment with an equal number of males and females. In the original population, all males are subsequently enumerated and identified. By using the simple random sampling method described earlier with the table of random numbers, a simple random sample of a designated number of males is selected.

Next, the females in the population are identified and enumerated. A simple random sample of females is also obtained in an identical fashion. Combining these two random samples of males and females into one larger sample of elements will yield a stratified random sample, stratified according to sex.

A distinction may be made between proportionate and disproportionate stratified random samples. *Proportionate stratified random samples* are those in which certain characteristics of interest to the researcher are represented in the same proportion that they exist in the population. For example, if the population is composed of 55 percent female and 45 percent male, the sample would be a proportionate one if it were composed of 55 percent female and 45 percent male. Of course, other characteristics could also be included in one's sampling plan (e.g., age, grade-point average, years of education, etc.) We would say that our sample is stratified according to sex, age, grade-point average, and years of education.

Disproportionate stratified random samples are randomly selected in such a way that certain characteristics are not distributed in the same proportion as they are distributed in the population. A sample consisting of 50 percent female and 50 percent male, for example, would be disproportionate if the original population breakdown on sex distribution were 55 percent female and 45 percent male.

The key control governing the inclusion of elements for both kinds of stratified random samples is our procedure of randomness. Regardless of the number of characteristics stratified in any sample, as long as we use our basic random selection procedure for simple random sampling defined above, our sample will qualify as a probability sample.

Cluster or Area Sampling. *Cluster samples* are used by ecologists and demographers who study larger populations, such as the population of the United States or the population of Canada. Rather than attempt to identify all persons individually in the population prior to sampling from them, the researcher will identify areas of the United States and subareas within these areas. Eventually, through the delineation of subareas within subareas, the investigator will observe that some subareas will be one city block in a large city or several acres of land in a rural area. The researcher proceeds to randomly select subareas, each of which contains clusters of dwelling units or families. This is accomplished by previously enumerating all of the smallest subareas to be sampled (the "population" of subareas) and selecting a simple random sample of subareas from it. All families are then used as a cluster if they happen to fall within given subareas sampled. The combination of all such clusters will yield a cluster or area sample. Because randomness was employed as the means of obtaining a random sample of subareas, such a sample is a probability sample.

Some of the practical advantages of cluster sampling should be apparent. Researchers can limit their travel to a few areas within a given community and "sample" all family heads who were included earlier in a particular subarea drawn. If the subarea happened to be a city block of apartment units, the investigator can concentrate research efforts within this narrow area. Considerable time and travel expense are saved as a result of sampling in this fashion.

A more thorough discussion of these sampling techniques and their relative strengths and weaknesses as research tools is beyond the scope of this text. An important point to remember is that these procedures permit *generalizations* to be made about population parameters from observed sample statistics or characteristics. These generalizations have a known amount of error that can be used strategically to evaluate the accuracy or precision of such sample statistics as estimates of population parameters. This is one reason why such samples are referred to as probability samples.

Nonprobability Sampling Plans

Nonprobability sampling plans are those that do not use randomness as the primary control for the inclusion of elements. Three of the many types of nonprobability sampling plans available will be discussed briefly here. They are (1) accidental sampling, (2) quota sampling, and (3) judgmental or purposive sampling.

Accidental Sampling. *Accidental sampling* occurs whenever the researcher takes a sample from whatever is available at the time. A roving reporter randomly interviewing passersby in a shopping center is, in fact, obtaining an accidental sample of persons and not a random one.

If one professor at a university assists another professor by allowing that person to give a questionnaire to the students of a large introductory sociology class, that sample of students obtained is purely accidental and cannot be regarded as random. If a researcher advertises in a newspaper for persons to participate in a harmless social experiment, the persons who respond to the advertisement and participate as a sample are purely accidental, not random.

Quota Sampling. A *quota sampling* plan is one step above the accidental sampling procedure. Quota samples are designed to insure the inclusion of certain types of persons in a subsequent draw of elements. For instance, if a researcher wished to interview male and female physicians, it is likely that a majority of physicians contacted initially would be male. In order to insure that female physicians would be represented in some significant number, a quota of female physicians would be specified. Therefore, a researcher would strive to achieve a sample of physicians in which a significant proportion of them would be female. Perhaps a sample of 100 physicians would include at least 30 or 40 female physicians. No attempt would be made by the researcher to randomize the selection of physicians. The selection of both male and female physicians would be "accidental" for all practical purposes.

Judgmental or Purposive Sampling. Whenever an investigator does not have time to enumerate all elements in the population for the purpose of drawing a random sample of them, a purposive or judgmental sample can be obtained. A *judgmental sample* is one that is handpicked by someone who knows the population fairly well and can be relied upon to designate persons who represent a reasonable sampling of viewpoints on a given issue. A person who has lived in a small community for many years, for instance, can be used as an "informant" to provide the researcher with the names of other community residents who might represent differing opinions toward political or social issues or who might have different attitudes about things. Samples obtained in this manner are not probability samples either. Again, this is because they have not been obtained randomly.

The one characteristic shared by all three sampling procedures described above is that they are easily obtained. They are cheap, and they require little time and effort on the part of the researcher.

The major drawback accompanying each of these samples is that they do not provide the researcher with any kind of sound foundation for making generalizations or inferences about populations from which they were drawn. The fact is that we have no way of knowing exactly what population they were obtained from, and it is impossible to determine any kind of meaningful measure of the accuracy or precision of any generalizations we might make.

But precisely because of the fact that these types of samples are easy to obtain and offer the researcher the opportunity of getting large quantities of elements for relatively little expenditure of time and effort, they are used with some regularity in social research. The researcher operating with a nonprobability sample of any kind should exercise the appropriate amount of caution in making interpretations of study findings and generalizations from them to larger populations of elements.

Most investigators will call these sampling limitations to the attention of the reader. However, some find it difficult to self-impose such restraints of caution and conservatism. It is on these occasions that readers of articles are misled by study findings that purportedly reflect population values and sentiments when, in fact, they do not. This is mentioned primarily as a warning so that the reader will be able to clearly evaluate research findings in view of how the sample was originally obtained.

Meeting the assumption of randomness is somewhat difficult for the researcher to accomplish. There are always problems that make it nearly impossible for the investigator to obtain all persons selected for inclusion in the sample. Some people simply do not want to be interviewed or bothered with filling out and returning a questionnaire. Others have illnesses that prevent the researcher from contacting them. Some persons die, move away, or are simply not to be found. Whatever the reason, the researcher inevitably ends up with a sample of a random sample. It is likely that the researcher will continue to label the sample a random one. In some respects, it still is. But it suffers from what is called *nonresponse.* To the extent that some persons did not respond or were not included in the sample, the subsequent sample obtained becomes less reliable as a basis for generalizations; at the very least, the sample becomes less representative of the population from which it was drawn. Inferences and generalizations are seriously affected whenever nonresponse has cut down sample size appreciably.

Unfortunately, there are no precise guidelines to follow when we evaluate our sample and the amount of nonresponse associated with it. The researcher uses a high degree of personal judgment in assessing the quality of the sample obtained. Although this may not sound very scientific, it is the best that can be done under the circumstances. In short, the researcher does the best that can be done with whatever sample has been obtained. Of course, the researcher should make every effort to comply with the rules governing probability samples, particularly if statistical inference is planned as a part of the methodological analysis of the data. All of the statistical tests and procedures discussed in this book have randomness as an underlying assumption.

□ SAMPLE SIZE

Most beginning researchers and social science students want to know how large their samples should be for various research purposes. Depending upon a person's area of specialization, *sample-size requirements will vary.* For instance, a person who studies small groups and small-group interactions will require samples of fewer than 25 elements. A demographer might require a sample of 300 to 400 or perhaps even larger for demographic research purposes.

A conventional approach would be to sample approximately $\frac{1}{10}$ of the population about which generalizations are to be made. This is referred to as the *sampling fraction* and is represented symbolically as

$$\frac{n}{N},$$

where

n = sample size,
N = population size

A sampling fraction of $\frac{1}{10}$ is considered reasonable, provided that the population size is not gigantic. If the investigator wished to draw a random sample of persons from New York City, for instance, the sample size would be several hundred thousand. This is a prohibitive figure. One solution to the problem of large sample size arising from an extremely large population would be to take a sample that is considerably smaller proportionately. If we were to take a random sample of 500 from the population of New York City, we would obviously have a sampling fraction many times smaller than the recommended $\frac{1}{10}$.

This is frequently satisfactory, however, because 500 itself is considered a large number. And we find that our generalizations about New York City residents, based on our random sample of 500, is nearly as good as generalizations we might make based on a larger sample of 300,000. The slight increase in the accuracy of our generalizations based on the larger sample size is plainly not justified by the additional expenditures of time and money. In short, there is a *diminishing return effect* taking place as we increase our sample size to enormous proportions.

Most statistical tests and measures discussed in Chapters 8 through 12 have accompanying recommended sample-size ranges. In other words, a given statistical test is fully effective when applied to sample sizes ranging from 30 to 60, or from 120 to 250, as examples. Some procedures are severely restricted and specify that the sample size should be no greater than 10 (e.g., the randomization tests). Others must not be applied if the sample size is below 30. With these many varied requirements associated with the tests to be discussed, it is indeed difficult to specify an across-the-board figure as an optimum sample size. If the $\frac{1}{10}$ rule of thumb results in a sample of great magnitude (i.e., a sample larger than 500), this rule can be relaxed, permitting the researcher to deal with a sample size which, although it is considerably smaller proportionately, will be adequate under the circumstances.

There is a point beyond which the application of statistical tests of significance is considered useless and not very meaningful. This matter will be discussed in greater detail in Chapters 7 and 8. It is sufficient here to consider the recommendation not to apply statistical tests whenever one's sample size is in excess of 500.[6]

□ OTHER ASSUMPTIONS

In some cases, additional assumptions will be found to accompany particular tests or measures. Whenever such assumptions are necessary for the proper application of the test, they will be mentioned and discussed. All statistical tests require randomness, however. Also underlying all statistical tests is the level-of-measurement assumption. Some tests require that the researcher have nominal data, whereas others require interval data. These are considered the basic assumptions associated with all statistical testing.

Varying sample-size recommendations will be found with each test covered as well. It is usually appropriate for the researcher to adhere fairly closely to such sample-size recommendations in certain statistical applications.

Before concluding this chapter, it should be noted that not everyone agrees about the extent to which we should comply with the assumptions underlying statistical tests as we apply them to social data. One extreme position is that no statistical test should be applied if any one or more assumptions is violated. This "purist" position is not a particularly popular one. Of course, there is the other extreme, which might be that any test can be applied regardless of assumption violations that might occur. On the basis of what we have observed in these first chapters, certain tests that require multiplication and division would be inappropriate if applied to data of the nominal or ordinal levels of measurement. An assumption violation of this sort can clearly be regarded as serious, inasmuch as the meaningfulness of the study results would be adversely affected.

If we were to adopt the purist position in every technical detail, it might be the case that few, if any, studies would lend themselves to statistical analysis of any kind. This would be attributable to the fact

[6] This may seem somewhat arbitrary, and some researchers may even take issue with this recommendation. There are logical reasons for not applying statistical tests and procedures whenever extremely large sample sizes are encountered, but it is beyond the scope of the present discussion to elaborate on these meaningfully at this time. Again, Chapters 7 and 8 will provide some key elements that will lend support to this position and recommendation.

that our samples would not be purely random (i.e., a certain amount of nonresponse would accompany any sample drawn).

Therefore, it seems that the wisest course of action under the circumstances would be to evaluate the data one has collected and determine which assumptions, if any, would be violated, given certain statistical test choices we might make. A careful evaluation of the implications of certain assumption violations may lead us to conclude that certain tests and procedures could be applied to sample data, to the extent that proper caution and conservatism were exercised in the resulting interpretations of our findings.

□ SUMMARY

This chapter has sought to acquaint the reader with various important assumptions that underlie the legitimate application of statistical tests and procedures. Although there is some controversy over whether all assumptions must be met in order for tests or measures to be applied meaningfully to collected data, three important assumptions were presented that serve to influence our choice of tests. These assumptions were levels of measurement, randomness, and sample-size specifications.

The level-of-measurement assumption means that numbers which stand for different subclasses of variables mean different things from one variable to the next. Given the nature of arithmetic operations involved in certain statistical applications, it is necessary to make an assumption about the level of measurement we have achieved with the data we have collected and measured.

Also, our samples should be randomly drawn. This will permit the researcher to make generalizations about population parameter values based upon observed sample statistics. Statistical inference is justified to the extent to which we have random samples at our disposal. If we should happen to lack randomness in a given sample, our generalizing will become increasingly limited, and we will be unable to evaluate accurately the precision of any inferences we might make about population values.

Finally, sample size is of concern to all researchers. It was mentioned that, usually, a recommended sample-size range will accompany each statistical procedure discussed to assist the researcher in making statistical choices. Although some statistical tests have additional assumptions associated with them, the discussion of these will be deferred until the particular technique or measure is presented in later chapters.

SELECTED STUDY TERMS

Assumptions
Level of measurement
Nominal level of measurement
Ordinal level of measurement
Interval level of measurement
Continuum
Ratio level of measurement
Randomness
Probability sampling plan
Simple random sample
Table of random numbers
Proportionate stratified random sample
Disproportionate stratified random sample
Cluster or area sample
Nonprobability sampling plan
Accidental sample
Quota sample
Judgmental or purposive sample
Sampling fraction

EXERCISES

1. Identify the level of measurement probably associated with the following variables: (a) weight; (b) union membership/nonmembership; (c) work motivation; (d) labor turnover; and (e) ethnic background. In each case, give a brief explanation of your rationale for labeling each variable as you did.
2. What are some factors that must be considered in determining the size of one's sample for research purposes? Discuss briefly.
3. Why is it important to consider the level of measurement associated with one's data? Explain.
4. How can random samples be obtained? What is a simple random sample and why do you think it is important in statistical inference? Explain.
5. Distinguish between probability sampling plans and nonprobability sampling plans. Give two examples of each.
6. What is meant by the "sampling fraction"?
7. Differentiate between proportionate and disproportionate stratified random samples. Why do you think it is important to "stratify" on several variables in research? Explain briefly.
8. Differentiate between purposive and accidental samples. Give an example of each.
9. What is it about nonprobability sampling plans that renders them inferior to probability sampling plans? Explain briefly. Why do people persist in utilizing nonprobability sampling plans in spite of their weaknesses and limitations?

10. What are the primary criteria that determine whether or not a person's sample is truly random?
11. Write a short essay on "meeting the assumptions." Include in your essay a discussion of the value of assumptions in social research.

REFERENCES

Black, James A., and Dean J. Champion, *Methods and Issues in Social Research.* New York: John Wiley & Sons, Inc., 1976.
Cochran, William G. *Sampling Techniques.* New York: John Wiley & Sons, Inc., 1963.
Conway, Freda, *Sampling: An Introduction for Social Scientists.* London: George Allen & Unwin Ltd., 1967.
Goode, William J., and Paul K. Hatt, *Methods in Social Research.* New York: McGraw-Hill Book Company, 1952.
The Rand Corporation, *A Million Random Digits.* New York: The Free Press, 1955.
Selltiz, Claire, Lawrence S. Wrightsman, and Stuart W. Clark, *Research Methods in Social Relations.* New York: Holt, Rinehart and Winston, 1976.
Walker, Helen M., and Joseph Lev, *Elementary Statistical Methods.* New York: Holt, Rinehart and Winston, 1958.
Winer, B. J., *Statistical Principles in Experimental Design.* New York: McGraw-Hill Book Company, 1971.

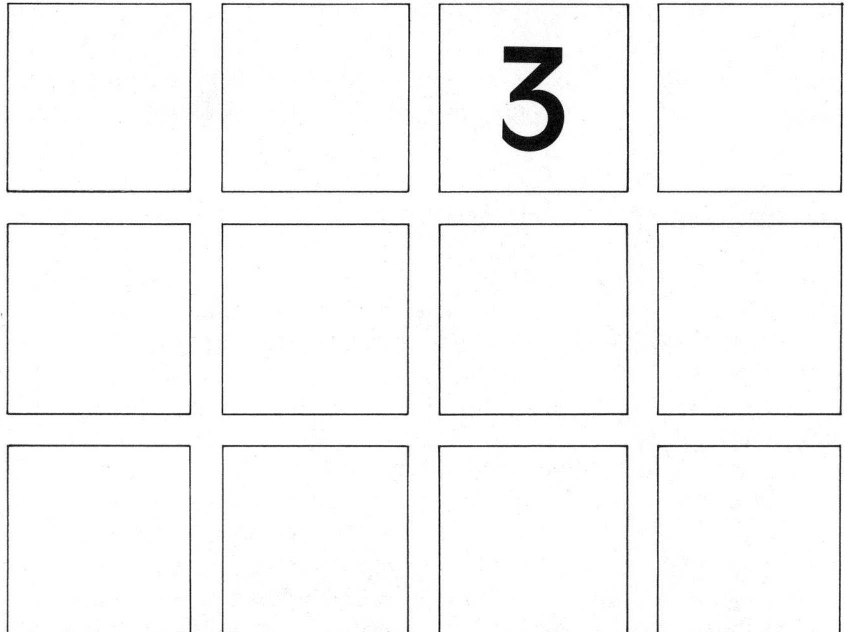

Graphic Presentation

□ THE VALUE OF ILLUSTRATIONS AND GRAPHS

The expression "a picture is worth a thousand words" is particularly appropriate when applied to presentations of social scientific findings in the research literature. Readers of articles and reports on scientific surveys are assisted in their understanding of the material read by the inclusion of supplementary tables, charts, and assorted graphs. Not only can a reader appreciate the written word, but the person can clearly see graphic and tabular evidence supporting one theoretical argument or another.

Tables, graphs, charts, figures, and diagrams are not only essential to increasing one's understanding of written material, but they also enhance our theory-building efforts by providing visual evidence of the outcomes of hypothesis tests.

This chapter deals with several of the more popular methods of presenting materials graphically in social scientific work. The discussion is not intended to be comprehensive, but it should provide the reader with a fairly good idea of the potential applications of graphic materials.

□ FREQUENCY DISTRIBUTIONS

One of the first things a researcher does when data have been collected is to *order* it in some fashion. We must organize the data in some meaningful way if we are to make any kind of systematic sense out of it.

Depending on the size of the sample, we will treat the data as either ungrouped or grouped. Conventionally, if the sample size is 25 or smaller, we will find it fairly easy to deal with the data from the sample in ungrouped form. *Ungrouped data analysis* means that we will deal with the raw scores directly. For instance, suppose that we have a sample of 10 students and are interested in their particular year in school. Table 3.1 shows the 10 students in our sample and the year in school associated with each. By recasting or reordering the data as shown in Table 3.2, we have a somewhat more meaningful presentation of year in school and the number of students in our sample who fall into each of the four categories shown.

In Table 3.2 we have entered a *tally* in each of the "year in school" categories for the 10 students in our sample. These data have been ordered to form a frequency distribution. A *frequency distribution* is the simple tally of scores or values of characteristics that have been taken from any collection of elements.

Table 3.2 contains some new symbols. The symbol f stands for "frequency." The symbol Σ stands for "the sum of." Together, Σf means the "sum of the frequencies" or the "total sample."

TABLE 3.1
Number of Years in School for a Sample of 10 Students. (Unorganized Data.)

Student Number	*Year in School*
1	Senior
2	Sophomore
3	Freshman
4	Freshman
5	Junior
6	Junior
7	Freshman
8	Freshman
9	Sophomore
10	Sophomore

TABLE 3.2
Frequency Distribution of 10 Students by Year in School

Year in School	*Tally*	*Frequency* *f*
Freshman	4	////
Sophomore	3	///
Junior	2	//
Senior	1	/
Sum of frequencies $(\Sigma f) = 10$		

Frequency distributions can be constructed for data of any level of measurement (i.e., nominal, ordinal, interval, or ratio). We might arrange a sample of elements into a frequency distribution for religious preference, political affiliation, or any number of other nominal categorizations. We could also arrange data according to various socioeconomic levels or social classes, reflecting some ordinal frequency distributional arrangement. There are seemingly endless applications of frequency distributions for social and/or psychological characteristics or information. The improvement in *informative value* as we have moved from one data arrangement (Table 3.1) to another (Table 3.2) is apparent. We can say that our data in Table 3.1 are to some degree in *disarray*. Our attempt to order these data in Table 3.2 has given us a much clearer picture of the distribution of students by year in school.

For sample sizes in excess of 25 (where $N > 25$–read "N is greater than 25"), frequency distributions of values are especially helpful for introducing clarity to one's research work. Table 3.3 presents raw scores for 82 students taking a junior English proficiency examination at a small college. The scores in Table 3.3 are in disarray in their present form. Our initial attempts to deal with these data in ungrouped form would be cumbersome, to say the least. We would experience considerable difficulty trying to enter tallies in a fre-

TABLE 3.3
Junior English Proficiency Examination Scores for 82 Students. (Data in Disarray.)

326	322	349	358	343	390	345	322	333	335	338	338	339
349	350	351	365	371	356	344	355	345	344	340	359	351
356	381	375	371	370	360	365	378	390	349	341	346	362
324	381	327	348	367	368	369	371	382	369	387	345	330
327	346	344	332	330	330	344	348	354	358	366	366	367
389	388	324	322	339	368	373	378	377	382	383	345	365
345	369	340	358									

TABLE 3.4
Frequency Distribution of Junior Proficiency Examination Scores for 82 Students. (Organized Data.)

Interval	*f*
320–324	5
325–329	3
330–334	5
335–339	5
340–344	8
345–349	12
350–354	4
355–359	7
360–364	2
365–369	12
370–374	5
375–379	4
380–384	5
385–389	3
390–394	2
	$\Sigma f = 82$

quency column for each and every different raw score in the table. Therefore, because our sample size is in excess of 25, we make the decision to treat our data as grouped. *Grouped data* are data that have been ordered into a series of intervals of a specified size. Table 3.4 is a frequency distribution of our data rearranged according to the intervals shown.

By placing our raw scores into intervals of some specified size, we are reducing the potential number of categories into which our data can be divided and grouped. In Table 3.4, our data have been grouped into 15 different intervals of size 5. (The method for achieving this frequency distribution will be illustrated shortly.) We have done this in preference to itemizing each and every score from the largest (390) to the smallest (322) in a long column and marking tallies of frequencies associated with the 82 raw scores in the appropriate intervals (e.g., 390, 389, 388, 387, 386, . . . , 322).

Constructing a Frequency Distribution

The construction of a frequency distribution such as that shown in Table 3.4 is fortunately based on a number of conventional guidelines that researchers tend to follow.

1. We must identify the largest and the smallest scores in the distribution of 82 raw scores. It happens that the largest score is 390 and the smallest score is 322.

2. We determine the difference between these scores, or 390 − 322 = 68. The value, 68, is the distance over which all 82 of the scores are spread and is referred to as the *range.* (This value will be discussed in greater detail in Chapter 5.)
3. We decide how large the interval size should be, given the range over which the scores are spread. Again, we are guided partially by conventional considerations, partially by practicality. If we were to have too few intervals, our data would be so cramped into so few categories that we would be unable to obtain a clear picture of the distribution of these scores. For instance, it would not be very helpful to have only two categories, 350–394 and 320–349. By the same token, if we had too many categories, we would observe that our data would be so dispersed that we would be unable to glean from it a clear picture of the distribution.

   Conventionally, a reasonable number of intervals would be between 10 and 20 of them. Fewer than 10 would be too few, and more than 20 of them would be too many. To determine the appropriate interval size and thus identify the intervals we would need to categorize the data, we will take the range of 68, in this case, and divide it by 15 (an appropriate number of intervals to have between 10 and 20 of them). Proceeding with our computations, 68/15 = 4.53. Since we want our intervals to be arranged in whole-number form, we will round 4.53 to 5.
4. With our interval size determined to be 5, we next start with the smallest score in the array of scores, 322, and construct our first interval in such a way that it (a) includes the smallest score, and (b) begins with a multiple of the interval size we are using.[1]

   The interval 315–319 could be used. The interval size is 5 and 315 is a multiple of the interval size of 5. But in this case, no scores would fall within this interval. The interval 320–324 is selected because (a) it is the appropriate size, 5; (b) it begins with a multiple of the interval size of 5, namely 320; and (c) it includes the smallest score in the distribution, 322.
5. We proceed in this fashion constructing intervals until we have reached the interval that includes the largest score in the distribution, in this case 390–394.
6. Finally, we enter the tallies associated with each and every raw score in the appropriate intervals associated with them. The score of 326 is entered in the interval 325–329; the score of

[1] Conventional interval sizes are 1, 2, 3, 4, and 5; or 10, 20, 30, 40, and 50; or 100, 200, 300, 400, and 500; and so on. Also, for values in decimal form (e.g., batting averages), .1, .2, .3, .4, .5; or .01, .02, .03, .04, .05; etc.

380 belongs in the interval 380–384, and so on. After we have done this, the tallies in each interval are summed and placed in numerical form as shown in Table 3.4. Then we sum the frequencies to complete construction of our frequency distribution.

The primary reasons we use intervals which begin with values that are multiples of the interval size are that (1) it is conventional to do so, and (2) it enables us to make a check on the accuracy of our work when we subsequently analyze the data in the frequency distribution. We are able to scan the column of first values in each interval and make a rapid determination that all values are multiples of interval size 5. The values from the "bottom" of the distribution (those intervals containing the smallest scores) to the "top" of it (those intervals containing the largest scores) which begin each interval are 320, 325, 330, 335, 340, 345, 350, 355, 360, 365, 370, 375, 380, 385, and 390, respectively. An interval such as 351–354 would be easily spotted as an error: 351 is not a multiple of 5. Also, the interval is really of size 4 rather than 5 (only four scores could be placed in the interval: 351, 352, 353, and 354). The interval 350–355 would begin with a multiple of the interval size of 5, but it is of size 6 in this case. No doubt the error would be detected when we examine the next adjacent interval, 356–359, again an error.

The importance of accuracy here cannot be overemphasized. Various measures of central tendency and dispersion or variability (discussed in Chapters 4 and 5, respectively) are computed for data, usually in grouped form. Maintaining the appropriate interval size throughout is important inasmuch as various statistical formulas employ the interval-size value as an integral component.

□ SOME INTERVAL CHARACTERISTICS

Several features of intervals are of interest to social researchers. If we happen to have interval-level data at our disposal, any frequency distribution we construct later with intervals of a given size will have the following features: (1) interval upper and lower limits, and (2) interval midpoints.

Upper and lower limits of intervals are particularly meaningful when we deal with data that are continuously distributed. All too often we think of scores in whole-number form (e.g., 10, 200, 85, etc.), although data are often expressed as fractions of numbers or in decimal form (e.g., 10.3, 200.889, 85.0035, etc.). If we had an array of values expressed in decimal form, we would need to have a system whereby numbers could be assigned to particular intervals. For instance, referring back to Table 3.4, suppose that we had the value 324.2. Where would we place this value? Would we place it in the interval 320–324 or in the interval 325–329? Fortunately, these intervals have upper and lower limits that will function to resolve most problems of categorization that we might face.

The interval 325–329 technically extends from 324.5 to 329.5, and the interval 320–324 technically extends from 319.5 to 324.5. 319.5 and 324.5 are the lower limits of the intervals 320–324 and 325–329, respectively. The values 324.5 and 329.5 are the upper limits of these two intervals, respectively. Since the value 324.2 lies between 319.5 and 324.5, we place it in the interval 320–324.

One minor problem might be encountered if the value we observe were 324.5. Would it belong in the interval 320–324 (whose upper limit is 324.5) or in the interval 325–329 (whose lower limit is 324.5)? In this kind of borderline situation, we must employ a *rounding rule.* We will round 324.5 to the nearest even number. This is purely arbitrary, inasmuch as some books recommend rounding to the nearest odd number. For all mathematical problems in this text, we will usually round all values in decimal form to the nearest *even* whole number. Rounding 324.5 to the nearest even number gives us 324. Therefore, we place this rounded value in the interval 320–324.

Interval midpoints are those points that divide intervals into two equal parts. If the interval is of size 5, the interval midpoint would divide the interval into 2.5 and 2.5. A convenient way of determining interval midpoints is simply to halve the interval size and add that to the lower limit of the interval. Therefore, given an interval size of 5, $5/2 = 2.5$, and adding 2.5 to the lower limit of the interval 320–324, or 319.5, would be

$$319.5 + 2.5 = 322.$$

So 322 is defined as the midpoint of the interval 320–324.

Table 3.5 contains some examples of intervals of various sizes, upper and lower limits that have been determined for them, interval sizes, and interval midpoints.

Occasionally, a researcher will encounter what are known as "open-ended intervals." Suppose the largest score in the distribution

TABLE 3.5
Interval Sizes, Upper and Lower Limits, and Midpoints.

Interval	*Lower Limit*	*Upper Limit*	*Midpoint*	*Interval Size*
15–19	14.5	19.5	17	5
500–509	499.5	509.5	504.5	10
.21–.23	.205	.235	.22	.03
1460–1479	1459.5	1479.5	1469.5	20
.0058–.0061	.00575	.00615	.00595	.0004

of values in Table 3.4 had been 475? This would have necessitated constructing more intervals up to and including the interval which would encompass the large score of 475. But the intervals from 395–399 to 470–474 would have no frequencies in them. Rather than go to the trouble of setting up all of these intervals, the researcher may decide to designate the last interval as 390+. This would become the open-ended interval. For the primary purpose of maintaining the simplicity of computational work to follow, it will be assumed that all intervals in grouped data form will be of the same size. Even though the interval 390+ would contain a score of 475, we would consider this interval to be of size 5 for all practical purposes.

Whenever data are grouped into intervals such as those shown in Table 3.4, a certain amount of accuracy is sacrificed. For instance, the eight frequencies in the interval, 340–344, are all presumed to be equal to the midpoint of that interval, or 342. In reality, the interval may contain eight scores of 344. But we group data into intervals because it makes the data easier to manage for analysis and descriptive purposes. Clearly, we trade a certain amount of accuracy for greater ease in data presentation and computation. This is an acceptable exchange.

□ SOME ASSUMPTIONS ASSOCIATED WITH FREQUENCY DISTRIBUTIONS

For data of the nominal level, frequency distributions can be constructed without restrictions. Acceptable mathematical operations would include determining proportions or percentages (to be discussed in the next section). In short, we would be able to designate for a given distribution that 40 percent would be Catholic, 30 percent Protestant, 20 percent Jewish, and 10 percent "other." Other nominal variables and categorizations could be treated similarly.

For data at the ordinal level of measurement, we are able to rank-order the various intervals, and limited calculations are permissible. (Centiles, deciles, and quartiles are points that can be computed for ordinal-level data. These will be discussed in the next section.) When we have data at the interval level of measurement, there are no restrictions in our mathematical operations as they are applied to frequency distributions of scores.

□ CUMULATIVE FREQUENCY DISTRIBUTIONS

A type of frequency distribution that shows us how many scores are below (or above) a given point is called a *cumulative frequency dis-*

TABLE 3.6
Cumulative Frequency Distribution of 100 Scores.

Interval	*f*	*Cf*[a]
16–19	3	3
20–23	4	7
24–27	10	17
28–31	12	29
32–35	4	33
36–39	9	42
40–43	10	52
44–47	7	59
48–51	8	67
52–55	9	76
56–59	12	88
60–63	0	88
64–67	2	90
68–71	9	99
72–75	1	100
	$\Sigma f = 100$	

[a]Cf = cumulative frequencies.

tribution. For example, Table 3.6 is a cumulative frequency distribution of 100 scores. In this table, we have summed scores in each successive interval, beginning with the smallest scores and proceeding to the largest scores in the distribution. Note that the frequencies in the first interval, 16–19, have been added to the frequencies in the next interval, 20–23; and so on. This accumulation of frequencies can be seen in the column labeled Cf, or cumulative frequencies.

Sometimes this type of frequency distribution is helpful in permitting us to see approximately where the middle of the distribution of scores might be. Also, some researchers prefer to construct a cumulative frequency distribution prior to certain applications of statistical values such as the median (see Chapter 4).

□ PERCENTAGES, PROPORTIONS, CENTILES, DECILES, AND QUARTILES

A *proportion* is determined by dividing a part of a sum of frequencies by the sum of the frequencies. For example, if we wanted to know what proportion 20 scores were of 50, we would divide 20 by 50 or 20/50 = .40. Here .40 is the proportion of scores that 20 is of 50.

Multiplying .40 by 100 will convert the proportion to a *percentage* (.40 × 100 = 40 percent). We can say, therefore, that 20 is 40 percent of 50. We can also accomplish this by moving the decimal point two spaces to the right and adding the word "percent."

TABLE 3.7
Centiles, Deciles, and Quartiles in a Hypothetical Distribution of Scores.

Intervals	*Quartiles*		*Deciles*		*Centiles*
Highest scores	Q_4	=	D_{10}	=	C_{100} (point leaving 100% of scores below it)
⋮			D_9	=	C_{90} (point leaving 90% of scores below it)
⋮			D_8	=	C_{80} (point leaving 80% of scores below it)
⋮	Q_3			=	C_{75} (point leaving 75% of scores below it)
⋮			D_7	=	C_{70} (point leaving 70% of scores below it)
⋮			D_6	=	C_{60} (point leaving 60% of scores below it)
⋮	Q_2	=	D_5	=	C_{50} (point leaving 50% of scores below it)
⋮	⋮		⋮		
⋮	Q_1		⋮	=	C_{25} (point leaving 25% of scores below it)
Lowest scores			D_1	=	C_{10} (point leaving 10% of scores below it)

In any frequency distribution of scores, there are points below (and above) which a certain percentage of scores will be found. A specific point in a distribution of scores below which a given proportion (or percentage) of scores will be found is called a *centile.* Centiles are represented symbolically by C. For instance, the 18th centile would be written symbolically as C_{18} and would be that point in a distribution of scores below which 18 percent of the scores would be found. C_{35} is that point in a distribution of scores below which 35 percent of the scores will be found; and so on.

Decile points (e.g., D_1, D_2, D_3, etc.) are points that systematically divide a distribution of scores into groups of 10 percent each. D_1 is the numerical equivalent of C_{10} and is that point below which 10 percent of the scores in the distribution are found. D_2 is the second decile, the numerical equivalent to C_{20}, and it is that point below which 20 percent of the scores in the distribution are found.

A third way of dividing distributions of scores is by using *quartiles.* Quartiles are 25 percent points in distributions of scores. For example, Q_1 would be equivalent to C_{25} or the 25th centile, and it would be that point below which 25 percent of the scores in the distribution would be found. The Q_3 is the numerical equivalent to C_{75} and would be that point leaving 75 percent of the scores in the distribution below it. Table 3.7 provides percentage cutoff points for centiles, deciles, and quartiles.

Centiles, deciles, and quartiles are computed as follows. First, we determine what centile (e.g., C_9, C_{20}, etc.) we are seeking in a distribution of scores. Suppose that we are seeking the 23rd centile or C_{23} with the data in Table 3.8. We are interested in determining that point in the distribution which leaves 23 percent of the scores below it. We must multiply our sample size, $N = 50$, by the proportion, .23, or $(.23)(50) = 11.5$. The C_{23} is, therefore, that point which leaves

TABLE 3.8
Frequency Distribution of 50 Scores.

Interval	*f*	*Cf*
20–24	5	5
25–29	6	11
30–34	11	22
35–39	4	26
40–44	3	29
45–49	2	31
50–54	9	40
55–59	10	50
	$\Sigma f = 50$	

11.5 scores below it. Beginning at the end of the distribution containing the smallest scores, we count the frequencies we are seeking.

The first interval, 20–24, contains five frequencies. The next interval, 25–29, contains six frequencies. So far, we have 11 frequencies in the first two intervals (in much the same way as we might construct a cumulative frequency distribution). We need only $\frac{1}{2}$ of one frequency in the next interval to give us our 11.5 frequencies. But since there are 11 frequencies in that interval, we will need to apply the following formula to obtain C_{23}:

$$LL' + \frac{fn}{ff}(i),$$

where

LL' = lower limit of the interval we are entering to obtain the frequencies we need to get our desired number of frequencies
fn = frequencies we need
ff = frequencies found in the interval
i = interval size

With this formula, we proceed as follows:

$$\begin{aligned} C_{23} &= 29.5 + \frac{.5}{11}(5) \\ &= 29.5 + \frac{2.5}{11} \\ &= 29.5 + .2 \\ &= 29.7. \end{aligned}$$

Here 29.7 is defined as the 23rd centile.

As an additional example, suppose that we are seeking the Q_3 or third quartile, that point leaving 75 percent of the scores below it. We must multiply our sample size, 50, by .75, or (50) (.75) = 37.5. Next, we count all frequencies from the first interval containing the smallest scores toward the intervals containing the larger scores, until we reach that point which has the desired frequencies we are seeking, or 37.5 of them. Using the same information in Table 3.8, we count up the distribution until we reach the interval, 50–54. Up to that point, we have 31 scores. We need 6.5 more scores for our desired 37.5 of them. But there are nine scores in the interval 50–54. Therefore, we enter that interval to get the frequencies we need by applying the formula we used for the 23rd centile:

$$\begin{aligned} Q_3 &= 49.5 + \frac{6.5}{9}(5) \\ &= 49.5 + \frac{32.5}{9} \\ &= 49.5 + 3.6 \\ &= 53.1. \end{aligned}$$

So 53.1 is Q_3, the third quartile, that point below which 75 percent of the scores are found.

This procedure will be useful in solving various problems in Chapters 4 and 5. At the end of this chapter are various mathematical problems to work for practice and to enhance your understanding of terms presented here. Answers to all mathematical problems in this and subsequent chapters are found in Appendix B.

In each of the examples given above, the frequencies we sought for various centiles and quartiles were rounded to the nearest tenth rather than rounded to whole numbers. All such problems to be worked at chapter ends have usually been rounded to the nearest tenth, unless other instructions have been given. This represents a slight improvement in the accuracy of our calculations for the various centiles computed [e.g., (50) (.75) = 37.5, not 38; (50) (.23) = 11.5, not 12].

Centiles, deciles, and quartiles are useful indicators. They give the researcher a better understanding of the distribution of any particular aggregate of values. These percentage points are also useful for computing several measures of variability to be discussed in Chapter 5, such as the interquartile range and 10–90 range. At the very least, it is assumed that the researcher has ordinal-level information for such centile computations where lower (and sometimes upper) limits of intervals are used. Preferably, the researcher should have interval-level data to justify fully such computations.

□ HISTOGRAMS

A *histogram* is a graph constructed to portray diagrammatically the frequency of occurrence in a distribution of scores. Figure 3.1 is a histogram of the information presented in Table 3.4.

The horizontal axis in Figure 3.1 marks off the various intervals from 320–324 to 390–394. The vertical axis to the far left identifies the frequency of occurrence of persons with scores falling within each interval.

Constructing the Histogram

Histograms may be constructed as follows. Graph paper will be helpful and is recommended for this purpose.

1. Draw the horizontal and vertical axes as shown in Figure 3.1. Make the vertical axis about two-thirds as long as the horizontal axis, as shown.

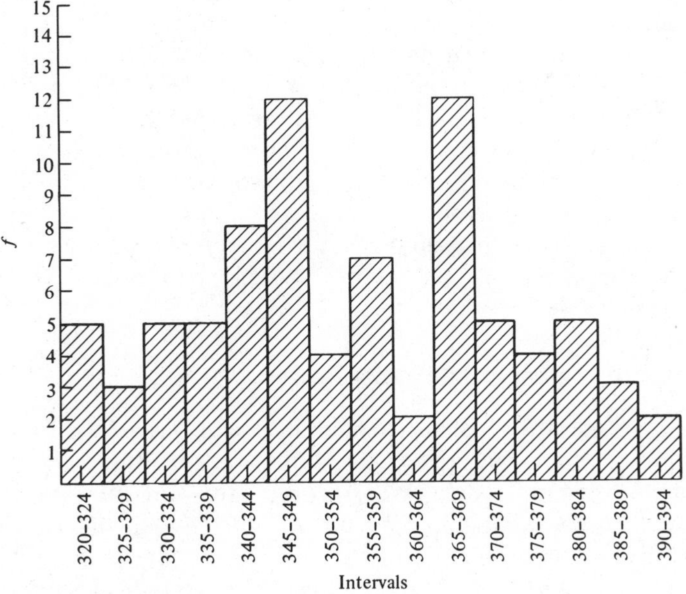

FIGURE 3.1. Histogram of the Data in Table 3.4.

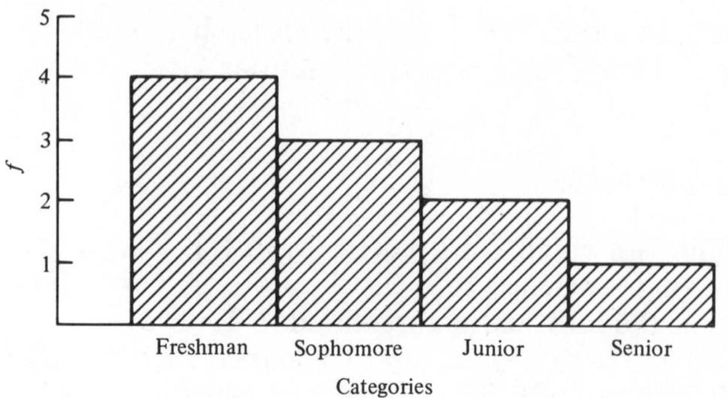

FIGURE 3.2. Histogram of the Data in Table 3.2.

2. Identify equal divisions along both axes, marking off numbers of frequencies on the vertical axis and equal spacings for intervals along the horizontal axis.
3. Draw vertical bars using as your dividing lines between bars the upper and lower limits of each adjacent interval. This will place the vertical bars in such a position that the center of each bar will be directly over the midpoint of the interval. This is the reason for constructing these bars in this fashion.

The height of each of the vertical bars is determined by the frequencies in each interval. Draw the first vertical bar to a height of five frequencies, the second bar to a height of three frequencies, and so forth, until all vertical bars have been drawn. The highest vertical bars will be for the intervals 345–349 and 365–369, respectively, with 12 frequencies each. The lowest vertical bars will be found in the intervals 360–364 and 390–394, respectively, as shown in Figure 3.1. You have now constructed a histogram that should closely resemble the one in this figure.

We may construct histograms for virtually any data we have. For example, Figure 3.2 is a histogram for the distribution of 10 students taken from Table 3.2.

Uses of Histograms in Social Research

The primary utility of histograms in social research is to illustrate graphically scores from a frequency distribution. Important features of distributions of scores will become apparent by a rapid visual inspection of the histogram. We will be able to make decisions about the nature and shape of the distribution. Such decisions will help us to determine which of several alternative statistical measures we might use to provide the most informative description of the data we have collected. The shape of distributions of scores will take on increasing significance as we cover material dealing with measures of central tendency and variability in Chapters 4 and 5.

□ FREQUENCY POLYGONS

In the case of histograms, we utilized vertical bars to represent the frequency of occurrence of various values. *Frequency polygons* do precisely the same thing, although a series of lines connecting points is used rather than vertical bars. Figure 3.3 is a frequency polygon drawn directly from the data presented in the histogram in Figure 3.1. If we were to place a dot at the top and in the center of each vertical bar in the histogram in Figure 3.1, and then if we were to connect the dots by straight lines, we would have a frequency polygon for the same information.

Notice in Figure 3.3 that we have "tied down" the ends of the frequency polygon to the far left and to the far right by attaching straight lines to the midpoints of the next intervals to the far left and far right. (These are the extreme intervals with no frequencies in them, and as such, the straight line we draw attaches directly to the horizontal axis at both "ends" of the distribution to provide "closure" for the frequency polygon.) Like histograms, frequency polygons portray the shape of distributions of scores.

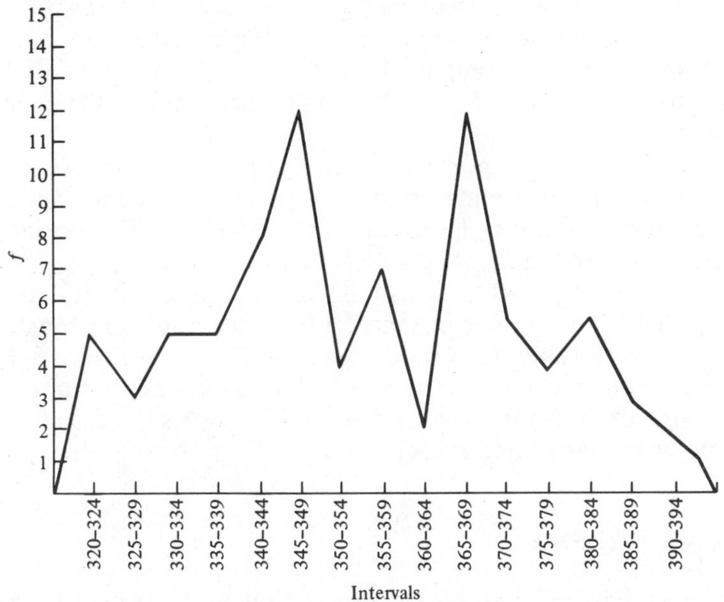

FIGURE 3.3. Frequency Polygon for the Data in Figure 3.1.

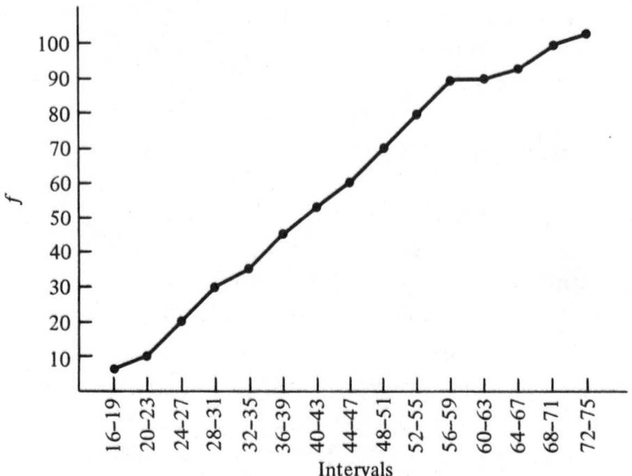

FIGURE 3.4. Ogive Curve for the Data in Table 3.6.

Uses of Frequency Polygons

Frequency polygons have essentially the same functions as histograms. However, there is additional flexibility in that frequency polygons from several different distributions of scores can be superimposed upon one another for comparative purposes. If a researcher wanted to know if two or more distributions of scores were similar in terms of their shape, frequency polygons could be drawn for both sets of scores and placed upon one another in the same graph. This would permit instant comparison of the two distributions of scores, and a decision could be made easily about their differences or similarities.

Because frequency polygons utilize upper and lower limits of intervals, it is recommended that they be used for data primarily at the ordinal or interval levels of measurement. This restriction is frequently relaxed in actual practice, however.

Frequency polygons can also be computed for cumulative frequency distributions. For instance, a frequency polygon constructed for the data in Table 3.6 would appear as shown in Figure 3.4. This type of frequency polygon is referred to as an ogive curve. *Ogive curves* give us an impression of how rapidly scores increase from low to high over a designated range.

□ BAR GRAPHS

Bar graphs are similar to histograms in that bars are used to portray the frequency of occurrence of particular values. However, bar

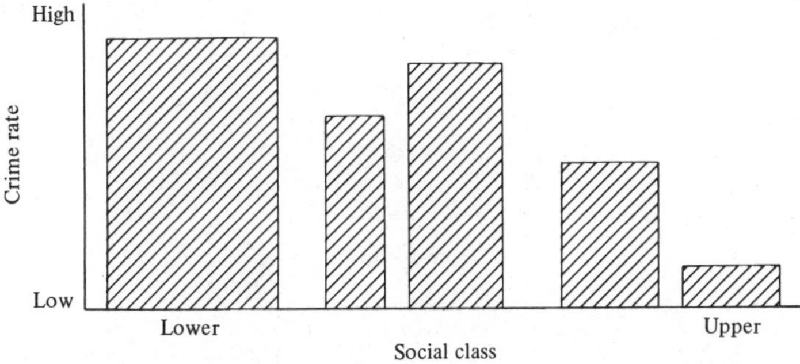

FIGURE 3.5. Bar Graph Reflecting Social Class and Crime. [With permission from Travis Hirschi, "Social Class and Crime," in Gerald W. Thielbar and Saul D. Feldman, *Issues in Social Inequality* (Boston: Little, Brown and Company, 1972), p. 508.]

graphs provide the researcher with considerably more flexibility. Bar graphs can be presented either vertically (as is the case with histograms) or horizontally. Figure 3.5 shows a bar graph reflecting varying crime rates by social class. Notice in Figure 3.5 that it is not necessary to maintain equal widths from one bar to the next or to make use of upper and lower limits of intervals.

The bar graph in Figure 3.5 consists of various vertical bars that are indicative of higher or lower crime rates. The horizontal axis is fluid, ranging from lower class at the far left to upper class at the far right. An inspection of the bar graph gives us some idea of the frequency of crime from one social class level to the next.

Bar graphs can also be used to illustrate many other things, including population age trends, mortality, birthrates for different countries, and crime incidence. Figure 3.6 portrays a bar graph constructed from data collected by Atkyns and Hanneman (1974).

These researchers were interested in communication behavior among drug users and nonusers as one part of a larger study they conducted. The bar graph in Figure 3.6 shows percentage distributions of the extent to which drug users and non-drug users turn to various sources for information about drugs and their effects. An inspection of Figure 3.6 shows, among other things, that drug users differ from non-drug users in the sources of information they utilize for drug knowledge and effects. Non-drug users are more inclined to use private physicians, telephone drug lines, and drug program information, whereas users turn most frequently to their friends.

Because of the fact that there are virtually no restrictions to the use of bar graphs, they can be used to present data at any measurement level. These graphs are perhaps the easiest to construct of those presented in this chapter, and they are used regularly in social research.

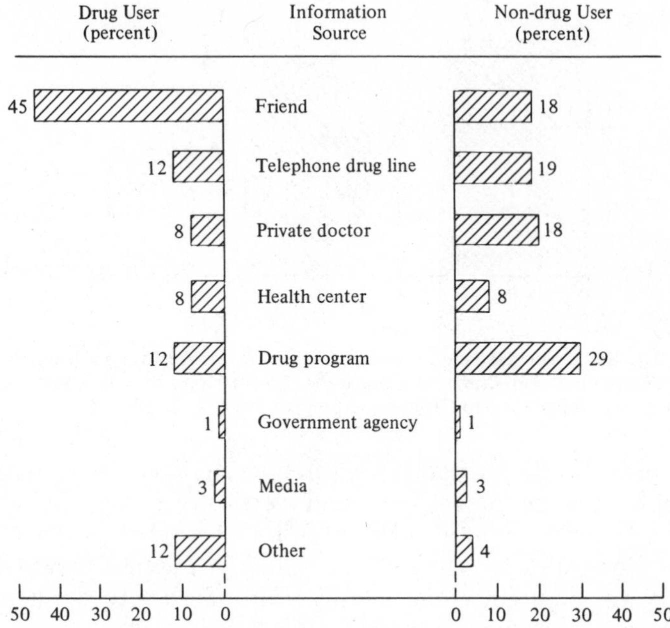

FIGURE 3.6. Percentage Distribution of Information Sources of Drug Users and Non-drug Users. (Adapted from Robert L. Atkyns and Gerhard J. Hanneman, "Illicit Drug Distribution and Dealer Communication Behavior," *Journal of Health and Social Behavior,* **15**:41, 1974.)

□ PIE CHARTS

Pie charts are circular graphs divided into various sectors that represent fractions of the total circle. One of the more frequent uses of pie charts is to illustrate the frequency of occurrence of different types of crime. For instance, the FBI publishes the *Uniform Crime Report Bulletin*, which includes various *crime clocks*—pie charts that show approximately how often different types of crime are committed. Figure 3.7 shows the number of burglaries committed each hour in the United States. The crime clock itself represents 1 hour, and the crimes are portrayed as occurring every so many minutes or seconds.

Pie charts can also be used to represent distributions of ethnic or racial categories for a given population, sex distribution, and political distribution. Figure 3.8 shows a pie chart of an hypothetical distribution of political affiliation for U.S. voters in the most recent national elections.

Pie charts have relatively fewer uses compared with histograms,

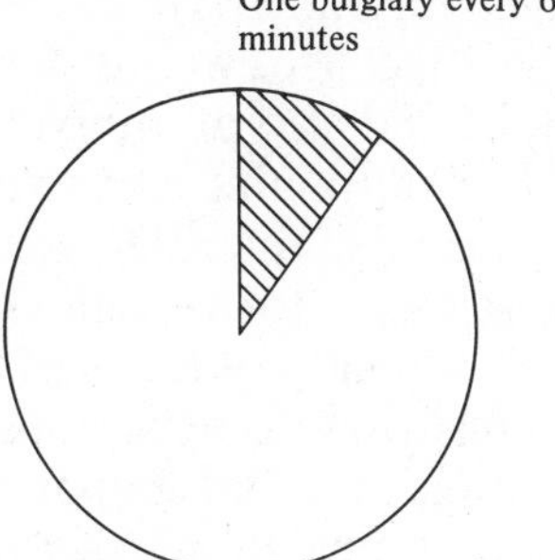

FIGURE 3.7. Crime Clock. [From the *FBI Uniform Crime Report Bulletin* (Washington, D.C.: U.S. Government Printing Office, 1979.)]

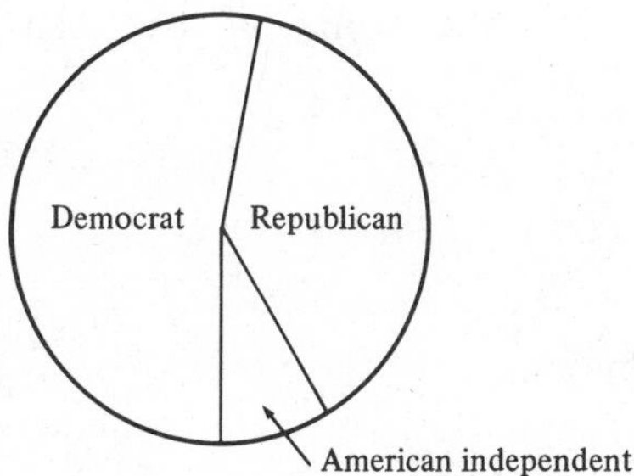

FIGURE 3.8. Pie Chart Showing U.S. Voter Political Affiliation.

frequency polygons, and bar graphs. Their primary limitation is that there are only so many divisions of the "pie" that can be made before it becomes cluttered. A pie chart with too many divisions or sectors makes it difficult for the researcher to label each sector adequately. Therefore, it is recommended that if pie charts are used to portray social data of one form or another, the number of divisions of the pie should be limited to six or seven at most. There are no special assumptions that would restrict the use of pie charts in research work.

□ SUMMARY

We have presented and discussed a number of useful strategies for portraying social and/or psychological data graphically. First, we must determine whether or not to treat our data in ungrouped or grouped form. Such a decision hinges on whether our sample is smaller or larger than approximately 25. When we group our data into intervals of a specified size, we must be mindful of upper and lower limits of intervals, and also of interval midpoints. These points will be helpful later in determining percentage cutoff points associated with centiles, deciles, and quartiles. Recasting our raw data into grouped form makes it easier for certain computations to be made that describe the distributional properties of the scores.

Also useful is the construction of various graphs known as histograms, frequency polygons, and bar graphs. These tools can be used to visually assess distributional properties of an array of scores. It should be understood that these graphic aids are not statistical methods, although they have considerable informative value and function as supplemental information when presented together with statistical procedures. In Chapter 4 we examine several statistical measures that describe some of the distributional properties of scores.

SELECTED STUDY TERMS

Ungrouped data
Frequency distribution
Grouped data
Upper and lower interval limits
Interval midpoints
Cumulative frequency distribution
Proportion
Percentage
Centile
Decile
Quartile
Histogram
Frequency polygon
Ogive curve
Bar graph
Pie chart
Crime clock

EXERCISES

1. Under what conditions would a researcher benefit by treating a set of scores in grouped fashion? Explain.
2. Differentiate between a frequency polygon and a histogram. In what ways would a bar graph be similar to a histogram?
3. Construct a frequency polygon for the following frequency distribution of scores.

Interval	*f*
10–14	6
15–19	7
20–24	13
25–29	8
30–34	6
35–39	10
40–44	19
45–49	15
50–54	7
55–59	3
60–64	9
65–69	12
70–74	13
75–79	5
	$\Sigma f = 133$

4. Determine upper and lower limits for the following intervals:
(a) 90–109 (b) 1500–1599 (c) .20–.29
(d) .0055–.0059 (e) 136–139 (f) 200–249
Next, determine the interval midpoints for these intervals.

5. Given the following array of scores, construct a frequency distribution beginning with an interval of 30–39.

33 44 57 38 92 111 103 152 188 159 57 45 50 60
70 42 79 68 62 165 158 35 49 82 95 18 99 102
91 94 39 40 110 115 56 84 137 126 145 176 164
138 156 148 186 67 58 92 30 49 90 54 87 96 76
94 100 103 100 105 110 110 182 167 173 128 119
177 115 115 83 49 68 58 190 187 154 139 168 150
112

6. For the data you have arranged into a frequency distribution in Exercise 5, determine the following centiles, deciles, and quartiles.
(a) C_{27} (b) Q_3 (c) D_8 (d) C_4
(e) D_5 (f) Q_1 (g) C_{90} (h) D_3
In each case, specify the proportion of scores that would be found below each of the points you have identified.

7. Given the following information, construct a pie chart.

Democrat	35 percent
Republican	42 percent
American Independent	20 percent
Other	3 percent

8. What are some of the major restrictions associated with histograms and frequency polygons? Discuss briefly. Are there any special requirements for application to social data of particular kinds?

9. Convert the following proportions to percentages.
(a) .0036 (b) .1560 (c) .9700
(d) .1158 (e) .5550 (f) .0004

10. Identify the interval midpoints and the upper and lower limits associated with the data in Table 3.4.

11. Construct an ogive curve for the data in Table 3.5.

REFERENCES

Atkyns, Robert L., and Gerhard J. Hanneman, "Illicit Drug Distribution and Dealer Communication Behavior," *Journal of Health and Social Behavior*, **15**:36-43, 1974.

F.B.I., *Uniform Crime Report Bulletin.* Washington, D.C.: U.S. Government Printing Office, 1979.

Hirschi, Travis, "Social Class and Crime," in Gerald W. Thielbar and Saul D. Feldman, eds., *Issues in Social Inequality.* Boston: Little, Brown and Company, 1972.

Miller, Delbert C., *Handbook of Research Design and Social Measurement*, 3rd. ed. New York: David McKay Co., Inc., 1977.

4 Measures of Central Tendency

Descriptive statistical values that depict central locations of distributions of scores are referred to as *measures of central tendency*. This chapter presents three such measures that assist the researcher in determining those points around which scores tend to focus.

For instance, if two classes of sociology students took separate examinations on some material studied by members of both groups, we could refer to certain measures of central tendency to see whether or not one group "outperformed" the other or did generally better (or worse) than the other.

Three measures of central tendency that are popularly applied to social data are (1) the mode, (2) the median, and (3) the mean.

□ THE MODE

In some distributions of scores or values, certain scores occur more frequently than any other scores. For data in *ungrouped form*, the *mode* is defined as that value in a distribution of scores which occurs most frequently.

Suppose that we have the following scores:

25 25 26 27 29 31 35 35 39 39 49 50 50
50 52 60.

The mode for these data would be the score 50 because it occurs more frequently than any of the other values. The values of 25, 35, and 39 occur twice each, but the value of 50 occurs three times.

In certain situations, several values occur most frequently. Suppose that we were to modify the set of scores above and rearrange them as follows:

25 25 25 26 27 29 31 35 35 35 39 39
39 50 52.

In this case, three values would be reported as the modes for these data (e.g., 25, 35, and 39) because all occur equally and with the greatest frequency.

A rule of thumb to apply when multiple modes occur would be to report a maximum of three modal values for the reader's information. If more than three modes exist, it would be best for the researcher to say that because an excessive number of values occur most frequently, an alternative measure of central tendency should be selected if possible. Or the researcher may say simply that there is no mode for these data.

For data in *grouped form*, the *mode* is defined as the midpoint of the interval containing the most frequencies. Some hypothetical data have been arranged in Table 4.1. For this information, the mode for these data would be the midpoint of the interval 30–39, or 34.5, because this interval contains the most frequencies.

In situations where more than one interval contains the most frequencies, we can apply the rule of thumb earlier applied to data in

TABLE 4.1
Distribution of Scores.

Interval	*f*
20–29	3
30–39	13 (midpoint 34.5 = mode)
40–49	8
50–59	4
60–69	9
70–79	10
80–89	12
	$\Sigma f = 59$

ungrouped form. Report up to three interval midpoints as modal values. If more than three intervals contain the most frequencies, the researcher should say that either (1) there is no mode, or (2) some alternative central tendency measure should be selected if possible because of the multiple-mode condition.

Assumptions, Advantages, and Disadvantages of the Mode

There are no restrictions governing the application of the mode. Data of the nominal level of measurement or higher are amenable to modal analysis.

The primary utility of the mode is that it reflects the most popular value or values in any distribution of scores. Of course, an accompanying disadvantage is that the most popular value may not be most descriptive of the central tendency of the distribution. In Table 4.1, for example, the mode of 34.5 fails to reflect the fact that there are also large concentrations of scores in the intervals 70–79 and 80–89, respectively. The central tendency of the distribution leans more toward the upper end of the distribution, where the larger scores occur.

It is important for the researcher to examine carefully the data collected before selecting a central tendency measure. To the extent that scores occurring most frequently lie in the extremes of the distribution (i.e., below most of the rest of the scores or above most of the rest of the scores), the mode would be a poor indicator of the central tendency of that distribution.

Compared with the other measures of central tendency to be presented in this chapter, the mode is by far the easiest to compute.

For data of the nominal level, such as political affiliation or religious preference, the mode would, of course, be the appropriate measure to apply. We could designate one political party or another or one religious faith or another as the modal party or faith for a given sample of elements such as a small group or a community.

When situations exist where higher levels of measurement can be assumed, the researcher will have a greater range of choices between other more useful and descriptive measures of central tendency, such as the median or the mean.

□ THE MEDIAN

The median is defined as that point which divides a distribution of ordered scores into two equal parts. For data in ungrouped form, such as the array of scores

55 56 57 58 59 60 61 62 63,

the median would be 59. 59 is that value which divides the nine scores into two equal parts.

If we were to drop one of the scores from the distribution, leaving the array

55 56 57 58 59 60 61 62,

the median would be that point between the two central scores in the distribution that would theoretically divide them into two equal parts. A simple way of obtaining this value is to sum the two central scores and divide by 2, or

$$\text{median} = \frac{58 + 59}{2}$$

$$= \frac{117}{2}$$

$$= 58.5.$$

One additional example would be helpful here. Suppose that we had the following score arrangement:

54 55 56 90 110 111 112 450.

We would simply take the two central values, 90 and 110, sum them, and divide by 2:

$$\text{median} = \frac{90 + 110}{2}$$

$$= \frac{200}{2}$$

$$= 100.$$

100 is the median for these data. It is the theoretical point that divides the distribution into two equal parts.

If the researcher finds an arrangement of ungrouped data where several identical scores occur near the center of the distribution, such as the array

15 18 19 20 22 23 23 23 23 24 25 26 27,

the most direct solution is simply to designate any one of the scores of 23 as the median for these data. This may be done by inspection without any calculation.

The primary requirement for computing the median for ungrouped data is that we must first arrange the scores into an array from low to high or high to low. Once we have ordered the scores in this fashion,

TABLE 4.2
Frequency Distribution of Graduate Record Examination Scores for 151 Students.

Interval	*f*	*Cf*
500–509	8	8
510–519	17	25
520–529	14	39
530–539	3	42
540–549	10	52
550–559	11	63
560–569	12	75
570–579	15	90
580–589	12	102
590–599	9	111
600–609	13	124
610–619	15	139
620–629	12	151
	$\Sigma f = 151$	

we can readily determine that point which divides equally the set of scores.

For data in grouped form, we are still interested in determining that point which divides the distribution of scores into two equal parts. But whenever data are arranged into intervals such as those shown in Table 4.2, we must use a *grouped data formula* to determine the median value.

Computing the Median for Grouped Data

First, we must divide the distribution of frequencies into two equal parts. In Table 4.2, there are 151 frequencies. Therefore, $\frac{151}{2} =$ 75.5. We need to determine that point in the distribution which leaves 75.5 scores above it and 75.5 scores below it. The median for grouped data involves a computation similar to that used for deciles, centiles, and quartiles. Arithmetically, the median is equal to C_{50}, D_5, and Q_2.

In Table 4.2, a cumulative frequency distribution has also been constructed. We can use this to our advantage as a means of determining which interval we will need to enter to find the median value. The sum of the frequencies up to and including those found in the interval 560–569 is 75. We need .5 frequencies in the next interval to obtain our desired 75.5 (or half) of them. The next interval contains 15 frequencies. With this information, we enter the interval at the lower limit of it and apply the following formula:

$$\text{median} = LL' + \frac{fn}{ff}(i),$$

where

LL' = lower limit of the interval we need to enter to obtain the frequencies we need to acquire half of them
fn = frequencies we need in the interval
ff = frequencies found in the interval
i = interval size

Based on the existing information in Table 4.2, the median is determined as follows:

$$\text{median} = 569.5 + \frac{.5}{15(10)}$$

$$= 569.5 + \frac{5}{15}$$

$$= 569.5 + .3$$

$$= 569.8.$$

The median for these data is 569.8.

Assumptions, Advantages, and Disadvantages of the Median

The primary assumption underlying the computation of the median is that the data are measured according to an ordinal scale. Rank-ordered information includes attitudinal scores of various kinds, socioeconomic status, and grade-point average.

Compared with the mode, the median is a very stable measure of *central tendency*. It is possible for several modes to occur in a given distribution. These modes may be located anywhere, thus giving us a poor picture of the central tendency of any score arrangement. There is only one median, however. It occurs precisely at the center of the distribution and always reflects that point which divides the total number of scores into two equal parts. In this sense, then, it is a more reliable measure of central tendency.

The median is also stable in another sense. Suppose that we were to rearrange the distribution of frequencies in Table 4.2 in such a way so as to create three additional intervals, 630–639, 640–649, and 650–659. Further suppose that we removed the frequencies from the interval 620–629 and distributed these 12 frequencies equally throughout the newly created additional intervals. We might have a situation such as that shown in Table 4.3.

If we were to recompute the median for this new arrangement of scores, the median value would remain unaffected. It would still be 569.8. This would be true in spite of the fact that additional intervals

TABLE 4.3
Rearrangement of the Data in Table 4.2.

Interval	*f*	*Cf*
500–509	8	8
510–519	17	25
520–529	14	39
530–539	3	42
540–549	10	52
550–559	11	63
560–569	12	75 (median = 569.8)
570–579	15	90
580–589	12	102
590–599	9	111
600–609	13	124
610–619	15	139
620–629	0	139 (frequencies removed)
630–639	4	143 (new interval)
640–649	4	147 (new interval)
650–659	4	151 (new interval)
	$\Sigma f = 151$	

with larger scores were created. The median can only be affected by (1) adding more scores to the distribution, or (2) modifying score arrangements near the center of the distribution.

This property of stability makes the median an attractive measure of central tendency, especially when compared with the mean. The statement that extreme scores (either very large or very small scores) have no effect on the median value holds for data in both ungrouped and grouped forms.

□ THE MEAN

Perhaps the most widely used (and abused) measure of central tendency is the mean. The *mean* is defined as the average value in any distribution of scores. For instance, the mean is determined for a set of ungrouped scores by summing them and dividing by the number of scores. The following formula would be applied:

$$\text{mean or } \overline{X} = \frac{\sum X_i}{N},$$

(read: X bar)

where

$\sum X_i$ = sum of the scores
N = number of scores

Suppose that we had the following set of raw scores:

55 56 59 60 61 65 69 72 75 79 80.

The mean would be determined as follows:

$$\overline{X} = \frac{55 + 56 + 59 + 60 + 61 + 65 + 69 + 72 + 75 + 79 + 80}{11}$$

$$= \frac{731}{11}$$

$$= 66.5.$$

So 66.5 would be the mean for these data.

The Mean Computation for Grouped Data

For data in grouped form, two fairly easy methods of mean computation are available. These are (1) the use of interval midpoints, and (2) the "arbitrary reference point" method. Table 4.4 shows a distribution of 116 scores that have been arranged into intervals of size 5. In Table 4.4, a column MP has been created immediately to the right of the frequency (f) column. This column contains all interval midpoints. A final column, (f) (MP), has been created which is the product of frequencies (f) and interval midpoints (MP).

The mean is determined by summing the products of frequencies

TABLE 4.4
Frequency Distribution Showing Interval Midpoints for the Mean Computation.

Interval	*f*	*MP*	*(f) (MP)*
325–329	6	327	1962
320–324	10	322	3220
315–319	11	317	3487
310–314	3	312	936
305–309	12	307	3684
300–304	2	302	604
295–299	6	297	1782
290–294	10	292	2920
285–289	9	287	2583
280–284	4	282	1128
275–279	8	277	2216
270–274	15	272	4080
265–269	11	267	2937
260–264	9	262	2358
	$\Sigma f = 116$		$\Sigma(f)$ (MP) = 33,897

and interval midpoints, Σ (f) (MP), and dividing by the total number of frequencies (N). Using the data in Table 4.4, we compute the mean from the interval midpoints as follows:

$$\overline{X} = \frac{\sum (f)\,(\text{MP})}{N},$$

where

$\sum (f)$ (MP) = sum of products of frequencies and interval midpoints
N = total number of frequencies

Therefore,

$$\overline{X} = \frac{33{,}897}{116}$$
$$= 292.2.$$

The mean for the data in Table 4.4 is 292.2.

As a way of illustrating the arbitrary-reference-point method, we will use the same data from Table 4.4 and arrange it somewhat differently, as shown in Table 4.5. The method of mean computation to be described below is also useful for computing the standard deviation for grouped data in Chapter 5.

In Table 4.5 we have established a column, x', which is determined as follows. First, we select any interval we wish as the one we believe

TABLE 4.5
Arbitrary-Reference-Point Method of Mean Computation.

Interval	*f*	*x'*	*fx'*
325–329	6	6	36
320–324	10	5	50
315–319	11	4	44
310–314	3	3	9
305–309	12	2	24
300–304	2	1	2
295–299	6	0	0
290–294	10	–1	–10
285–289	9	–2	–18
280–284	4	–3	–12
275–279	8	–4	–32
270–274	15	–5	–75
265–269	11	–6	–66
260–264	9	–7	–63
	$\Sigma f = 116$		$\Sigma fx' = -111$

contains the mean and which will also contain the *arbitrary reference point.* The interval selected in this case is 295–299. Although any interval may be selected, it is usually wise to select an interval near the center of the distribution rather than one far away from it. This will minimize the magnitude of numbers to be manipulated arithmetically later in our work.

We place a 0 in the x' column adjacent to the interval we have selected. Next, we number consecutively away from zero 1, 2, 3, 4, and so on, until the "top" of the distribution is reached (that end of the distribution containing the largest scores). Also, we number consecutively away from zero in the opposite direction–that is, -1, -2, -3, and so on–until the "bottom" of the distribution is reached (that end of the distribution containing the smallest scores).

Once we have these values in place as shown in Table 4.5, we multiply the various frequencies in the f column by their respective x' values. We place each of these products in the final column, fx'. Finally, we sum the products to obtain $\Sigma fx'$, or -111 in this case, as shown in Table 4.5. Now we apply the following formula, given the existing information:

$$\overline{X} = MP' + \frac{\sum fx'}{N}(i),$$

where

MP' = midpoint of the interval we selected as the arbitrary reference point
$\sum fx'$ = sum of the products of frequencies and their adjacent x' values
N = sample size
i = interval size

With this information, we have

$$\begin{aligned}\overline{X} &= 297 + \frac{-111}{116}(5)\\ &= 297 + \frac{-555}{116}\\ &= 297 - 4.8\\ &= 292.2.\end{aligned}$$

The mean for these data in Table 4.5 is 292.2, the same as we obtained when using the interval midpoint method. Both methods yield identical results.

For the beginning student in statistics, it should be reassuring to know that at least with this method for computing the mean for grouped data, it is impossible to be wrong when selecting an arbitrary reference point. You may select any interval you wish for this purpose. But again, your objective is to minimize the mathematical work involved, and you can accomplish this task by selecting an interval that is somewhere near the mean (i.e., you make an educated guess after visually inspecting the distribution of scores). As an example, suppose that you had selected as the interval containing the arbitrary reference point, 325–329. Table 4.6 shows our computational rearrangement to accommodate this selection. We begin by placing a 0 in the interval 325–329. Next, we number away from 0 consecutively, -1, -2, -3, and so on, until the bottom of the distribution is reached, as shown in the table. After we have obtained our x' values, we determine the products of frequencies and x' values as shown. Summing these products gives us a $\Sigma fx' = -807$. With the information from Table 4.6, we may carry out our mean computation as follows:

$$\overline{X} = 327 + \frac{-807}{116}(5)$$

$$= 327 + \frac{-4035}{116}$$

$$= 327 - 34.8$$

$$= 292.2.$$

TABLE 4.6
Arbitrary-Reference-Point Method of Mean Computation with a Different Point from That Selected in Table 4.5.

Interval	*f*	*x'*	*fx'*
325–329	6	0	0
320–324	10	–1	–10
315–319	11	–2	–22
310–314	3	–3	–9
305–309	12	–4	–48
300–304	2	–5	–10
295–299	6	–6	–36
290–294	10	–7	–70
285–289	9	–8	–72
280–284	4	–9	–36
275–279	8	–10	–80
270–274	15	–11	–165
265–269	11	–12	–132
260–264	9	–13	–117
	$\Sigma f = 116$		$\Sigma fx' = -807$

The mean for the data in Table 4.6 is again 292.2. This illustrates that the arbitrary-reference-point method is self-correcting, regardless of the interval you select to begin your computations.

Assumptions, Advantages, and Disadvantages of the Mean

The mean or arithmetic average assumes at least an interval-level scale underlying the variable measured. Technically, data at the ordinal level or nominal level of measurement would not be amenable to mean computations. But the mean is the best-known measure of central tendency. From our earliest years as children, we are bombarded with batting averages, grade-point averages, and the like. Because of the fact that the mean is so well known, there is the tendency on the part of some researchers to apply it to social data indiscriminately, without first seeing whether the level-of-measurement assumption has been met. This is the reason for the most frequent misapplication of mean values in social research.

In addition to being well-known and frequently used, the mean is often used for statistical inference purposes. The reasons for using the mean in this manner are beyond the scope of the present chapter. However, a more detailed explanation will be provided in Chapter 7, where the mean will occur once again but in a role different from that of sheer description of data.

The mean has one primary disadvan age. It is extremely sensitive to the presence of very large or very small scores compared with other scores in distributions. Such scores (i.e., very large or very small ones) are called *deviant scores.* Consider the following example:

(A)	10	11	12	13	14	15	16
(B)	10	11	12	13	14	15	100.

The mean for the A set of scores above is 13. However, the mean for the B set of scores is 25. The great difference in mean values is explained by the presence of the deviant score of 100. No other score in the B distribution is in excess of 15 except that single score. Therefore, using the mean in this instance to depict the central tendency of the scores would be extremely misleading to the reader. We would be led to believe that the scores were, on the average, much higher than would actually be the case. The presence of the deviant score led to this large mean value and is indicative of the instability associated with the mean on such occasions where unusually large or small scores are encountered. Means should never be computed when deviant scores are present. This statement holds for data in grouped form, as well. On such occasions, the researcher should select the median because of its insensitivity to the presence of deviant scores. It would be a more reliable measure of central tendency compared with the mean. Note that for examples A and B above, the median for each distribution of scores would be identical: 13.

☐ THE MODE, MEDIAN, AND MEAN COMPARED

Briefly reviewing, we recall that the mode is the least frequently used measure of central tendency. It is useful for data at the nominal level of measurement, but because the most frequently occurring values in distributions are not necessarily the most central values, the mode is not always the best measure to use.

For data at the ordinal level of measurement, the median is appropriate. There are various statistical tests and procedures that involve the median, but such tests have been overshadowed in statistical work by tests utilizing the better-known mean. The median is the most stable measure of central tendency, however. Deviant scores have absolutely no influence on the magnitude of the median. This particular property of the median renders it superior to the mean whenever deviant scores are encountered.

The mean has the advantage of being useful in statistical inferential work, to be discussed in detail in Chapter 7. Some researchers prefer to present their descriptive statistical information in greater detail than others. In certain instances, all three measures of central tendency have been reported for distributions of scores being analyzed. This gives the reader an opportunity to evaluate the distribution more effectively. We might conclude from this that it is better for statistical description purposes to have too much information rather than too little.

☐ THE MEAN OF MEANS

Whenever the researcher has the opportunity of evaluating information derived from several samples drawn from a given population, it is possible to "average" the means from those samples as the overall best indicator of what that particular characteristic is like for the population. For instance, if we were to have three means at our disposal from three separate samples drawn from a given population, the *grand mean*, or mean of means, would be the best guess of the population mean, rather than using any single mean value separately. Therefore, we may say that in this sense, the mean is the best as well

TABLE 4.7
Computational Illustration for Determining the Grand Mean.

Sample Number	N_i	*Unweighted* $\overline{X}_i$	*Weighted* $(N_i)\ (\overline{X}_i)$
1	$N_1 = 50$	$40\ (\overline{X}_1)$	$2000\ (N_1)\ (\overline{X}_1)$
2	$N_2 = 25$	$65\ (\overline{X}_2)$	$1625\ (N_2)\ (\overline{X}_2)$
3	$N_3 = 40$	$30\ (\overline{X}_3)$	$1200\ (N_3)\ (\overline{X}_3)$
4	$N_4 = 10$	$80\ (\overline{X}_4)$	$800\ (N_4)\ (\overline{X}_4)$
5	$N_5 = 45$	$35\ (\overline{X}_5)$	$1575\ (N_5)\ (\overline{X}_5)$
	$\Sigma N_i = 170$	$\Sigma \overline{X}_i = 250$	$\Sigma (N_i)\ (\overline{X}_i) = 7200$

as the most stable estimate of its population parameter compared with other measures of central tendency. This statement holds only on the condition that several samples are available for analysis. Unfortunately, the researcher rarely has the opportunity of analyzing data from several samples that have been drawn from the same population.

On occasions when we do possess information from several samples, we may wish to average the mean values obtained. Suppose that we had information from five samples, such as those shown in Table 4.7.

If a researcher wants to average mean values, there is a tendency to want to sum the means themselves and then divide by the number of means. If we were to do this for the data in Table 4.7, we would have the sum of the means, $\Sigma \overline{X}_i = 250$, divided by the number of means, 5, or $250/5 = 50$. This procedure would be satisfactory provided that all samples were of equal size. But as can be seen from the data in Table 4.7, the sample sizes are unequal. The sample mean of 80, for instance, has a sample size of 10 associated with it. When this is averaged with the sample mean of 40 (which has a sample size of 50 associated with it), it is given *equal weight.* This causes a misleading grand mean or mean of means to be computed. Summing the means and dividing by the number of means is legitimate only when all sample sizes are equal. For the researcher to make the proper grand mean computation, the means must be *weighted* according to their respective sample sizes. In the example in Table 4.7, each sample mean is weighted by multiplying the mean value by its sample size. These products are shown in the column "$(N_i)\ (\overline{X}_i)$," to the far right in the table. These products are then summed and divided by the sum of the sample sizes for all five samples, or

$$\text{grand mean } (\overline{X}_T) = \frac{\sum (N_i)\ (\overline{X}_i)}{\sum N_i},$$

where

$\sum(N_i)(\overline{X}_i)$ = sum of products of sample sizes and sample means
$\sum N_i$ = sum of the sample sizes

With the information found in Table 4.7, we may compute the grand mean as follows:

$$\overline{X}_T = \frac{7200}{170}$$
$$= 42.4.$$

The grand mean, $\overline{X}_T$, is equal to 42.4. This is the accurate mean of means because each mean has been weighted according to its sample size.

The grand mean has application for certain statistical decision-making problems in later chapters. It is important at this point to recognize the value of weighting each sample mean with the sample size associated with it for maximizing the accuracy of the mean of means computation. It was also stated earlier than whenever the researcher has several means available from different samples taken from the same population, the grand mean becomes the best estimate of the population mean rather than any single mean considered separately.

□ SUMMARY

This chapter has surveyed three popular averages or measures of central tendency.[1] Measures of central tendency describe points around which scores in distributions tend to focus. The mode or most frequently occurring value is the least frequently used measure compared with the median and mean. However, it is suitable for data at the nominal level of measurement and reflects the most typical or most prominent category.

The median is associated with data at the ordinal level of measurement and is considered to be the most stable measure compared with the mean and mode. It is unaffected by deviant scores that may be present in a distribution. The median is not well known, however, and it is less frequently used in research work compared with the mean. The mean is by far the most popular measure of central tendency. But it has the distinct disadvantage of being quite sensitive to deviant scores. Its value is easily influenced by scores that are

[1] Over the years, researchers have referred to these measures collectively as "averages," although technically, only the mean reflects the average score or value for a distribution.

considerably larger or smaller than the rest. The mean is the most frequently used measure of central tendency and is involved extensively in tests of significance to be discussed in later chapters.

Finally, for those occasions when the researcher has several samples available for statistical analysis and description, means of samples may be averaged. The grand mean can be computed, which is the overall mean for several samples. The grand mean is the most accurate estimate of whatever the true population mean happens to be.

Measures of central tendency provide only a partial picture of score distributions, however. Another set of measures, which we study in Chapter 5, provides us with descriptions of the ways in which scores tend to focus around various central tendency measures.

SELECTED STUDY TERMS

Mode
Median
Central tendency
Mean
Arbitrary reference point
Deviant score
Grand mean
Weighting

EXERCISES

1. Given the following information, determine the values requested.

Interval	*f*
550–554	2
545–549	3
540–544	6
535–539	8
530–534	4
525–529	6
520–524	19
515–519	0
510–514	0
505–509	4
500–504	5
	$\Sigma f = 57$

Determine the mode, median, and mean for these data.

2. For the following *ungrouped data*, determine the mode, median, and mean.

8 9 10 11 12 13 14 14 15 20.

3. Given the following information, determine the mode, median, and mean.

Interval	*f*
150–159	8
140–149	7
130–139	6
120–129	5
110–119	12
100–109	9
90–99	10
80–89	8
70–79	3
60–69	10
50–59	8
40–49	7
30–39	7
	$\Sigma f = 100$

4. Given the following information, determine the mode, median, and mean.

15 17 17 18 22 68 120 15 60 45
13 19 26 31 28 15 22 29 41 95.

5. In what sense is the median a more stable measure of central tendency than the mean? Explain. In what sense is the mean more stable than the median?
6. Given the following information, determine the grand mean.

Sample	N_i	$\overline{X}_i$
1	52	47.8
2	65	28.3
3	29	52.5
4	70	40.1
5	10	65.3
6	23	55.4

7. Compute the mean of means for the data in Exercise 6 by summing the means and dividing by the number of means. Compare your answer with that obtained through weighting. What can you say about the influence of sample size on the grand mean when weighting is not carried out by the researcher? Explain.
8. Given the following scores, determine the mean, mode, and median.

55 75 82 41 28 41 55 67 69 75
78 75 55 24 38 42 46 49 57 76.

9. Under what conditions would it not be advisable to use the mean for describing the central tendency of a distribution? Explain.
10. Given the following information, determine the mode, median, and mean.

Interval	*f*
115–119	5
120–124	10
125–129	11
130–134	15
135–139	10
140–144	9
145–149	10
150–154	7
155–159	8
160–164	13
165–169	3
170–174	6
175–179	4
	$\Sigma f = 111$

REFERENCES

Anderson, Theodore R., and Morris Zelditch, Jr., *A Basic Course in Statistics.* New York: Holt, Rinehart and Winston, 1968.

Downie, N. M., and R. W. Heath, *Basic Statistical Methods.* New York: Harper & Row, Publishers, 1974.

Huff, Darrell, and Irving Geis, *How to Lie with Statistics.* New York: W. W. Norton & Company, Inc., 1966.

Williams, Frederick, *Reasoning with Statistics.* New York: Holt, Rinehart and Winston, 1968.

5 Measures of Variability

Descriptions of frequency distributions of scores are incomplete if we refer only to measures of central tendency. It is important to know those points around which scores tend to focus. But it is equally important for us to know *how* scores are distributed around those points. Suppose that we had the following hypothetical sets of raw scores:

(A) 110 111 112 113 114 *115* 116 117 118 119 120
(B) 40 55 70 85 100 *115* 130 145 160 175 190.

The scores in distributions A and B both have identical means of 115. But the scores in both distributions are dispersed differently about the mean. For instance, in distribution A, the scores are closely dispersed around the mean. In distribution B, the scores are widely dispersed about the same point. These distributions have identical central tendency (i.e., equal means), but they have quite different *dispersion* or *variability*.

We can describe the way in which scores focus around various values of central tendency by turning to what are called measures of variability or dispersion. *Measures of variability* depict the way in which distributions of scores are distributed or spread about a central point.

This chapter presents eight measures of dispersion, all of which are used in research work to varying degrees. They include Mueller's and Schuessler's Index of Qualitative Variation (IQV), range, 10–90 range, interquartile range, semi-interquartile range or quartile deviation, average deviation, variance, and standard deviation. All of these measures, with the exception of the IQV, assume that the data are measured according to an interval scale. The IQV assumes that data are measured according to a nominal scale.

□ MUELLER'S AND SCHUESSLER'S INDEX OF QUALITATIVE VARIATION

The *Index of Qualitative Variation* (IQV) is a measure of *attribute heterogeneity*. This means that the IQV measures the degree to which any nominal characteristic (e.g., race, religion, ethnic background, political affiliation, etc.) is evenly (or unevenly) distributed for a given sample of elements.

The usefulness of the IQV in social research is illustrated by a study of group cohesiveness (the degree to which persons in a group "stick together" and are supportive of one another) and the degree of similarity among group members according to the types of tasks they perform. Cramer and Champion (1975) collected four random samples from a bank, a high school, a church administrative organization, and a naval reserve training center. These samples of persons were administered questionnaires that sought to determine the type of individual task performed and each person's perceived group cohesion. The four groups were rank-ordered according to the degree of their perceived group cohesion, and IQV's were computed for each group to see to what extent there was task similarity among them. The researchers reasoned that the greater the task similarity, the greater the degree of cohesion. If this reasoning were true, we would expect to find increasing task similarity as we moved from less cohesive to more cohesive groups. Table 5.1 shows the distributions of the four samples ranked by cohesiveness and distributed throughout a variety of task categories.

Table 5.1 lists five task categories, referring to the number of

TABLE 5.1
IQV's for Four Groups.

Type of Task	Group 1 (Bank)	Group 2 (School)	Group 3 (Naval)	Group 4 (Church)
	(low cohesion)			(high cohesion)
A	10	3	7	3
B	12	7	3	19
C	13	10	3	8
D	14	4	10	
E	11	6	2	
	$N_1 = 60$	$N_2 = 30$	$N_3 = 25$	$N_4 = 30$
	$\text{IQV}_1 = 99.7\%$	$\text{IQV}_2 = 95.8\%$	$\text{IQV}_3 = 90.8\%$	$\text{IQV}_4 = 77.7\%$

different tasks performed by any group. Group 1 performs five different tasks, and group 4 performs three different tasks. It is not necessary that all groups perform the same number of tasks. It is also not necessary that the tasks performed in one group be the same as those performed in another. IQV's may be computed for groups of any size, subdivided into any number of categories.

The IQV formula is

$$\text{IQV} = \frac{\text{observed heterogeneity}}{\text{maximum heterogeneity}} \times 100,$$

where

observed heterogeneity = sum of products of all observed category totals
maximum heterogeneity = sum of products of all expected category totals

Suppose that we observed the three subclassifications of some variable X for a group of 30 in Table 5.2 as a hypothetical illustration. According to these data, there are 5 persons in category A, 15 in category B, and 10 in category C. We can obtain the maximum distribution of these elements (the column labeled "maximum") by dividing our total sample, 30, by k, the number of categories (i.e.,

TABLE 5.2

Category	Observed	Maximum
A	5	10
B	15	10
C	10	10
	$N = 30$	$N = 30$

A, B, and C). In this case, $N/k = 30/3 = 10$. Therefore, 10 elements belong in each of the 3 categories for maximum heterogeneity to exist. The IQV we subsequently compute will reflect the *percent of maximum heterogeneity* associated with our observed distribution of frequencies throughout the k categories.

Based on the information in the hypothetical illustration above, we may compute the observed and maximum heterogeneity values as follows:

$$\begin{aligned}\text{observed heterogeneity} &= (A)(B) + (A)(C) + (B)(C)\\ &= (5)(15) + (5)(10) + (15)(10)\\ &= 75 + 50 + 150 = 275.\\ \text{maximum heterogeneity} &= (A')(B') + (A')(C') + (B')(C')\\ &= (10)(10) + (10)(10) + (10)(10)\\ &= 100 + 100 + 100 = 300.\end{aligned}$$

There are always equal numbers of products in the numerator and denominator terms for samples of any size and for any number of subcategories. The A', B', and C' above refer to each of the subclass or subcategory totals in the maximum heterogeneity column. The IQV for these data becomes

$$\begin{aligned}\text{IQV} &= \frac{275}{300}(100)\\ &= .916(100)\\ &= 91.6 \text{ percent.}\end{aligned}$$

We would say that there is 91.6 percent of maximum heterogeneity for these data. This is almost a perfectly even distribution of frequencies throughout the three categories.

Table 5.3 shows maximum heterogeneity distributions of frequencies for each of the four groups from the information provided in Table 5.1. In each of the four cases, the sample size has been divided by the number of task categories associated with the distribution of frequencies. The computations for each group are as follows:

$$\text{IQV}_1 = \frac{\begin{array}{c}(10)(12) + (10)(13) + (10)(14)\\ + (10)(11) + (12)(13) + (12)(14)\\ + (12)(11) + (13)(14) + (13)(11) + (14)(11)\end{array}}{\begin{array}{c}(12)(12) + (12)(12) + (12)(12) + (12)(12)\\ + (12)(12) + (12)(12) + (12)(12)\\ + (12)(12) + (12)(12) + (12)(12)\end{array}}(100)$$

TABLE 5.3
Observed and Maximum Heterogeneity Values for Cramer and Champion's Four Groups.[a]

Type of Task	Group 1		Group 2		Group 3		Group 4	
	Obs.	Max.	Obs.	Max.	Obs.	Max.	Obs.	Max.
A	10	12	3	6	7	5	3	10
B	12	12	7	6	3	5	19	10
C	13	12	10	6	3	5	8	10
D	14	12	4	6	10	5		
E	11	12	6	6	2	5		
	60	60	30	30	25	25	30	30

[a] Obs. = observed distribution of frequencies for k categories. Max. = maximum distribution of frequencies for k categories.

$$= \frac{\begin{array}{c}120 + 130 + 140 + 110 + 156 \\ + 168 + 132 + 182 + 143 + 154\end{array}}{\begin{array}{c}144 + 144 + 144 + 144 + 144 \\ + 144 + 144 + 144 + 144 + 144\end{array}}(100)$$

$$= \frac{1435}{1440}(100)$$

$$= .997(100) = 99.7 \text{ percent.}$$

$$\text{IQV}_2 = \frac{\begin{array}{c}(3)(7) + (3)(10) + (3)(4) + (3)(6) + (7)(10) \\ + (7)(4) + (7)(6) + (10)(4) + (10)(6) + (4)(6)\end{array}}{\begin{array}{c}(6)(6) + (6)(6) + (6)(6) + (6)(6) + (6)(6) \\ + (6)(6) + (6)(6) + (6)(6) + (6)(6) + (6)(6)\end{array}}(100)$$

$$= \frac{21 + 30 + 12 + 18 + 70 + 28 + 42 + 40 + 60 + 24}{36 + 36 + 36 + 36 + 36 + 36 + 36 + 36 + 36 + 36}(100)$$

$$= \frac{345}{360}(100)$$

$$= .958(100) = 95.8 \text{ percent.}$$

$$\text{IQV}_3 = \frac{\begin{array}{c}(7)(3) + (7)(3) + (7)(10) + (7)(2) + (3)(3) \\ + (3)(10) + (3)(2) + (3)(10) + (3)(2) + (10)(2)\end{array}}{\begin{array}{c}(5)(5) + (5)(5) + (5)(5) + (5)(5) + (5)(5) \\ + (5)(5) + (5)(5) + (5)(5) + (5)(5) + (5)(5)\end{array}}(100)$$

$$= \frac{21 + 21 + 70 + 14 + 9 + 30 + 6 + 30 + 6 + 20}{25 + 25 + 25 + 25 + 25 + 25 + 25 + 25 + 25 + 25}(100)$$

$$= \frac{227}{250}(100)$$

$$= .908(100) = 90.8 \text{ percent.}$$

$$\text{IQV}_4 = \frac{(3)(19) + (3)(8) + (19)(8)}{(10)(10) + (10)(10) + (10)(10)}(100)$$

$$= \frac{57 + 24 + 152}{100 + 100 + 100}(100)$$

$$= \frac{233}{300}(100)$$

$$= .777(100) = 77.7 \text{ percent.}$$

According to the information in Table 5.1, group 1 has the highest amount of maximum heterogeneity, with $\text{IQV}_1 = 99.6$ percent. A high heterogeneity index also means a low degree of homogeneity or *similarity.* Observe the IQV values as we move from group 1 to group 4. The IQV values decrease accordingly. This means that as the heterogeneity of the groups decreases, task similarity increases. It would appear from these data that as task similarity increases (as indicated by lower IQV values), there is a corresponding increase in the cohesiveness of group members. IQV's range from 0 percent (no heterogeneity) to 100 percent (maximum heterogeneity).

Assumptions, Advantages, and Disadvantages of the IQV

The IQV has no assumption for application beyond being able to subcategorize data into k subclasses. This is the nominal-level-of-measurement assumption. IQV's can be determined for religious, political, or racial characteristics. They are useful for portraying the heterogeneity (or the homogeneity) of groups on any nominal characteristic for comparative purposes. In the example from Table 5.1, IQV values were used to see whether or not task similarity (or dissimilarity) tended to vary with group cohesion. Students of small-group behavior might be interested in whether similarities in a group's age or sex characteristics are related to group cohesion or to efficiency in problem-solving activities.

Persons studying race relations might be interested in the ethnic or racial heterogeneity of communities where racial violence is absent compared with communities where acts of racial violence occur fairly frequently. These are a few of the many potential applications of IQV's in social research.

The primary advantage of such a measure is that it is amenable to data at the nominal level of measurement. Most other measures of variability require that the researcher has interval measurement achieved before application is indicated.

□ THE RANGE

The range is defined as the distance over which 100 percent of the scores in a distribution are spread. For data in ungrouped form, the range is defined as the distance between the upper limit of the largest score and the lower limit of the smallest score:

$$\text{range} = UL' - LL',$$

where

UL' = upper limit of the largest score
LL' = lower limit of the smallest score

For the data in ungrouped form below, the range would be determined by taking the difference between the upper limit of 92 and the lower limit of 14.

14 15 19 21 23 26 28 29 33 35 41 45 49
51 59 67 69 72 92.

The range for these data would be 92.5 - 13.5 = 79. Another way of saying this is that 79 is the distance over which 100 percent of the scores in the distribution are spread or dispersed.

For grouped data, the range is defined in one of the following two ways: as (1) the distance between the midpoints of the intervals containing the largest and smallest scores in a distribution, or (2) the distance between the upper limit of the interval containing the largest scores and the lower limit of the interval containing the smallest scores in a distribution. The data in Table 5.4 provide a simplified range computation using both of the methods defined above.

The range for the data in Table 5.4 using the midpoints of extreme intervals would be 73.5 - 25.5 = 48. The range based on the upper and lower limits of the extreme intervals would be 75.5 - 23.5 = 52. Although either range computation would be acceptable, more researchers would probably prefer the method where the upper and lower limits of extreme intervals are used.

TABLE 5.4
Frequency Distribution Showing Different Values for the Range Computation.

Interval	*f*	
24–27	10	(lower limit = 23.5) (midpoint = 25.5)
28–31	6	
32–35	5	
36–39	3	range = 75.5 - 23.5 = 52
40–43	0	
44–47	9	*or*
48–51	12	
52–55	10	range = 73.5 - 25.5 = 48
56–59	9	
60–63	11	
64–67	11	
68–71	13	
72–75	1	(upper limit = 75.5) (midpoint = 73.5)
	$\Sigma f = 100$	

Assumptions, Advantages, and Disadvantages of the Range

The range assumes interval-level measurement associated with the data being analyzed. The primary advantage of the range is that it is used to determine the interval size and the number of intervals a researcher should have for presenting data in grouped form. This was discussed in Chapter 3. The main disadvantage of the range is that although it does indicate the distance over which 100 percent of the scores are spread, it does not necessarily mean that most of the scores are spread that sparsely. For instance, if a researcher were to have the 10 scores

$$6 \quad 7 \quad 8 \quad 9 \quad 10 \quad 11 \quad 12 \quad 13 \quad 14 \quad 100,$$

the range for these data would be 100.5 - 5.5 = 95. But 9 of the 10 scores are spread over a 9-point distance (i.e., 14.5 - 5.5 = 9). The deviant score of 100 is responsible for the larger range.

In many respects, this is reminiscent of the major disadvantage of the mean. A deviant score will lead to an unusually high (or low) mean value for a group of scores, which is atypical for that score grouping. By the same token, a deviant score such as 100 will mislead us into thinking that the scores are fairly evenly distributed across a distance of 95. Although this is true in a technical sense, a more stable measure of the score range would be 9, reflecting the distance over which most of the scores are spread. Therefore, the range is an unstable and unreliable measure of variability whenever deviant scores are present in a distribution. In an effort to compensate for the presence of deviant scores, researchers have devised a variety of alternative "ranges," presented in the next few sections.

□ THE 10–90 RANGE (INTERDECILE RANGE)

The 10–90 range (sometimes called the interdecile range) is defined as the distance over which the central 80 percent of the scores are spread.[1] The 10–90 range is computed as follows:

$$\text{10–90 range} = C_{90} - C_{10},$$

where

C_{90} = 90th centile (or 9th decile, D_9)
C_{10} = 10th centile (or 1st decile, D_1)

The 10–90 range computation will be illustrated using the data in Table 5.5:

$$\begin{aligned}\text{10–90 range} &= C_{90} - C_{10}\\ &= 146.6 - 43.8\\ &= 102.8.\end{aligned}$$

The distance over which the central 80 percent of the scores are spread is 102.8, or the 10–90 range. Had we computed the range for these data, it would have been either 120 or 130, depending upon the method of computation selected. Therefore, a slight correction or compensation for extreme scores has been effected by using as the variation measure the distance between the 10th and the 90th centiles.

Advantages and Disadvantages of the 10–90 Range

The major advantage of the 10–90 range is that it overcomes the distorting effect of the presence of deviant scores in a distribution. It is superior to the range as a dispersion measure whenever deviant scores are present. The primary assumption underlying the application of the 10–90 range is that the researcher has interval-level data.

[1] It seems appropriate here to mention that percentages are usually most meaningful when computed for samples of size 50 or larger. It would be possible to compute a percentage for any sample less than 50, but imagine how misleading it would be to say that 66 percent of our sample of three persons favors such and such an issue. For this reason, examples of some of the ranges to follow will be limited to grouped data examples where larger sample sizes are typically found.

TABLE 5.5
Frequency Distribution Showing 10-90 Range and Interquartile Range Computations.

Interval	*f*	
150–159	8	$C_{90} = 149.5 - \frac{2}{7}(10)$
140–149	7	$= 149.5 - 2.9 = 146.6$
130–139	6	$Q_3 = 129.5 - \frac{4}{5}(10)$
120–129	5	$= 129.5 - 8 = 121.5$
110–119	12	
100–109	9	$C_{90} - C_{10} = 146.6 - 43.8 = 102.8$
90–99	10	$Q_3 - Q_1 = 121.5 - 62.5 = 59$
80–89	8	
70–79	3	
60–69	10	$Q_1 = 59.5 + \frac{3}{10}(10)$
50–59	8	$= 59.5 + 3 = 62.5$
40–49	7	$C_{10} = 39.5 + \frac{3}{7}(10)$
30–39	7	$= 39.5 + 4.3 = 43.8$
	$\Sigma f = 100$	

□ THE INTERQUARTILE RANGE

The interquartile range is defined as the distance over which the central 50 percent of the scores are spread. This is thought by some researchers to be an improvement over the 10–90 range and gives the reader a more informed appraisal of the true dispersion of scores. Assuming that there are several deviant scores present in a distribution, it may not be sufficient to compensate for the lowest and highest 10 percent of scores by the 10–90 range. The interquartile range compensates even further by moving into the distribution to the first and third quartiles, Q_1 and Q_3, respectively. The difference between these two values defines the interquartile range:

$$\text{interquartile range} = Q_3 - Q_1,$$

where

Q_3 = third quartile
Q_1 = first quartile

For the data in Table 5.5, these quartiles are computed as follows:

$$Q_3 = 129.5 - \frac{4}{5}(10)$$
$$= 129.5 - 8$$
$$= 121.5.$$

$$Q_1 = 59.5 + \frac{3}{10}(10)$$

$$= 59.5 + 3$$

$$= 62.5.$$

The interquartile range would be $Q_3 - Q_1 = 121.5 - 62.5 = 59$. Therefore, 59 is defined as the interquartile range or the distance over which the central 50 percent of the scores are spread.

Assumptions, Advantages, and Disadvantages of the Interquartile Range

The interquartile range assumes the interval level of measurement. Its primary advantage is that it more than compensates for deviant scores in any distribution, to give the researcher a conservative appraisal of the variation of the central 50 percent of the scores. It is commonly viewed as the standard variation measure for compensating for deviant scores in any distribution. It is used more frequently compared with the 10–90 range. It has no disadvantages.

□ THE SEMI-INTERQUARTILE RANGE OR QUARTILE DEVIATION

The semi-interquartile range or quartile deviation is defined as the interquartile range divided by 2:

$$\text{semi-interquartile range} = \frac{Q_3 - Q_1}{2},$$

where

Q_3 = third quartile
Q_1 = first quartile

This measure of variability represents no improvement whatsoever over the interquartile range. The primary reason for including it here is to illustrate the fact that convention sometimes obligates us to perform various statistical procedures that have little or no rational explanation. For instance, the quartile deviation has been used by some researchers to give them some indication of the approximate value of the standard deviation, a measure of variability to be discussed in a later section of this chapter. But there is no mathematical link between the quartile deviation and the standard deviation. In fact, it is probably more meaningful for the researcher to know that

50 percent of the central scores are distributed over a given distance than it is to know the value of half that distance. However, the fact that more than a few researchers continue to use the quartile deviation in their descriptions of social and/or psychological information is ample explanation for including it here.

□ THE AVERAGE DEVIATION

The average deviation is another measure of variability that is seldom used in research work. It is defined as a value that specifies the average departure of scores from the mean of their distribution. The inclusion of the average deviation in this chapter serves to introduce the idea of score deviations from the mean and thus provides a logical connection between the standard deviation and deviations of scores from mean values.

Suppose that we have the following 10 scores:

10 12 14 15 17 19 20 23 24 26.

The mean for these data would be the sum of scores divided by the number of scores, or 180/10 = 18. If we were to arrange these scores in a column and then identify the departure of each score from the mean of 18 in a second column, x', we would have Table 5.6. The score of 10 is 8 points below the mean of 18, and we give this a *deviation score* of −8. The score of 24 is 6 points above the mean of 18, and therefore we give this a deviation score of +6. Each raw score in the distribution has been assigned a deviation score, x', as shown. Deviation scores are determined as follows:

$$\text{deviation score } (x') = X_i - \overline{X},$$

TABLE 5.6

Score	x'	$\lvert x' \rvert$
10	−8	8
12	−6	6
14	−4	4
15	−3	3
17	−1	1
19	+1	1
20	+2	2
23	+5	5
24	+6	6
26	+8	8
	$\Sigma x' = 0$	$\Sigma\lvert x' \rvert = 44$

where

X_i = any raw score
$\overline{X}$ = mean for the distribution of scores

The sum of the deviation scores will always be equal to zero, provided that we started with the correct mean value. To determine the average deviation for this distribution of 10 scores, we must take the absolute deviations of scores from the mean ($|x'|$), sum them, and then divide by the number of scores. The formula for the average deviation is

$$\text{average deviation} = \frac{\sum |x'|}{N},$$

where

$\sum |x'|$ = sum of the absolute score deviations from the mean
N = sample size

For these data, the average deviation would be

$$\text{average deviation} = \frac{44}{10}$$
$$= 4.4.$$

On the average, scores in this distribution fluctuate about the mean by 4.4 points.

For data in grouped form, the average deviation would be determined as follows. First, a mean is determined for the distribution. Next, a value is assigned each interval based on the departure of each interval midpoint from the mean of the distribution. In Table 5.7, interval midpoints are shown. In a column labeled "$|x'|$," the absolute deviation of each midpoint from the mean of 639.2 is shown. The column to the far right contains the products of absolute deviations of interval midpoints from the mean and the frequencies found in each interval, or $f|x'|$. We are weighting each interval-midpoint departure from the mean according to the number of frequencies found in each interval. We sum these products to provide $\Sigma f|x'|$. Finally, we apply these values from Table 5.7 to the following formula:

$$\text{average deviation} = \frac{\sum f|x'|}{N},$$

TABLE 5.7
Frequency Distribution Showing the Average Deviation Computation.

Interval	*f*	*Midpoint*	$\|x'\|$	$f\|x'\|$
652–653	3	652.5	13.3	39.9
650–651	3	650.5	11.3	33.9
648–649	5	648.5	9.3	46.5
646–647	5	646.5	7.3	36.5
644–645	9	644.5	5.3	47.7
642–643	15	642.5	3.3	49.5
640–641	3	640.5	1.3	3.9
638–639	15	638.5	.7	10.5
636–637	9	636.5	2.7	24.3
634–635	10	634.5	4.7	47.0
632–633	13	632.5	6.7	87.1
630–631	10	630.5	8.7	87.0
	$\Sigma f = 100$			$\Sigma f\|x'\| = 513.8$
		$\overline{X} = 639.2$		

where

$\sum f|x'|$ = sum of products of absolute midpoint departures from the mean and frequencies found in each interval

N = sample size

Supplying the information from Table 5.7, we have

$$\text{average deviation} = \frac{513.8}{100}$$

$$= 5.1.$$

We may now say that on the average, the scores in Table 5.7 fluctuate about the mean, 539.2, by 5.1 points.

Assumptions, Advantages, and Disadvantages of the Average Deviation

The assumption underlying the computation of the average deviation is that the data be measured according to an interval scale. There are no particular advantages of the average deviation for social research.

The average deviation has no precise or consistent interpretation and cannot be compared meaningfully with other average-deviation values from one sample to the next. For this reason, it has lapsed into disuse over the years. The primary utility of the average deviation, however, is to introduce the idea of deviation scores, actual numerical departures of scores from the means of their distributions. It is possible to obtain a more precise estimate of the departure of scores from a mean value, but we must continue several steps beyond where the average deviation computation leaves us. For a more detailed look at additional computations that are necessary to give us a more informed appraisal of any distribution of scores, we next examine the variance and the standard deviation.

□ THE VARIANCE AND STANDARD DEVIATION

The variance is defined as the mean of the sum of all squared deviation scores about the mean of a given distribution. For instance, suppose that we had the set of raw scores given in Table 5.8. If we were to square the deviation scores about the mean of 18, we would have an additional column, x^2. Then, if we were to sum these squared deviation scores, we would have the sum of the squared deviation scores, $\Sigma x^2 = 256$, as shown. Finally, if we divide this sum by N, or 10, we would have $256/10 = 25.6$. 25.6 is the variance for these data. It is represented by the symbol s^2 and is computed symbolically as follows:

$$s^2 = \frac{\sum x^2}{N},$$

where

$\sum x^2$ = sum of the squared deviation scores
N = sample size

By itself, the variance tells us very little about the distribution of scores. However, if we obtain the square root of the variance, we will have the best measure of variability available, the *standard deviation.*

TABLE 5.8

X_i	x	x^2
10	−8	64
12	−6	36
14	−4	16
15	−3	9
17	−1	1
19	+1	1
20	+2	4
23	+5	25
24	+6	36
26	+8	64
	$\Sigma x = 0$	$\Sigma x^2 = 256$

The standard deviation, s, is defined symbolically as

$$s = \sqrt{s^2} = \sqrt{\frac{\sum x^2}{N}},$$

where

$\sum x^2$ = sum of the squared deviation scores
N = sample size

The method for computing the standard deviation (and the variance) from ungrouped data using the deviation scores becomes tedious when decimal values are encountered. If the mean were 88.35 for some distribution of scores, one single deviation score might be 13.65. If we squared this value, we would get 186.3225. Imagine how cumbersome it would be to manipulate values this large in an effort to compute the variance and standard deviation. A more direct method of computing these variability measures is based on the raw scores themselves and the squares of these scores.

The key term in the variance and standard deviation formulas is the sum of the squared deviation scores, Σx^2. Knowing this value permits us to determine readily the variance and standard deviation for any distribution. Therefore, the following shortcut is recommended, which bypasses the need to compute a mean for a group of scores or individual deviation scores.

Using the same 10 scores used in the variance computation above, we square each score in the distribution and obtain two sums: (1) the sum of the scores; and (2) the sum of the squared scores. This has been done in Table 5.9. We may then enter these values in the following formula for Σx^2:

$$\sum x^2 = \sum X_i^2 - \frac{(\sum X_i)^2}{N},$$

TABLE 5.9

X_i	X_i^2
10	100
12	144
14	196
15	225
17	289
19	361
20	400
23	529
24	576
26	676
$\Sigma X_i = 180$	$\Sigma X_i^2 = 3496$

where

$\sum X_i^2$ = sum of the squared raw scores
$\sum X_i$ = sum of the raw scores
N = number of scores

Using the sums we have determined for the data above, we can solve for Σx^2:

$$\sum x^2 = 3496 - \frac{(180)^2}{10}$$

$$= 3496 - \frac{32{,}400}{10}$$

$$= 3496 - 3240$$

$$= 256.$$

Once we have determined this value, we can solve for the variance:

$$s^2 = \frac{256}{10} = 25.6.$$

Finally, we can solve for the standard deviation:

$$s = \sqrt{25.6}$$

$$= 5.1.$$

Observe that this value, $s = 5.1$, matches the one obtained in the original solution using the mean and deviation scores from the mean. To further minimize one's computational work in such problems, a table of squares and square roots has been provided in Table A1, Appendix A.

For data in grouped form, the variance and standard deviation are computed as follows. Suppose that a researcher had information such as that shown in Table 5.10.

For these data an arbitrary reference point is selected in precisely the same way as it was selected for the mean computation for grouped data. The arbitrary reference point is an interval near the center of the distribution.

We place a 0 in the column labeled x', and we number +1, +2, +3, and so on, away from 0 until the top of the distribution is reached (i.e., the end of the distribution containing the largest scores). Next, we number away from 0—that is, −1, −2, −3, and so on—until the end of the distribution is reached, which contains the smallest scores. Once we have these values in place as shown in Table 5.10, we multiply the frequencies found in each interval by the corresponding x' value. This provides us with an fx' column, as shown.

TABLE 5.10
Frequency Distribution Showing the Variance and Standard Deviation Computations.

Interval	f	x'	fx'	fx'^2
845–849	6	4	24	96
840–844	4	3	12	36
835–839	3	2	6	12
830–834	7	1	7	7
825–829	2	0	0	0
820–824	2	–1	–2	2
815–819	8	–2	–16	32
810–814	4	–3	–12	36
805–809	2	–4	–8	32
800–804	12	–5	–60	300
	$\Sigma f = 50$		$\Sigma fx' = -49$	$\Sigma fx'^2 = 553$

The final step is to multiply the values in the fx' column by the corresponding values in the x' column to yield a final fx'^2 column as shown. We must sum the values for the f, fx', and fx'^2 columns. Once these values have been obtained, we can enter them into the following formula, which will determine the value of Σx^2:

$$\sum x^2 = (i)^2 \left[\sum fx'^2 - \frac{(\sum fx')^2}{N} \right],$$

where

i = interval size
$\sum fx'^2$ = sum of products of the fx' and x' columns
$\sum fx'$ = sum of products of the f and x' columns
N = sample size

From the information provided in Table 5.10, we can solve for Σx^2:

$$\sum x^2 = (5)^2 \left[553 - \frac{(-49)^2}{50} \right]$$

$$= (25) \left[553 - \frac{2401}{50} \right]$$

$$= (25)\,[553 - 48]$$

$$= (25)(505)$$

$$= 12{,}625.$$

We can now solve for the variance, which would be

$$s^2 = \frac{\sum x^2}{N}$$
$$= \frac{12{,}625}{50}$$
$$= 252.2.$$

The standard deviation would be

$$s = \sqrt{252.5}$$
$$= 15.9.$$

Assumptions, Advantages, and Disadvantages of the Standard Deviation

The principal reason why the standard deviation is the best measure of variability available is that it has a consistent meaning from one distribution to the next. One standard deviation value of 5.1 means the same thing for its particular distribution as 15.9 means for its distribution. And a standard deviation of 200 for a third distribution of scores would have an equivalent meaning as well. This property of *consistency of interpretation* makes the standard deviation distinctive among other variability measures.

When applied to any distribution of raw scores, the standard deviation usually refers to a given distance on either side of the mean, which will include a specific proportion of scores. For instance, if we knew that a $\overline{X} = 100$ and an $s = 10$, a specific proportion of scores would be included between the mean of 100 and 1 standard deviation above and below the mean, or 100 ± 10, or from 90 to 100 and from 100 to 110. It will soon be seen that a knowledge of the mean and standard deviation for any given distribution of scores will tell us about the proportion of scores between any pair of points in the distribution. We will be able to appreciate more fully the importance of standard deviations and means when the normal distribution is examined in Chapter 6.

The primary assumption underlying the application of the standard deviation is the interval level of measurement. In order for the meaning of the standard deviation to be maximized, we must make a further assumption about the *shape* of the distribution of scores. Since Chapter 6 examines distributions of varying shapes in considerable detail and includes the standard deviation as a critical part of this examination, we defer additional discussion of the weaknesses and strengths of the standard deviation for use in social research.

□ SUMMARY

This chapter has presented several measures of dispersion that describe the way in which scores focus around various points of central tendency. All measures presented, with the exception of the IQV, assume the interval level of measurement. The IQV is a useful measure of attribute heterogeneity and is easy to apply where severe restrictions exist that hamper the use of any higher level-of-measurement dispersion computation.

The range is the distance over which 100 percent of the scores in a distribution are dispersed. It is primarily useful for determining interval size for grouped data. It is the most sensitive and unstable measure of variability, however. This is because deviant scores influence the range's magnitude easily. As a means of compensating for deviant scores in a distribution, researchers have created the 10–90 range and interquartile range, respectively, which give the distances over which the central 80 percent and 50 percent of the scores are spread. Thus the deviant scores in a distribution are virtually ignored by these computations.

The power of convention was illustrated through the relatively meaningless computation of the semi-interquartile range or quartile deviation, which is nothing more than the interquartile range halved.

The average deviation was also presented. However, because of its imprecise interpretation and inconsistency in application from one distribution of scores to the next, it has been rendered obsolete as a measure of variability.

The most useful and meaningful measure of variability is the standard deviation. This was presented together with its square, the variance. The standard deviation almost always has a uniform interpretation from one distribution to the next. It has other properties of interest to us, as well. But for these to be discussed most profitably and meaningfully, additional information about score distributions must be presented, which will be done in Chapter 6.

SELECTED STUDY TERMS

Dispersion or variability
Index of Qualitative Variation
Attribute heterogeneity
Range
10–90 range
Interquartile range
Semi-interquartile range or quartile deviation
Average deviation

Deviation score
Variance
Standard deviation

EXERCISES

1. Given the information in the table, compute the values listed below.

Interval	f
640–643	8
644–647	10
648–651	3
652–655	2
656–659	9
660–663	14
664–667	12
668–671	11
672–675	9
676–679	15
680–683	14
684–687	12
688–691	5
	$\Sigma f = 124$

   (a) The variance and standard deviation.
   (b) The 10–90 range.
   (c) The semi-interquartile range.

2. Given the information in the table, compute the values listed below.

Interval	f
900–909	3
910–919	7
920–929	13
930–939	14
940–949	15
950–959	4
960–969	10
970–979	15
980–989	10
990–999	11
1000–1009	5
1010–1019	10
	$\Sigma f = 117$

   (a) The 10–90 range.
   (b) The standard deviation.
   (c) The average deviation.
   (d) The interquartile range.

3. Determine IQV values for each of the following groups distributed according to various religious categories.

Religion	*Group 1*	*Group 2*	*Group 3*	*Group 4*
Catholic	20	15	12	4
Jewish	25	30	22	6
Protestant	15	30	12	15

4. Why is the standard deviation preferred to a measure of dispersion such as the interquartile range? Explain.
5. Compute the values requested for the following raw scores.

21 21 35 36 38 39 40 41 42 42
43 55 66 66 67 67 67 71 75 78.

(a) The range.
(b) The standard deviation.

6. Given the information in the table, compute the values listed below.

Interval	*f*
145–149	13
140–144	9
135–139	10
130–134	11
125–129	15
120–124	10
115–119	10
110–114	10
105–109	12
100–104	9
95–99	7
90–94	3
85–89	14
80–84	12
75–79	10
	$\Sigma f = 160$

(a) The range.
(b) The variance.
(c) The average deviation.
(d) The semi-interquartile range.

7. Compute the values requested for the following ungrouped data.

2 5 7 8 8 8 9 12 13 13 13 14 15 15 16.

(a) The range.
(b) The standard deviation.
(c) The average deviation.

8. Compute the values requested for the following ungrouped data.

3 8 12 14 9 16 12 29 58 22 4 14 14.

(a) The standard deviation.
(b) The range.

9. Determine IQV's for the following three groups for political affiliation.

Political Party	*Group 1*	*Group 2*	*Group 3*
Democrat	55	28	32
Republican	29	15	10
American Independent	10	10	52

Which group is most heterogeneously distributed regarding political affiliation?

10. Determine the mean for the data in Exercise 8. Next, determine deviation scores for each of the raw scores. Does the sum of the deviation scores equal zero or nearly zero?
11. Given the information in the table, compute the values listed below.

Interval	*f*
40–41	6
38–39	3
36–37	14
34–35	3
32–33	11
30–31	9
28–29	3
26–27	14
24–25	10
22–23	7
	$\Sigma f = 80$

(a) The range.
(b) The standard deviation.
(c) The variance.
(d) The semi-interquartile range.
(e) The average deviation.

REFERENCES

Cramer, James A., and Dean J. Champion, "Toward the Clarification of Solidarity: A Factor-Analytic Study," *Pacific Sociological Review*, **18**: 292–309, 1975.

Edwards, Allen, *Statistical Methods.* New York: Holt, Rinehart and Winston, 1967.

Hauser, Philip M., *Social Statistics in Use.* New York: Russell Sage Foundation, 1975.

Maxwell, Albert E., *Analyzing Qualitative Data.* New York: John Wiley & Sons, Inc., 1961.

Tanur, Judith, M. F. Mosteller, W. H. Kruskal, R. F. Link, R. S. Pieters, and

G. R. Rising, *Statistics: A Guide to the Unknown.* San Francisco: Holden-Day, Inc., 1972.

Wike, Edward L., *Data Analysis: A Statistical Primer for Psychology Students.* Chicago: Aldine Publishing Company, 1971.

Zeisel, Hans, *Say It with Figures.* New York: Harper & Row, Publishers, 1968.

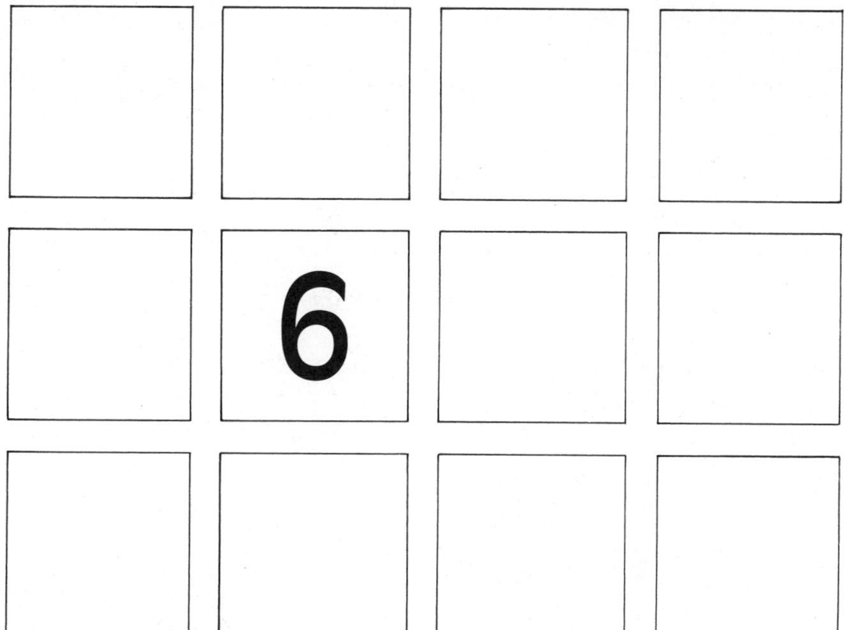

6

The Unit Normal Distribution and Standard Scores

Social scientists can use any one of several sampling plans for obtaining elements from some designated population of them. However, a limited number of sampling plans will permit the researcher to make generalizations about the population from the sample drawn. These sampling plans, designated probability sampling plans, include simple random sampling, stratified proportionate or disproportionate random sampling, and cluster or area sampling. It was shown in Chapter 2 that these plans use randomness, with a computer-determined drawing or table of random numbers as the means of selecting elements for inclusion in a sample.

A primary value of selecting a sample through probability sampling is that the resulting sample statistics can be used in conjunction with the *unit or standard normal distribution.* A distribution that is

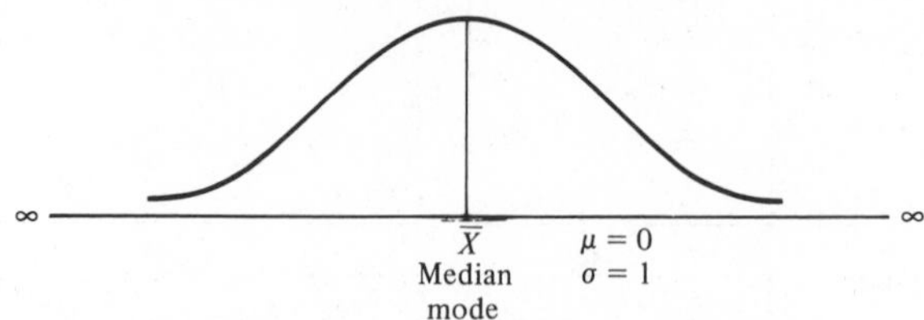

FIGURE 6.1. Unit Normal Distribution.

normal in form is said to conform to the characteristics of a theoretically derived distribution known as the *standard* or *unit normal distribution.* The unit normal distribution is derived mathematically by the following formula:

$$Y = \left(\frac{1}{\sigma\sqrt{2\pi}}\right) e^{-1/2\left(\frac{X-\mu}{\sigma}\right)^2},$$

where

$\pi = 3.1416$
$e = 2.7183$
σ = parameter equal to the standard deviation of the distribution
μ = parameter equal to the mean of the distribution
X = abscissa–measurement or score marked on the horizontal axis
Y = ordinate–height of the curve at a point corresponding to an assigned value of X

Figure 6.1 shows the unit normal distribution and depicts several important characteristics of it. These characteristics are:

1. The curve of the unit normal distribution, known as the *normal curve*, is bell-shaped and perfectly symmetrical. The highest point in the distribution is at the center of it, and the curve ends or "tails" taper off in opposite directions in an identical manner.
2. The mean, median, and mode are at the same point in the center of the distribution and are therefore equal to one another.
3. The tails of the curve extend toward the baseline in opposite directions, but they never touch the horizontal axis. Therefore, the ends of the curve extend toward infinity. This is the asymptotic property of the unit normal distribution.
4. The mean, μ, of the unit normal distribution is equal to zero, and the standard deviation, σ, is equal to 1. These values are the two parameters of the unit normal distribution and are designated as μ and σ of zero and 1, respectively. The unit of

measurement along the horizontal axis of the unit normal distribution is a $\sigma = 1$, and various points to the left or to the right of a $\mu = 0$ are a certain number of σ's of 1 above or below the mean. Values to the left of μ are negative, and values to the right of the mean are positive.

5. The mean of the unit normal distribution divides the distribution into two equal parts. This is true because the median is also located at the same point in the distribution. Because of the fact that the unit normal distribution is perfectly symmetrical, the same distance of σ values to the left or right of the mean will cut off an identical portion of curve area.
6. The total area under the curve of the unit normal distribution is equal to unity, or 1.0000. Portions of curve area are represented as various proportions of 1.0000, or .3366, .4495, .9946, or .0028. (Four-place proportion values are used because tabled proportions of curve area in Table A3, Appendix A, are also expressed to four places.)

The unit normal distribution exists only in theory, and it has been derived mathematically through the formula presented above. Over the years, scientists have found that distributions of a wide variety of variables often approximate the unit normal distribution in their dispersion and central tendency. For instance, political conservatism–liberalism might be approximately normally distributed in a given sample of elements. Various attitudes that have been converted into numerical quantities appear to be normally distributed in particular samples. Distributions of scores that approximate several characteristics of the unit normal distribution are said to be normally distributed. Statements that can be made about the unit normal distribution can also be applied to distributions that approximate the unit normal distribution. In short, if we have a distribution of attitudinal scores that is approximately normal in form, we can say things about the distribution of attitudinal scores that can also apply to the unit normal distribution. The functional utility of the unit normal distribution is discussed below.

□ STANDARD SCORES

Points along the horizontal axis of the unit normal distribution that cut off various portions of curve area are referred to as *Z values* or *standard values.* Standard or Z values depict the direction and distance of a given point along the horizontal axis of the unit normal distribution in relation to its mean. This distance is measured in terms of standard deviation units of 1 because one of the parameters

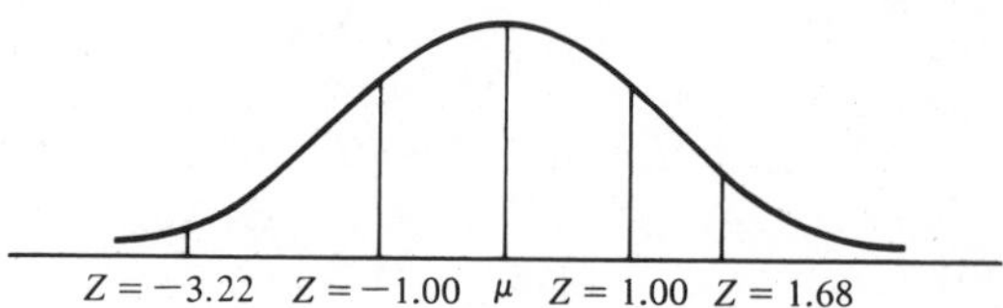

FIGURE 6.2. *Z* Values on the Unit Normal Distribution.

of this distribution is $\sigma = 1$. For instance, Figure 6.2 shows a normal curve with several *Z* values depicted.

Each of the *Z* values in Figure 6.2 cuts off a constant portion of curve area. Each of these values is a given distance from $\mu = 0$ expressed in sigmas of 1. These are translated as shown in Table 6.1. We can identify the proportion of curve area cut off by any *Z* value by turning to Table A3, Appendix A. In Table A3, the left-hand column contains *Z* values expressed to the nearest tenth. Values across the top of the table provide additional precision to the nearest hundredth. Therefore, if we are looking up a *Z* value of 1.68 in this table, we must find 1.6 down the left-hand column and then .08 across the top of the table. Where these values intersect in the body of the table identifies the proportion of curve area that lies between $\mu = 0$ and a *Z* value of 1.68, or .4535. In other words, approximately 45 percent of the curve area lies between the mean of 0 and a *Z* of 1.68 (which is 1.68σ's above the mean). More precisely, the proportion, .4535, would represent the amount of area between these two points, as shown in Figure 6.3.

Note that an additional *Z* value of −1.68 has been provided in Figure 6.3. An identical amount of curve area will be found between the mean and a *Z* of −1.68, or .4535, as shown. This is because of the *symmetry* of the unit normal distribution. Therefore, if we want to identify the proportion of curve area cut off by any *Z* value, regardless of whether it is above or below the mean (i.e., positive or negative), we simply examine the absolute *Z* value shown in Table A3. A *Z* value of 1.00 cuts off .3413 of the curve area, and a *Z* value of −1.00 cuts off the same amount of curve area in the opposite direction, or .3413 of it. For additional examples, the *Z* values

TABLE 6.1

Z Value Is	*Direction and Distance from $\mu = 0$ in Sigmas Equal to 1*
1.00	1.00σ's or 1.00σ above the mean
−1.00	-1.00σ's or 1.00σ below the mean
1.68	1.68σ's or 1.68σ's above the mean
−3.22	-3.22σ's or 3.22σ's below the mean

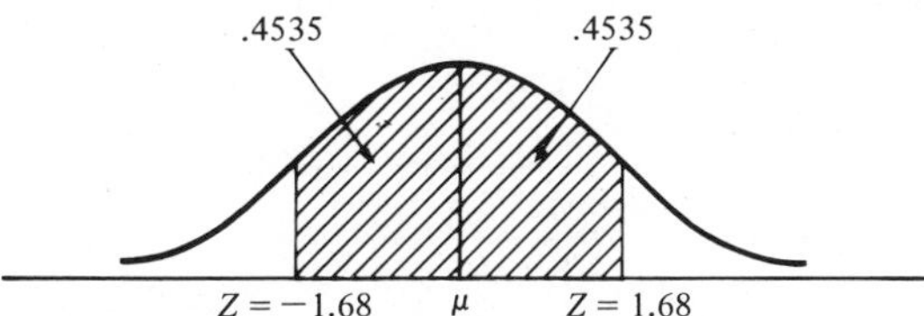

FIGURE 6.3. *Z* Values on the Unit Normal Distribution.

TABLE 6.2

Z Value	*Proportion of Curve Area from Mean to Z Value*
2.26	.4881
−2.26	.4881
−3.14	.4992
.03	.0120
1.45	.4265
1.96	.4750
2.33	.4901
−2.33	.4901

in Table 6.2 are provided with the amount of curve area cut off by each. These proportions of curve area are *constant proportions* that are included between the mean of 0 and some designated number of sigmas above or below the mean. Another way of looking at these is to regard them as *standard proportions.* These standard or "constant" proportions always exist for each sigma departure from the mean of the unit normal distribution. If we encounter distributions of scores in our research that are approximately normal in form, we can make fairly reliable estimates about the proportion of scores included within a given distance of the mean, whatever it may be, in terms of standard deviation units.

Suppose that we were to draw a random sample of elements from a population and construct a frequency distribution of ages for the sample. Table 6.3 shows a frequency distribution of ages for a sample of 199 elements. These age values have also been arranged into a curve of ages shown in Figure 6.4. We have merely constructed a frequency polygon for these data and smoothed the lines connecting various frequencies. It will be observed that the curve for these data looks bell-shaped or normal. Statements that can be made about the unit normal distribution will also apply to our distribution of ages to the extent that this distribution is also approximately normal in form.

Some preliminary computations for the data in Table 6.3 will

TABLE 6.3
Frequency Distribution of Ages for 199 Elements.

Interval	*f*
10–14	3
15–19	7
20–24	9
25–29	12
30–34	13
35–39	14
40–44	15
45–49	16
50–54	17
55–59	16
60–64	15
65–69	14
70–74	13
75–79	12
80–84	9
85–89	7
90–94	3
95–99	2
	$\Sigma f = 199$

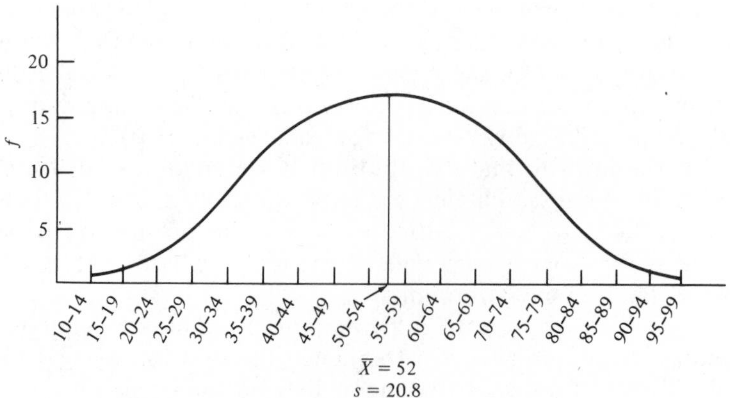

FIGURE 6.4. Curve Drawn for the Data in Table 6.3.

show that the mean, mode, and median are identical, or 52. The standard deviation for these data is 20.8. Knowing the mean and standard deviation of any distribution that is approximately normally distributed will enable us to determine any number of things about the distribution. For instance, we will be able to determine the approximate proportion of ages that occur between the mean and 1 standard deviation above or below the mean. Given a $\overline{X} = 52$ and $s = 20.8$, we will know that .3413 or 34 percent of the ages will occur between 52 and 20.8 points above or below 52. We know this because (1) our distribution of ages is approximately normally distributed; and (2) .3413, or the curve area for the unit normal distribution lies between the $\mu = 0$ and 1 σ to the left or right of μ.

A Z value of +1.00 or -1.00 cuts off .3413 of the curve area or approximately 34 percent of it. Therefore, a point in our distribution of ages that is one standard deviation (s) above or below the mean ($\overline{X}$) will cut off and include an identical proportion of .3413 or 34 percent. The point of -1.00 on the unit normal distribution is analogous to the point 31.2 on the distribution of ages, which is 1 standard deviation of 20.8 below the mean of 52. The Z value of -1.00 is 1σ below the mean of 0, whereas the value 31.2 is 1 standard deviation of 20.8 below the mean of 52. 31.2 is at the same point in its distribution as -1.00 is in the unit normal distribution. If we were to superimpose the two distributions on one another, the points would be identical. This statement holds to the extent that our distribution of scores is normal in form or approximates the unit normal distribution with its characteristics.

If we know that a given person's age is 75, we can determine the proportion of persons aged 52 to 75. We must convert our age "score" of 75 to a standard score in order to determine the proportion of curve area (and hence the approximate number of ages) between the mean and the observed age. This is accomplished as follows:

$$Z \text{ score} = \frac{X_i - \overline{X}}{s},$$

where

X_i = any raw score in a frequency distribution
$\overline{X}$ = mean of the distribution
s = standard deviation of the distribution

Given a $\overline{X} = 52$ and $s = 20.8$, we compute the Z score for our age of 75 as follows:

$$Z = \frac{75 - 52}{20.8}$$

$$= \frac{23}{20.8}$$

$$= 1.11.$$

The Z value associated with our raw score of 75 (the age value in this case) is 1.11. Turning to Table A3, we determine that .3665 of the curve area lies between 0 (the mean) and 1.11. This also means that approximately .3665 or 36.6 percent of the curve area lies between the mean of 52 and the age value of 75.

In the general case, raw scores for any distribution may be converted to Z scores by using the Z-score formula above. Once we have converted raw scores to Z scores, we can use Table A3, the table of areas of the normal curve, as a way of knowing where our raw score might be located in the distribution.

□ STANDARD SCORES AND THE UNIT NORMAL DISTRIBUTION

One of the major uses of Z scores is in the area of educational testing and the measurement and comparison of abilities and skills. For instance, if we wanted to use scores from an abilities and aptitudes test for diagnostic purposes in advising students on their course of study in school, we would probably want to convert their raw scores to Z scores or standard scores in an effort to better evaluate their weaknesses and strengths. Suppose that we had the information given in Table 6.4 for a student who had taken a battery of tests together with a large freshman college class. It would appear at first glance that our student did the best on test B and the worst on test D, with raw scores of 3000 and 15, respectively. But this preliminary appraisal would be in error. We cannot make direct comparisons of test scores from different tests. Test A may be an English proficiency test, whereas test B may be an assessment of mathematical aptitude. The tests would differ in degree of difficulty, the actual range of scores, the mean and standard deviation of each, the conditions under which the tests were administered, and any number of other factors. In order to get a crude appraisal at best of our student's test performances, we must convert each of the test scores into a Z score and compare them on the unit normal distribution. The unit normal

TABLE 6.4

Test	*Raw Score*
A	25
B	3000
C	150
D	15

TABLE 6.5

Test	*Raw Score*	*Mean*	*Standard Deviation*	*Z Score*
A	25	20	5	1.00
B	3000	3300	300	-1.00
C	150	165	7.5	-2.00
D	15	12	1	3.00

distribution becomes our common standard for comparative purposes, therefore.

To determine the person's standard scores or Z scores for the raw scores received, we must first know the class means and standard deviations of all tests taken. These values are provided in Table 6.5. Using the Z-score formula,

$$\frac{X_i - \overline{X}}{s},$$

we can determine Z values for each of the raw scores as follows:

Test A: $$\frac{25 - 20}{5} = \frac{5}{5} = 1.00 = Z_1.$$

Test B: $$\frac{3000 - 3300}{300} = \frac{-300}{300} = -1.00 = Z_2.$$

Test C: $$\frac{150 - 165}{7.5} = \frac{-15}{7.5} = -2.00 = Z_3.$$

Test D: $$\frac{15 - 12}{1} = \frac{3}{1} = 3.00 = Z_4.$$

Next, we may place each of these Z scores on the unit normal distribution as shown in Figure 6.5. It appears that our student did best on test D, even though the raw score was the smallest (in magnitude) of the four scores. The Z score of 3.00 tells us that the raw score of

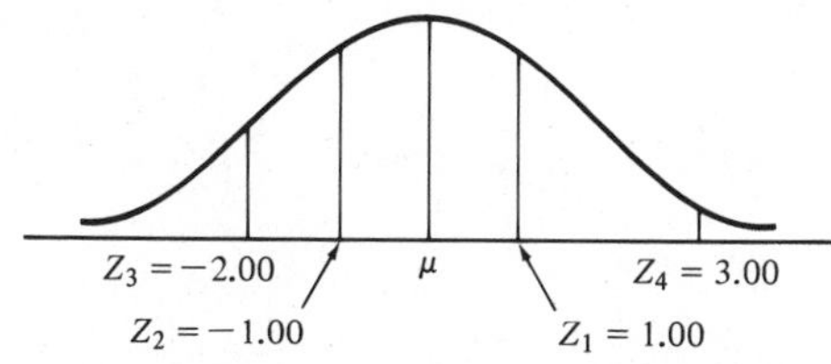

FIGURE 6.5. Unit Normal Distribution Showing Four Z Scores.

15 is 3 standard deviations of 1 above the mean of 12. We can also see that the score of 3000 was actually below the mean of its distribution, 3300, by 1 standard deviation of 300. This score received a Z score of -1.00. Test C was the student's "worst" performance compared with the other tests. We might use this information to advise the student to pursue a curriculum in school which might remedy the deficiency indicated by the Z-score results. Of course, a person's test scores are not the only criteria that we would use in educational advising or diagnostic work. It is somewhat more complicated than that. The point is that such score results may be helpful in assessing one's weaknesses and strengths.

The unit normal distribution serves an important comparative function. We may convert any number of sets of raw scores to Z scores for comparative purposes. Once we have determined Z scores for any set of raw scores, it is possible to determine other interesting information about these scores as well. For instance, we will be able to determine (1) the amount of curve area above or below (to the left or to the right of) a given Z value, and (2) the amount of curve area between two Z values. Some examples of these operations are discussed and described below.

Determining Curve Area to the Left or Right of a Z Value

Two Z values of 1.45 and -1.26 are shown in Figure 6.6. Suppose that we wish to know how much curve area lies below (or to the left of) each of these Z values. For the Z value of 1.45, we first determine the amount of curve area (from Table A3, Appendix A) between the mean of 0 and the Z of 1.45, which is .4265. The amount of curve area below or to the left of 1.45 would not only include the .4265 between $\mu = 0$ and a Z of 1.45, but it would also include the entire left half of the curve as well, or .5000 of it. Therefore, we add .4265 to .5000 to give us .9265, the amount of all curve area to the left of or below the Z value of 1.45. This is the shaded area shown in Figure 6.7.

For the Z value of -1.26, we are also interested in the amount of curve area lying below or to the left of it. Again, we must determine

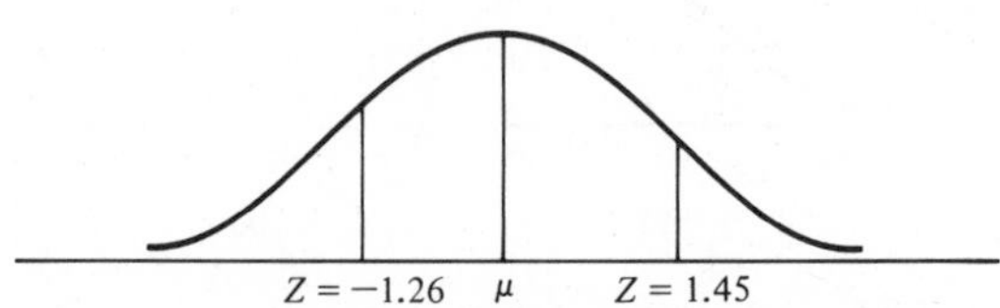

FIGURE 6.6. Unit Normal Distribution Showing Two Z Values.

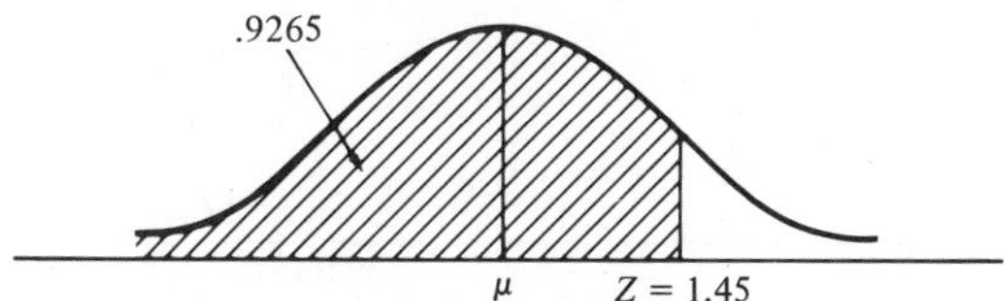

FIGURE 6.7. Unit Normal Distribution Showing the Curve Area to the Left of 1.45.

how much of the curve area occurs between the mean of 0 and our Z value of -1.26, which is .3962. Next, we must subtract .3962 from .5000. This will tell us how much of the curve area lies to the left of -1.26, or $.5000 - .3962 = .1034$. This is also shown as the shaded area in Figure 6.8. The reason we took the difference between .3962 and .5000 is that .5000 is exactly one-half of the curve area, and .3962 is the amount of curve area between the mean of 0 and the Z score of -1.26 to the left of the mean. The remaining area to the left of the Z score of -1.26 is the remaining area between .3962 and .5000, or .1034. We are simply taking what we know about the unit normal distribution and solving for the unknown proportion of curve area.

As an additional example, suppose that we were interested in determining the amount of curve area to the right of the same two Z values of 1.45 and -1.26, respectively. Again, we must determine the amount of curve area between the mean, 0, and a Z value of 1.45, which is .4265. Using our knowledge of the unit normal distribution that one-half of the curve is equal to .5000, we must take the difference between .5000 and .4265 to determine the amount of curve area to the right of 1.45. Completing this arithmetic, we have $.5000 - .4265 = .0735$. This is the proportion of curve area lying to the right of a Z of 1.45 and is the shaded portion shown in Figure 6.9.

For the Z value of -1.26, we again determine the proportion of curve area between the mean, 0, and -1.26, which is .3962. Next, we must add to this the entire right half of the curve area of .5000, or $.5000 + .3962 = .8962$. This is the shaded area shown in Figure 6.10 and is the amount of curve area to the right of -1.26.

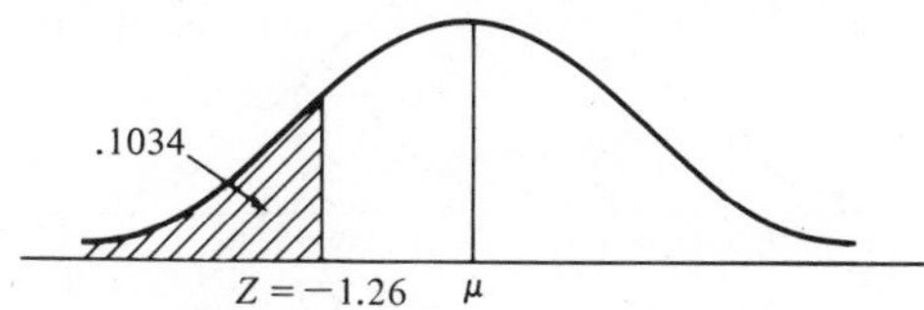

FIGURE 6.8. Unit Normal Distribution Showing the Curve Area to the Left of $Z = -1.26$.

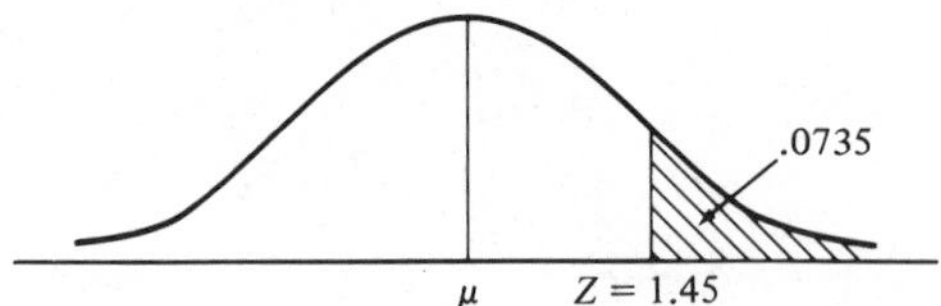

FIGURE 6.9. Unit Normal Distribution Showing the Curve Area to the Right of Z Value = 1.45.

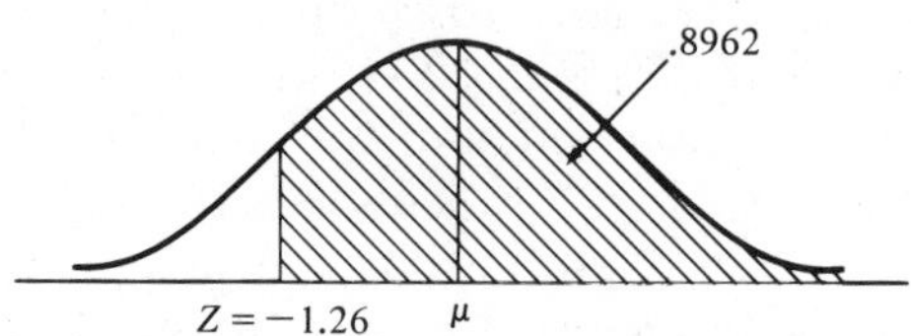

FIGURE 6.10. Unit Normal Distribution Showing the Curve Area to the Right of Z Value = −1.26.

Determining Proportions of Curve Area Between Two Z Values

If we wished to determine the proportion of curve area between any two Z values, we would first determine the amount of curve area included between the mean, 0, and each Z value. Suppose that we had the Z values of −1.55 and 1.86, respectively. The amount of curve area included between the mean, 0, and −1.55 is equal to .4394. The amount of curve area between the mean, 0, and the Z value of 1.86 is .4686. Summing these two proportions will give us the total amount of curve area lying between the two Z values, or .4394 + .4686 = .9080. This is the shaded area shown in Figure 6.11.

If the two Z values happen to be on the same side of the mean in the case of −1.23 and −2.66, we would again determine the amount of curve area between the mean, 0, and each of these Z values. The Z value, −1.23, includes .3907 of curve area, and the Z value of −2.66 cuts off .4961 of curve area. The amount of curve area between these two Z values is the difference between the two propor-

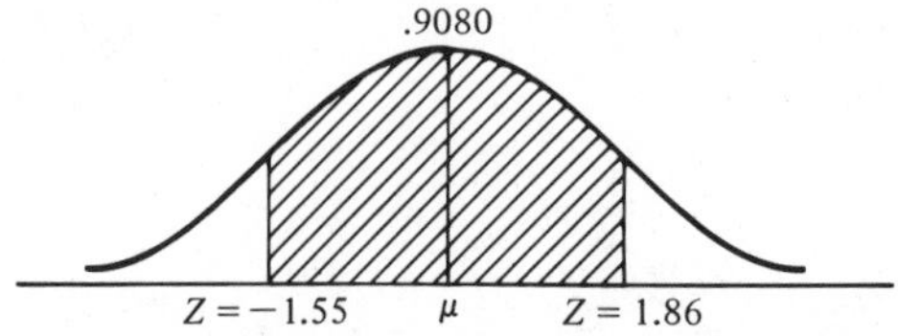

FIGURE 6.11. Unit Normal Distribution Showing the Curve Area Between the Z Values −1.55 and 1.86.

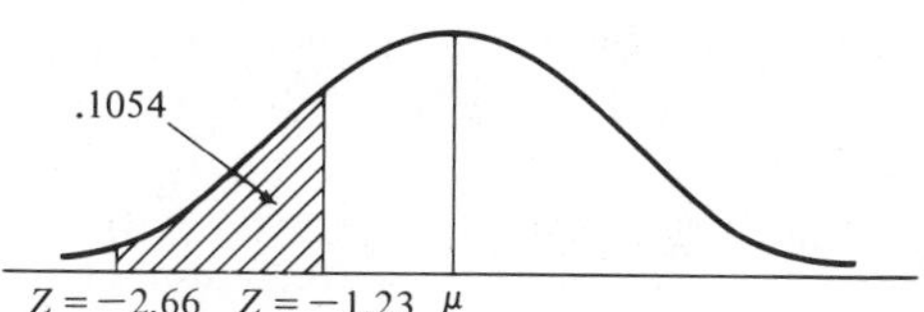

FIGURE 6.12. Unit Normal Distribution Showing the Curve Area Between Z Values of −1.23 and −2.66.

tions, or .4961 - .3907 = .1054. This is the shaded area shown in Figure 6.12.

It is important to note that this type of problem (i.e., determining the proportion of curve area lying between two Z values located on the same side of the mean) must be solved in the fashion outlined above. It is not possible to get a correct answer by taking the difference in Z values (e.g., −2.66 and −1.23) and looking up the curve area cut off by the difference in these Z values. This is an erroneous procedure. Only the difference in proportions cut off by each Z value provides the accurate and correct response.

These exercises dealing with normal-curve areas are important for persons engaged in diagnostic work, advising, or in other assistance or educational testing activity. Raw scores from different tests and from different distributions can be roughly compared and the information obtained can be helpful in providing assistance and advice to those persons being tested or evaluated.

Social researchers benefit from a knowledge of these normal-curve functions as well. The normal distribution is one of several important assumptions made about arrangements of scores that have been collected from samples. If researchers know that the scores they are analyzing are normally distributed, this permits them to consider various statistical tests and procedures for more extensive data analysis. Some of the tests discussed in Chapters 8 through 12 have underlying them the assumption of normality before they can be properly applied to the analysis of social information.

□ CONVERTING Z SCORES TO RAW SCORES

Occasionally, the researcher will wish to convert standard scores or Z scores back into their original raw-score form. Perhaps the raw scores must be included in a portion of the researcher's report about the analyzed data. Or perhaps the researcher wants to provide the reader with the more familiar raw scores rather than the scores in standardized form, which may be somewhat confusing. There are also occasions when a researcher wishes to translate standard scores into raw scores from a report or an article written by someone else. Whatever the reason, the following procedure can be applied.

To transform Z scores or standard scores into raw scores, the original mean, $\overline{X}$, and the original standard deviation, s, must be known. With a knowledge of these values and with a knowledge of the particular Z score to be transformed, the following formula is used:

$$X_i \text{ (raw score)} = \overline{X} + (Z)(s),$$

where

$\overline{X}$ = original mean
s = original standard deviation
Z = standard score to be transformed

For instance, suppose that a person had a Z score of 1.50. Given a hypothetical mean of 65 and a standard deviation of 4, we would determine the person's raw score as follows:

$$\begin{aligned} X_i &= 65 + (1.50)(4) \\ &= 65 + 6 \\ &= 71. \end{aligned}$$

So 71 is the person's original raw score.

If another person had a Z score of -2.75, we would determine the original raw score as follows (using the same mean and standard deviation values):

$$\begin{aligned} X_i &= 65 + (-2.75)(4) \\ &= 65 + (-11) \\ &= 65 - 11 \\ &= 54. \end{aligned}$$

So 54 is this person's original raw score. Note that we must subtract the product from the mean in the case of a negative Z value such as the one shown above.

With this formula, it is possible to convert Z scores into raw scores with any mean and standard deviation the researcher wishes to use. After all, Z scores are simply raw scores transformed into values that fit a distribution with a mean = 0 and a standard deviation = 1. If the researcher prefers not to deal with Z values (which may be positive or negative), other forms of "standardization" are possible.

Suppose that an investigator had the test-score information shown in Table 6.6. The researcher would have the option of converting

TABLE 6.6

Test	Raw Score	Mean	Standard Deviation	Z Score
A	500	420	40	+2.00
B	2000	1800	200	+1.00
C	75	100	25	−1.00

each of the raw scores for tests A, B, and C into standard scores for comparative purposes. Each raw score would be converted into a Z value. The score of 500 for test A would have a Z value of +2.00, for instance. The raw score of 2000 (test B) would have a standard score of +1.00, and the raw score of 75 would have a Z score of −1.00. If the researcher did not want to deal with negative values (i.e., any Z value to the left of or below the mean would be negative), an alternative set of parameters could be substituted. In other words, the raw scores above could be changed into a new form, where they could be compared and where no negative values would be encountered.

Suppose that the researcher wanted to convert all of the raw scores to a "standard form" with a new mean of 5000 and a new standard deviation of 200. This could be accomplished quite easily by substituting these new values for the original mean and standard deviation values associated with each of the raw scores. Converting the raw score of 500 to a new form in which it could be compared with a $\overline{X} = 5000$ and $s = 200$ would be accomplished as follows:

$$\begin{aligned}\text{new score} &= \text{new mean} + (Z)\,(\text{new standard deviation})\\ &= 5000 + (2.00)\,(200)\\ &= 5000 + 400\\ &= 5400.\end{aligned}$$

So 5400 is the new form of the original raw score of 500. 5400 may be compared directly with a mean of 5000. Note that this new score is 2 standard deviations of 200 above the mean of 5000. This is at the same location where 500 occurs in relation to its mean of 420 (i.e., 2 standard deviations of 40 above 420).

The other raw scores would be converted to this new form by using the standard scores associated with them:

For 2000, we have

$$\begin{aligned}5000 + (1.00)\,(200) &= 5000 + 200\\ &= 5200.\end{aligned}$$

So 5200 is the new score associated with the original raw score of 2000.

For 75, we have

$$\begin{aligned} 5000 + (-1.00)(200) &= 5000 + (-200) \\ &= 5000 - 200 \\ &= 4800. \end{aligned}$$

So 4800 is the new score associated with the original raw score of 75.

The primary advantage of converting raw scores to standard forms such as distributions with means of 5000 and standard deviations equal to 200 is that we do away with having to manipulate negative Z values. The various branches of the armed forces often standardize test results in this fashion, where large numbers of recruits are barraged by numerous tests. Diagnostic activity is made somewhat easier by eliminating complex-appearing negative Z values.

□ SOME NON-NORMAL DISTRIBUTIONS

When the social investigator is able to assume normality with the data collected, the mean and standard deviation can be used to provide a systematic and consistent interpretation of raw scores from one distribution to the next. This is the valuable comparative function provided by the unit normal distribution when applied to all distributions of scores approximating it.

Unfortunately, the researcher cannot always assume normality with the data collected. Score arrangements that are not normal in form are occasionally encountered.[1] Two kinds of conditions may be present to disqualify a distribution of scores from being normal in form. These are skewness and kurtosis.

Skewness occurs whenever the scores in a distribution "bunch up" or accumulate at one end or the other of the distribution. Two illustrations of skewness are presented in Figures 6.13 and 6.14. The distribution in Figure 6.13 is positively skewed. Positive skewness is indicated because the curve "tail" tapers off toward the right end of the distribution, as shown. The distribution in Figure 6.14 is negatively skewed because the curve tail tapers off toward the left end of the distribution.

[1] In the real world, it is seldom the case that perfectly normal distributions of raw scores will be found. Usually, there are minor departures from normality where the mean, mode, and median are slightly different from one another, or where the curve is not exactly bell-shaped. These slight departures from normality are frequently disregarded and treated (correctly) as unimportant. The conditions of kurtosis and skewness to be discussed in this section are, however, important departures from normality.

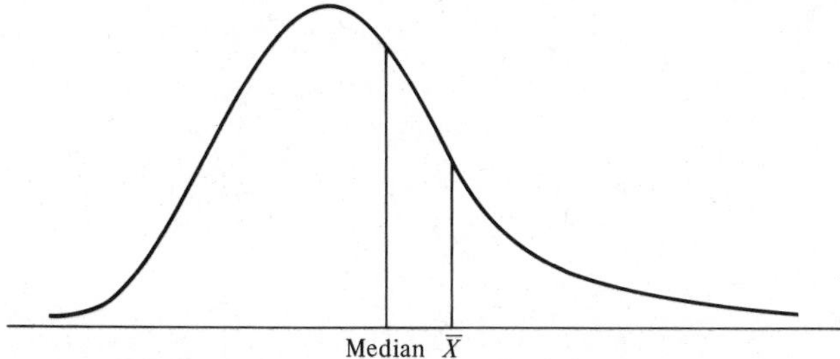

FIGURE 6.13. Distribution That Is Positively Skewed.

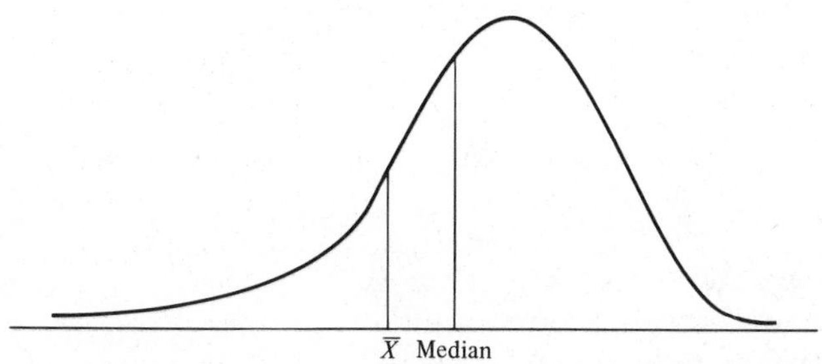

FIGURE 6.14. Distribution That Is Negatively Skewed.

A simple formula for skewness is

$$\text{skewness} = \frac{3(\overline{X} - \text{Mdn})}{s},$$

where

$\overline{X}$ = mean
Mdn = median
s = standard deviation
3 = a constant

When the mean is larger than the median, positive skewness will be found. In Figure 6.13, the mean is to the right of the median and is therefore the larger central tendency value. When the skewness value is computed, the skewness will be positive. In Figure 6.14, the mean is to the left of or smaller than the median. The skewness formula will yield a negative skewness value in that instance.

Suppose that the distribution in Figure 6.13 had the following values: $\overline{X} = 50$; median = 40; $s = 5$. Skewness for this first distribution would be

$$\text{skewness} = \frac{3(50 - 40)}{5}$$

$$= \frac{30}{5}$$

$$= 6.00.$$

Skewness would be +6.00.

Suppose that the second distribution had the following observed statistics: $\overline{X} = 70$; median = 85; $s = 10$. Skewness would be

$$\text{skewness} = \frac{3(70 - 85)}{10}$$

$$= \frac{-45}{10}$$

$$= -4.50.$$

Skewness would be negative or −4.50.

There is no precise interpretation of skewness. Researchers are not in agreement as to how much skewness must be present before deciding that a distribution is not normal in form. One rule of thumb we might apply would be to seriously question normality for any distribution whenever skewness is greater than +1.00 or −1.00. This is purely arbitrary, however. Ultimately, the researcher exercises personal judgment in the matter.

The problem posed by a skewed distribution is that we cannot make good use of the table of areas of the normal curve. For one thing, if we were to move 1 standard deviation to the left of the mean or to the right of it, we would cut off different proportions of curve area. Figure 6.15 shows the unit normal distribution and the fact that the area cut off by a movement of 2σ's in one direction is the same as that cut off by a movement of 2σ's in the other direction. Area A is equal to area B in the curve in Figure 6.15.

Figure 6.16 shows a skewed distribution. Note that a movement of 2σ's in both directions from the mean will cut off different propor-

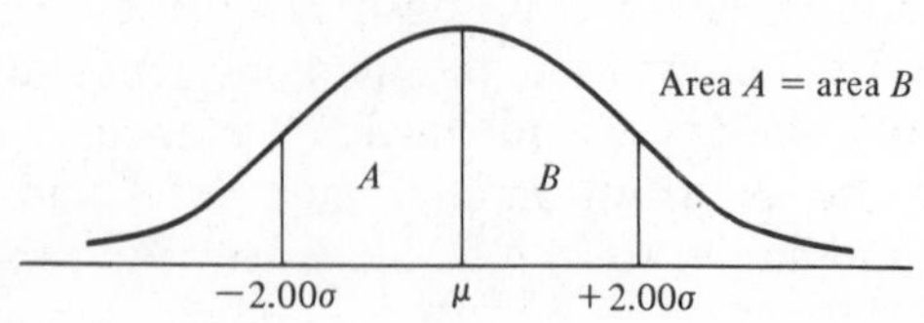

FIGURE 6.15. Normal Distribution Showing Equal Areas Within Two Sigmas of the Mean.

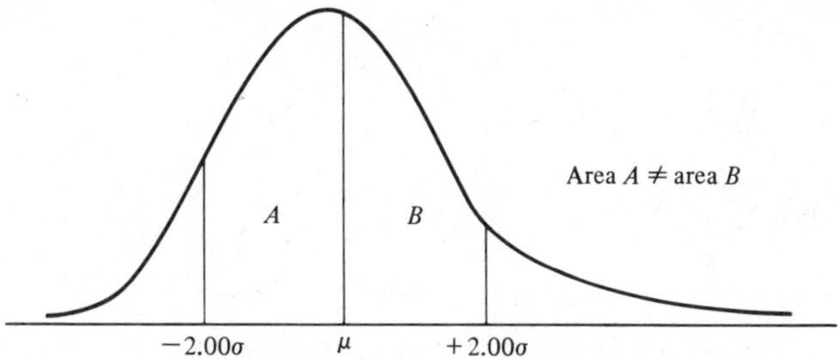

FIGURE 6.16. Skewed Distribution Showing Two Sigma Areas Above and Below the Mean That Are Not Equal to One Another.

tions of curve area. Area *A* will not equal area *B* in a skewed distribution. Therefore, in a skewed distribution situation, the standard deviation cannot be relied upon to give us consistent information about the distribution of scores.

The second condition that might serve to disqualify a distribution from being normal in form is *kurtosis* or *curve peakedness.* Three types of kurtosis have been identified. These are leptokurtosis, platykurtosis, and mesokurtosis, shown in Figures 6.17, 6.18, and 6.19, respectively.

Leptokurtic or tall *distributions* such as the one portrayed in Figure 6.17 may be symmetrical and totally free of skewness. But an unusually large number of scores will be found near the center of the

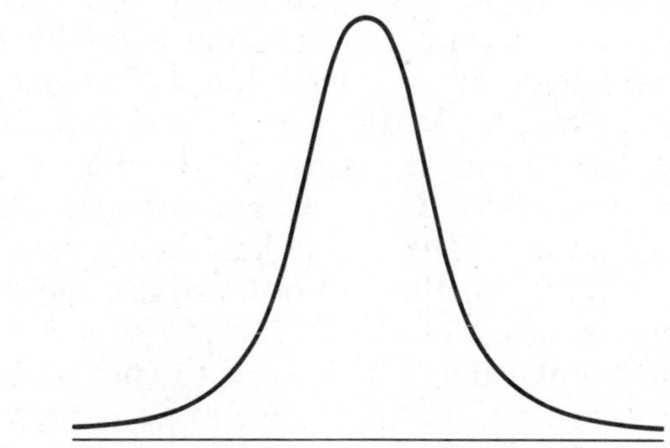

FIGURE 6.17. Leptokurtic Distribution.

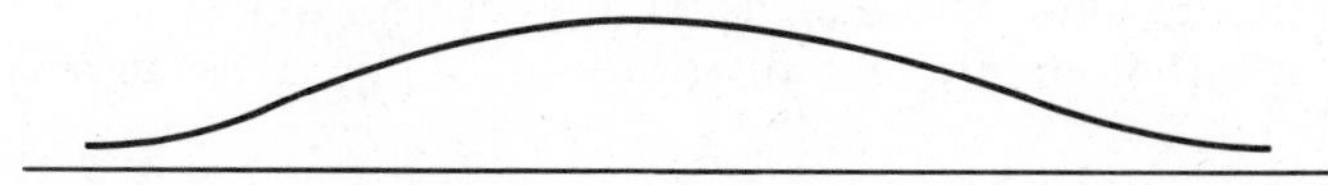

FIGURE 6.18. Platykurtic Distribution.

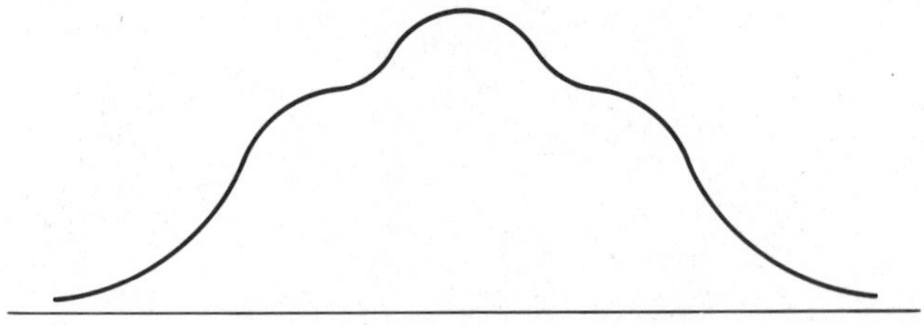

FIGURE 6.19. Mesokurtic Distribution.

distribution. Compared with the unit normal distribution, there will be larger portions of curve area cut off by a movement of 1 standard deviation to the left or right of the mean of a leptokurtic distribution.

Platykurtic distributions such as the one shown in Figure 6.18 are flat distributions. Again, the departure of 1 standard deviation to the left or right of the mean of a platykurtic distribution will cut off a portion of curve area unequal to that cut off on the unit normal distribution. There will be a substantial proportionate difference between the amount of curve area within specified distances of the mean of the unit normal distribution and each of these types of distributions illustrated here.

The *mesokurtic distribution* shown in Figure 6.19 is the most normal-appearing of the three. Again, there are serious departures from normality in this type of distribution.

Any distribution of scores that is severely skewed or suffers from any one of these three types of kurtosis cannot be considered normal in form. By definition, a normal distribution is totally free of skewness and kurtosis. Sometimes a distribution will appear to be leptokurtic, mesokurtic, or platykurtic, but will, in fact, be normal in form. There are such things as normal distributions that are flatter or more peaked than others. This does not automatically disqualify them from being normal. The researcher should make some preliminary checks to verify whether or not kurtosis is present.

If the researcher suspects that a distribution is seriously skewed or is platykurtic or leptokurtic, it is possible to empirically determine the number of scores within 1 or 2 standard deviations of the mean of the distribution. In addition to comparing proportions of curve area between a distribution of raw scores and the unit normal distribution, the researcher can also examine the shape of the curve drawn for the data. Often, a visual inspection will assist one in determining whether or not the distribution of scores is approximately normal.

When the researcher cannot assume that the distribution of scores is truly normal in form, this does not mean that the standard devia-

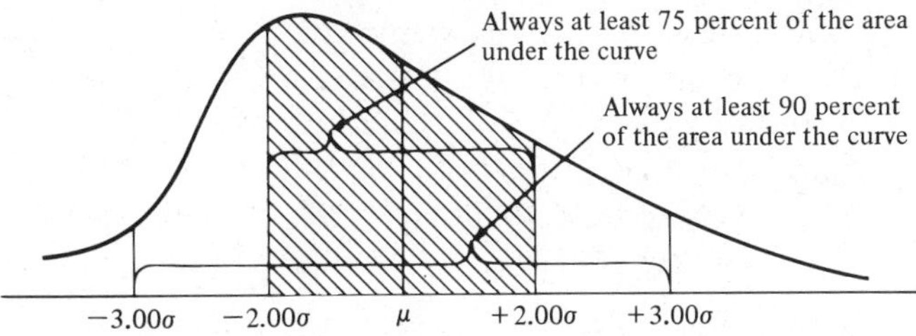

FIGURE 6.20. Areas of Curve Always Included Within Two and Three Standard Deviations from the Mean.

tion and mean computations for that distribution are without value. There are several things a researcher can say about the distribution, regardless of how skewed it may be. For one thing, at least 75 percent of the curve area will always be included within 2 standard deviations on either side of the mean. Also, at least 90 percent of the curve area will always be included within 3 standard deviations on either side of the mean. Figure 6.20 illustrates the proportions of curve area included within 2 and 3 standard deviations of the mean for skewed distributions. Of course, if the unit normal distribution were truly approximated, these percentages would be appreciably higher. In the final analysis, the meaning of the standard deviation and mean are maximized when the normal distribution can be assumed with the data under investigation.

□ THE PROBABILITY FUNCTION OF THE UNIT NORMAL DISTRIBUTION

In addition to being useful for comparative purposes in educational testing and diagnostic activities, the unit normal distribution serves a probability function. Proportions of curve area can be translated into probabilities. Scores that occur within 1 standard deviation on either side of the mean have a 68 percent chance of occurring within this general area. In short, the proportions of curve area encompassed by any standard score or Z value can be translated into probabilities. Scores found in the extremes of the distribution (i.e., in the "tails" to the left or to the right) are less plentiful compared with scores near the center of the distribution, and therefore there is a much lower probability associated with their occurrence.

In some of the statistical procedures to be presented in later chapters, a Z value will be the result of a statistical test application. We will evaluate each Z value according to where it is located on the unit normal distribution. A probability will be assigned that will tell us how significant the Z value is within a chance context. Considerably more will be presented in Chapters 7 and 8, which will make clear the probability function of the unit normal distribution and how it is used in statistical hypothesis-testing work. For the time being, it is important only to recognize that the unit normal distribution serves several key roles in our statistical activities.

□ SUMMARY

The standard or unit normal distribution is a mathematically derived, theoretical distribution that serves a probability function as well as a comparative one. In research work, social scientists often approximate the unit normal distribution with distributions of raw scores they have collected. To the extent that a similarity in distributions occurs, statements about the unit normal distribution can also apply to distributions of raw scores that approximate it.

Some of the characteristics of the unit normal distribution include the fact that it is bell-shaped, symmetrical, and has a $\mu = 0$ and a $\sigma = 1$ as its primary parameters. Points along the horizontal axis of the unit normal distribution are designated by Z scores or standard scores. These represent various departures to the left or to the right of the mean in standard deviation units. Researchers can translate their raw scores into standard scores for purposes of comparison and in the educational testing and advising activities they perform.

Not all distributions of scores are truly normal, however. Distributions may be skewed; that is, scores tend to bunch up or accumulate in the left or right tails of the curve. Also, distributions may be affected by kurtosis of one sort or another. Three kinds of kurtosis or curve peakedness were identified: leptokurtosis (tall distribution), platykurtosis (flat distribution), and mesokurtosis. These types of kurtosis cause a distribution of scores to be non-normal. When a distribution is severely skewed or has serious kurtosis, by definition it cannot be considered normal in form. The meaningfulness of the mean and standard deviation is seriously reduced when such non-normal distributions are encountered.

It has been shown that normal-curve areas can be translated into probabilities. The probability function of the unit normal distribution will take on greater significance in later chapters when various statistical tests are presented.

SELECTED STUDY TERMS

Unit normal distribution
Normal curve

Z score or standard score
Skewness
Kurtosis
Leptokurtosis
Platykurtosis
Mesokurtosis

EXERCISES

1. Determine the proportion of curve area lying to the right of the following Z values.
   (a) 1.45 (b) -2.33 (c) 0.00
   (d) -.40 (e) 1.99 (f) 1.00
2. Determine the proportion of curve area lying between the following pairs of Z values.
   (a) -1.95 and -1.26 (b) -1.66 and 1.66
   (c) 2.11 and .04 (d) 2.33 and 2.44
3. Convert the following raw scores to Z scores, where $\overline{X} = 115$ and $s = 10$.
   (a) 156 (b) 115 (c) 100 (d) 85
4. Convert the following Z scores to raw scores, where $\overline{X} = 220$ and $s = 15$.
   (a) -5.55 (b) 1.44 (c) 3.11 (d) 0.00
5. Standardize the following raw scores with an old mean = 100 and an old standard deviation = 20 to a new mean = 500 and a new standard deviation = 50 (round to the nearest whole number).
   (a) 120 (b) 65 (c) 200 (d) 100
6. Determine the proportion of curve area lying to the *left* of the following Z values.
   (a) .32 (b) -2.18 (c) .99
   (d) -.03 (e) 1.11 (f) 2.23
   (g) -.81 (h) 1.00
7. Determine the *raw score* associated with the following Z values, given $\overline{X} =$ 40 and $s = 4.2$ (round to the nearest whole number).
   (a) -1.09 (b) .11 (c) 3.48
   (d) -6.00 (e) -0.00 (f) -2.26
8. Determine the amount of curve area lying between the following Z values (express to four places, .0000).
   (a) .26 and 1.21 (b) 1.09 and -2.18
   (c) .00 and 1.00 (d) 1.45 and -1.02
   (e) 2.32 and 2.33 (f) 2.88 and -1.18
   (g) 1.86 and -1.23 (h) -.09 and -1.10
9. Transform the following raw scores into standard scores, given $\overline{X} = 400$ and $s = 32$.
   (a) 442 (b) 496 (c) 448
   (d) 411 (e) 465 (f) 480
10. Transform the following raw scores into standard form with a new mean = 1300 and a new standard deviation = 300 (old mean = 55, old standard deviation = 7).

(a) 60 (b) 55 (c) 42
(d) 66 (e) 71 (f) 30

11. With $\overline{X} = 60$ and $s = 4$, what proportion of scores theoretically lies above the following values?
(a) 64 (b) 49 (c) 46 (d) 55

12. What proportion of scores (and curve area) would be included between the following Z values?
(a) .94 and -.75 (b) 2.33 and 1.70
(c) -1.08 and -1.09 (d) -1.40 and -.300
(e) 2.66 and -1.77 (f) -2.16 and .09

13. Determine the amount of curve area to the right of the following Z values.
(a) 3.11 (b) .03 (c) -1.54
(d) 2.27 (e) -2.55 (f) -.07

14. Determine the amount of curve area between each of the following pairs of Z values.
(a) -1.55 and .03 (b) 1.66 and -1.66
(c) -2.23 and -2.25 (d) 3.03 and 1.45
(e) .09 and -1.78 (f) 1.30 and 1.00

15. Convert the following raw scores to Z values, given $\overline{X} = 60$ and $s = 12$.
(a) 60 (b) 48 (c) 22
(d) 69 (e) 72 (f) 84

16. Convert the following Z values to original raw scores, rounding to the nearest whole number, given $\overline{X} = 25$ and $s = 3$.
(a) 2.45 (b) -4.60 (c) -1.99 (d) 8.88

REFERENCES

Arkin, Herbert, and Raymond R. Colton, *An Outline of Statistical Methods.* New York: Barnes & Noble Books, 1968.

Bernstein, Allen L., *A Handbook of Statistical Solutions for the Behavioral Sciences.* New York: Holt, Rinehart and Winston, 1964.

Crowley, Francis J., and Martin Cohen, *Basic Facts of Statistics.* New York: Collier Books, 1963.

Tanur, Judith M., F. Mosteller, W. H. Kruskal, R. F. Link, R. S. Pieters, and G. R. Rising, *Statistics: A Guide to the Unknown.* San Francisco: Holden-Day, Inc., 1972.

Weiss, Robert S., *Statistics in Social Research.* New York: John Wiley & Sons, Inc., 1968.

Wike, Edward L., *Data Analysis: A Statistical Primer for Psychology Students.* Chicago: Aldine Publishing Company, 1971.

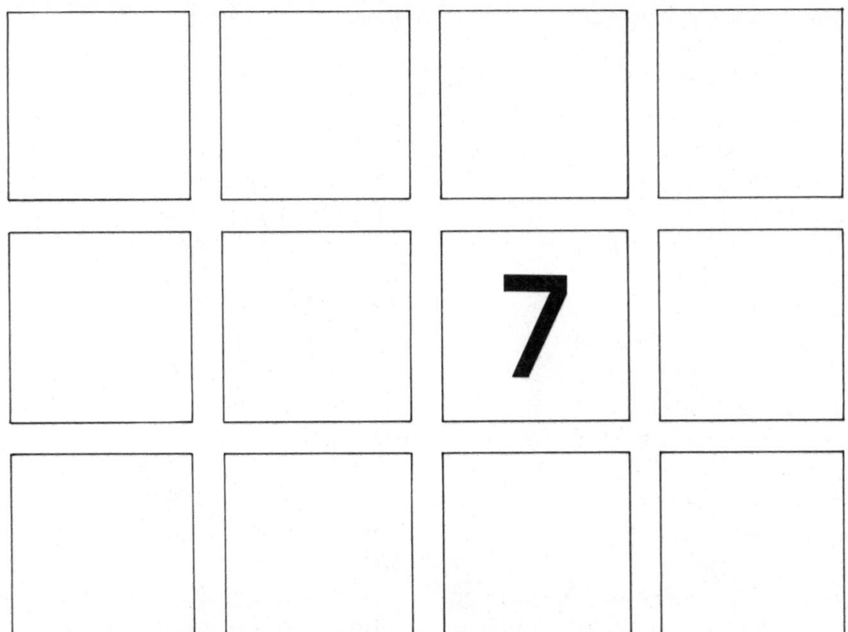

Hypothesis Testing and Statistical Inference

A primary function of statistical procedures is to assist in evaluating the outcomes of hypothesis tests. Hypotheses are statements that usually have been derived from a theoretical scheme or theory; they are statements about a portion of the theory that has been rendered amenable to an empirical test. Sometimes researchers refer to hypotheses as *statements of theory in testable form.* Sometimes hypotheses are defined as *tentative statements about reality* that can be either supported or refuted on the basis of collected evidence or relevant information.

Three kinds of hypotheses will be identified and described here: (1) research hypotheses, (2) null hypotheses, and (3) statistical hypotheses.

□ RESEARCH HYPOTHESES

Research hypotheses are statements that have been derived directly from our theoretical schemes. For instance, if we were studying the influence of home environment on juvenile delinquency, we might examine the impact of homes broken by desertion or divorce on the incidence of juvenile delinquency. Perhaps we would collect interview and/or questionnaire information from social caseworkers, friends, or relatives of persons who have been identified as "delinquent." Our general explanatory scheme or theory might seek to relate broken homes directly with delinquency. If we know that homes have been broken by desertion or divorce, we might expect that the incidence of delinquency among children in those homes would be fairly high. At the very least, we would expect delinquency to be more prevalent in broken homes compared with the amount of delinquency in homes not broken by divorce.

One research hypothesis might be that delinquency rates will be higher in broken homes compared with more stable home settings. If we were able to show empirically that higher delinquency rates existed in broken homes compared with more stable home settings, this could be interpreted as support for our research hypothesis. In turn, support for our research hypothesis would be partial support for the theory from which this hypothesis was originally derived. We would probably be inclined to take a closer look at the stability of the home environment as we attempted to account for differences in delinquency rates from one type of home condition to the next.

A variety of competing theoretical schemes exists for any phenomenon we wish to explain in our social and psychological world. For instance, the phenomenon "delinquency" may be explained by paying attention to socioeconomic factors and cultural deprivation (e.g., children might become delinquent if they do not have access to the same material goods as other children or if they are "deprived" of the things they want), or to peer group influences (e.g., children become delinquent if they associate with other delinquents). In each of these situations, a different explanatory scheme must be created, linking delinquency with types of companions or type of socioeconomic background, or to home stability or instability. Some researchers will find arguments favoring one point of view compelling while other researchers will pursue alternative explanations. Regardless of the explanation we select to account for the existence of some phenomenon, we will proceed in our scientific investigations utilizing common principles or procedures of inquiry.

After we collect the necessary information pertaining to the phenomenon we are attempting to explain, we subject our explanation to an empirical test. We do this by formulating research hypotheses that provide connecting links between the phenomenon to be explained and the variable or variables we are using to explain it.

Some examples of research hypotheses might be as follows:

1. There is a relation between job satisfaction and pay for employees of the American National Bank.
2. A sample of Republicans will differ from a sample of Democrats in the degree of conservatism.
3. Couples from interfaith marriages will have higher divorce rates compared with couples from intrafaith marriages.
4. Students who learn history through programmed-learning instruction will exhibit higher history examination scores compared with students learning history through the lecture method of instruction.
5. Nutrition program X will cause greater weight loss than will nutrition program Y.

In each of the hypotheses, some phenomenon is being investigated and explained by some variable. In hypothesis 1, our interest in factors associated with job satisfaction of employees might include the potential influence of pay. In the case of hypothesis 4, we might be interested in the effects of new and different learning methods on learning potential, level of achievement, or performance in history comprehension. And in attempting to predict the most successful weight-loss programs for obese persons in hypothesis 5, we might examine the effectiveness of two competing nutritional programs, X and Y.

Preceding each of these hypothesis statements is an explicit (or sometimes implicit) theoretical scheme. Hypotheses are usually deduced from the theoretical scheme and arranged in some kind of testable form. The *hypothesis test* is a real situation where real data are presented, compared, and evaluated. Suppose that we were conducting a test of hypothesis 5, concerning weight loss associated with two alternative nutritional programs. If we found that the mean weight loss for a sample of persons in nutrition program X was 15.5 pounds, and if we determined that the mean weight loss for a sample of persons in nutrition program Y was 13.3 pounds, we would have instant "evidence" of a weight-loss difference between the two groups. A visual inspection of the data would indicate that 15.5 pounds is obviously different from 13.3 pounds. Assuming that the two groups participating in the weight-loss programs were similar to one another in almost all respects, it would be logical to assume that the different weight-loss programs accounted for the differences in mean weight lost by each group.

As researchers, we may believe that the two weight-loss programs effect different weight losses for the program participants. In an effort to "back up" our belief that one program is actually better or more effective than the other at causing or contributing to greater weight loss, the research hypothesis is subjected to a statistical test. After applying a statistical test to the difference between means (the difference between the average weight lost by both groups), we will have *numerical or quantitative confirmation* of the observed difference. We will be able to assign a *probability value* to the difference we have observed between the groups. This probability will help us to decide whether or not the difference between 15.5 pounds and 13.3 pounds is *statistically significant.*

We will soon see that there are at least three kinds of significance associated with our observations. The first kind of significance is *substantive.* What are the practical advantages of following one type of nutritional program rather than another? A second type of significance is *theoretical.* Does our knowledge of weight-loss programs help us to learn more about a person's self concept, early childhood socialization, or sociocultural development? Have we increased our knowledge of human metabolism or biochemical balance? A third type of significance is *statistical.* Is the difference in weight loss between groups more likely due to chance or to the different nutritional programs? Have we observed a chance fluctuation or a crucial and meaningful difference in mean weight lost for both groups?

Although this book promotes statistical significance more than substantive or theoretical significance, it is important to recognize that researchers are actually concerned to some extent with all three types. Each type of significance complements the other types: a degree of interdependency exists among them. When we learn about statistical significance, however, we run the risk of neglecting or "playing down" the value of other types of significance. We realize that we have gone too far or have taken statistical significance too seriously whenever it can be said that "what we have observed is statistically significant–but it doesn't mean anything." The role of statistical tests is first and foremost a supporting one. Without carefully constructed theoretical schemes and well-formulated hypotheses, our statistical testing would be so much meaningless activity.

Research hypotheses, therefore, are logically deduced from theoretical schemes. As scientific investigators, we are interested in determining whether or not they are true statements. Rather than subjecting these research hypotheses to a direct empirical test, however, it has become conventional to test our research hypothesis statements indirectly through the use of null hypotheses.

□ NULL HYPOTHESES

Null hypotheses are negations or denials of research hypothesis statements. Some people regard null hypotheses as the "reverse" of research hypotheses, although this view is somewhat inaccurate. Technically, a null hypotheses is a statement which, if refuted, will lead to the support of some true research hypothesis.

In view of the research hypotheses stated in the last section, null hypotheses associated with these (and derived directly from them) are:

1′. There is no relation between job satisfaction and pay for employees of the American National Bank. (If this hypothesis is refuted or demonstrated by real data to be false, it must be true that there is an association between job satisfaction and pay for employees of the American National Bank.)

2′. There is no difference in degree of conservatism between a sample of Republicans and a sample of Democrats. (If this hypothesis is refuted or "denied" as true, it must be true that there is a difference between Republicans and Democrats in their degree of conservatism.)

3′. Divorce rates will be the same for couples from interfaith marriages and intrafaith marriages; or if there is a difference, divorce rates will be higher for couples from intrafaith marriages. (If this hypothesis is not true, it must be true that divorce rates will be higher for couples from interfaith marriages compared with couples from intrafaith marriages.)

4′. There will be no difference in history examination scores for students learning history through programmed learning and lecture instruction; if there is a difference, the lecture instruction group will have higher history examination scores. (If this hypothesis is refuted or rejected, it must be true that the programmed learning student group will do better on the history examination compared with the group learning history through the lecture method.)

5′. There is no difference in weight loss between groups participating in nutrition program X and nutrition program Y; if there is a difference, greater weight loss will occur in the sample participating in program Y. (If this hypothesis is rejected or shown not to be true, it must be true that persons in nutrition program X will have greater weight loss compared with persons in nutrition program Y.)

Why Use Null Hypotheses?

The use of null hypotheses in social research and hypothesis testing situations is sometimes confusing for the beginning student. The most frequently asked question is: Why use null hypotheses in the first place? There are at least four answers to this question. The first three are weak at best. The fourth answer is perhaps the most valid for hypothesis-testing purposes. Null hypotheses are used in research because:

1. It is easier to "prove" a hypothesis statement false than it is to prove it true—this reason has led some persons to think that null hypotheses are somehow easier to test than research hypotheses. There is no proof to show that either type of hypothesis is easier to support (or refute).
2. It is more objective to test null hypotheses rather than research hypotheses—the reason given for testing null hypotheses is that this presents an "objective picture" to the layman. After all, if the researcher were to test the research hypothesis directly, an accusation might be made that the researcher was trying to "prove" a hypothesis true that was believed to be true to begin with. Therefore, putting forth a null hypothesis gives the appearance of starting out testing a hypothesis that is not believed to be true. At least this gives the appearance of greater objectivity.
3. It is conventional to use null hypotheses in hypothesis testing—perhaps this is the most compelling reason of these first three. The researcher is swayed toward one method of procedure or another as a result of powerful conventional rules. The fact that so many researchers employ null hypotheses in hypothesis tests as a matter of convention is sufficient justification for the novice researcher to do so as well.
4. Null hypotheses fit a probability model underlying all hypothesis testing. Probability theory is always utilized as the means of evaluating or assessing the significance of whatever we observe. We couch all of the decisions we make about hypothesis tests in terms of probability. For instance, there is a 90 percent chance or likelihood that some hypothesis is true. Or, there is a 99 percent chance or likelihood that some hypothesis is supported.

Whenever null hypotheses are subjected to empirical test, we will make a decision to either *reject* or *fail to reject* them. Rejecting null hypotheses or refuting them is tantamount to supporting or accepting research hypotheses. By the same token, failing to reject null hypothesis statements is equivalent to failing to support research hypotheses which are their counterparts.

As an example, suppose that we have the following null hypothesis and research hypothesis set:[1]

H_0: Height and weight for members of group A are not related.
H_1: Height and weight for members of group A are related.

Conventionally, a statistical test will be made of H_0, the null hypothesis, directly. A decision made about H_0 directly will indirectly influence our decision about the truthfulness or falsity of H_1, the research hypothesis. Suppose that we show from our collected data that H_0 is not true. If H_0 is refuted, then, automatically, H_1 is supported. If it is not true that height and weight for members of group A are not related, it must be true that height and weight for members of group A are related.

The support or lack of support for any H_1 (the research hypothesis) is, of course, dependent upon the rejection of or failure to reject H_0 (the null hypothesis). Therefore, if a null hypothesis is rejected or refuted by our research findings, our research hypothesis is supported, and there is a fixed probability or likelihood that it is true or that we have made the correct decision to support it.

The probability value we assign to any hypothesis test is our measure of the statistical significance associated with that test. A simple illustration will indicate what is usually done in general hypothesis testing:

H_0: Height and weight for members of group A are not related.
H_1: Height and weight for members of group A are related.

$$P \leqslant .05$$

First, note that H_0 and H_1 are presented as a pair of hypotheses. This format will be followed throughout the remaining chapters in all hypothesis tests presented. This is an accepted and conventional procedure, although it is certainly not the only procedure followed by all social scientists in their hypothesis presentations. Some researchers prefer to present H_1's only, or H_0's only, with their respective counterparts implied in their accompanying discussion of test results.

[1] Null hypotheses and research hypotheses are frequently presented as a pair or "set" of hypotheses. Also, null hypotheses are symbolically portrayed as H_0's, and research hypotheses are portrayed as H_1's. Some notation systems designate these same hypotheses as H_1 and H_2, respectively, although in this text we will follow the symbol format shown above.

Accompanying the pair or set of hypotheses presented above is a *probability* (P). In this instance, $P \leqslant .05$. The $P \leqslant .05$ means that if H_0 is tested and refuted or rejected, H_1 will be supported . . . and there is a 5 percent chance (.05) that we will be wrong in supporting our H_1 and rejecting H_0. If $P \leqslant .01$, we would say that our chances would be 1 in 100 (.01) or 1 percent of being wrong in deciding to reject H_0 and support H_1.

We establish or determine the probability level used to test hypotheses. The .05 represents our willingness to accept an error factor of 5 percent in making a wrong decision. The .01 might represent our willingness to accept an error factor of 1 percent in making a wrong decision. A more detailed explanation of probability and its role in hypothesis testing will be presented later in this chapter.

□ STATISTICAL HYPOTHESES

When research and null hypotheses are expressed in symbolic and numerical terms, they are often called statistical hypotheses. *Statistical hypotheses* are statements about statistical populations that, on the basis of information obtained from observed data, one seeks to support or refute (Winer, 1971, p. 10). The observations we make about statistical populations (i.e., people or things) based on samples drawn from them are typically reduced to numerical quantities that are examined. If we subsequently determine that differences exist in numerical expressions of variables for two or more groups, we will infer that the groups are different regarding those variables. In short, our research and null hypotheses are transformed into numerical expressions designated as statistical hypotheses. These statistical hypotheses can be tested by applying statistical procedures which are purely mathematical. The relationship among research, null, and statistical hypotheses is shown in Table 7.1.

In Table 7.1, the statistical hypothesis set reads as follows: H_1 says that the relation (r) between height and weight (x and y are subscripts that stand for variables X and Y) is not equal to zero (meaning that a relation exists somewhere between -1.00 and $+1.00$, perfect negative and perfect positive associations, respectively). Also, H_0 reads that the association (r) between height and weight (x and y subscripts) is equal to zero (meaning "no association"). If there is any association (r) between height and weight, it will be reflected in a departure from zero, either above or below it. The degree of departure from zero will indicate the significance or strength of the association between the variables height (X) and weight (Y).

As an additional example, suppose that we examine history test

TABLE 7.1
Relationship Among Research, Null, and Statistical Hypotheses.

Research Hypothesis ⟶	Null Hypothesis
(Example: X and Y are related.)	(Example: X and Y are not related.)
Statistical Hypotheses 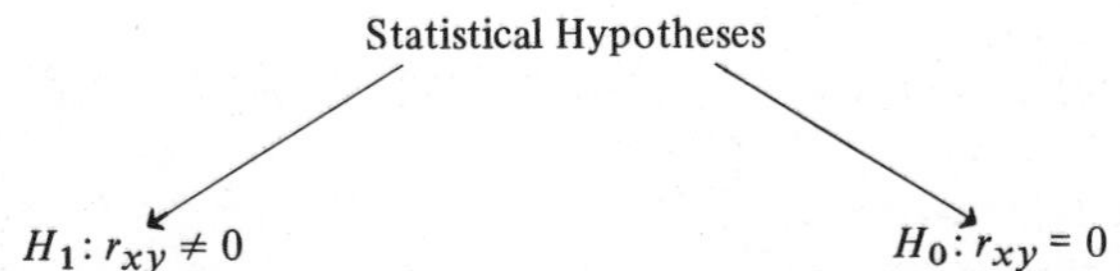	
$H_1: r_{xy} \neq 0$	$H_0: r_{xy} = 0$
[Research hypothesis symbolically expressed says that variables X and Y are related (r).]	[Null hypothesis symbolically expressed says that there is no relation (r) between variables X and Y.]

scores for two samples of freshman college students. The samples consist of different sections of an introductory history class taught by the same professor. The professor uses a different teaching method in each class and wants to know whether differences in average history test performance will be observed at the end of the term. The mean test score for the first section of history students is designated as $\overline{X}_1$, and the mean history test score for the second section of students is designated as $\overline{X}_2$. The professor believes that differences in average test scores will be observed between the two sections of students, and therefore the research hypothesis is

> H_1: There will be a difference between two sections of history students on their history examination scores.

The null hypothesis, derived from H_1, will be

> H_0: There is no difference in average test scores for the two sections of history students.

The statistical hypothesis set for the research and null hypotheses stated above will be

$$H_0: \overline{X}_1 = \overline{X}_2$$
$$H_1: \overline{X}_1 \neq \overline{X}_2.$$

The null hypothesis, H_0, says that the two groups will be the same, or that the mean for the first group ($\overline{X}_1$) will be equal to the mean for the second group ($\overline{X}_2$); H_1 says that the mean score for the first group ($\overline{X}_1$) will not be equal to ($\neq$) the mean score for the second group ($\overline{X}_2$).

For most research and null hypotheses tested in later chapters, variables can be reduced to numerical quantities and symbolic expressions can be substituted for wordy statements. Occasionally, it will not be possible to reduce research and null hypotheses statements to numerical expressions because of the complexity of the hypotheses to be tested. In such instances, a rationale will be provided for the procedures followed in hypothesis presentations and tests.

□ DECISION RULES GOVERNING HYPOTHESIS TESTS

Whenever a statistical test is made of any null hypothesis, the result of that test is interpreted by the researcher. The result may lead the researcher to believe that the null hypothesis is not true and ought to be rejected. Or the result may indicate that the null hypothesis should not be rejected. Guiding the researcher's decision making regarding the outcomes of hypothesis tests and how such outcomes ought to be interpreted are decision rules.

Decision rules consist of a set of conditions specified in advance of any statistical test which define how test outcomes should be properly interpreted. If a researcher were to proceed with hypothesis testing without using a set of decision rules, the results would be subject to any interpretation we would care to make. One researcher's interpretation would be just as valid as another researcher's interpretation, even if both researchers reached opposite or contradictory conclusions. Decision rules are employed, therefore, as impartial arbiters that remove all subjectivity and guesswork from the researcher's grasp. Following the canons of scientific inquiry, researchers are obligated to abide by decision rules in judging hypothesis test outcomes. Decision rules include the following: (1) the sampling distribution of a statistic, (2) the level of significance, and (3) the critical region or region of rejection.

The Sampling Distribution of a Statistic

A sampling distribution of a statistic is the distribution of all possible values a given statistic may assume for samples of a specified size drawn from a specified population. Every statistic presented in Chapters 4 and 5 has a sampling distribution. In fact, all known statistics have sampling distributions. If a researcher were to draw all possible samples of size 3 from a population of 10 persons, the number of samples drawn would be equal to N^n or $(10)^3$, where N is the population size and n the sample size. In this case, there would be $(10)^3$ or (10) (10) (10) or 1000 samples of size 3 that could be drawn from a population of 10. How many samples of size 500 could be drawn from a population of 30,000? $30{,}000^{500}$ or (30,000) (30,000) (30,000) $\cdots$, until 500 products had been obtained.

Returning to our smaller-scale example of drawing all possible samples of size 3 from a population of 10, we would be able to draw 1000 samples. Let us assume that for each sample drawn, the researcher will compute a mean, a median, a standard deviation, and a range. The results of such computations will yield 1000 means, 1000 medians, 1000 standard deviations, and 1000 ranges. Now, if the researcher arranges all the means into a frequency distribution, the result will be a sampling distribution of 1000 sample means. If the medians are arranged into a frequency distribution as well, the resulting distribution will be called a sampling distribution of 1000 sample medians. Similarly, if all standard deviation values are arranged into a frequency distribution, the researcher will have a sampling distribution of 1000 standard deviations. Finally, all range values can be arranged into a frequency distribution that will be called the sampling distribution of 1000 sample ranges.

In each case described above, the researcher has arranged all observed statistical values into a frequency distribution. The sampling distribution of means is a distribution of all possible values that the mean can assume for samples of a specified size (in this case, 3) drawn from a specified population (in this case, 10). The sampling distribution of standard deviations is a distribution of all possible values that the standard deviation can assume for samples of a specified size (in this case, 3) drawn from a specified population (in this case, 10).

A sampling distribution of a statistic can be illustrated (again, on a small scale) by the following example. Suppose that we have a population of six drill-press operators. Also, suppose that we have the number of units of product produced per day by each drill-press operator. We designate each drill-press operator by a different letter: A, B, C, D, E, and F. Units of product produced per day are shown to the right of each identifying letter, and are designated as various X_i values. For instance, in Table 7.2, operator A produces 10 units per day and operator C produces 12 units per day. Further suppose that we wish to draw all possible random samples of size 2 from this population of 6. The possible number of random samples of $n = 2$ that

TABLE 7.2

Operator	*Units of Product Produced*
A	10
B	11
C	12
D	13
E	14
F	15

could be drawn from a population $N = 6$ would be N^n or $(6)^2 = 36$ possible samples.

The possible samples of size 2 that the researcher can draw from the population of 6 are represented by the following letter combinations:[2]

AA	*BA*	*CA*	*DA*	*EA*	*FA*
AB	*BB*	*CB*	*DB*	*EB*	*FB*
AC	*BC*	*CC*	*DC*	*EC*	*FC*
AD	*BD*	*CD*	*DD*	*ED*	*FD*
AE	*BE*	*CE*	*DE*	*EE*	*FE*
AF	*BF*	*CF*	*DF*	*EF*	*FF*.

After these 36 samples of size 2 have been drawn, the researcher computes all the sample means. These means would be symbolically portrayed as $\overline{X}_1, \overline{X}_2, \ldots, \overline{X}_{36}$:

$\overline{X}_1$	$\overline{X}_2$	$\overline{X}_3$	$\overline{X}_4$	$\overline{X}_5$	$\overline{X}_6$	10.0	10.5	11.0	11.5	12.0	12.5
$\overline{X}_7$	$\overline{X}_8$	$\overline{X}_9$	$\overline{X}_{10}$	$\overline{X}_{11}$	$\overline{X}_{12}$	10.5	11.0	11.5	12.0	12.5	13.0
$\overline{X}_{13}$	$\overline{X}_{14}$	$\overline{X}_{15}$	$\overline{X}_{16}$	$\overline{X}_{17}$	$\overline{X}_{18}$	11.0	11.5	12.0	12.5	13.0	13.5
$\overline{X}_{19}$	$\overline{X}_{20}$	$\overline{X}_{21}$	$\overline{X}_{22}$	$\overline{X}_{23}$	$\overline{X}_{24}$	11.5	12.0	12.5	13.0	13.5	14.0
$\overline{X}_{25}$	$\overline{X}_{26}$	$\overline{X}_{27}$	$\overline{X}_{28}$	$\overline{X}_{29}$	$\overline{X}_{30}$	12.0	12.5	13.0	13.5	14.0	14.5
$\overline{X}_{31}$	$\overline{X}_{32}$	$\overline{X}_{33}$	$\overline{X}_{34}$	$\overline{X}_{35}$	$\overline{X}_{36}$	12.5	13.0	13.5	14.0	14.5	15.0

To the far right of these means are the actual mean values computed. We observe that the smallest mean, $\overline{X}_1$, is 10.0, and the largest mean, X_{36}, is 15.0.

Next, the researcher constructs a frequency distribution of these sample means as shown in Table 7.3. The resulting frequency distribution of sample means is called the sampling distribution of means for samples of size 2 drawn from a population of size 6.

It is possible for the researcher to determine any other statistic desired for these samples of size 2 and arrange these statistical values into a similar frequency distribution of them. In these cases, the researcher would have sampling distributions of whatever statistic has been computed.

[2] The letter combinations *AA*, *BB*, *CC*, *DD*, *EE*, and *FF* are possible because of *sampling with replacement*, a procedure by which a person once drawn randomly can be drawn again randomly. This is a purely theoretical sampling consideration. Ordinarily, in social research, samples would consist entirely of *n* different elements. For instance, we would not interview the same person twice if that person happened to be randomly drawn twice. Rather, we would interview *n* different elements.

TABLE 7.3
Sampling Distribution of $\overline{X}$'s for Samples of Size 2 from a Population of Size 6.

Observed $\overline{X}$'s	*f*	*Proportion*	*Probability*
10.0	x	$\frac{1}{36}$	.03
10.5	xx	$\frac{2}{36}$	.06
11.0	xxx	$\frac{3}{36}$	.08
11.5	xxxx	$\frac{4}{36}$	.11
12.0	xxxxx	$\frac{5}{36}$	.14
12.5	xxxxxx	$\frac{6}{36}$	.16
13.0	xxxxx	$\frac{5}{36}$	.14
13.5	xxxx	$\frac{4}{36}$	.11
14.0	xxx	$\frac{3}{36}$	.08
14.5	xx	$\frac{2}{36}$	.06
15.0	x	$\frac{1}{36}$	.03
	$\Sigma f = 36$	$\frac{36}{36}$ or 1.00	1.00

The sampling distribution of sample means has a number of desirable properties. For one thing, the distribution is usually approximately normal in form. The data in Table 7.3 have been arranged into a smoothed frequency polygon shown in Figure 7.1. The distribution of $\overline{X}$ values shown in Figure 7.1 is approximately bell-shaped, symmetrical, and otherwise normal in form. In fact, the sampling distribution of means, under random sampling, approaches the normal form as N gets larger when sampling large populations. With Ns exceeding 30, the normality approximation is quite close. Of all the statistics we have considered thus far (e.g., the mean, mode, median, standard deviation, 10–90 range, etc.), only the mean has a sampling distribution with these properties. The sampling distributions of all other statistics we have examined are not normal in form.

Another characteristic of the sampling distribution of the means

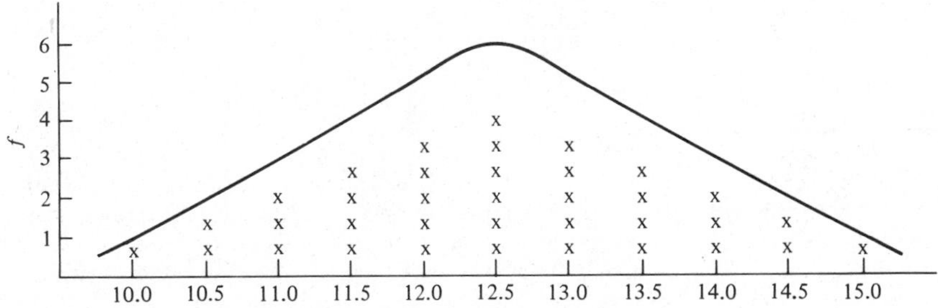

FIGURE 7.1. Curve Drawn for the Data in Table 7.3.

is that the mean of it (the mean of means or grand mean) is equal to the population mean. If we were to compute the population μ of the units of product produced per day by the population of six workers, we would have the sum of the six individual productivity scores divided by 6, or

$$\frac{10 + 11 + 12 + 13 + 14 + 15}{6} = \frac{75}{6} = 12.5.$$

$12.5 = \mu$, the population mean. If we were to compute the mean for the sampling distribution of sample means, it would also be equal to 12.5 or μ, the population mean.

The mean of *any* sampling distribution of *any* statistic is called the *expected value* of that statistic. Therefore, the mean of the sampling distribution of means is called the expected value of the mean. The mean of the sampling distribution of sample medians would be called the expected value of the median, and so on. In the general case, the *expected value of a statistic* is the mean of the sampling distribution of that statistic.

All sampling distributions of statistics have means. All sampling distributions of statistics have standard deviations as well. However, standard deviations of sampling distributions of statistics are given a special name–*standard errors of statistics.* Therefore, instead of referring to the standard deviation of a sampling distribution, we will refer to this value as the standard error of the sampling distribution, or more simply, the standard error of the statistic. For example, the standard error of the mean is the standard deviation of the sampling distribution of sample means. The standard error of the standard deviation is the standard deviation of the sampling distribution of sample standard deviations, and so on.

Let us examine the sampling distribution of sample means more closely. It has two parameters–a population mean, μ, and a standard error term, the standard error of the mean, or $s_{\overline{x}}$.[3] An estimate of the standard error of the mean, $s_{\overline{x}}$, is computed as follows:

$$s_{\overline{x}} = \frac{s}{\sqrt{N - 1}},$$

[3] Sometimes, the standard error of the mean is shown as $\sigma_{\overline{x}}$. This assumes that we have a knowledge of the population standard deviation, where $\sigma_{\overline{x}} = \sigma/\sqrt{N}$ (where σ is the population standard deviation and N is the sample size). It is usually unrealistic to assume a knowledge of population values, inasmuch as the statistical tests we use are designed to estimate such values, which are usually unknown. Therefore, $s_{\overline{x}}$ will be used as our estimate of it because it is based on known sample values computed from randomly drawn samples.

where

s = sample standard deviation
N = sample size

If we obtained a sample of two elements, persons A and F, with scores of 10 and 15, respectively, the resulting $s_{\overline{X}}$ would be equal to 2.5, as an example. (The student can prove this as an exercise.)

The sampling distribution of sample means is illustrated in the general case in Figure 7.2. Note the two parameters, μ and $s_{\overline{X}}$. Almost always, the sampling distribution of means is bell-shaped, symmetrical, and approximates the unit normal distribution. It is also a probability distribution.

Referring to Table 7.3, for instance, the observed mean of 10.0 occurs once in 36 times. The observed $\overline{X}$ of 12 occurs five times out of 36 times, and so on. Probabilities can be assigned to the frequency of each $\overline{X}$ occurrence, as shown to the far right in Table 7.3. As an illustration, if the researcher were to draw a random sample with an $\overline{X} = 12.5$, there would be a probability of .16 or 16 times out of 100 of drawing a sample with such a mean value. This is because 12.5 occurs 6 times in 36, or approximately 16 percent of the time. If the researcher were to draw a sample with a mean of 14.5, a probability of .06 or 6 times in 100 would be associated with this $\overline{X}$ occurrence. This is because there are two samples with $\overline{X}$ values equal to 14.5, and they therefore occur twice in 36 times, or 6 percent of the time.

The odds of the researcher drawing a sample with a mean of 10.0, 10.5, or 11.0 would be the sum of the individual probabilities associated with their occurrence, or $.03 + .06 + .08 = .17$. Therefore, .17 or 17 percent of the time the researcher would probably draw a sample with a mean of *either* 10.0, 10.5, or 11.0.

The most likely samples (and sample $\overline{X}$'s) drawn are those occurring in and around the center of the sampling distribution of means. This is an *area of high probability*, referring to the fact that there is a strong likelihood of getting a sample with an $\overline{X}$ equal to 12.0, 12.5 (the population μ), or 13.0. These mean values occur with the great-

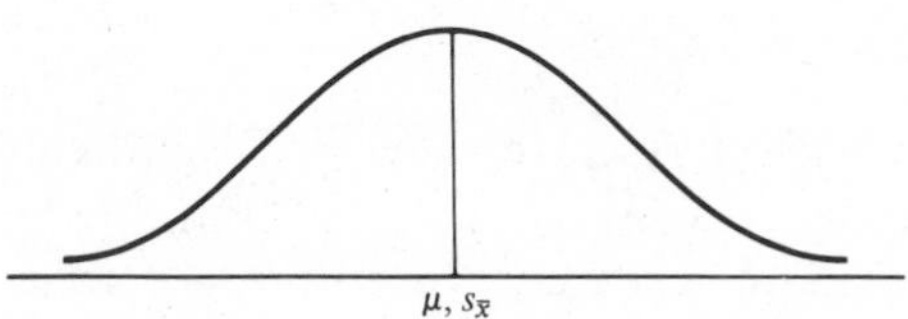

FIGURE 7.2. Sampling Distribution of $\overline{X}$'s.

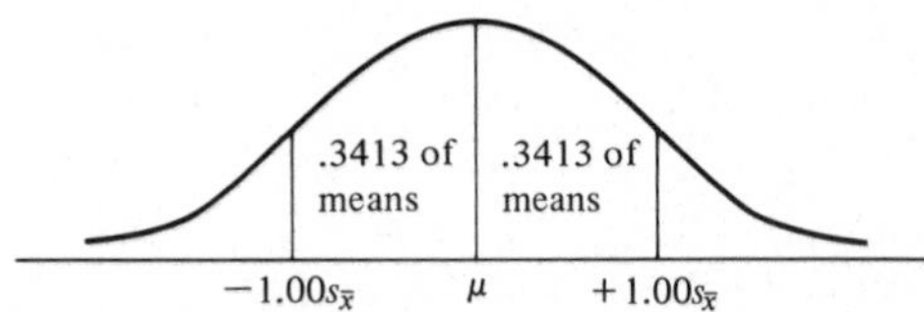

FIGURE 7.3. Sampling Distribution of $\overline{X}$'s Showing the Curve Area Cut Off by $+1.00s_{\overline{X}}$ and $-1.00s_{\overline{X}}$.

est frequency. Those mean values to the far left and to the far right in the "tails" of the sampling distribution occur least frequently. The $\overline{X}$ values of 10.0 and 15.0 lie in an *area of low probability*. If the researcher were to draw a sample randomly, there would be a greater likelihood of obtaining a sample with a mean of 12.0, 12.5, or 13.0 compared with getting means equal to 10.0 or 15.0. Again, this is attributable to the differential frequency of occurrence of these $\overline{X}$ values.

The standard error of the mean, $s_{\overline{X}}$, on the sampling distribution of sample means functions in precisely the same way as σ functions on the unit normal distribution in relation to μ. For instance, if we were to move 1.00σ's to the left or right of μ on the unit normal distribution, we would probably cut off .3413 of curve area in either direction. By the same token, if we were to move $1.00s_{\overline{X}}$'s to the left or right of μ on the sampling distribution of sample means, we would cut off approximately .3413 of the sample means in either direction. Figure 7.3 illustrates the proportion of curve area cut off by a movement of $+1.00s_{\overline{X}}$ or $-1.00s_{\overline{X}}$ in relation to μ. This underscores the similarity between the unit normal distribution and the sampling distribution of sample means. This also provides an important reason why researchers prefer to use sample $\overline{X}$ values in their statistical inference and estimation work compared with alternative statistics. The fact that the unit normal distribution principles can apply to the sampling distribution of means supplies researchers with an important advantage which they would not have if other sampling distributions of statistics were used.

The Level of Significance

As a second decision rule, the level of significance is the probability the researcher assigns to the decision made about the null hypothesis tested. The researcher is interested in rejecting null hypotheses and supporting research hypotheses. Research hypotheses have usually been derived from theoretical schemes that are believed by the researcher to be reasonably sound explanations of phenomena. If a research hypothesis is supported or confirmed by observed data, there is a good chance that the theory from which that hypothesis was derived is also confirmed or supported by the investigator's findings. But as we have seen, it is conventional to test null hypotheses directly and to infer support or lack of support for some research hypothesis as the result of rejecting or failing to reject some null hypothesis counterpart.

In advance of making the test of the null hypothesis, the researcher specifies a probability (*P*), known as the level of significance, at which the null hypothesis is tested. Usually, this probability is set at 5 percent or 1 percent as a matter of convention, although other probability values can be set by the researcher. The probability, *P*, refers to the amount of error the researcher is willing to accept in a subsequent decision about the null hypothesis. Specifically, if the researcher decides on the basis of empirical evidence or data collected that the null hypothesis is not true and should be rejected, a probability of error (*P*) would accompany that decision. If the level of significance is set at .05 (5 percent), there is a 5 percent chance that the researcher is wrong in making a decision to reject the null hypothesis. If the level of significance is set at .01 (1 percent), there is a 1 percent chance that the researcher is wrong in making the decision to reject the null hypothesis. Levels of significance always define the amount of error involved in a decision to reject null hypotheses and support their accompanying research hypotheses.

Table 7.4 provides a more complete picture of statistical decision making and the probable implications of these decisions for hypothesis tests. We always make the assumption that the null hypothesis being tested is potentially true or false. We must make this assumption because we never know absolutely that the data we have

TABLE 7.4
Type I and Type II Errors in Statistical Decision-Making Situations.

Decision is to:	H_0 is True	H_0 is False
Reject H_0:	Type I error, α	$1 - \beta$
Fail to reject H_0:	$1 - \alpha$	Type II error, β

collected in our research (including the sample drawn, the measures used, etc.) are perfectly representative of the phenomenon we are investigating. The research studies we conduct are single instances of tests of theories. We lack the certainty of knowing that our particular research represents a true picture of reality. Therefore, a probability always exists that any hypothesis we test may or may not be true, regardless of the outcome of that hypothesis test and the decisions we make.

If we decide on the basis of collected data that the null hypothesis we are testing should be rejected, there is always some likelihood that we are wrong in our decision. This is one source of error known as *type I error* or *alpha* (α) *error*, shown in Table 7.4.

Another type of error exists as well. This is known as *type II error* or *beta* (β) *error*. It occurs whenever we decide to fail to reject the null hypothesis and there is some likelihood that it is false and ought to be rejected. Since there is always a likelihood that the null hypothesis we are testing is both true and false simultaneously, we will always be subject to making either types of errors (i.e., rejecting H_0 when H_0 is true and should not be rejected, and failing to reject H_0 whenever H_0 is false and ought to be rejected).

Of course, we want to make the right decision whenever null hypotheses are tested. We want to reject false null hypotheses, and we want to fail to reject them whenever they are true. In short, we wish to minimize both kinds of errors that occur whenever hypothesis tests are made. It is not possible to eliminate these errors in any absolute sense.

One way of reducing type I error, for instance, is to simply lower the level of significance from .05 to .01 to .001. By reducing our chance of error from 5 times in 100 to 1 time in 1000, we make it considerably more difficult to commit the error of rejecting H_0 when it is true and should not be rejected. Unfortunately, by making it more difficult to make type I error, we increase our chances of making type II error, or failing to reject H_0 when it is actually false and ought to be rejected.

By now, the reader may, understandably, be perplexed. If we lower one type of error, we raise the other. If we raise one type of error, we lower the other. In order to live comfortably with this apparent dilemma, we must accept the fact that both types of error exist and cannot be overcome totally. It is only within our power to reduce these errors to minimal levels. Since type I error is directly within our control, we merely set it at a reasonable level. Usually, what is reasonable is whatever is conventional. Conventional significance levels (and type I errors) are .05 and .01. Chances of being wrong 5 times or 1 time in 100 times are considered by many researchers to be acceptable error levels.

Type II error or beta error is only indirectly within our control. Of course, it is partially influenced by whatever type I error happens to be. Although there is not a one-to-one correspondence between type I and type II errors (i.e., a 1-unit increase in type I error will not mean a 1-unit decrease in type II error), greater type I error will usually mean less type II error, and vice versa.

Type II error is also influenced by fluctuations in sample size. Increasing one's sample size (by following any probability sampling plan) will generally effect a decrease in type II error, regardless of whatever type I error happens to be.[4]

The Critical Region or Region of Rejection

A third decision rule is the specification of a critical region or region of rejection, which is an area on the sampling distribution of sample means. (The sampling distribution of means is used here because our hypothesis test deals with observed sample means; other sampling distributions of statistics would be used if other sample statistics were used in hypothesis tests.)

The area designated as the critical region is determined directly by the level of significance as selected by the researcher. If the .05 level of significance has been selected for a hypothesis test, then 5 percent (.05) of the sampling distribution of means will become the critical region. If the .01 level of significance has been selected for some hypothesis test, then 1 percent (.01) of the sampling distribution of means will be established as the critical region.

Critical regions of sampling distributions of statistics are located in the tails or extremes of such sampling distributions. Consider the following hypothesis set as an illustration:

H_0: $\mu = 75$
H_1: $\mu \neq 75$

$$P \leqslant .05 \text{ (also, } \alpha = .05\text{)},$$

where H_0 says that the population mean, μ, is equal to 75, and H_1 says that the population mean, μ, is not equal to 75. The level of significance at which H_0 (and H_1) are tested has been set at .05.[5] Here H_0 is actually a guess or, more accurately, an estimate of the population mean, μ. Since the mean of the sampling distribution of sample means (the expected value of the mean) is also equal to μ,

[4] It is beyond the scope of the present section to show precisely how this reduction in type II error takes place, but more will be presented about such error in a subsequent chapter.

[5] This is an alpha level of .05, type I error, or the probability at which the hypothesis is tested, or the level of significance—all of these designations mean the same thing.

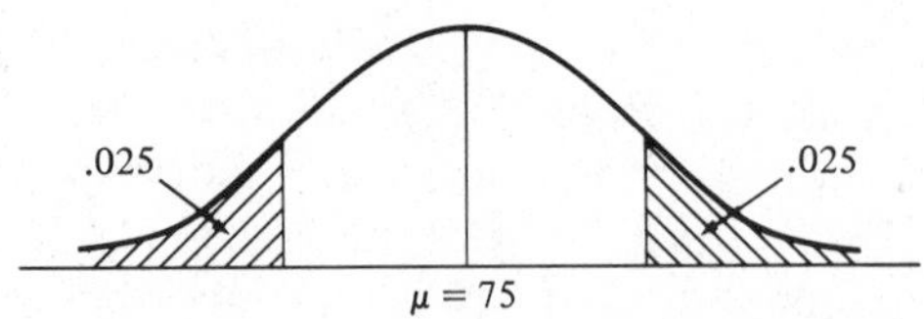

FIGURE 7.4. Sampling Distribution of Means Showing Critical Regions.

H_0 is also specifying that the expected value of the mean is equal to 75. Figure 7.4 shows a sampling distribution of sample $\overline{X}$ values with our guessed or estimated $\mu = 75$ at its center as illustrated.[6]

An area on the sampling distribution of means will be designated as the critical region. We know that 5 percent of the area of this distribution will be set aside as the critical region. This is because our level of significance has been set at .05. We also know that the area will be located in one or both tails of the distribution. Note that H_0 hypothesizes that μ is equal to 75 and that H_1 says that μ is not equal to 75. Therefore, we could conceivably reject the null hypothesis by observing a sample mean that is substantially higher or lower than 75. Since we are not concerned about the direction of the departure of an observed sample mean from our hypothesized μ value, we will establish critical regions in both tails of the sampling distribution. This is easily accomplished by dividing our probability of .05 into two equal parts and placing .025 (2.5 percent) in one tail and .025 (2.5 percent) in the other tail, as shown in Figure 7.4. These tails of the distribution are our critical regions for the hypothesis test. If we happen to observe a sample mean that is located in one or the other of these critical regions, we will be able to reject the null hypothesis H_0 that $\mu = 75$. This is why these regions are also called "regions of rejection." Mean values lying in these critical regions are sufficiently far away from the hypothesized μ value to be considered significantly different from it.

How do we know if an observed sample $\overline{X}$ is far enough away from a hypothesized μ value to be significantly different from it? How do we know if an observed sample mean lies in one critical region or the other? We will use our knowledge of the unit normal distribution to answer these questions. We will proceed systematically through a hypothetical problem to illustrate the solution to our apparent dilemma.

A researcher is conducting a study of entering freshmen at a small

[6] We do not have to know the value of all sample means to construct a sampling distribution of sample means—we have previously illustrated the fact that for fairly large N's, the sampling distribution of means will approximate normality.

college. Based on previous entrance examination scores for entering freshmen, the researcher hypothesizes that the current year's mean will be 100. The researcher actually believes that the mean entrance examination score for this year's freshman group will be different from 100. The level of significance is set at .05. The following hypothesis set is provided:

H_0: $\mu = 100$
H_1: $\mu \neq 100$

$$P \leqslant .05$$

Suppose that the researcher observes a sample $\overline{X} = 108$. The question to be answered is whether 108 is sufficiently different from the hypothesized μ of 100 so that the null hypothesis can be rejected and H_1 supported.

A sampling distribution of $\overline{X}$'s is constructed by the researcher. The hypothesized μ under H_0 is supplied and critical regions for the distribution are indicated. These are illustrated in Figure 7.5. To determine if the *observed value*, here $\overline{X}$ of 108, lies in one critical region or the other, we must assign a Z value to both the observed $\overline{X}$ and to each of the points that identify the critical regions on the sampling distribution of means. The critical regions each contain 2.5 percent of the curve area (i.e., the level of significance, .05, divided by 2 or .05/2 = .025 or 2.5 percent). The Z values associated with the points that identify the critical regions are simply those which cut off 47.5 percent (.4750) of the curve area to the left and to the right of the hypothesized μ. The Z values that cut off .4750 of curve area (47.5 percent of it), leaving 2.5 percent of the curve in each tail, are −1.96 and +1.96, as shown in Figure 7.5. These Z values were obtained directly from Table A3, Appendix A, the table of areas of the normal curve. These Z values leave 2.5 percent (.025) of curve area in each tail of the unit normal distribution. Since the sampling distribution of means approximates the unit normal distribution in form, the same Z values cut off 2.5 percent of the curve

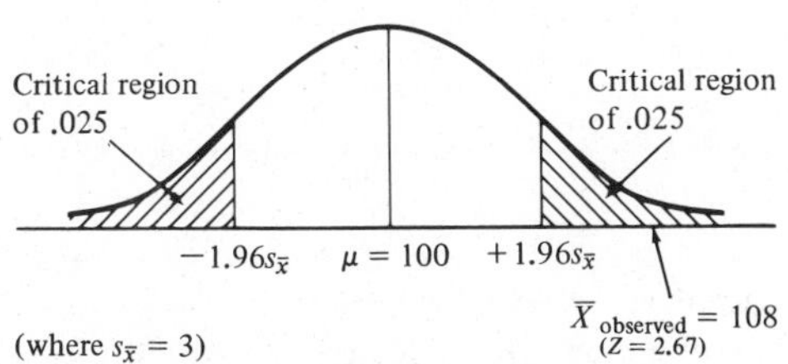

FIGURE 7.5. Sampling Distribution of $\overline{X}$'s with a Hypothesized $\mu = 100$ and the .05 Level of Significance.

area for the sampling distribution of means. If our observed mean of 108 is one of those means lying in the critical regions in the left or right tails of the sampling distribution of means, we conclude that 108 is significantly different from 100. There will be a 5 percent chance of our being wrong in this decision, however, because the level of significance was originally set at .05.

Before we can make this decision, we must translate the mean of 108 into a Z value. To accomplish this transformation, we need some additional information. Specifically, we need to know the value of the standard error of the mean, $s_{\overline{x}}$. This is the unit of measurement along the horizontal axis of the sampling distribution of sample means, and it functions in precisely the same fashion as σ functions on the unit normal distribution. Instead of identifying how many σ's 108 is from 100, we will identify how many $s_{\overline{x}}$'s 108 is from 100. Assuming a sample $s = 21, N = 50$, our $s_{\overline{x}}$ would be equal to $s/\sqrt{N-1}$, or $21/\sqrt{50-1}$, or $21/7 = 3$. The $s_{\overline{x}} = 3$. Now we know that the unit of measurement along the horizontal axis of the sampling distribution of means, $s_{\overline{x}}$, is equal to 3. How far is 108 from 100 in terms of $s_{\overline{x}}$? We may determine this by taking the difference between the two mean values, $\overline{X}$ observed and μ, the hypothesized population mean, and dividing this difference by $s_{\overline{x}}$:

$$Z = \frac{\overline{X}_{\text{obs}} - \mu}{s_{\overline{x}}},$$

where

$\overline{X}_{\text{obs}}$ = observed sample mean
μ = hypothesized population mean
$s_{\overline{x}}$ = standard error of the mean

Using the information from the foregoing problem, we can determine a Z value for the $\overline{X}$ of 108 as follows:

$$Z = \frac{108 - 100}{3}$$
$$= \frac{8}{3}$$
$$= +2.67.$$

The Z value associated with our observed mean of 108 is 2.67. Since this Z value of 2.67 is equal to or larger than the absolute value of Z identifying the critical regions (1.96), we conclude that H_0 can be rejected and H_1 can be supported. It is likely that the $\mu \neq 100$, and we run the risk of being wrong 5 percent of the time in making that decision.

The values of Z that identify the critical regions on the sampling distribution of means are called *critical values* of Z. Any time an observed Z value (associated with an $\overline{X}$ observed) equals or exceeds the critical value of Z (set by the level of significance), the H_0 being tested can be rejected. The error involved in that particular decision is equal to or smaller than the level of significance we have chosen initially.

The foregoing problem was solved by translating our observed mean into a Z value and comparing that Z value with a critical value of Z established to identify the critical region (s) on the sampling distribution of means. We can also deal with this problem by translating the critical value of Z into a form that can be compared directly with the observed mean of 108.

For instance, the critical values of Z for the .05 level of significance in the earlier problem were -1.96 and $+1.96$, respectively. These Z values are a given distance from the hypothesized μ value of 100. Specifically, they are 1.96 standard errors of the mean above and below 100. If $s_{\overline{x}} = 3$, these points become $100 \pm (3)(1.96) = 100 \pm 5.88$ or 94.12 to the left of 100 (or below it) and 105.88 to the right of 100 (or above it). In the general case, we may determine these values by the following formula:

$$\mu \pm (s_{\overline{x}})(Z),$$

where

μ = hypothesized population mean under H_0
$s_{\overline{x}}$ = standard error of the mean
Z = critical value of Z identifying the critical region (s)

Suppose that the researcher studying the entering freshmen believed that the population mean would be lower than 100. The hypothesis set would now be slightly different:

H_0: $\mu \geqslant 100$
H_1: $\mu < 100$

$$P \leqslant .05.$$

Here H_0 says that the population mean, μ, is equal to or greater than ($\geqslant$) 100 and H_1 says that μ is less than ($<$) 100. Again, the significance level or probability is set at .05. Suppose that $s_{\overline{x}}$ continues to be 3, but in this instance the observed $\overline{X} = 90$ instead of 108. The researcher proceeds to make the hypothesis test as follows.

A sampling distribution of means is constructed as shown in Figure 7.6. The hypothesized μ of 100 is placed in the distribution

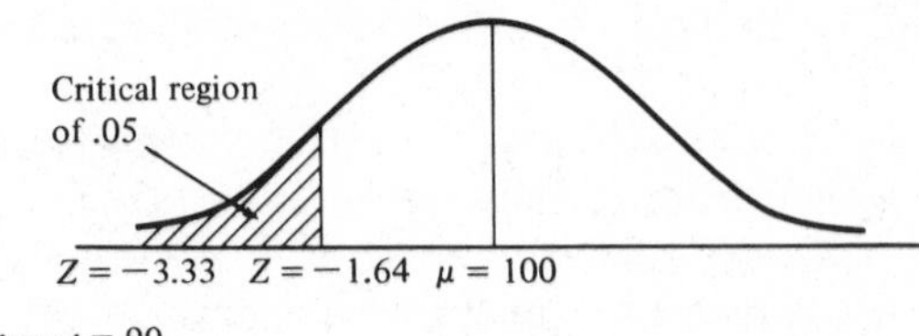

FIGURE 7.6. Sampling Distribution of Means Showing a One-Tailed Hypothesis Test.

as shown. This time, however, a modification must be made in our designation of the critical region. Note that in the present instance, the researcher believes that μ will be less than 100 or below it (or to the left of 100). This is called a *directional* or *one-tailed hypothesis test*, because the researcher has predicted under H_1 that the $\overline{X}$ observed will be less than (or greater than) some value rather than simply different from it.[7]

All hypothesis tests that utilize the signs less than ($<$) or greater than ($>$), or equal to or less than ($\leqslant$), or equal to or greater than ($\geqslant$) are directional or one-tailed tests. All hypothesis tests that utilize the signs equal to or not equal to ($=$ or $\neq$) are, by definition, two-tailed or nondirectional tests.

The researcher examines H_1 and determines that the observed $\overline{X}$ value is expected to occur below or to the left of 100, the hypothesized μ. This is the reason for hypothesizing that μ is less than 100. The left tail of the sampling distribution of means will contain the critical region, therefore. This time, we will designate the extreme left 5 percent (.05) of curve area as the critical region. Because directionality has been specified under H_1 as being to the left of μ, we may ignore the right tail of the curve. We can assign a critical value of Z to the point that identifies the critical region by examining Table A3, Appendix A, and determining the Z value which cuts off 45 percent (.4500) of the curve area, leaving 5 percent (.05) in the left tail of it. This Z value is -1.64.[8]

[7] In the original problem, where μ was specified as being equal to or not equal to 100, this represented a *nondirectional* or *two-tailed hypothesis test.* Two tails of the sampling distribution of means were used for critical regions. This is the reason for designating such an hypothesis test as two-tailed or nondirectional.

[8] Actually, we select the Z closest to cutting off .4500. Note in Table A3 that a Z of 1.64 cuts off .4495 while a Z of 1.65 cuts off .4505. Since both Z values cut off curve areas that are the same distance from .4500, we make the decision to use the Z value that ends in an even number (e.g., 1.64 instead of 1.65). Had 1.65 been closer to .4500 in the area cut off from μ to that point, we would have used that Z value to identify the critical region on the sampling distribution of means. The minus sign ($-$) is used in front of 1.64 because this Z value lies in the left tail of the curve.

The question we must answer is whether 90, the observed $\overline{X}$, is sufficiently different from 100, the hypothesized μ value, to be considered significantly different from it. We must assign a Z value to our observed mean of 90. The $\overline{X}$ of 90 differs from a μ of 100 by a distance of so many $s_{\overline{x}}$'s. Taking the difference between the two mean values, 90 and 100, and dividing the difference by $s_{\overline{x}}$ will supply us with a Z value for the $\overline{X}$ of 90, or

$$Z = \frac{90 - 100}{3} \quad \text{or} \quad \frac{\overline{X}_{\text{obs}} - \mu}{s_{\overline{x}}}$$

$$= \frac{-10}{3}$$

$$= -3.33.$$

Our observed Z value for the observed $\overline{X}$ of 90 is -3.33. By inspection of Figure 7.6, we can see that -3.33 is either on the line of or in the critical region to the left of 100. A $Z = -3.33$ is well beyond the critical value of Z, which is -1.64. Since -3.33 lies in the region of rejection, H_0 can be rejected and H_1 can be supported. We may conclude tentatively that the population mean, μ, is less than 100, and we run the risk of being wrong in making that decision 5 percent of the time (again, this is because of the fact that the level of significance has been set at .05).

□ SUMMARIZING DECISION RULES

Decision rules are always specified in advance of all hypothesis tests. A sampling distribution of a statistic is specified depending on the statistics we choose to examine from collected data. A level of significance is set to enable us to assess objectively the outcomes of hypothesis tests. A critical region or regions on the sampling distribution of the statistic selected are determined, based upon the level of significance we have originally designated.

Our hypothesis testing proceeds according to these rules we have specified, and our statistical decision making is rendered more objective as a result. We must not forget the fact that all studies we conduct are couched in the context of probability theory. The data we collect may or may not be representative of the real world and the problems we have selected for scientific examination. Therefore, any decisions we make about hypotheses tested may be incorrect—but they may also be correct.

Two sources of error are always present in hypothesis tests—type

I error, alpha error (rejecting H_0 when H_0 is true and should not be rejected); and type II error, beta error (failing to reject H_0 when H_0 is false and ought to be rejected). We can never eliminate these errors entirely, but we are in the position of being able to reduce or minimize their magnitude by direct or indirect means.

□ HYPOTHESIS TESTING THROUGH POINT AND INTERVAL ESTIMATION

Persons engaged in social research often find themselves in the business of attempting to estimate population parameters by examining sample statistics. If we want to learn about the characteristics of some population, we will usually draw a sample of elements from it. Then, we will make inferences about the population and its parameters based upon an examination of those characteristics shared by the sample elements. *Statistical inference* is the process of estimating population parameters by studying sample statistics. Two alternative forms of estimation have been used by researchers for years. These are (1) point estimation, and (2) interval estimation.

Point Estimation

We have already had a taste of point estimation in the discussion of critical regions in an earlier section of this chapter. Point estimation is the process of forecasting or predicting the value of a population parameter and then comparing the sample statistic counterpart with it. For instance, we might predict that the population $\mu = 100$, as we did in an earlier example. Then we will draw a sample of elements and compare the sample mean with the population mean. The degree of discrepancy between our observed $\overline{X}$ and the hypothesized μ will indicate the accuracy of our inference or estimation. In short, we estimate a "point" at which the population μ occurs. We compare this point estimate with an actual observed $\overline{X}$ value to determine the accuracy of our estimation.

The primary problems with point estimation are: (1) we must guess what the population parameters are in advance, and (2) unless we know a great deal about the population we are studying, we will have little basis for justifying the guesses we make.

Point estimation bothers a great many people, because the question always exists as to where the point estimates should come from. More often than not, the population parameters that are of interest to us are unknown. We draw samples of elements from populations in order to learn more about the population parameters.

Interval Estimation

A superior form of estimation is known as interval estimation. The logic of interval estimation is as follows. If we obtain a sample of elements (through some probability sampling plan) and compute various statistics for it, there is a strong likelihood that our sample statistics are close to their parametric counterparts in the population. For example, a sample $\overline{X}$ is probably near the true population μ value. A sample median is probably near the population median value. In fact, for any random sample of elements we select, any mean we compute is more likely to be closer to the population mean than far away from it.

Recalling the nature of the sampling distribution of means, we may say with considerable assurance that there are far more sample means occurring in and around the center of the distribution than occur at its extremes. We might designate the general area near the center of the sampling distribution of means as an area of high probability. Similarly, we can designate the tails of the sampling distribution of means as areas of low probability. The area of high probability near the center of the distribution is where a majority of sample means are located. Relatively few means are found in the extremes of the distribution. Utilizing what we know about the sampling distribution of means and the unit normal curve that it approximates, about 68 percent of the sample means are within $\pm 1.00 s_{\overline{x}}$ on either side of the population μ. This is because approximately 68 percent of the normal curve area lies between -1.00σ and $+1.00\sigma$ on either side of μ on the unit normal distribution.

To make this statement, we do not have to know the value of μ for the sampling distribution of means. We merely need to know that the sampling distribution of means is normal in form. A given distance to the left or to the right of the unknown μ value will cut off a certain amount of curve area, which is also equivalent to a portion of mean values occurring there.

Therefore, whenever we draw a random sample of elements from a designated population, the probability is in our favor of obtaining a sample with an $\overline{X}$ that is nearer μ rather than far away from it. It is logical to assume that if we place our observed $\overline{X}$ value on the horizontal axis of the sampling distribution of means, it will probably be near μ, the true population mean. Furthermore, if we advance a short distance to the left and to the right of our observed $\overline{X}$, it is probable that the true μ value will be overlapped. In short, an interval can be created around our observed $\overline{X}$ value which will probably include or overlap μ at some point. The interval created around an observed $\overline{X}$ value is referred to as a *confidence interval* and is the subject of interval estimation.

□ THE CONSTRUCTION OF CONFIDENCE INTERVALS

Confidence intervals are designated distances above and below an observed sample $\overline{X}$ value that have a specified likelihood of overlapping the true μ value at some point. Confidence intervals are labeled as 95 percent confidence intervals, 90 percent confidence intervals, or 99 percent confidence intervals, and so forth. These percentage values refer to the likelihood that any given confidence interval determined will overlap the true population mean, μ.

Since the true population mean is almost always unknown, we are never absolutely sure that any confidence interval we construct will truly overlap μ. As a way of illustrating the logic of confidence interval construction, imagine that a researcher were to draw all possible samples of size 50 from a designated population of 2000. As we have discussed earlier, there would be N^n or 2000^{50} samples that could be drawn. Furthermore, suppose that the researcher were to compute a mean for each sample drawn. Obviously, this would require much work, but eventually, the researcher would have 2000^{50} $\overline{X}$'s.

Next, imagine that a 95 percent confidence interval were to be constructed around each and every one of the 2000^{50} means. There would be 2000^{50} confidence intervals constructed. Since all of these would be 95 percent confidence intervals, we could say with certainty that 95 percent of these confidence intervals would overlap the true population μ at some point. We could also say with certainty that 5 percent of these confidence intervals would not overlap μ.

Had we created 99 percent confidence intervals for all observed mean values, we would have 2000^{50} 99 percent confidence intervals. We could say that 99 percent of them would overlap μ and that 1 percent of them would not overlap it. Had we created 80 percent confidence intervals for all observed $\overline{X}$ values, 80 percent of those confidence intervals would overlap the population mean and 20 percent of them would fail to overlap it. The confidence interval that we designate defines the number of confidence intervals that would overlap the true population mean value if we were to construct such intervals for all possible $\overline{X}$ values that could be computed.

What does the researcher do in reality? Usually, one sample is drawn randomly rather than 10 samples or 1000 samples. The researcher observes a single $\overline{X}$ rather than 2000^{50} of them. A single confidence interval of some magnitude is created around that single observed $\overline{X}$. The researcher then specifies the likelihood associated with that confidence interval (e.g., 99 percent, 90 percent, 95 percent) of overlapping the true (and unknown) population μ value. The researcher is never in the position of knowing which sample has been drawn of all the possible samples that could be drawn. Therefore, the researcher cannot possibly know which mean has been obtained of all possible means that could have been computed. Again, the probability theory of which we have spoken comes to the rescue. We do know that the random draw of a single sample will be more likely to yield a sample that is near the population mean rather than far away from it. Therefore, the probability of observing sample mean that lies near the population mean is in our favor. Therefore, a confidence interval we construct around that mean will be more likely to overlap μ at some point than not to overlap it.

Suppose that the researcher has drawn a random sample of 226 elements and has observed a sample $\overline{X} = 25$ and a sample $s = 5$. Further suppose that the researcher wants to construct a 90 percent confidence interval about the observed $\overline{X}$ of 25. The 90 percent confidence interval is constructed as follows:

$$\text{90 percent confidence interval} = \overline{X}_{\text{obs}} \pm (s_{\overline{x}})\,(Z),$$

where

$\overline{X}_{\text{obs}}$ = observed sample mean
$s_{\overline{x}}$ = standard error of the mean
Z = standard score associated with cutting off $\frac{1}{2}$ of the confidence interval percent (in this case, 90 percent/2 = 45 percent, or .4500)

Using the information supplied above, we have

$$\begin{aligned}
\text{90 percent confidence interval} &= 25 \pm \frac{5}{\sqrt{226-1}}\,(1.64)\\
&= 25 \pm \frac{5}{15}\,(1.64)\\
&= 25 \pm (.33)\,(1.64)\\
&= 25 \pm .54\\
&= 24.46 \text{ to } 25.54.
\end{aligned}$$

The 90 percent confidence interval around the observed mean of 25 extends from 24.46 to 25.54 and has a 90 percent chance of overlapping the population μ at some point.

In the general case, if we wish to construct any confidence interval around any observed $\overline{X}$, the following formula can be used:

$$\text{percent confidence interval} = \overline{X}_{\text{obs}} \pm (s_{\overline{x}})\,(Z),$$

where

$\overline{X}_{obs}$ = observed mean

$s_{\overline{x}}$ = standard error of the mean

Z = standard score associated with cutting off normal curve area equal to $\frac{1}{2}$ of whatever percent the confidence interval happens to be

To determine which Z value should be used in this formula, we must first divide the percent of the confidence interval desired by 2. If we are computing the 90 percent confidence interval, we would divide 90 percent by 2, or 90 percent/2 = 45 percent (.4500). If we are computing the 80 percent confidence interval, we would divide 80 percent by 2, or 80 percent/2 = 40 percent (.4000); and so on. Once we have determined this result, we look up the equivalent proportion in Table A3.

For example, the Z value to use for the 90 percent confidence interval would be the Z that cuts off 90 percent/2 = 45 percent or .4500 of curve area, or a Z of 1.64. The Z value for the 80 percent confidence interval would be the Z value cutting off .4000 of the curve area (i.e., $\frac{1}{2}$ of 80 percent or 40 percent or .4000) or 1.28; and so on.

Given an observed $\overline{X}$ = 25 and an $s_{\overline{x}}$ = .33, we could determine the following confidence intervals as shown:

$$\begin{aligned} \text{95 percent confidence interval} &= 25 \pm (.33)(1.96) \\ &= 24.35 \text{ to } 25.65. \\ \text{99 percent confidence interval} &= 25 \pm (.33)(2.58) \\ &= 24.15 \text{ to } 25.85. \\ \text{80 percent confidence interval} &= 25 \pm (.33)(1.28) \\ &= 24.58 \text{ to } 25.42. \end{aligned}$$

In each case we have added to and subtracted from the observed mean the product of the $s_{\overline{x}}$ and the Z value associated with cutting off one-half of whatever the confidence interval percent happens to be.

The 95 percent confidence interval above means that there is a 95 percent chance that the true (unknown) population μ lies somewhere between 24.35 and 25.65. The 99 percent confidence interval means that there is a 99 percent chance that the true (unknown) population μ lies somewhere between 24.15 and 25.85. And finally, the 80 percent confidence interval means that there is an 80 percent likelihood that the true (unknown) population mean lies somewhere between 24.58 and 25.42.

It will be observed that the confidence interval gets larger as the percentage increases. Also, the confidence interval decreases in magnitude as the percentage decreases. This reflects either an "increase" or a "decrease" in our "confidence" that the population mean will be found within any given confidence interval. Thus we are provided with another reason for the use of the term "confidence interval."

Confidence intervals have the distinct advantage over point estimation of providing a *range* wherein the population μ might occur. We begin our estimation with an observed $\overline{X}$ value and create an interval around it which likely overlaps μ. This is superior to the method of guessing a population mean value in advance, with little or no information, and then comparing a sample mean value with our point estimate.

□ SUMMARY

Hypothesis testing involves the establishment of decision rules in advance, which provide a set of criteria against which hypothesis test outcomes may be compared. Research hypotheses are usually derived directly from a theoretical scheme and subjected to empirical test. Null hypotheses, based on research hypothesis statements, are negations of whatever the researcher believes to be true. They are statements which, if rejected, will lead to the direct support of some true alternative research hypothesis. Both types of hypotheses are frequently converted into symbolic and numerical expressions and designated as statistical hypotheses.

Decision rules governing the test of statistical hypotheses (and of their research and null hypothesis equivalents) include the specification of a sampling distribution of a statistic, a level of significance, and a region on the sampling distribution referred to as a critical region or region of rejection. Observed statistical values such as $\overline{X}$'s are compared with hypothesized μ values and a decision is reached about the accuracy of the estimates made. Observed statistical values that lie in critical regions of sampling distributions of statistics lead to the rejection of null hypotheses, symbolically designated H_0's. The rejection of an H_0 will lead to the support of some true research hypothesis, designated H_1.

There is an amount of error associated with all statistical decision making, however. Whenever an H_0 is rejected and it is true and should not be rejected, type I error (or alpha error) results. Whenever the researcher tests H_0 and fails to reject it, it may be false and ought to be rejected. Type II error (beta error) occurs in this event. It is impossible for the researcher to eliminate entirely these error terms. These can be minimized, however. Conventional guidelines exist for establishing levels of significance at which hypothesis tests are made and for evaluating test outcomes.

Researchers engage in two types of estimation in the course of their inferential work. Point estimation involves stating in advance a hypothetical population value and comparing it with a sample statistic as its counterpart in a subsequent sample randomly drawn. Interval estimation is the preferred alternative, inasmuch as the researcher obtains an estimate of a range around an observed sample mean which has a likelihood of including the population μ.

Population values are the targets of estimation work. Sample statistics function as estimates of population parameters. Normally, probabilities are assigned to the intervals estimated by the researcher, which specify a likelihood of including population parameter values.

In the chapters to follow, a variety of statistical tests and procedures will be presented that assist the researcher in hypothesis testing and statistical decision making. These are arranged according to the level of measurement associated with the data being analyzed. The internal portions of chapters are typically arranged according to single-sample tests, two-sample (independent and related) tests, and k-sample (independent and related) tests. Later chapters deal with an array of association measures that are useful in assessing relationships between k variables. These are also structured according to levels of measurement associated with data analyzed.

SELECTED STUDY TERMS

Research hypothesis, H_1
Null hypothesis, H_0
Probability
Statistical hypothesis
Decision rules
Sampling distribution of a statistic
Expected value of a statistic
Standard error of a statistic
Level of significance
Type I error
Type II error
Critical region or "region of rejection"
Observed value
Critical value
One-tailed test
Two-tailed test
Point estimation

Interval estimation
Confidence interval

EXERCISES

1. Given $s_{\overline{X}} = 2.55, N = 108$, and $\overline{X}_{obs} = 100$, determine the following:
   (a) 90 percent confidence interval.
   (b) 80 percent confidence interval.
   (c) 99 percent confidence interval.
2. Determine the following around $\overline{X}_{obs} = 75$, where $s_{\overline{X}} = 3.5$.
   (a) 90 percent confidence interval.
   (b) 95 percent confidence interval.
   (c) 85 percent confidence interval.
   (d) 75 percent confidence interval.
3. Given the following H_0's, supply the corresponding H_1 statements as symbolic statistical hypotheses.
   (a) H_0: $r_{xy} > 105$
   H_1: ?
   (b) H_0: $\mu_1 = \mu_2$
   H_1: ?
   (c) H_0: $\overline{X} \leqslant 55$
   H_1: ?
   (d) H_0: $r_{xy_1} \neq r_{xy_2}$
   H_1: ?
4. With an $\overline{X}$ observed $= 100, N = 65$, and $s = 24$, determine the following.
   (a) 95 percent confidence interval.
   (b) 80 percent confidence interval.
   (c) 85 percent confidence interval.
5. How much type I error is associated with the following hypothesis tests?
   (a) H_0: $\overline{X} = 90$
   H_1: $\overline{X} \neq 90$
   $P \leqslant .05$
   (b) H_0: $\overline{X}_1 \neq \overline{X}_2$
   H_1: $\overline{X}_1 = \overline{X}_2$
   $P \leqslant .001$
   (c) H_0: $\overline{X} \geqslant 200$
   H_1: $\overline{X} < 200$
   $P \leqslant .01$
   Determine whether each is a one-tailed test (directional) or a two-tailed test (nondirectional).
6. Given the following information, determine the confidence intervals requested: $\overline{X}_{obs} = 500$ and $s_{\overline{X}} = 12$.
   (a) 90 percent confidence interval.
   (b) 80 percent confidence interval.
7. Define what is meant by type I error. Define what is meant by type II error. Which type of error does the researcher control directly? How? Explain.
8. With an $\overline{X}_{obs} = 100, N = 101$, and $s = 15$, determine the following.
   (a) 95 percent confidence interval.
   (b) 90 percent confidence interval.
   (c) 99 percent confidence interval.
9. Determine the confidence intervals for each of the following, where $\overline{X}_{obs} = 330, s = 25$, and $N = 145$.
   (a) 88 percent confidence interval.
   (b) 95 percent confidence interval.
   (c) 70 percent confidence interval.

10. Determine the following confidence intervals given $s = 3.4$, $\overline{X}_{obs} = 70$, and $N = 65$.
    (a) 95 percent confidence interval.
    (b) 70 percent confidence interval.
    (c) 50 percent confidence interval.
    (d) 98 percent confidence interval.
    On the basis of the magnitudes of the confidence intervals you have established in Exercise 10, what can be said generally about increasing and decreasing the percentages associated with the confidence intervals you have determined?
11. Identify the Z values you used in determining the confidence intervals for Exercise 1. Do the same for Exercise 2.
12. Determine the critical values of Z that you would use on the sampling distribution of means for the following hypothesis test:

$$H_0: \mu = 300$$
$$H_1: \mu \neq 300$$

$$P \leqslant .01$$

13. Supply the following null hypothesis statements for the research hypotheses stated below.
    (a) H_1: there is no difference in working hours between three work groups in plant X.
    H_0: ?
    (b) H_1: the relation between reading level and study time in group 1 is different from the relation between reading level and study time in group 2.
    H_0: ?
    (c) H_1: the mean of group 1 is equal to 50.
    H_0: ?
    (d) H_1: there is greater delinquency among children from homes where the mothers work compared with homes where the mothers do not work.
    H_0: ?
    (e) H_1: as pay increases, motivation to work increases.
    H_0: ?
14. With $s = 15$, $N = 220$, and an $\overline{X}_{obs} = 122$, determine the following:
    (a) 85 percent confidence interval.
    (b) 95 percent confidence interval.
    (c) 65 percent confidence interval.

REFERENCES

Blalock, Hubert M., *Social Statistics.* New York: McGraw-Hill Book Company, 1972.

Downie, N. M., and R. W. Heath, *Basic Statistical Methods*, 4th ed. New York: Harper & Row, Publishers, 1974.

Grant, D. A., "Testing the Null Hypothesis and the Strategy and Tactics of Investigating Theoretical Models," *Psychological Review*, **69**:54-61, 1962.

Hays, William, *Statistics for Psychologists.* New York: Holt, Rinehart and Winston, 1963.

Lehmann, E. L., *Testing Statistical Hypotheses.* New York: John Wiley & Sons, Inc., 1959.

Levy, Sheldon G., *Inferential Statistics in the Behavioral Sciences.* New York: Holt, Rinehart and Winston, 1968.

Loether, Herman J., and D. McTavish, *Descriptive and Inferential Statistics: An Introduction.* Boston: Allyn and Bacon, Inc., 1976.

Walker, Helen M., and J. Lev, *Statistical Inference.* New York: Holt, Rinehart and Winston, 1953.

Winer, B. J., *Statistical Principles in Experimental Design.* New York: McGraw-Hill Book Company, 1971.

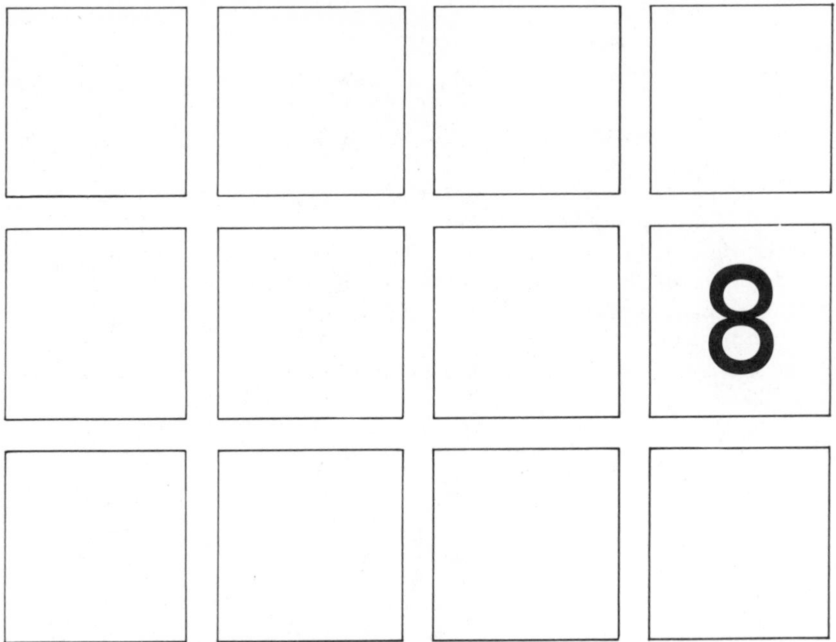

8 Interval-Level Tests of Significance

This chapter examines a variety of statistical techniques that researchers can apply to hypothesis tests involving data measured according to an interval scale. Briefly recalling our discussion of levels of measurement in Chapter 2, data are usually measured according to nominal, ordinal, interval, and ratio level-of-measurement requirements. The lowest level of measurement, the nominal level, appropriately applies to classifications of data into several discrete categories that are merely different from one another.

Ordinal-level data are measured according to scale properties that permit the researcher to make "greater than" or "less than" statements with respect to different "ordinal" scores. Interval-level data not only include classification (i.e., differentiation associated with nominal scales) and rankable quantities (i.e., gradated differentiation associated with ordinal scales), but such information is amenable to interval spacing along some continuum of values from low to high. In short, if a researcher can assume that data are measured according to an interval scale, then equal distances between measured units of some variable can be assumed to exist. Such an assumption of the interval level of measurement permits the researcher to engage in arithmetic operations that would not be permissible if data at lower levels of measurement were encountered.[1]

This chapter includes statistical procedures that have as a common underlying assumption the interval level of measurement. Before any of the procedures presented in this chapter can be applied to the researcher's data, it must be demonstrated that an interval scale of measurement underlies and is directly associated with the data to be analyzed. This is the basic assumption associated with any statistical procedure or measure.

One point of clarification needs to be made here. We have presented levels of measurement in order, from lowest to highest (e.g., nominal → ordinal → interval, etc.), but this chapter begins with tests of hypotheses where data at the interval level of measurement are involved. Although it might make more sense to present tests of hypotheses involving nominal data prior to introducing tests involving data of a higher level of measurement, there are several reasons why this has not been done here.

First, many of the tests to be presented in this and later chapters (i.e., nominal and ordinal tests of significance) will be compared with several of the tests in this chapter. Researchers will be in the position of evaluating tests in later chapters more effectively by observing such comparisons. The advantages and disadvantages associated with many tests in later chapters will frequently be linked meaningfully with various tests presented here. In a sense, the tests in the present chapter are often used as standards against which other tests are compared and contrasted. Selecting an appropriate statistical method for an hypothesis test is not as cut and dried a procedure as one might suspect. All tests have different weaknesses and strengths, depending upon the circumstances associated with their proposed applications. Selecting the appropriate test, therefore, is more of an "art" rather than following a simple set of steps in one chapter or another.

Another reason for the presentation of interval-level tests in advance of others at lower levels of measurement is that there is a logical transition from the discussion of confidence intervals and hypothesis testing (Chapter 7) to *t* tests and other procedures included in this chapter. Several of the tests presented at the beginning of this chapter focus upon differences between means. The sampling distri-

[1] The ratio level of measurement is seldom assumed by most statistical tests and procedures in the social sciences. Therefore, only tests assuming nominal, ordinal, or interval levels of measurement will be treated in this book.

bution of means is used, therefore, in subsequent statistical decision making. These topics are quite compatible with the discussion of sampling distributions in Chapter 7.

In later chapters, where several measures of association are presented, several of these coefficients have tests of significance associated with them. Again, it would be proper to consider tests of significance first, given the fact that they will be usefully applied to evaluate the significance of observed relationships between variables.

□ A NOTE ON CHAPTER ORGANIZATION

This chapter presents statistical tests in the following order: (1) tests involving single samples of elements; (2) tests involving two samples of elements, where such samples are considered "independent"; (3) tests involving two samples of elements, where such samples are considered "related"; (4) tests involving *k* samples, where such samples are considered independent; and (5) tests about *k* samples, where the samples are considered related. Several specialized tests are presented near the end of the chapter for making multiple-mean comparisons. Such tests typically follow the application of procedures designed to evaluate differences between *k* groups.

□ SINGLE-SAMPLE TESTS OF SIGNIFICANCE

Two tests will be presented in this section. The first test, the t test, is designed to test hypotheses about estimates of population means based upon sample $\overline{X}$ values. The second test, the Z test, also tests hypotheses about estimates of population means. The t test assumes that the population standard deviation, σ, is unknown, whereas the Z test usually assumes that σ is known.

The *t* Test

Perhaps the best single-sample test of significance when data at the interval level can be assumed, the *t test* is designed to determine the significance of difference between some hypothesized population μ and some observed $\overline{X}$. The following example demonstrates this.[2]

[2] Examples used throughout the text have been taken largely from real data. Such data have often been rearranged so as to present clear illustrations of statistical techniques. Most statistical tests have associated with them interpretive tables, as in Appendix A, which are approximations of sampling distributions of statistics associated with each test presented. The examples have been arranged so as to maximize the potential usefulness of these interpretive tables for the researcher whenever decisions of hypothesis-testing outcomes are necessary.

Minton (1975) was interested in assessing the potential impact of the television program, "Sesame Street," on the readiness of a sample of prekindergarten children to enter and participate successfully in kindergarten school and its related activities. Such research might prove helpful in defining those prekindergarten experiences that enable children to adjust more smoothly to the educational setting. Better adjustment might mean better performance in one's school subjects, better self-concept development, and the emergence of a better "product" at the end of one's school years.

Minton used the Metropolitan Readiness Test (MRT) to measure such "readiness" factors as word meanings, copying, and listening (Hildreth et al., 1964). A sample of 41 parochial school children using video instruction as a part of their study program was selected for the research. Mean MRT performance scores were collected for this sample and compared with an hypothesized $\mu = 64$ for a larger sample of children from the year preceding the introduction of "Sesame Street" to educational programming. The larger the score on the MRT, the more "ready" the child is to enter kindergarten. An observed $\overline{X} = 68.5$ was found for the sample of 41 parochial school children and compared with the hypothesized $\mu = 64$. Was there a significant difference between the two means? The following hypothesis set was tested:

H_0: $\mu \leqslant 64$
H_1: $\mu > 64$

$$P \leqslant .05 \text{ (one-tailed test).}$$

The null hypothesis, H_0, says that the mean for the population (in this case, the mean MRT score of children in the year preceding Minton's research) is equal to or less than 64; whereas H_1 says that the population mean is greater than 64. Minton probably believed that the "Sesame Street" program would contribute to readiness (larger MRT scores) among the parochial school children observed, and therefore a directional or one-tailed test of the hypothesis was conducted.

To test H_0 (and indirectly test H_1), the following t test was conducted:

$$t = \frac{\overline{X} - \mu}{s_{\overline{x}}},$$

where

$\overline{X}$ = observed sample mean
μ = hypothesized population mean
$s_{\overline{x}}$ = *standard error of the mean* $(s/\sqrt{N-1})$

Assume that Minton has the following information: $s = 12.2, N = 41$, and $\overline{X}_{obs} = 68.5$. With this information, we may compute t as follows:

$$t = \frac{68.5 - 64}{\dfrac{12.2}{\sqrt{41 - 1}}}$$

$$= \frac{4.5}{\dfrac{12.2}{6.3}}$$

$$= \frac{4.5}{1.94}$$

$$= 2.320.$$

The observed value of t for these data is 2.320.

In order to determine the statistical significance of our observed t value, we must turn to Table A5, Appendix A. This table contains critical values of the t statistic that must be equaled or exceeded by our observed t values in order for our observed t values to be significant at the levels of probability indicated across the top of the table. Note in Table A5 that both one- and two-tailed probabilities are provided. Since H_0 is being tested at the .05 level of significance and is a one-tailed (directional) test, we locate the .05 one-tailed probability across the top of the table. Next we must determine *degrees of freedom.*[3] Degrees of freedom in this instance are $N - 1$, or $41 - 1$ or 40. With df = 40, we may now locate that point where .05 (one-tailed test level of significance) and df = 40 intersect in the body of the table. This defines the critical value of t that must be equaled or exceeded by our observed t value in order for H_0 to be rejected and H_1 supported. The critical value of t from this table is 1.684. Given an observed t value of 2.320, which clearly equals or exceeds the critical t value, the null hypothesis may be rejected and H_1 supported. Therefore, Minton has supporting evidence that the observed $\overline{X}$, the average MRT score for her 41 prekindergarten children, is significantly larger than the hypothesized μ of 64.

This result is tentatively interpreted as support for the notion that "Sesame Street" as an educational device is probably instrumental in improving the readiness of children to enter school settings and adapt

[3] Degrees of freedom are frequently used for the purpose of entering statistical tables. They are designated "df" and refer to the number of values in a set of them which are free to vary. For single-sample t tests of significance, degrees of freedom are defined as $N - 1$, where N = sample size.

successfully to these new experiences and encounters. Obviously, more research would be needed as additional confirmation before anything conclusive could be determined about the television medium as an effective educational tool. Minton's study is one of many studies. But in this instance, a sample of children did appear more ready to accept kindergarten responsibilities after an exposure to the educational program "Sesame Street."

Had Minton not predicted that the television program "Sesame Street" would improve children's MRT scores but merely change them, a two-tailed hypothesis test would have been in order. The hypothesis set might have been revised as follows:

H_0: $\mu = 64$
H_1: $\mu \neq 64$

$$P \leqslant .05 \text{ (two-tailed test).}$$

With a two-tailed test of the hypothesis being made, the only difference in our strategy for determining the significance of the resulting observed t value would be to examine the two-tailed probability line in Table A5 rather than the original one-tailed probability line.

All facts in the original research situation would remain the same. The same t test would be conducted with the same observed t value of 2.320. But our inspection of Table A5 would provide us with a different critical value of t to equal or exceed. In this instance, we would determine the point where df = 40 intersected the two-tailed probability of .05. The new critical value of t would be 2.021 instead of 1.684. Again, Minton's observed t value of 2.320 equals or exceeds the critical t value of 2.021 and H_0 can be rejected. It should be noted that because this is a two-tailed test, the observed $\overline{X} = 68.5$ would be just as significantly different from the hypothesized μ of 64 as would an observed $\overline{X} = 59.5$. (This is a hypothetical mean value but differs from 64 to the same degree as the original observed mean value of 68.5.) In each situation, the difference between means would be 4.5 points. Minton would only be interested in the significance of any difference, regardless of the direction of the observed $\overline{X}$ above or below the hypothesized μ.[4]

Critical values of statistics such as t for two-tailed tests are generally larger than critical values for one-tailed tests. This is because

[4] The t table includes specific instructions on how to deal with degrees of freedom (df) that cannot be found in the table. For instance, 78 df cannot be found in Table A5, and yet a researcher may have df = 78 in a particular study. Instructions for dealing with this situation are provided in a table footnote. In fact, most tables in Appendix A have interpretive instructions accompanying them to assist the researcher in evaluating observed values of statistics in relation to critical values shown in the tables.

there is less risk involved in predicting a hypothesis test outcome in a two-tailed test situation. The researcher has less information about the sample studied and the nature of the experiment conducted. In one-tailed or directional test situations, there is some justification for assuming that the hypothesis test outcome will be in one direction or the other. "Sesame Street" as an educational program was believed to enhance the learning experiences of children. Therefore, Minton predicted that exposure to this television program would be helpful and lead to an improvement in MRT scores. In the early days of television broadcasting, relatively little was known about the effect of programming schedules on learning effectiveness. It is more likely, therefore, that earlier hypothesis tests would have been two-tailed ones than one-tailed ones.

The less we know about a sample we are examining, the effects of an experiment we are conducting, or anything of a new or revolutionary nature used in social research projects, the more inclined we are to use two-tailed, nondirectional hypothesis tests in our initial research activity. Of course, the more we learn about any area of study, the more precise we can be about hypothesis test outcomes, and one-tailed, directional hypothesis tests are increasingly justified.

One embarrassing implication of one-tailed hypothesis tests, however, is to predict a hypothesis test outcome in one direction and observe an outcome in the opposite direction. We do not run this risk in two-tailed hypothesis tests, and therefore, nondirectional predictions are more conservative (and typically less informative and less risky) compared with their one-tailed, directional counterparts.

Large-Sample-Size Considerations. When the researcher tests hypotheses about population means where the sample size exceeds 120, a decision can be made to use either the infinity (∞) sign line of Table A5 for determining critical values of t, or Table A3. If Table A3 is used, the t test becomes, in effect, a Z test of significance of difference. The format of the Z test is the same as the t test, where

$$Z = \frac{\overline{X} - \mu}{s_{\overline{x}}},$$

where

$\overline{X}$ = observed sample mean
μ = hypothesized population mean
$s_{\overline{x}}$ = standard error of the mean

The magnitude of Z increases as the discrepancy between the observed $\overline{X}$ and the hypothesized μ increases. The larger the Z value, the more significant the difference between the two means. Critical

TABLE 8.1

Level of Significance	*Critical Values of Z*	
	One-Tailed Test	*Two-Tailed Test*
.05	1.64	1.96
.01	2.33	2.58

values of Z for the .05 and .01 (conventional) levels of significance are provided in Table 8.1 for both one- and two-tailed hypothesis tests. It will be observed that these values correspond with the critical values of t associated with those same levels of significance (.05 and .01) for one- and two-tailed tests on the df infinity (∞) line in Table A5. In fact, when sample sizes exceed 120, the t distribution becomes identical to the unit normal distribution, for all practical purposes.[5]

Assumptions of the t Test. The primary assumptions of the t test (in addition to randomness and the interval level of measurement) include the assumption of a normal distribution associated with the observed scores. It is important that a normal or approximately normal distribution of scores be assumed, inasmuch as $\overline{X}$ values are used in hypothesis tests. It will be recalled that means are especially sensitive to deviant scores. Therefore, if means are computed from distributions where deviant scores exist, the true central tendency of the distribution will be somewhat misleading. Applications of such means in hypothesis tests can lead to highly unreliable test results. The researcher could reject (or fail to reject) H_0, and this decision would be faulty or incorrect primarily because of a misleading mean value rather than any real discrepancy between a hypothesized μ and an observed $\overline{X}$ from a distribution that has substantial skewness or kurtosis.

There is no true sample-size limitation imposed for t-test applications. Extremely small sample sizes, where $N < 30$, are amenable to the t test provided that the other assumptions are met. It has been

[5] In some statistics texts, discussions may be found of tests of hypotheses about population means when population standard deviations, σ values, are assumed to be known. In these instances, the Z test presented above is used, with a minor modification in the denominator term. Instead of $s_{\overline{x}}$ (defined as $s/\sqrt{N-1}$), the designation for the standard error of the mean is $\sigma_{\overline{x}}$, where the revised formula for this value becomes $\sigma/\sqrt{N}$, where σ is the population standard deviation and N the sample size. The more common of the two hypothesis-testing situations is that the population σ is assumed to be unknown. It is highly unlikely that circumstances would exist where we would have a knowledge of one population parameter and not have a knowledge of the other. Therefore, the t test presented earlier is preferred here. In any case, it will suffice for all single-sample tests at the interval level, regardless of whether σ is known or unknown.

shown that for larger sample sizes (i.e., where $N > 30$ or even where $N > 120$), the t test may also be applied.

Advantages and Disadvantages of the t Test. The primary advantages of the t test are (1) it is easy to use, (2) a table of critical values exists for quick and convenient interpretations of observed t values, (3) there are no sample-size restrictions, (4) many researchers are familiar with the t test and it is conventional to apply such a test in research work, and (5) it is the most powerful test a researcher can use when all assumptions associated with the data have been met.

Power is defined as the probability associated with rejecting H_0, the null hypothesis, when it is false and ought to be rejected. It will be recalled that two sources of error always exist in hypothesis tests: (1) type I error (alpha error), when H_0 is rejected when it is true and should not be rejected; and (2) type II error (beta error), when H_0 is not rejected and it is false and ought to be rejected.

The researcher wishes to minimize these errors as well as maximize the likelihood of making the correct decisions. The probabilities of making correct statistical decisions are $1 - \alpha$ (1 - alpha error) and $1 - \beta$ (1 - beta error), respectively. $1 - \beta$ is the power of the test of H_0, referring to the researcher's likelihood of being correct in rejecting H_0 when it is false and ought to be rejected.

The t test assists the researcher by being the most powerful procedure to apply whenever hypotheses involving population μ values are tested and when all assumptions underlying it have been met. In fact, the t test functions as a "standard" against which many other tests of significance are often compared regarding their relative power in rejecting H_0's that are false. We will find, for example, that test A is 95 percent as powerful as the t test, or that test B is 80 percent as powerful as the t test. This means that if all such tests (the t test, test A, and test B, whatever these other tests may be) are applied to the same hypothesis set (H_0 and H_1), the t test will usually be the one most likely to result in the rejection of H_0. The alternative tests designated as test A and test B are designed to accomplish the same function as the t test, but they will not be as powerful. Therefore, they will be less likely to lead to a decision to reject H_0 in favor of H_1 (compared with the more powerful t test).

The primary disadvantage of the t test is that it has rather stringent assumptions. The two most likely to bother social scientists are the interval-level-of-measurement assumption and the normal distribution assumption. The t test is often incorrectly applied to attitudinal data that have been measured according to Likert, Thurstone, or Guttman scaling procedures. Since these procedures yield an ordinal scale of measurement at best, the interval-level scale requirement of the *t* test is immediately violated (Edwards and Kenney, 1946; Labovitz, 1967). Also, many distributions of scores are not normal in form. If the researcher persists in applying the *t* test to such nonnormal distributions, then another important assumption is violated.[6] Since the *t* test has such restrictive and stringent assumptions, the researcher often finds it difficult to apply this test legitimately to collected data. Of course, the *t* test is excellent whenever the assumptions associated with it have been satisfied.

□ TWO-SAMPLE TESTS OF SIGNIFICANCE

Frequently, researchers have the opportunity of analyzing data obtained from two samples of elements. Normally, statistical questions about two samples concern any possible differences that may exist on some trait or characteristic shared by both samples. Do two samples differ on trait *X*? Depending upon how trait *X* (whatever it may be) is measured initially (i.e., at the interval level of measurement in this case), several statistical techniques exist for helping the researcher to decide whether two samples are significantly different from one another.

Before the selection of a statistical test can be made, the investigator must determine whether or not the samples are *independent* of one another or *related* in some fashion. Samples that are independent are mutually exclusive of one another. For instance, the researcher can actually draw two samples from the same or different populations at the same or different times. A random sample of St. Louis residents could be drawn by researcher Jones and compared with a random sample of residents from Kansas City. Clearly, the two samples would be independent of one another. Or the researcher could draw two random samples of students from some university and examine differences between them. This procedure would be one way of achieving independence in sampling.

Another way of obtaining two independent samples for statistical analysis purposes (and avoiding the methodological headache of drawing two separate samples) is to draw a single sample of elements and separate them according to some logical categorical division such as male–female, Democrat–Republican, Protestant–Catholic, or rich–poor. This procedure makes it impossible for a person to be a mem-

[6] Several statistical procedures designed to perform a similar function as the *t* test are presented in this and later chapters. Although they perform a similar *t* test function, they do not have the restrictive assumption of normality associated with them. They are often referred to as "nonparametric" or "distribution-free" tests. These will be discussed in detail when the first of these tests is presented later in this chapter.

ber of both groups simultaneously, thus implementing the mutual exclusivity property associated with independent samples. Actually, this procedure can be extended to drawing *k* samples (two or more samples) as well.[7] For instance, we could draw a sample of students and separate them logically into freshman–sophomore–junior–senior categories. Members of one category could not possibly be members of another category at the same time. Of course, the researcher could actually draw *k* different samples if desired.

Related samples are usually obtained by one of three methods. The most popular procedure is to examine one sample in one time period and then examine the same sample in a later period. This is referred to as using each element as his/her own *control*, usually in a *before–after experiment.* The effects of alcohol on reaction time in driving motor vehicles is an example of how persons function as their own controls. Blood alcohol levels for a designated number of persons are measured prior to an experiment. Each person drinks a measured amount of some alcoholic beverage. Then, perhaps an hour later, blood alcohol levels are checked again by the researcher. During the first time period (prior to the introduction of the alcoholic beverage), a test is conducted to determine the time it takes a person to apply the brakes of their car in a simulated driving incident. After the hour interval, another test is conducted of reaction time.

A comparison of differences in reaction time from one time period to the next involves a *two-related-sample statistical test.* Two groups are involved, even though the same persons are members of both groups. When the same people are examined at two or more different points in time, this is called a two-related-sample or *k*-related-sample test situation. The persons are related because of the fact that they are functioning as their own controls in a before–after experiment.

A second way of achieving related samples is by *matching* individuals. Persons are matched whenever they share a fairly large number of characteristics with one another. A researcher might obtain one sample and attempt to match each person in the sample with someone else. A second sample is eventually obtained, matched with the first sample on an individual-by-individual basis. A brief example might be two persons matched with one another who are 19-year-old freshmen female Democrats with 3.5 grade-point averages living in the same dormitory. Both are 5 feet 2 inches tall, have blue eyes, blonde hair, and are psychology majors. They might even share several attitudinal traits as well (e.g., similar anxiety levels, similar achievement motivation, etc). This is obviously an exaggeration. Re-

[7] In this book, chapter subdivisions refer specifically to two-sample cases and to *k*-sample cases. Therefore, the letter, *k*, will refer here to any situation where three or more samples are encountered, even though *k* literally means "two or more."

searchers would probably not find a sample matched on an individual basis on so many different traits. A reasonable number of traits considered sufficient for matching purposes might be five or six. Although it is beyond the scope of this book to explore the weaknesses and strengths of matching as a sampling tool, it is clear that matching is extremely difficult for the researcher to accomplish. This is the primary reason it is seen so infrequently in research publications.

A third way of obtaining related samples is through *frequency distribution matching.* Rather than match individuals with other individuals on a selected number of characteristics, a researcher matches one group with another on group characteristics. For example, we might find two groups of approximately the same size whose mean ages are similar. The male–female composition may be the same. They may be of the same religious preference, political affiliation, and racial composition. To this extent, at least, the two groups may be considered matched on the basis of the similarity of distributions of common traits or characteristics. By comparison, matching groups is easier to accomplish than matching individuals.

Whenever two or more samples are involved in a researcher's study, it must be determined whether the samples are independent or related. Associated with all two- and k-sample tests is the assumption that one or the other of the two conditions exists (i.e., independent or related samples). A related-sample statistical test is inappropriate for investigating differences between two independent samples. By the same token, any two- or k-independent sample test would be wrongly applied to two- or k-related samples.

□ TWO INDEPENDENT SAMPLE TESTS

In this section two tests of significance will be examined: (1) the t test for differences between means, and (2) the randomization test for two independent samples.

The t Test for Differences Between Means

The t test for differences between means is an extension of the t test for a single sample. Therefore, almost all of the assumptions, advantages, and disadvantages associated with the application of the t test in the single-sample case also pertain to the two-sample case. An example of the t test is provided.

Spitzer et al. (1966) explored various differences between persons who hold different opinions of themselves. Specifically, Spitzer et al. found two samples of university students, who they identified as "derogators" and "nonderogators." Derogators were defined as persons making at least one derogatory self-statement on a test assessing "self" characteristics. Nonderogators were defined as persons who made no statements of a derogatory nature about themselves on the measuring instruments. Later, the two samples were compared to see whether they differed from one another on another test that measured degree of self-satisfaction. Spitzer et al. expected the derogators would have lower self-satisfaction scores than the nonderogators. Probably, their argument was that persons who make unfavorable statements about themselves are more likely to be less satisfied with themselves than the nonderogators. Therefore, a one-tailed or directional hypothesis test was in order. The hypothesis set was

H_0: Derogators will have the same or larger (higher) self-satisfaction scores compared with nonderogators.
H_1: Derogators will have smaller (or lower) self-satisfaction scores compared with nonderogators.

The level of significance was set at .01. The degree of self-satisfaction was measured by Bill's (1958) Index of Adjustment and Values, and mean satisfaction scores were computed for both samples. The mean self-satisfaction score of derogators was labeled $\overline{X}_1$, and the mean for the nonderogators was $\overline{X}_2$. Using these symbols, the hypothesis set is restated as

H_0: $\overline{X}_1 \geqslant \overline{X}_2$
H_1: $\overline{X}_1 < \overline{X}_2$

$$P \leqslant .01 \text{ (one-tailed test).}$$

The following information was made available from the collected data:

$$\overline{X}_1 = 61.71 \qquad s_1 = 7.46 \qquad N_1 = 305$$
$$\overline{X}_2 = 69.38 \qquad s_2 = 5.16 \qquad N_2 = 50.$$

With this information, the following hypothesis test was made using the t formula:

$$t = \frac{\overline{X}_1 - \overline{X}_2}{s_{\overline{X}_1 - \overline{X}_2}},$$

where

$\overline{X}_1$ = mean for the first sample
$\overline{X}_2$ = mean for the second sample
$s_{\overline{X}_1 - \overline{X}_2}$ = standard error of the difference between the two means

the standard error of the difference between the two means is determined as follows:

$$s_{\bar{x}_1 - \bar{x}_2} = \sqrt{\frac{s_1^2}{N_1} + \frac{s_2^2}{N_2}},$$

where

N_1 and N_2 = two sample sizes
s_1^2 and s_2^2 = two sample variances

Substituting our information for the symbols in the formula, we have

$$t = \frac{61.71 - 69.38}{\sqrt{\frac{(7.46)^2}{305} + \frac{(5.16)^2}{50}}}$$

$$= \frac{-7.67}{\sqrt{\frac{55.6}{305} + \frac{26.6}{50}}}$$

$$= \frac{-7.67}{\sqrt{.71}}$$

$$= \frac{-7.67}{.84}$$

$$= -9.13.$$

The observed value of $t = -9.13$. We may enter Table A5 to determine the statistical significance of this observed t value. Degrees of freedom are determined by the following formula for a two-sample situation:

$$\text{Df} = (N_1 - 1) + (N_2 - 1).$$

In this instance, we have $(305 - 1) + (50 - 1)$ or $304 + 49 = 353$ degrees of freedom. With a df this large, we can use the infinity line in Table A5. Where this df of "infinity" intersects with the .01 significance level for a one-tailed test gives us a critical value of $t = -2.326$, which we must equal or exceed with our observed t value. Clearly, our observed $t = -9.13$ equals or exceeds the critical value, and H_0 can be rejected. We may conclude that the derogators have significantly lower self-satisfaction scores compared with the nonderogators.[8]

[8] The t table is similar to the normal-curve table in that both positive and negative critical values of t can be obtained. We must pay attention to the direction of mean differences predicted by H_1 in order to determine whether the critical value will be positive or negative. Since $\bar{X}_1$ is predicted to be smaller than $\bar{X}_2$, the resulting mean difference is negative rather than positive. We merely assign a negative sign (–) to the critical value of t when it is time to compare this value with our observed t.

Had Spitzer et al. elected to make a two-tailed, nondirectional hypothesis test, they would have constructed the hypothesis set as follows:

H_0: $\overline{X}_1 = \overline{X}_2$
H_1: $\overline{X}_1 \neq \overline{X}_2$

$$P \leqslant .01 \quad \text{(two-tailed test).}$$

The critical value of t that must be equaled or exceeded in order for these researchers to reject H_0 is found again where the infinity line in Table A5 intersects with .01 (two-tailed test). It can be seen that the new (two-tailed) critical value of $t = -2.576$. Again, H_0, which says that the derogators and nonderogators have the same mean self-satisfaction scores ($\overline{X}_1 = \overline{X}_2$), can be rejected. This is because the observed t value of -9.13 also equals or exceeds -2.576.

Assumptions of the t Test for Differences Between Means. The primary assumptions of the t test in this case are (1) the interval level of measurement associated with the data analyzed, (2) randomness, and (3) normal distributions for both groups on the variable measured. One additional assumption is sometimes made by researchers. Investigators sometimes desire that the standard deviations (and variances) for the two groups should be similar. If there is some reason to believe that the two variances are substantially dissimilar, the following formula may be applied, which usually increases the magnitude of $s_{\overline{x}_1 - \overline{x}_2}$ and renders the difference between means slightly less significant (hence a more conservative result):

$$t = \frac{\overline{X}_1 - \overline{X}_2}{s_{\overline{x}_1 - \overline{x}_2}},$$

where

$\overline{X}_1$ and $\overline{X}_2$ = two sample means

$$s_{\overline{x}_1 - \overline{x}_2} = \sqrt{(s^2)\left(\frac{N_1 + N_2}{N_1 N_2}\right)},$$

where

$$s^2 = \frac{(N_1 - 1)s_1^2 + (N_2 - 1)s_2^2}{N_1 + N_2 - 2}.$$

Using our knowledge of values from the original hypothesis test by Spitzer et al., we will first solve for s^2:

$$s^2 = \frac{(305 - 1)(55.6) + (50 - 1)(26.6)}{305 + 50 - 2}$$

$$= \frac{18{,}205.8}{353}$$

$$= 51.6.$$

Then the new t is computed as follows:

$$t = \frac{61.71 - 69.38}{\sqrt{(51.6)\left(\frac{305 + 50}{(305)(50)}\right)}}$$

$$= \frac{-7.67}{\sqrt{(51.6)(.023)}}$$

$$= \frac{-7.67}{\sqrt{1.1868}}$$

$$= \frac{-7.67}{1.09}$$

$$= -7.04.$$

It is observed that the new $s_{\bar{x}_1 - \bar{x}_2}$ value becomes 1.09, somewhat larger than the original denominator term of .84. Applying this new denominator term to the original observed mean difference of -7.67 (sign is unimportant in a two-tailed, nondirectional test), we obtain an observed t value = -7.04. This compares with an original observed t value of -9.13. Although H_0 will continue to be rejected even with this lower observed t value, there is the possibility that it could make a difference in the hypothesis-testing outcome if the critical value and observed value of t were closer together.

If the researcher follows sound sampling principles initially, however, the original denominator-term formula would be much simpler to apply. In practice, it emerges as the more popularly applied error term in t tests for differences between means.

Advantages and Disadvantages of the t Test for Mean Differences. The fact that two means are being analyzed rather than one makes this test slightly more cumbersome to apply than the single-sample version of it. The denominator term, $s_{\bar{x}_1 - \bar{x}_2}$, is more complex as well, inasmuch as two variances are combined or "pooled." Other than these minor differences, the same advantages and disadvantages associated with the single-sample t test also apply here.

The test is appropriate for data at the interval level of measurement (sometimes a disadvantage where ordinal attitudinal scales are used). It is easy to apply and interpret with available tables of critical values, and it is the most powerful test for assessing mean differences between groups.

On the negative side, the stringent level of measurement and normality assumptions as well as the "equal variances" recommendation made by some researchers are significant constraints and limit the *t* test's utility in a large number of research projects. Again, when the assumptions are met, it is the best test to use to assess differences between two groups for a characteristic measured at the interval level.

The Randomization Test for Two Independent Samples

The randomization test is designed to determine whether two groups differ on some characteristic measured according to an interval scale. The groups are presumed to be small, where $N_1 + N_2 \leqslant 12$. This procedure is frequently applied in small-group research, where small numbers of individuals would be encountered. An example of the application of the randomization test is provided by Blau (1966).

Blau studied 10 agents who were members of a law enforcement agency charged with investigating complaints against business establishments (e.g., contract violations, labor laws, etc.). The agency was staffed with a fairly large number of subordinates who made frequent reports to the agents during the workday. The subordinates were generally at liberty to contact any agent regarding problems associated with a business investigated by the agency. Initially, Blau observed that not all agents were equally adept at handling complaints brought to them. Consequently, some agents received more contacts from subordinates, and other agents received fewer contacts.

On the basis of ratings provided by the agent supervisor, Blau labeled one sample of five agents as "more competent" and the other sample of five agents as "less competent." Blau believed that social interaction as well as the processing of complaints would be influenced significantly by whether the agents were judged competent by their subordinates. Blau determined the actual number of contacts each agent received per hour during a 30-hour observation of the work setting. These numbers of contacts by subordinates for both samples of agents are shown in Table 8.2. The following hypothesis set was tested:

H_0: There is no difference in the number of contacts received by more competent or less competent agents; if there is a difference, less competent agents will receive more contacts.

TABLE 8.2
Observed Subordinate Contact Scores for Two Groups of Law Enforcement Agency Agents.

Numbers of Contacts per Hour	
More Competent Agents ($N_1 = 5$)	*Less Competent Agents* ($N_2 = 5$)
9	4
6	3
12	1
7	8
11	2

Source: Adapted from general information provided by Peter M. Blau, "Patterns of Interaction Among a Group of Officials in a Government Agency," in A. H. Rubenstein and C. J. Haberstroh, eds., *Some Theories of Organization* (Homewood, Ill.: Richard D. Irwin, Inc., and The Dorsey Press, 1966), pp. 397–408.

H_1: More competent agents will receive more contacts from subordinates compared with less competent agents.

$$P \leqslant .01 \quad \text{(one-tailed test)}.$$

The score distribution (number of contacts per hour) for the two groups in Table 8.2 is called the *observed outcome.* We are interested in determining whether this observed outcome is significant enough to warrant rejection of the H_0. Are the two groups significantly different regarding their contacts per hour by subordinates? To answer this question and test the hypothesis, we must determine all possible outcomes that could occur. This will help us decide whether the observed outcome is really significant or is simply due to chance. The possible number of outcomes that could be observed (all possible score arrangements) is determined by the following formula:

$$\binom{N_1 + N_2}{N_1} = \binom{a}{b} = \frac{a!}{b!(a-b)!},$$

where N_1 and N_2 are the respective sample sizes. This formula involves factorials, the symbol for which is !. Numbers followed by a factorial sign are treated as follows:

$$3! = (3)(2)(1) = 6$$

$$5! = (5)(4)(3)(2)(1) = 120$$

$$6! = (6)(5)(4)(3)(2)(1) = 720$$

$$0! = (1).$$

In the present situation, where $N_1 = 5$ and $N_2 = 5$, the formula for the possible number of outcomes is

$$\binom{5+5}{5} = \binom{10}{5} = \frac{10!}{5!(10-5)!},$$

which becomes

$$\frac{(10)(9)(8)(7)(6)(5)(4)(3)(2)(1)}{(5)(4)(3)(2)(1)(5)(4)(3)(2)(1)} = 252.$$

There are 252 possible outcomes of score arrangements for the present problem, where $N_1 = 5$ and $N_2 = 5$.

Next, we must determine whether the outcome observed in Table 8.2 is substantially different from what would be expected according to chance. We know that there are 252 possible outcomes. A greater portion of these outcomes of score arrangements are more common or expected, and the most radical distributions of scores between the two groups are least expected. One extreme arrangement might be where the more competent agents had all of the higher contact scores, and the less competent agents had all of the lower contact scores. The other extreme arrangement would be if all of the higher contact scores were located within the less-competent-agent sample, while the lower contact scores occurred within the more-competent-agent sample.

The distribution of all possible outcomes of score arrangements is like a sampling distribution of means, although the shapes of each differ considerably. There are "tails" of this distribution to the left and right. We might envision the general type of outcome arrangements in distributional form shown in Figure 8.1.

The arrangement of scores of interest to us will be found somewhere in the right tail of the distribution of outcomes. A *critical number of outcomes* must be determined in order to see whether the outcome observed in Table 8.2 is consistent with any of them. We

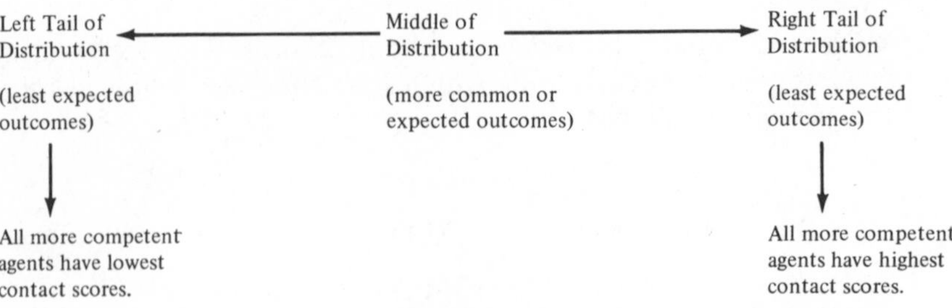

FIGURE 8.1

TABLE 8.3
The Three Most Extreme Arrangements of Scores.

	Extreme Score Arrangements (A One-Tailed Hypothesis Test)	
Number Outcome	*Less Competent Agents* ($N_1 = 5$)	*More Competent Agents* ($N_2 = 5$)
1	1 2 3 4 6	7 8 9 11 12
2	1 2 3 4 7	6 8 9 11 12
3	1 2 3 4 8	6 7 9 11 12[a]

[a]Matches our observed outcome of scores.

obtain the critical number of outcomes by multiplying the possible number of outcomes, 252, by the level of significance associated with the hypothesis test, or .01, or (.01) (252) = 2.52, which we will round to three outcomes. Therefore, we are interested in the three most extreme outcomes in the right tail of the distribution.

Given the score distribution in Table 8.2, we have rearranged these scores, regardless of where they occurred originally in the two groups, and this information is presented in Table 8.3.

Table 8.3 is constructed as follows. The most extreme score arrangement (outcome 1) would place all of the higher scores in the more competent agent group and all of the lower scores in the less competent agent group. The next most extreme outcome (outcome 2), as shown in Table 8.3, involves an exchange of the largest score among the smallest scores with the smallest score among the largest scores. In short, the score 6 in the first group is exchanged with the score 7 in the second group. The next most extreme score arrangement (outcome 3) involves a similar switch of the score 6 in the first group with the score 8 in the second group; and so on.

It will be observed from the data presented in Table 8.3 that extreme outcome 3 matches our observed outcome of score arrangements. Since this is the case, we may reject H_0 and support H_1 at the .01 level of significance. The more competent agents do receive more contacts from subordinates than do the less competent agents.

Had a two-tailed, nondirectional test been made, the following hypothesis set would have been presented:

H_0: There is no difference in contacts received from subordinates by more and less competent agents.

H_1: There is a difference in contact scores between the two group of agents.

$$P \leqslant .01 \quad \text{(two-tailed test).}$$

To determine the critical number of outcomes, we would use the

	Less Competent Agents ($N_1 = 5$)	More Competent Agents ($N_2 = 5$)
Most extreme outcome (left tail) →	7 8 9 11 12	1 2 3 4 6
Most extreme outcome (right tail) →	1 2 3 4 6	7 8 9 11 12

FIGURE 8.2

same factorial formula as before, yielding 252 possible outcomes. But this time, two tails of the distribution of outcomes would be used instead of one. Therefore, we must multiply the 252 possible outcomes by .01/2 or .005, or (.005) (252) = 1.26, rounded to one outcome. The most extreme outcome in each tail of the distribution would comprise the critical regions and contain the two critical outcomes (see Figure 8.2). In the two-tailed case, we are unable to reject H_0 at the .01 level of significance because our observed score distributional arrangement fails to match either extreme outcome.

Assumptions of the Randomization Test. The assumptions for this test include (1) randomness, (2) interval level of measurement, (3) two independent samples, and (4) combined sample sizes of $N_1 + N_2 \leqslant 12$.

Advantages and Disadvantages of the Randomization Test. The randomization test makes no distributional assumption for its legitimate application. It is somewhat restrictive in that interval-level data are required. Also, the sample-size limitation functions as a restriction. The test itself is approximately 90 percent as powerful as the t test for mean differences if both tests were applied to the same data. Therefore, it is considered as a reasonable alternative whenever small samples are encountered.

The primary usefulness of the randomization test is in the area of small-group research or any situation where the researcher has extremely small sample sizes under investigation. Where sample sizes ($N_1 + N_2$) exceed 12, either the t test should be used (if assumptions are met) or the researcher should consider another equally powerful test, the Mann–Whitney U test, presented in Chapter 10. The Mann–Whitney U test will not utilize as much information; it requires only that the data be measured according to an ordinal scale. But it is a powerful alternative, nevertheless.

The primary disadvantage of the randomization test is that it is somewhat cumbersome to apply. The fact that the researcher must work with factorials in determining critical numbers of outcomes is sometimes sufficient to frustrate all but the most patient of investigators.

Earlier it was indicated that some statistical tests are known as nonparametric procedures. The randomization test for two independent samples is the first such nonparametric test of many to be covered in this and later chapters. A *nonparametric test* usually has associated with it the following characteristics: (1) the assumption of a normal distribution is not a requirement of any nonparametric procedure; (2) most nonparametric procedures are applicable to data measured according to ordinal and nominal scales, although a limited number of interval-level tests such as the randomization test are available; (3) nonparametric tests are generally not as powerful as parametric tests (although in many instances, the power difference between them is insignificant); and (4) nonparametric procedures are quite suitable for analyzing smaller samples of elements, probably more so than their parametric counterparts.

Nonparametric tests have fewer restrictive assumptions associated with them. Most are rapid to compute and easy to apply to a wide variety of social and psychological investigations. The use of nonparametric statistical procedures in the social sciences has been growing steadily over the years. Our increasing familiarity with such procedures and a recognition of the kinds of tasks they can potentially accomplish accounts for such increased usage of them in research work. Contributing to their popularity in social investigations is the fact that many measures of attitudinal variables are at (but not entirely restricted to) the ordinal level of measurement. The following scaling methods are encompassed within the ordinal level: (1) Likert-type scaling, (2) Thurstone scaling, (3) Guttman scaling, and (4) Osgood's Semantic Differential scaling procedure.[9]

If a recommendation were to be made for using one kind or another of statistical procedure for data analysis, a preference could be expressed for the application of a parametric test, provided that all assumptions were met. Should any one or more assumptions be violated, the meaningfulness of such a test is seriously questioned. As a safe and conservative alternative to parametric tests whenever assumption violations are known or suspected, nonparametric tests designed to accomplish the same function are recommended.

[9] For an extended discussion of such scaling procedures and the justification of level of measurement associated with each, see James A. Black and Dean J. Champion, *Methods and Issues in Social Research* (New York: John Wiley & Sons, Inc., 1976), especially Chaps. 6 and 7.

□ TWO-SAMPLE TESTS: RELATED SAMPLES

In this section we examine two procedures to measure the significance of difference between two samples that are related in some manner. Either persons are matched (according to individual properties) or persons are used as their own "controls" in before–after experimental designs. Two tests appropriate for such related-sample situations when the interval level of measurement is achieved are (1) the randomization test for matched pairs (related samples), and (2) the Wilcoxon matched pairs–signed ranks test.

The Randomization Test for Matched Pairs (Related Samples)

The present version of the randomization test is similar in many respects to the randomization test for two independent samples. Small samples are again required, where $N_1 + N_2 \leqslant 12$. The researcher would use this test to determine the significance of difference between some interval-level characteristic in a matching or before–after situation. An illustration of the application of the randomization test is provided by available data in a study conducted by Morse and Reimer (1956).

These researchers focused upon one department of a large nonunionized industrial organization. Morse and Reimer examined the influence of increased decision-making power on job satisfaction among a group of clerical workers performing routine tasks in the department studied. The decision-making power of employees in this organization was altered over the course of several weeks through an "autonomy" program implemented by departmental supervisors. Gradually, employees were given greater decision-making power during the program. Morse and Reimer believed that a change toward greater involvement in the decision-making process among these employees would ultimately increase their job satisfaction level as well.

Job satisfaction scores for five employees were obtained prior to the introduction of the autonomy program. After a period of 6 months, job satisfaction scores for the same five employees were recorded again. Did the program have any effect on the job satisfaction level of these employees? Did increased involvement in the decision-making process contribute to greater job satisfaction levels among them? Before and after job satisfaction scores for the five employees are presented in Table 8.4. The possible value of job satisfaction scores ranged from 6 (the lowest possible score) to 25 (the highest possible score) according to this scale. The larger the score,

TABLE 8.4
Job Satisfaction Scores Before and After an Autonomy Program.

Employee	*Before Autonomy Program*	*After Autonomy Program*	*Score Differences*
1	15	19	+4
2	18	21	+3
3	14	15	+1
4	12	10	−2
5	11	13	+2
		Sum of score differences =	8

the greater the job satisfaction of these employees. Since it was anticipated by Morse and Reimer that job satisfaction scores would increase among employees from one time period to the next, the following hypothesis set was subjected to test:

H_0: Employees will have no change in their level of job satisfaction after exposure to an autonomy program; if there is a change, job satisfaction scores will be lower after the program.
H_1: Employees will have higher job satisfaction scores after exposure to an autonomy program.

$$P \leqslant .10 \quad \text{(one-tailed test).}$$

Before we proceed with the actual statistical test, we first examine Table 8.4 to see whether the score differences in the last column are generally consistent with the prediction we have made under H_1. It is observed that most of the score differences are positive, or that generally higher job satisfaction scores are found after the autonomy program. The question is: Does this pattern of score differences reflect a statistically significant change in job satisfaction scores?

In order to apply the randomization test, we first need to determine all possible outcomes of score differences from the data in the last column of Table 8.4. The factor 2^N, where N is the number of pairs of elements, is used. Since there are five pairs of clerical employees (five pairs of scores for the same five employees), the number of possible outcomes is $2^5 = 32$. Knowing the possible number of outcomes will enable us to determine how many outcomes will belong in the critical region of this distribution. We multiply the possible number of outcomes, 32, by the level of significance at which the hypothesis is tested, .10, or $(.10)(32) = 3.2$ outcomes. Rounding this result to 3, we are interested in the three most extreme outcomes in the direction predicted under H_1 (toward the end of the distribution where score differences are all positive).

The three most extreme outcomes of score differences are

(1)	+4	+3	+1	+2	+2	sum equals	12
(2)	+4	+3	−1	+2	+2	sum equals	10
(3)	+4	+3	+1	−2	+2	sum equals	8
(4)	+4	+3	+1	+2	−2[10]	sum equals	8.

The most extreme outcome is determined by assigning positive signs (+) to all score differences. The second most extreme outcome is determined by assigning a negative sign (−) to the smallest score difference and positive signs to all other score differences. The third most extreme outcome is determined by assigning a negative sign to the next smallest score difference, 2; positive signs to all other score differences; and so on. Since there are two scores of 2, one of these 2's receives a negative sign in the third outcome. The other 2 receives a negative sign for the fourth outcome. The researcher continues in this fashion until the critical number of outcomes has been reached.

Does our observed outcome of score differences match any of those lying in the critical region of outcomes? The third most extreme outcome is matched by our observed outcome; therefore, H_0 can be rejected and H_1 supported. There is a significant difference at the .10 level. Job satisfaction scores do increase significantly from one time period to the next. One implication of these findings is that the greater involvement in decision making probably contributed to the change in job satisfaction scores, as H_1 predicted.

Had the researchers elected to make a two-tailed, nondirectional test of the hypothesis set, the following modifications would have been made:

> H_0: There is no difference in employee's job satisfaction scores after participation in an autonomy program.
>
> H_1: There is a difference in employee's job satisfaction scores after participation in an autonomy program.

$$P \leqslant .10 \quad \text{(two-tailed test).}$$

In this instance, we are interested in the extreme outcomes in both tails of the distribution of outcomes. In short, we direct our attention to the tail that contains all positive score differences, and to the other tail, which contains all negative score differences. All steps are followed in determining the possible number of outcomes. But since a two-tailed test is involved, we will halve the significance level, .10,

[10] Since the fourth outcome can also result in the same sum of score differences, 8, it is treated as though it were actually a part of the third outcome and placed in the critical region.

and multiply the possible number of outcomes by this result, or (.10/2) (32) = (.05) (32) = 1.6 outcomes. We will round this to two outcomes. This means that our attention will be focused upon the two most extreme outcomes in both tails of the distribution. These are, respectively,

(1) +4 +3 +1 +2 +2

(2) +4 +3 −1 +2 +2

and

(3) −4 −3 −1 −2 −2

(4) −4 −3 +1 −2 −2.

This time, our observed outcome of score differences fails to match one of these extreme arrangements, and H_0 cannot be rejected at the .10 level of significance. The complete distribution of 32 score difference outcomes is shown in Table 8.5. Notice in the table that several score difference outcomes yield identical sums of score differences. This is the primary reason for treating such outcomes as identical for all practical purposes.

Figure 8.3 shows a vertical bar graph which identifies the frequency of occurrence associated with each of the outcomes shown in Table 8.5. Again, observe the interesting distributional properties associated with these possible outcomes of score differences. The more common outcomes are near the center of the distribution and the less frequently occurring outcomes are located in the tails.

Assumptions of the Randomization Test. The assumptions underlying the randomization test for matched pairs (related samples) are (1) randomness, (2) interval-level measurement associated with the data, (3) related samples, and (4) no more than six pairs of scores yielding an $N_1 + N_2 \leqslant 12$ elements.

Advantages and Disadvantages of the Randomization Test. The randomization test is a nonparametric procedure that does not require normality for its legitimate application. Compared with the randomization test for two independent samples, it is somewhat less cumbersome to work with in determining all possible outcomes and for identifying the critical regions. Primarily a small-sample test, it finds wide application in the small-group literature. Its primary limitations are the small-sample size restriction and the interval level of measurement that must be achieved. With attitudinal information, it is often difficult to meet the interval-level assumption. It is approximately 90 percent as powerful as the t test for deter-

TABLE 8.5
All Possible Score Difference Combinations Where $N = 5$.

Score Difference Arrangements					*Sum of Score Differences*
+4	+3	+1	+2	+2	12
+4	+3	−1	+2	+2	10
+4	+3	+1	−2	+2	8
+4	+3	+1	+2	−2	8
+4	−3	+1	+2	+2	6
+4	+3	−1	−2	+2	6
+4	+3	−1	+2	−2	6
+4	−3	−1	+2	+2	4
−4	+3	+1	+2	+2	4
+4	+3	+1	−2	−2	4
−4	+3	−1	+2	+2	2
+4	−3	+1	−2	+2	2
+4	−3	+1	+2	−2	2
+4	+3	−1	−2	−2	2
−4	+3	+1	−2	+2	0
−4	+3	+1	+2	−2	0
+4	−3	−1	−2	+2	0
+4	−3	−1	+2	−2	0
−4	−3	+1	+2	+2	−2
−4	+3	−1	−2	+2	−2
−4	+3	−1	+2	−2	−2
+4	−3	+1	−2	−2	−2
+4	−3	−1	−2	−2	−4
−4	−3	−1	+2	+2	−4
−4	+3	+1	−2	−2	−4
−4	+3	−1	−2	−2	−6
−4	−3	+1	−2	+2	−6
−4	−3	+1	+2	−2	−6
−4	−3	−1	−2	+2	−8
−4	−3	−1	+2	−2	−8
−4	−3	+1	−2	−2	−10
−4	−3	−1	−2	−2	−12

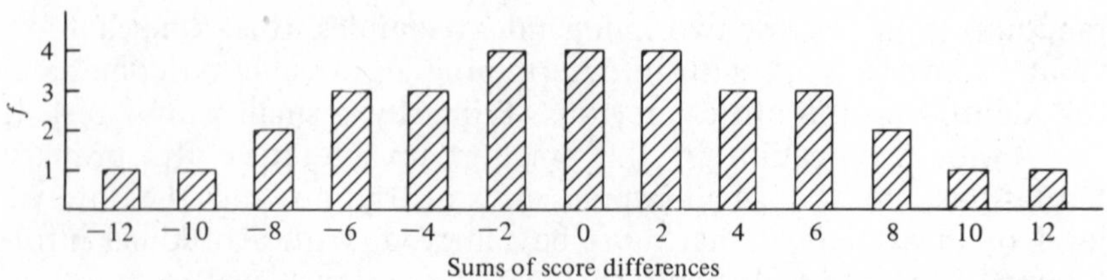

FIGURE 8.3. Bar Graph of the Score Difference Outcomes Shown in Table 8.5.

mining differences between groups. Whenever larger related samples are encountered (i.e., where $N_1 + N_2 > 12$), the researcher might turn to the Wilcoxon matched pairs–signed ranks test, which is comparatively more flexible and slightly more powerful.

The Wilcoxon Matched Pairs–Signed Ranks Test

The Wilcoxon test is designed to determine whether two related samples differ according to some variable measured at the interval level. It may be used whenever the researcher has samples that are related through matching or where persons are used as their own controls in before–after experiments. The following example is provided.

Ivancevich (1974) was interested in determining the effect of a "management by objectives" (MBO) program on subordinates of the Palos manufacturing corporation. This corporation produces machine parts and electrical products used by other firms. MBO is a program designed to influence an entire authority hierarchy in an organization and improve the performance and productivity of persons at all levels of supervision. In one department of the company, marketing, 21 employees were subsequently studied. These employees were exposed to the MBO program over a 36-month period. At specified intervals during the program, these employees were evaluated on a number of dimensions including job performance (a quantitative as well as a qualitative assessment of personal productivity). Between two given time periods, Ivancevich probably wanted to know whether the MBO program was affecting job performance. Does MBO change the job performance of participating employees from one time period to the next? The following hypothesis set is suggested by Ivancevich's research:

H_0: MBO will have no effect on employee job performance.
H_1: MBO will change employee job performance.

$$P \leqslant .05 \text{ (two-tailed test).}$$

Table 8.6 shows the productivity scores of 21 employees both before and after exposure to the MBO program. The larger the score, the higher the productivity.

The table is constructed as follows. Productivity scores are recorded for each employee both before and after the MBO program is introduced. The difference in each employee's score from one time period to the next is recorded in a third column, "D," as shown. Next, the *absolute score difference values* are ranked (regardless of sign) from 1 to 21, beginning with the smallest score difference. In the column of score differences, there are four score changes of 1. We assign to each of these values the average of the ranks they would

TABLE 8.6
Before and After Score Differences for 21 Employees on the Productivity Level.

Employee Number	*Productivity Scores*		*Difference, D*	*Rank, |D|*	*Rank with Less Frequent Sign, (T)*
	Before	*After*			
1	21	31	10	18	
2	28	29	1	2.5	
3	26	25	−1	−2.5	2.5
4	23	25	2	5.5	
5	25	28	3	7.5	
6	25	33	8	15.5	
7	22	20	−2	−5.5	5.5
8	19	23	4	10	
9	28	33	5	12.5	
10	31	30	−1	−2.5	2.5
11	32	31	−1	−2.5	2.5
12	20	31	11	19	
13	24	33	9	17	
14	27	35	8	15.5	
15	24	28	4	10	
16	23	29	6	14	
17	20	25	5	12.5	
18	24	28	4	10	
19	22	34	12	20	
20	28	42	14	21	
21	33	36	3	7.5	$\Sigma T = \overline{13.0}$

otherwise occupy if they were slightly different. They would occupy ranks 1, 2, 3, and 4. The average of these ranks is 2.5 and is assigned to each of the four 1 values. The next smallest score change is 2, and since there are two score differences of 2, these are given the average of the next two ranks of 5 and 6, or 5.5. We continue this procedure until all absolute score differences have been ranked.

In the final column, we enter all ranks associated with the less frequently occurring sign (+ or −). Since there are fewer score differences that reflect a decrease from one time period to the next, we will enter all ranks in this column associated with score decreases. The final step is to sum these ranks for a ΣT value as shown. The $\Sigma T = 13$. With this value we may enter Table A20, and determine the statistical significance of it.

Table A20 contains critical values of ΣT for both one- and two-tailed tests and for an N ranging from 6 to 50. In this table, N refers to the number of matched or paired scores. For our sample, $N = 21$. Where $N = 21$ intersects with the .05 level of significance (two-tailed test) identifies the critical value of ΣT. We must observe a ΣT equal to or smaller than the ΣT critical value shown in the table. We have observed an $\Sigma T = 13$, which is equal to or smaller than the critical

ΣT value of 59. We can reject H_0 at the .05 level of significance and conclude that the MBO program has probably affected employee productivity.

When larger samples are encountered (i.e., whenever $N > 50$), Table A20 cannot be used. Instead, an approximation of Z may be computed by the formula

$$Z = \frac{\Sigma T - \dfrac{N(N+1)}{4}}{\sqrt{\dfrac{N(N+1)(2N+1)}{24}}},$$

where

ΣT = sum of the ranks with the less frequent sign
N = number of pairs of scores

The values 4 and 24 are constants and are used regardless of the value of N or ΣT.

The resulting Z value is interpreted as we would interpret any Z value for the Z test of significance for either one- or two-tailed situations. For instance, if we were to use the observed $\Sigma T = 13$ in this formula, we would have

$$Z = \frac{13 - \dfrac{(21)(21+1)}{4}}{\sqrt{\dfrac{(21)(21+1)(42+1)}{24}}}$$

$$= \frac{-102.5}{\sqrt{\dfrac{19{,}866}{24}}}$$

$$= \frac{-102.5}{\sqrt{827.75}}$$

$$= \frac{-102.5}{28.8}$$

$$= -3.56.$$

An observed Z value of -3.56 (the direction of the Z value is irrelevant for a two-tailed test) would be significant at less than .01, where a critical value of + or − 2.58 would be exceeded.

Assumptions of the Wilcoxon Test. The primary assumptions of the Wilcoxon matched pairs–signed ranks test are (1) randomness, (2) the interval level of measurement, and (3) related samples. Since the magnitudes of score differences are ranked, some researchers have utilized the Wilcoxon test for data at the ordinal level. Conventionally, this test is applied to ordinal data, although a strict application of the level of measurement rule would restrict it to the interval level only.

Advantages and Disadvantages of the Wilcoxon Test. One advantage of the Wilcoxon test is that it may be applied to a larger number of pairs of scores compared with the more restricted randomization test. In a sense, the Wilcoxon test in application begins where the randomization test ends. It is amenable to both one- and two-tailed test interpretations, and the researcher can readily determine the direction associated with score changes if this has been predicted. Of course, a table for quick interpretation of ΣT values for N's ranging from 6 to 50 is also an advantage.

This test is easy to compute. For larger sample sizes where N exceeds 50 an approximation of Z can be obtained by an alternative formula provided. Although this formula appears somewhat complex, it has contributed to the flexibility and popularity of this nonparametric procedure. The Wilcoxon test is probably the best nonparametric procedure equivalent to the t test when related samples are found. It is approximately 95 percent as powerful as t.

□ k-SAMPLE TESTS: INDEPENDENT SAMPLES

When the researcher has data measured according to an interval scale and is examining differences between three or more groups, one possible option might be to examine differences between two groups at a time with the t test. But the researcher would be faced with multiple applications of the t test in order to examine differences between all group pairings. For instance, if the investigator were looking at differences among eight groups, there would be

$$\frac{k(k-1)}{2} \quad \text{or} \quad \frac{(8)(8-1)}{2} = \frac{56}{2} = 28$$

different t tests to be computed (where k is the number of groups). The results of 28 separate t tests would tell the researcher which groups differed from one another, but an inordinate amount of time would be spent in tedious computational work. Fortunately, a procedure is available that examines differences between k samples simultaneously. Such a procedure is called the *one-way analysis-of-variance* or *F* test.

The *F* Test

The *F* test for analysis of variance is a procedure that examines *k* groups and determines whether a significant difference exists between them on some interval-level characteristic. The *F* test answers the question: Does a significant difference exist anywhere between *k* samples on the variable measured? It has several stringent assumptions underlying its appropriate application in the social science literature, but if these assumptions are met, it is as powerful as the *t* test regarding tests of H_0. The following example is provided.

Giacquinta (1975) examined various attitudes of school officials and other persons connected with school administration. As a part of his research, he wanted to know whether different groups of educators were equally receptive to the idea of introducing sex education into elementary schools. Four groups of educators were subsequently examined: 15 school board members, 19 classroom teachers, 14 school administrators, and 18 sex education specialists.

Measures of different variables, including receptivity, were obtained from all persons involved in the study. Receptivity refers to the degree to which any person would consider a change or innovation in an organization, in this case an elementary school. Associated with any innovation is a degree of risk. Not all persons are in agreement as to when sex education ought to be introduced in the schools. In some communities, hostile reactions from parents could place a teacher's position in jeopardy as well as the positions of other school officials. Therefore, we might expect that different groups of educators with different vested interests might also differ on their degree of receptivity to the idea of sex education being taught in elementary schools. Based on such theorizing by Giacquinta, the following hypothesis set is suggested:

H_0: There is no difference among four groups of educators in their degree of receptivity toward sex education in elementary schools.

H_1: There is a difference among four groups of educators in their degree of receptivity toward sex education in elementary schools.

$$P \leqslant .01 \text{ (two-tailed test).}$$

Table 8.7 shows four groups of educators distributed according to their raw scores on a receptivity scale. The larger the score, the greater the receptivity to change. Table 8.7 contains the following relevant information: (1) the raw scores of all group members, (2) the sums of scores for each group, (3) the sums of the squared scores

TABLE 8.7
Receptivity Scores for Four Groups of Educators.

Sex Education Specialists ($N_1 = 18$)		*Classroom Teachers* ($N_2 = 19$)		*School Administrators* ($N_3 = 14$)		*School Board Members* ($N_4 = 15$)	
X_i	X_i^2	X_i	X_i^2	X_i	X_i^2	X_i	X_i^2
22	484	19	361	19	361	3	9
19	361	14	196	18	324	9	81
14	196	13	169	12	144	12	144
24	576	22	484	12	144	9	81
21	441	28	784	14	196	7	49
20	400	17	289	12	144	18	324
24	576	14	196	10	100	7	49
23	529	15	225	7	49	9	81
17	289	12	144	9	81	14	196
16	256	9	81	11	121	10	100
29	841	19	361	12	144	9	81
15	225	22	484	21	441	8	64
26	676	20	400	11	121	8	64
23	529	19	361	13	169	10	100
23	529	17	289			11	121
28	784	11	121				
21	441	14	196				
25	625	17	289				
		17	289				
$\Sigma X_1 = \overline{390}$	$\Sigma X_1^2 = \overline{8758}$	$\Sigma X_2 = \overline{319}$	$\Sigma X_2^2 = \overline{5719}$	$\Sigma X_3 = \overline{181}$	$\Sigma X_3^2 = \overline{2539}$	$\Sigma X_4 = \overline{144}$	$\Sigma X_4^2 = \overline{1544}$
$\overline{X}_1 = 21.7$		$\overline{X}_2 = 16.8$		$\overline{X}_3 = 12.9$		$\overline{X}_4 = 9.6$	

$\overline{X}_T = 15.7$

for each group, (4) the mean receptivity score for each group, (5) the grand mean or mean of means for all groups combined, and (6) each sample size. These values will be instrumental in determining "variation" between and within the four groups.

It is apparent from an inspection of Table 8.7 that there is some variation from one group to the next. Each group has a different mean score. We label this type of variation *between-group variation.* It is also observed that the members of each group generally have different scores from one another. Such score variations within each group is termed *within-group variation.*

The sum of between-group variation and within-group variation is equal to *total variation.* A mathematical definition of each type of variation is provided below:

Between-group variation is determined by squaring the differences of each sample mean from the grand mean, weighting the squared difference by each sample N, and summing these products. The sum of these products is called SS_{bet} or "sums of squares for between-group variation." Algebraically, we would have

$$SS_{bet} = \sum N_k(\overline{X}_k - \overline{X}_T)^2,$$

where

N_k = sample size for the kth sample
$\overline{X}_k$ = mean for the kth sample
$\overline{X}_T$ = grand mean of all elements

Within-group variation is determined by summing all squared deviations of each raw score from its sample mean across all samples, or

$$SS_{within} = \sum (X_{ik} - \overline{X}_k)^2,$$

where

X_{ik} = each individual score across k samples (i.e., ith score, kth sample)
$\overline{X}_k$ = kth sample mean

Finally, the sum of SS_{bet} and SS_{within} equals SS_{total}, or the total sums of squares. The total sums of squares is computed by summing the squared deviation of each raw score from the grand mean across all samples:

$$SS_{total} = \sum (X_{ik} - \overline{X}_T)^2,$$

where

X_{ik} = ith raw score in the kth sample
$\overline{X}_T$ = grand mean

The SS_{bet} and SS_{within} are key elements in the solution of our problem, the test of H_0. The SS_{total} is primarily useful in that it provides us with a check on our computational accuracy. The methods of computing SS_{bet} and SS_{within} (and subsequently, SS_{total}) involve laborious, but not difficult, calculator work. A short method for computing these values can be used which is based exclusively on the data provided in Table 8.7. This method involves the calculation of three terms:

(1) $$\left(\frac{\sum X_T}{\sum N_k}\right)^2$$

where

$\sum X_T$ = sum of all scores across all groups
$\sum N_k$ = sum of all sample sizes

(2) $\sum X_k^2$ or the sums of all squared scores across all samples

(3) $$\sum \frac{(\sum X_k)^2}{N_k}$$

where

$\sum X_k$ = sum of scores for each sample
N_k = sample size for each sample

Carrying out these computations from the data in Table 8.7, we have:

(1) $$\frac{(390 + 319 + 181 + 144)^2}{(18 + 19 + 14 + 15)} = \frac{(1034)^2}{66}$$

$$= \frac{1{,}069{,}156}{66}$$

$$= 16{,}199.333.$$

(2) $$(8758 + 5719 + 2539 + 1544) = 18{,}560.$$

(3) $$\frac{(390)^2}{18} + \frac{(319)^2}{19} + \frac{(181)^2}{14} + \frac{(144)^2}{15}$$

$$= \frac{152{,}100}{18} + \frac{101{,}761}{19} + \frac{32{,}761}{14} + \frac{20{,}736}{15}$$

$$= 8450 + 5355.842 + 2340.071 + 1382.4$$

$$= 17{,}528.313.$$

With these terms, SS_{bet}, SS_{within}, and SS_{total} can be computed as follows.

$$SS_{bet} = (3) - (1) = 17{,}528.313 - 16{,}199.333 = 1328.98.$$

$$SS_{within} = (2) - (3) = 18{,}560 - 17{,}528.313 = 1031.687.$$

$$SS_{total} = (2) - (1) = 18{,}560 - 16{,}199.333 = 2360.667.$$

Slight differences may result when using both the long and the shorter methods presented above. This is not serious and only reflects rounding error. With these values we may now construct an analysis-of-variance summary table, or ANOVA summary, such as that shown in Table 8.8.

The information in Table 8.8 is determined as follows. The first column, "source of variation," simply identifies the different kinds of variation that exist between and within groups. The sum of these two kinds of variation equals total variation.

The second column, SS, refers to sums of squares. The principal components are SS_{bet}, SS_{within}, and their sum, SS_{total}. We enter the values for these determined from the short method as shown.

The third column, df, refers to degrees of freedom. The df's for between groups are determined by $k - 1$, or the number of groups (k) less 1, or $4 - 1 = 3$. If we were dealing with 10 groups, the df for between groups would be $10 - 1 = 9$. If we were dealing with seven groups, df would be $7 - 1 = 6$; and so on. Df for within-group variation are determined by summing each sample size less 1 for each of the samples, or $(N_1 - 1) + (N_2 - 1) + (N_3 - 1) + (N_4 - 1)$ or $(18 - 1) + (19 - 1) + (14 - 1) + (15 - 1) = 17 + 18 + 13 + 14 = 62$ df for within groups. These values are entered in Table 8.8 as shown.

Total df are determined by summing all N's and subtracting 1

TABLE 8.8
Analysis-of-Variance Summary Table.

Source of Variation	SS	df[a]	MS	F_{obs}[b]
Between groups	1328.98 (SS_{bet})	3	442.99 (MS_{bet})	26.62
Within groups	1031.69 (SS_{within})	62	16.64 (MS_{within})	
Total	2360.67 (SS_{total})	65		

[a]Between-groups df = $k - 1$ (k = number of groups); within-groups df = $\Sigma(N_k - 1)$ (N_k = each sample size); and total df = $\Sigma N_k - 1$.

[b]$F_{obs} = \dfrac{MS_{bet}}{MS_{within}} = \dfrac{442.99}{16.64} = 26.62.$

from this sum. Given the information in Table 8.6, we would have df total = (18 + 19 + 14 + 15) - 1 or (66 - 1) = 65 df. Algebraic expressions for computing all of these df values are provided in a footnote to Table 8.8.

Once we have determined df for between, within, and total variation, we divide SS_{bet} by df for between groups. Also, we divide SS_{within} by df for within groups. These results are shown in the fourth column, labeled MS. This refers to mean square. Our resulting division of df into SS yields these MS values.

For the data in Table 8.8, MS_{bet} and MS_{within} are determined as follows:

$$MS_{bet} = \frac{SS_{bet}}{df_{bet}} = \frac{1328.98}{3} = 442.99.$$

$$MS_{within} = \frac{SS_{within}}{df_{within}} = \frac{1031.687}{62} = 16.64.$$

There is no such thing as MS_{total}, and therefore there is no need to make this computation.

We are now ready to determine our F_{obs}, the observed value of F. The F *statistic* is a measure of the degree to which differences exist between k samples. The larger the F value we observe, the more significant the difference between the groups. We obtain our F_{obs} as follows:

$$F_{obs} = \frac{MS_{bet}}{MS_{within}} = \frac{442.99}{16.64} = 26.62.$$

We must now take our observed value of F to Table A16. This table contains critical values of F for both the .01 and .05 levels of significance. We must equal or exceed the critical value of F shown in the body of the table with our observed F value in order to reject H_0.

Which F value we must equal or exceed is determined by where our df values intersect in the body of the table. With df's of 3 and 62, respectively (df for between groups = 3, and df for within groups = 62), we may examine Table A16.

Across the top of the table are various degrees of freedom for between groups. Down the sides of the table are df for within groups. We move across the top of table to df = 3, and then down the side of the table to df = 62. It will be noted that we do not have exactly 62 df tabled here. Df's for within groups are provided for 60 and 65. Since interpolation is not appropriate for the F distribution, we simply use the smaller df point, 60 df, to determine the critical F value. Where 3 df and 60 df intersect in the body of the table identifies two critical F values. The first, lightface critical F value is for the .05 level of significance; the second, boldface critical value is for the .01 level. Our hypothesis test is being made at the .01 level of significance in this case, and therefore the critical value of F shown in the table is 4.13. If our observed F value equals or exceeds 4.13, we can reject H_0 and support H_1. Given an observed F value = 26.62, H_0 is clearly rejected. We may tentatively conclude that a difference in receptivity scores exists somewhere between the groups of educators.

It should be noted that a two-tailed test of the hypothesis set was conducted. In almost all situations involving k samples of elements, the researcher is interested primarily in determining if a difference exists between the groups regardless of the direction of the difference. If the investigator wants to specify directionality for some reason, the mean scores of the different groups can be examined. For the data in Table 8.7, the sex education specialists had the highest degree of receptivity ($\overline{X}_1 = 21.7$); the school board members had the lowest degree of this variable ($\overline{X}_4 = 9.6$). Directionally, there was a declining receptivity to sex education in elementary schools from sex education specialists, to classroom teachers, to school administrators, and finally to school board members. In this fashion, commentary about directional differences between groups can be made despite the fact that a two-tailed test of the hypothesis has been conducted.

Assumptions of the F Test. The assumptions underlying the F test are (1) randomness, (2) the interval level of measurement, (3) an approximation of the unit normal distribution for each set of scores throughout the k samples, (4) independent samples, and (5) homogeneity of variance or "equal variances."

The *homogeneity-of-variance* assumption does not mean literally that the sample variances have to be identical to one another. But the variances should be sufficiently similar in magnitude to avoid potential distortion of the resulting F value.

A simple procedure designed to determine whether or not homogeneity of variance exists among k samples is Hartley's F_{max} test. The F_{max} test yields an F_{max} statistic based on the ratio of the largest variance to the smallest variance for k samples. The formula for the Hartley F_{max} test is

$$F_{max} = \frac{s^2_{largest}}{s^2_{smallest}},$$

where

$s^2_{largest}$ = largest observed sample variance for the k samples
$s^2_{smallest}$ = smallest observed sample variance for the k samples

The largest and smallest variances are used because if a significant difference does not exist between them, the other variance differences will not be significant either. The sample variance for the four groups of educators in Table 8.7 are

$$s_1^2 = 17.1 \quad s_2^2 = 19.1 \quad s_3^2 = 14.2 \quad s_4^2 = 10.8$$
$$N_1 = 18 \quad N_2 = 19 \quad N_3 = 14 \quad N_4 = 15.$$

We observe that the largest variance is 19.1 and that the smallest variance is 10.8. Using the F_{max} formula, we determine our F_{max} as follows:

$$F_{max} = \frac{s^2_{largest}}{s^2_{smallest}}$$
$$= \frac{19.1}{10.8}$$
$$= 1.77.$$

With an F_{max} observed = 1.77, we turn to Table A19 to determine the critical value of F_{max}. Across the top of the table are various values of k. In this case, k refers to the number of sample variances from the original data in Table 8.7. There are four variances, and therefore $k = 4$.

Down the left-hand side of the table are various df (degrees of freedom). Df are equal to $N - 1$, where N is any sample size when sample sizes are equal. When sample sizes are unequal, N is the largest sample size. The largest sample size is 19, and therefore 19 is used for entering this table.

Since Table A19 does not have precisely 19 - 1 or 18 df, we will make the decision to use the larger df point on either side of 18 df. Since 18 df is between 15 df and 20 df, we will use 20 df for purposes of entering the table. We locate the F_{max} critical value where

$k = 4$ and df = 20 intersect in the body of the table. The body of the table contains pairs of critical values. The first of these values is for the .05 level of significance; the second $F_{\max}$ critical value is for the .01 level. Since our original F test was made at the .01 level of significance, we will follow through with this same level of significance in the $F_{\max}$ test. Never change levels of significance here.

The critical value of $F_{\max} = 4.3$. If our observed $F_{\max}$ value equals or exceeds 4.3, we do not have homogeneity of variance. If our observed $F_{\max}$ is smaller than 4.3, we do have homogeneity of variance, and this important assumption is not violated. Our observed $F_{\max}$ of 1.77 is definitely smaller than 4.3, and therefore it can be safely assumed that homogeneity of variance exists for the data in Table 8.7.

An alternative test for homogeneity of variance is the *Cochran C test.* This test is computed as follows:

$$C = \frac{s^2_{\text{largest}}}{\sum s^2_k},$$

where

s^2_{largest} = largest sample variance

$\sum s^2_k$ = sum of all sample variances

Using the information about the sample variances provided above, we would compute C as follows:

$$\begin{aligned} C &= \frac{19.1}{17.1 + 19.1 + 14.2 + 10.8} \\ &= \frac{19.1}{61.2} \\ &= .31. \end{aligned}$$

We turn to Table A10 and determine the critical value of C.

First, we select k across the top of the table, which is equal to the number of sample variances, $k = 4$. Next, we move down the left-hand column, df (degrees of freedom). Here the df's are determined in the same way they were determined for the Hartley $F_{\max}$ test, or df $= N - 1$ (where N = any sample size if sample sizes are equal; N = largest sample size if sample sizes are unequal). In this instance, the largest sample size is 19. Therefore, df $= N - 1$ or $19 - 1$ or 18. Since this df is between the 16 and 36 df shown, we will select the larger of the two df points as our reference.

Where $k = 4$ and 36 df intersect in the body of the table identifies critical values of C. There are pairs of values presented in this table as well. The first of the two values of C is the critical value for the .05 level of significance. The second critical value of C is appropriate for the .01 level. The critical value of C from this table is .4057 (.01 level of significance). If we observe a C equal to or larger than .4057, we do not have homogeneity of variance among the samples. Our observed $C = .31$, and therefore homogeneity of variance is achieved.

Advantages and Disadvantages of the F Test. When the assumptions have been met, the F test is the most powerful measure of differences between k samples. It is an extension of the t test in a sense, and it has equivalent power. It is not particularly difficult to apply, especially using the short method of sums of squares computation, and tables exist for determining the significance of F observed values.

The stringent assumptions associated with this procedure make it difficult to apply legitimately in social research. Often, the normality assumption will be violated, or the homogeneity of variance assumption will not be met. Add to this the fact that the interval level of measurement is technically required, and the result is a test where assumptions are difficult to achieve. Some researchers have shown that under certain conditions where assumptions have been violated (particularly the normality and homogeneity of variance assumptions), the effect on the magnitude of the F observed value has been negligible. This has led to the questionable practice of using the F test without paying any attention to the important assumptions associated with it. Since there are alternative k sample tests that are nearly as powerful as the F test but have few restrictive assumptions, it does not make sense to knowingly violate assumptions of the F test simply because other people do it. When the F test cannot safely be applied to k independent samples because of possible assumption violations that have occurred, a useful alternative is the Kruskal–Wallis one-way analysis-of-variance or H test. This will be presented in Chapter 10.

One drawback of the F test is that it does not reveal where significant differences between groups exist. It simply says that a difference exists somewhere among the groups. We can assume that at least the largest and smallest sample means are different statistically if H_0 is rejected by applying the F test. But what about the largest and the second smallest sample means? To determine where significant differences between groups are, we could resort to using the t test and compare each mean with every other mean. But this is a cumbersome process, as has already been noted. Fortunately, there exists a number of procedures that permit the researcher to make a single test of significance of difference for k samples.

Tests that examine the significance of difference of all sample means after an initial F test has revealed that a difference exists somewhere among them are often referred to as *postmortem tests.* These procedures make it possible to assess all mean differences in one neat series of steps, thereby avoiding multiple t tests to probe all mean differences.

The Newman-Keuls Procedure

A rapid test for determining the significance of difference between all sample means simultaneously is the *Newman–Keuls procedure.* To carry out this test, we must arrange all observed means into a *table of ordered means* such as that shown in Table 8.9. All sample means are arranged from smallest to largest across the top of the table and down the left-hand side, as shown. Next, all differences between means are entered where the various means intersect in the body of the table. In the column immediately to the right of the mean differences, q, a value is entered that is taken from Table A17.

Turning to Table A17, we determine the q values as follows. Across the top of the table is r, the number of steps between ordered means. The r of interest to us is equal to the number of means we are examining. In this case, $r = 4$. (If we were examining 10 means, $r = 10$; if we were examining eight means, $r = 8$; and so on.) Down the left-hand side of the table are df. These degrees of freedom are determined by the df for within-group variation from the ANOVA summary table, Table 8.8. From Table 8.8, we determine that df = 62. Since we are between two df points (60 and 120), we will select the smaller df point for our reference, 60 df. Where these values, $r = 4$ and df = 60, intersect in the body of the table defines the first value of q, which we will place in the table of ordered

TABLE 8.9
Table of Ordered Means.

	9.6	*12.9*	*16.8*	*21.7*	q	$(q)(s_{\bar{t}})$
9.6	–	3.3	7.2[a]	12.1[a]	4.60	5.01
12.9		–	3.9	8.8[a]	4.28	4.66
16.8			–	4.9[a]	3.76	4.10
21.7				–		

[a]Significant mean difference.

means, Table 8.9. Again, we encounter a pair of values of q in the body of the table. The first value is the .05 level of significance q; the second is the .01 value of q. Since our original hypothesis test (the F test) was carried out at the .01 level of significance, we will continue using this same level of significance in the Newman–Keuls procedure.

The first value of q is 4.60 (for the .01 level), and we enter it in the q column in Table 8.9 as shown. The other q values in the column are derived by moving exactly one space to the left of the $q = 4.60$ (to the column in Table A17 where $r = 3$) and identifying the next adjacent $q = 4.28$. The final q value is found by moving to the next column to the left (where $r = 2$) and picking up this $q = 3.76$.

The final column in Table 8.9 is the product of each q value and $s_{\bar{t}}$. The value of $s_{\bar{t}}$, the standard error of the group means, is determined as follows:

$$s_{\bar{t}} = \sqrt{\frac{\text{MS}_{\text{within}}}{N}},$$

where

$\text{MS}_{\text{within}}$ = value shown in the ANOVA summary table (in this case, Table 8.8)

N = any sample size if the samples are equal, or the smallest sample size if the samples are unequal

Since the smallest sample size is 14 and $\text{MS}_{\text{within}}$ from Table 8.7 is 16.64, we may solve for $s_{\bar{t}}$ as follows:

$$s_{\bar{t}} = \sqrt{\frac{16.64}{14}}$$

$$= \sqrt{1.188}$$

$$= 1.09.$$

With an $s_{\bar{t}}$ value of 1.09, we multiply all values of q by this value, or

$$(4.60)\,(1.09) = 5.01$$

$$(4.28)\,(1.09) = 4.66$$

$$(3.76)\,(1.09) = 4.10.$$

These products are placed in the last column in Table 8.9 as shown. These values are critical values that the mean differences in the body of the table must equal or exceed in order to be significantly different at the .01 level.

Lines are drawn in the table of ordered means as shown to identify "sectors" associated with each of the critical values in the final column. The first sector will contain one mean difference (12.1), the second sector two mean differences (8.8 and 7.2), and the third sector three mean differences (4.9, 3.9, and 3.3). Critical values are used only in their designated sector as follows.

The first critical value, 5.01, is compared with the first mean difference to the left adjacent to it, 12.1. Since this mean difference equals or exceeds 5.01, it becomes the first significant mean difference. The second critical value, 4.66, is compared with the two mean differences to the left of it in its sector–8.8 and 7.2, respectively. Since both of these mean differences equal or exceed 4.66, they are significant at the .01 level. Finally, the critical value of 4.10 is compared with the three mean differences to the left of it in its sector–4.9, 3.9, and 3.3, respectively. Only the mean difference of 4.9 equals or exceeds the critical value of 4.10 and it is also significant. The other mean differences fail to equal or exceed this value and are not significant statistically.

The researcher is now ready to report a summary of findings concerning which mean differences (and which means) are significantly different at the .01 level:

9.6 is significantly different from 21.7

9.6 is significantly different from 16.8

12.9 is significantly different from 21.7

16.8 is significantly different from 21.7.

All other mean differences are not significant (i.e., 9.6 is not significantly different from 12.9, and 12.9 is not significantly different from 16.8). The Newman–Keuls procedure is completed.

The Scheffé Procedure

An alternative procedure for determining the significance of difference between k sample means is the Scheffé procedure. It is somewhat more conservative compared with the Newman–Keuls procedure, in that it yields fewer significant mean differences when applied to the same data in most research situations. A critical F value is determined by the following formula:

$$F_{\text{critical value}} = (k - 1)(F),$$

where

k = number of samples studied
F = critical value of F in the original F test (for the data in Table 8.8 in this instance)

Since $k = 4$ and our original critical value of F with 3 df and 62 df was 4.13, we may determine $F_{\text{critical value}}$ for the Scheffé test as follows:

$$F_{\text{critical value}} = (4 - 1)(4.13) = (3)(4.13) = 12.39.$$

All mean differences are evaluated by computing a special F observed value for each pair of means by the following formula:

$$F_{\text{obs}} = \frac{(\overline{X}_1 - \overline{X}_2)^2}{\dfrac{(\text{MS}_w)(N_1 + N_2)}{(N_1)(N_2)}},$$

where

$\overline{X}_1$ and $\overline{X}_2$ = any pair of sample means to be compared
MS_w = mean-square within-group variation taken from the ANOVA summary table
N_1 and N_2 = sample sizes for the two means being compared in the numerator term

As an example, suppose that we assess the difference between $\overline{X}_1$ and $\overline{X}_2$ from Table 8.7. $\overline{X}_1 = 21.7$ ($N_1 = 18$) and $\overline{X}_2 = 16.8$ ($N_2 = 19$). With these data and with the $\text{MS}_{\text{within}}$ value of 16.64 taken from Table 8.8, we may determine our first observed F value:

$$F_{1\ \text{obs}} = \frac{(21.7 - 16.8)^2}{\dfrac{(16.64)(18 + 19)}{(18)(19)}} = \frac{24.01}{\dfrac{615.68}{342}} = \frac{24.01}{1.80} = 13.34.$$

A second computation will be helpful here. Let us examine a second F value by comparing $\overline{X}_1$ and $\overline{X}_3$:

$$F_{2\ \text{obs}} = \frac{(21.7 - 12.9)^2}{\dfrac{(16.64)(18 + 14)}{(18)(14)}}$$

$$= \frac{77.44}{\dfrac{532.48}{252}}$$

$$= \frac{77.44}{2.11}$$

$$= 36.70.$$

We continue in this fashion until all mean comparisons have been made. All mean comparisons have been evaluated and placed in Table 8.10. Asterisks have been placed by all F observed values that are significant at the .01 level. All observed values of F that equal or exceed the F critical value of 12.39 are significant at the .01 level of significance.

It is clear from Table 8.10 that the mean differences judged significant by the Newman-Keuls procedure in Table 8.9 are also significant using the Scheffé method. In the majority of instances, however, the Scheffé method will generally yield fewer significant mean differences compared with the Newman-Keuls procedure. To that extent, the Scheffé method is more conservative.

A short statement on some differences between the Newman-Keuls procedure and the Scheffé method are in order. First, the Scheffé method is somewhat more involved in computing observed F values compared with the Newman-Keuls procedure. The New-

TABLE 8.10
Table of Ordered Means Showing Significant Mean Differences by the Scheffé Method.

	9.6	*12.9*	*16.8*	*21.7*
9.6	–	$F_6 = 4.74$	$F_5 = 26.05$*	$F_3 = 71.98$*
12.9		–	$F_4 = 7.38$	$F_2 = 36.70$*
16.8			–	$F_1 = 13.34$*
21.7				–

Note: Critical value of F for the Scheffé method = 12.39. All observed F values in body of table above are significant at .01 where asterisks are designated. These are F observed values that equal or exceed the critical value of 12.39.

man–Keuls procedure is simply more rapid to apply. The results of the Newman–Keuls procedure will yield more significant mean differences compared with the Scheffé method. To that extent, the Scheffé method is more conservative. There are at least seven or eight different procedures for determining where significant differences between means occur after an overall significant *F* value has been observed in the *F* test. The Scheffé method is the most conservative; the Newman–Keuls procedure is toward the less conservative side. Depending on the rigor the researcher wishes to introduce in evaluating significant mean differences, both procedures offer more or less conservative alternatives which are perfectly acceptable in research work.

□ TWO-WAY ANALYSIS OF VARIANCE

In the last section we examined a study of four samples of educators and the degree to which they differed according to their receptivity toward sex education in the elementary school. The *F* test or one-way analysis of variance allowed us to determine whether a difference existed among sex educational specialists, classroom teachers, school board members, and school administrators.

Under certain conditions, a researcher may want to determine if other factors contribute to variations in scores between persons in different groups in addition to their occupational or professional designations. For instance, suppose that we were to speculate about educators and reason that their "receptivity" toward sex education in the elementary school might be partially a function of their "length of service in education." In the original research by Giacquinta (1975), a total of 66 educators was studied. If we asked these persons to indicate how long they had been associated with education as a profession, we may find that classroom teachers would vary considerably in years of teaching, that school administrators varied according to how long they had performed administrative tasks, and so on. Our reasoning might be that those persons affiliated with education longer would tend to have more rigid and traditional views and would be less inclined to favor sex education in the elementary school. By the same token, those persons who had been in their profession a briefer period might be more inclined to try new and different instructional methods and innovative programs such as sex education.

Recasting the data presented in Table 8.7 by *cross-tabulating* each of the four groups of educators with "length of educational service," we might have a table similar to Table 8.11.

Two-Way Analysis of Variance, Educators by Length of Service.

Length of Service	Educational Group								
	Sex Education Specialists		Classroom Teachers		School Administrators		School Board		
	X_i	X_i^2	X_i	X_i^2	X_i	X_i^2	X_i	X_i^2	
1 to 6 years	22	484	19	361	19	361	3	9	
	14	196	13	169	12	144	7	49	
	21	441	28	784	14	196	9	81	
	24	576	14	196	10	100	9	81	
	17	289	12	144	9	81	8	64	
	29	841	19	361	12	144	8	64	$\overline{X}_{1R} = 15.5$
	26	676	20	400	11	121	10	100	
	23	529	17	289					
	21	441	14	196					
			17	289					
	$\Sigma X_1 = \overline{197}$	$\Sigma X_1^2 = \overline{4473}$	$\Sigma X_2 = \overline{173}$	$\Sigma X_2^2 = \overline{3189}$	$\Sigma X_3 = \overline{87}$	$\Sigma X_3^2 = \overline{1147}$	$\Sigma X_4 = \overline{54}$	$\Sigma X_4^2 = \overline{448}$	$\Sigma N = 33$
	$\overline{X}_1 = 21.9$		$\overline{X}_2 = 17.3$		$\overline{X}_3 = 12.4$		$\overline{X}_4 = 7.7$		$\Sigma X_T^2 = 9257$
	$N_1 = 9$		$N_2 = 10$		$N_3 = 7$		$N_4 = 7$		$\Sigma X_T = 511$
7+ years	19	361	14	196	18	324	9	81	
	24	576	22	484	12	144	12	144	
	20	400	17	289	12	144	9	81	
	23	529	15	225	7	49	18	324	
	16	256	9	81	11	121	7	49	$\overline{X}_{2R} = 15.8$
	15	225	22	484	21	441	14	196	
	23	529	19	361	13	169	10	100	
	28	784	11	121			11	121	
	25	625	17	289					
	$\Sigma X_5 = \overline{193}$	$\Sigma X_5^2 = \overline{4285}$	$\Sigma X_6 = \overline{146}$	$\Sigma X_6^2 = \overline{2530}$	$\Sigma X_7 = \overline{94}$	$\Sigma X_7^2 = \overline{1392}$	$\Sigma X_8 = \overline{90}$	$\Sigma X_8^2 = \overline{1096}$	
	$\overline{X}_5 = 21.4$		$\overline{X}_6 = 16.2$		$\overline{X}_7 = 13.4$		$\overline{X}_8 = 11.2$		$\Sigma N = 33$
	$N_5 = 9$		$N_6 = 9$		$N_7 = 7$		$N_8 = 8$		$\Sigma X_T^2 = 9303$
	$\overline{X}_{1C} = 21.7$		$\overline{X}_{2C} = 16.8$		$\overline{X}_{3C} = 12.9$		$\overline{X}_{4C} = 9.6$		$\Sigma X_T = 523$

Table 8.11 represents a cross-tabulation of "years of service" (down the left-hand column) and educational group (across the top of the table). "Length of service" has been dichotomized according to 1–6 years and 7 or more years of service. Those persons who have been affiliated with education for 1 to 6 years are in the first row in the upper half of the table. Those persons who have been in education 7 or more years are placed in the lower half of the table. Receptivity scores for each subgrouping of educators according to length of service make up eight subparts of the table. For instance, the first subpart of the table consists of sex education specialists with 1 to 6 years of service. Their mean receptivity score is shown as $\overline{X}_1 = 21.9$. In another subpart of the table, school administrators with 7 or more years of service are shown with an $\overline{X}_7 = 13.4$.

Means are computed for each of the eight subparts of the table as shown from $\overline{X}_1$ to $\overline{X}_8$. Grand means are computed for both rows and columns as well. The first grand mean for the upper row, $\overline{X}_{1R} = 15.5$, is the mean of means, where $\overline{X}_1$, $\overline{X}_2$, $\overline{X}_3$, and $\overline{X}_4$ have been averaged (and weighted according to each N). The second grand mean for the second row, $\overline{X}_{2R} = 15.8$, is the average of $\overline{X}_5$, $\overline{X}_6$, $\overline{X}_7$, and $\overline{X}_8$ (again, weighted by each sample N).

Grand means for the columns are also computed. $\overline{X}_{1C} = 21.7$, and is made up of $\overline{X}_1$ and $\overline{X}_5$ (weighted according to each sample N). $\overline{X}_{2C} = 16.8$ and is made up of the average of $\overline{X}_2$ and $\overline{X}_6$ (weighted according to each sample N); and so on.

We will label "length of service" factor 1. Factor 2 will be assigned to "educational grouping" across the top of the table.

We are interested in three things: (1) What is the main effect of factor 1 (length of service in education) on receptivity scores? (2) What is the main effect of factor 2 (educational grouping) on receptivity scores? (3) What is the interaction effect of both factors jointly on receptivity scores? *Main effects* are effects on score values (dependent variables) which are likely attributable to independent variables such as length of service in education or educational grouping. *Interaction effects* give us an indication of the significance of interplay between different factors on receptivity scores.

The main effect of factor 1 (length of educational service) is evaluated by determining whether there is a significant difference between row grand means. The main effect of factor 2 (educational grouping) is evaluated by seeing whether differences exist between grand means for the columns. Interaction effects are determined to exist if substantial differences are found on mean receptivity scores for persons in each group with different lengths of educational service. Differences between the following pairs of means do not appear to be substantial: $\overline{X}_1$ and $\overline{X}_5$, $\overline{X}_2$ and $\overline{X}_6$, and $\overline{X}_3$ and $\overline{X}_7$. The difference between $\overline{X}_4$ and $\overline{X}_8$ is the largest mean difference, but we do

TABLE 8.12
Two-Way ANOVA Summary Table.

Source of Variation	SS	df	MS	*F*
Between				
Factor 1	2.3	1[a]	2.3	.137 n.s.
Factor 2	1329.0	3[b]	443.0	26.350* ($P < .01$)
Interaction				
1 × 2	54.3	3[c]	18.1	1.077 n.s.
Within	975.1	58[d]	16.812	
	2360.7	65[e]		

[a]Factor 1 df = number of row categories − 1 or 2 − 1 = 1.
[b]Factor 2 df = number of column categories − 1 or 4 − 1 = 3.
[c]Interaction of 1 and 2 df = (factor 1 df) (factor 2 df) = 1 × 3 = 3.
[d]Within df = N − number of subcategories or N − 8 or 66 − 8 = 58.
[e]Total df = total N − 1 or 66 − 1 = 65.

not yet know if this difference is sufficient to trigger a significant interaction effect.

To evaluate the two main effects (factor 1 and factor 2) on receptivity and to learn of the significance of any interaction effect on this dependent variable, we need to construct a two-way analysis-of-variance summary table such as that shown in Table 8.12. Table 8.12 is computed as follows: We must determine sums of squares (SS) for six different terms: (1) SS total, (2) SS between groups, (3) SS within groups, (4) SS for factor 1 (length of service), (5) SS for factor 2 (educational grouping), and (6) SS for factor 1 and factor 2 interaction. These terms are computed from the following formulas:

$$SS_{\text{total}} = \sum X_T^2 - \frac{\left(\sum X_T\right)^2}{N_T},$$

where

$\sum X_T^2 = \sum X_i^2$, sum of the squared scores across all samples (eight subsamples in this case)

$\sum X_T$ = sum of scores across all samples (eight subsamples in this case)

N_T = sum of all sample sizes across all samples

$$SS_{\text{total}} = 18{,}560 - \frac{(1034)^2}{66}$$
$$= 18{,}560 - 16{,}199.3$$
$$= 2360.7.$$

$$SS_{\text{bet}} = \sum\left[\frac{\left(\sum X_i\right)^2}{N_i}\right] - \frac{\left(\sum X_T\right)^2}{N_T},$$

where

$\sum X_i$ = sum of scores for each sample or the ith sample
N_i = sample size for the ith sample
$\sum X_T$ = sum of the scores across all samples
N_T = sum of all sample sizes across all samples

Therefore,

$$SS_{\text{bet}} = \left[\frac{(197)^2}{9} + \frac{(173)^2}{10} + \frac{(87)^2}{7} + \frac{(54)^2}{7} + \frac{(193)^2}{9} + \frac{(146)^2}{9} + \frac{(94)^2}{7} + \frac{(90)^2}{8}\right] - \frac{(1034)^2}{66}$$

$$= (4312.1 + 2992.9 + 1081.3 + 416.6 + 4138.8 + 2368.4 + 1262.3 + 1012.5) - 16{,}199.3$$

$$= 17{,}584.9 - 16{,}199.3$$

$$= 1385.6.$$

$$SS_{\text{within}} = SS_{\text{total}} - SS_{\text{bet}}$$

$$= 2360.7 - 1385.6$$

$$= 975.1.$$

$$SS_{\text{f1}} \text{ (SS for factor 1)} = \sum\left[\frac{\left(\sum X_{TR}\right)^2}{N_{iR}}\right] - \frac{\left(\sum X_T\right)^2}{N_T},$$

where

$\sum X_{TR}$ = sum of scores for each row
$\sum X_T$ = sum of scores across all samples
N_T = sum of all sample sizes across all samples
N_{iR} = sum of sample sizes for each row

Therefore,

$$SS_{\text{f1}} = \left[\frac{(511)^2}{33} + \frac{(523)^2}{33}\right] - \frac{(1034)^2}{66}$$

$$= (7912.8 + 8288.8) - 16{,}199.3$$

$$= 16{,}201.6 - 16{,}199.3$$

$$= 2.3.$$

$$SS_{\text{f2}} \text{ (SS for factor 2)} = \sum\left[\frac{\left(\sum X_{TC}\right)^2}{N_{iC}}\right] - \frac{\left(\sum X_T\right)^2}{N_T},$$

where

$\sum X_{TC}$ = sum of scores for each column

N_{iC} = sum of sample sizes for each column

$\sum X_T$ = sum of the scores across all samples

N_T = sum of all sample sizes across all samples

Therefore,

$$SS_{f2} = \left[\frac{(390)^2}{18} + \frac{(319)^2}{19} + \frac{(181)^2}{14} + \frac{(144)^2}{15}\right] - \frac{(1034)^2}{66}$$

$$= (8450 + 5355.8 + 2340.1 + 1382.4) - 16{,}199.3$$

$$= 17{,}528.3 - 16{,}199.3$$

$$= 1329.$$

$SS_{interaction}$ 1×2 = SS for interaction between factor 1 and factor 2

$$= SS_{between} - SS_{f1} - SS_{f2}$$

$$= 1385.6 - 2.3 - 1329$$

$$= 54.3.$$

These values are now placed in the two-way ANOVA summary table, Table 8.12, as shown in the SS column.

The degrees of freedom for each SS value are determined as follows. For factor 1 df, we determine the number of row categories and subtract 1, or 2 - 1 = 1 df. For factor 2 df, we determine the number of column categories and subtract 1, or 4 - 1 = 3 df. For interaction df, we multiply factor 1 df by factor 2 df, or (1)(3) = 3 df. For within df, we take the total N and subtract from this the number of subcategories or rows × columns, or N - (2)(4) = 66 - 8 = 58 df. For total df, we take the total N and subtract 1, or 66 - 1 = 65 df. These df computations are also provided as a footnote to Table 8.12.

Once we have determined df for each SS value, we divide each SS value by its accompanying df. This result will yield the various mean-square values (MS values) in the fourth column. For instance, 2.3/1 = 2.3 = MS for factor 1. For factor 2, we have 1329.0/3 = 443.0, or MS for factor 2, and so on. To maximize our computational accuracy, the various SS values in the second column should sum to SS_{total} or 2360.7, as shown. The df for each SS should also sum to df_{total} or 65 df.

We are now ready to determine the significance of the main effects (factors 1 and 2) and the interaction effects (factor 1 by factor 2) on the dependent variable, "receptivity." The significance of these effects will be evaluated by the magnitude of various F values computed from the MS terms. The F observed value for factor 1 is determined by dividing the MS for factor 1 by MS within groups or 2.3/16.812 = .137. This F observed is placed in the table as shown.

The F observed for factor 2 is determined by dividing the MS for factor 2 by MS within groups, or 443.0/16.812 = 26.350. This second F observed value is placed in the table as shown. Finally, the F observed for interaction of factor 1 and factor 2 is determined by dividing the MS for interaction by the MS within groups, or 18.1/16.812 = 1.077. This F observed value is placed in the table as shown.

We now enter Table A16 to determine the critical values of F that we must equal or exceed with each of our F observed values for the .01 level of significance. The .01 level of significance is used here inasmuch as it was used earlier in the F-test example with Giacquinta's research. The critical value of F for factor 1 will be the boldface value, where 1 df and 58 df intersect in the body of the table. We find 1 df across the top of the table and 58 df down the side. Since there is no 58 df value, we will return to the closest df value to 58 that is smaller. Where 55 df and 1 df intersect defines the critical F value = 7.12. Our first observed F value, .137, must equal or exceed 7.12 in order for factor 1 to be considered significant as a main effect at the .01 level of significance. In this case, the main effect of factor 1, years of service in education, is not significant statistically (n.s. is placed beside the F observed in Table 8.12 as shown to indicate "not significant").

For factor 2, the critical value of F is determined where 3 df and 58 df intersect in the body of the table. Moving across the top of the table to 3 df and down the left-hand side to 58 df, we again return to 55 df. Where 3 df and 55 df intersect in the body of the table defines the critical F value, which is 4.16 in this case. Our observed F value for factor 2, educational grouping, is 26.350. Since this observed F value equals or exceeds the critical value of F of 4.16, we conclude that factor 2, educational grouping, acts upon receptivity scores as a significant main effect. It does appear to make a difference in receptivity scores depending on the group to which one belongs.

Finally, to assess the significance of any interaction effect between factor 1 and factor 2 upon receptivity, we determine the critical value of F where 3 df and 58 df intersect in the body of the table. Again, we return to 4.16, the F value where 3 df across the top of the table intersects with 55 df down the side (55 df is the closest smaller df to our 58 df for MS within groups). Our observed F value of 1.077 fails to equal or exceed 4.16, and, we therefore conclude that there is no significant interaction effect on receptivity scores. It seems to make little difference how many years persons have been affiliated with educational activity professionally and how these years might influence one's receptivity to sex education in the elementary school. This completes the two-way analysis-of-variance test.

Assumptions of the Two-Way ANOVA

The assumptions of the two-way ANOVA are (1) randomness, (2) the interval level of measurement for the variable measured, (3) homogeneity of variances, (4) independent samples, and (5) normality of distribution.

Advantages and Disadvantages of Two-Way ANOVA

One of the primary advantages of the two-way ANOVA test is that it permits us to see the effects of different variables on whatever we have selected as the dependent variable. Also, it permits us to assess the significance of interaction between several independent variables as they jointly act upon the dependent variable. More complex ANOVA's exist, as researchers can add any number of independent variables to their research schemes. It is beyond the scope of this text to present three-way ANOVA tests or more elaborate procedures beyond the two-way ANOVA scheme presented here. Several textbooks listed at the end of the chapter describe complex ANOVA procedures that may be selectively applied to research problems.

One of the primary drawbacks to this procedure is the tediousness associated with the computational work. When one's sample size exceeds 100, two-way ANOVA becomes extremely cumbersome to apply. There are computer programs available that will be able to solve two-way (and any number of other complex ANOVA procedures) ANOVA tests rapidly, thus avoiding a significant amount of calculation work. The stringent assumptions underlying this procedure tend to restrict its application in much the same way as the F test is restricted. However, tables that contain critical values of F are readily available and function to assist the researcher in decision-making situations regarding tests of H_0.

□ SUMMARY

This chapter has sought to acquaint the reader with a variety of parametric and nonparametric statistical tests for application at the interval level of measurement. Some of the more popular tests to apply for single-sample situations include the t test and the Z test (where larger samples are encountered). It was shown that the t test is virtually identical to the Z test where sample sizes are in excess of 120. These procedures are the most powerful tests the researcher can apply.

Two-sample tests include the t test for difference between means. This is one of the two most powerful independent-sample procedures available. When certain critical assumptions have not been met because of data quality, the randomization test for two independent samples is recommended. If the samples exceed 12 combined, the researcher might find it appropriate to use the Mann–Whitney U test as an alternative. It is the most powerful nonparametric equivalent to the t test. The Mann–Whitney U test is treated in Chapter 10.

For two related-sample situations, the randomization test for matched pairs (related samples) is recommended for samples less than 12. When sample sizes exceed 12, the Wilcoxon matched pairs–signed ranks test is appropriate. Both procedures are almost as powerful as the t test with respect to decisions made about two related samples of elements on some interval characteristic.

When the researcher has more than two samples for investigation, the F test is appropriate, provided that all assumptions have been met. These assumptions include normality, independent samples, homogeneity of variance, and randomness. The restrictive nature of such assumptions tends to exclude the F test from many applications in social science literature. One alternative to the F test is the Kruskal–Wallis H test for analysis of variance. This will be treated in Chapter 10. The Kruskal–Wallis H test functions well without requiring the interval level of measurement, homogeneity of variance, and normality of distribution. It is 95 percent as powerful as the F test and answers the basic question: Does a difference exist between k samples regarding some measured characteristic?

Two tests were presented for determining whether the researcher has homogeneity of variance. The easier of the two is the Hartley F_{max} test. This involves minimal computational work and yields a reasonably conservative result. Another procedure, Cochran's C, was also indicated as a suitable means for determining whether or not homogeneity of variance exists.

Once the researcher has determined that a significant difference exists among k sample means on some interval characteristic, an additional test is necessary to answer the question about where the significant mean differences are located. The Newman–Keuls procedure is one way of resolving this problem. It determines where significant differences between means occur, and it involves computational work equivalent to that required to compute two or three t tests. An alternative procedure is one developed by Scheffé. This is more conservative and yields fewer significant mean differences under most conditions.

Finally, a procedure was presented to indicate whether additional factors might be influential in affecting score changes or differences. The two-way ANOVA procedure is a method of ascertaining whether any interaction exists between some dependent variable and two independent variables. It has assumptions that are similar to the F test and utilizes Table A16 for determining critical values of F for evaluating main and interaction effects.

In Chapter 9 we examine several measures that are useful when the researcher can assume only nominal-level measurement associated with variables analyzed. Such procedures can be applied to almost all problems presented in this chapter, although a considerable amount of information would be wasted as a result.

SELECTED STUDY TERMS

t test
Standard error of the difference between two means
Degrees of freedom
Independent and related samples
Control group
Before–after or matching samples
F test
Homogeneity of variance
Postmortem tests of significance
Main effects
Interaction effects

EXERCISES

1. Given the following data, determine whether the two groups are the same or different using the randomization test for matched pairs. Use the .05 level of significance.

Individual	*Time 1*	*Time 2*
1	25	28
2	29	24
3	22	30
4	24	29
5	26	31
6	28	27

2. Carry out a simple one-way ANOVA for the following five groups at the .01 level of significance. Does a significant difference exist between these five groups at the .01 level?

Group 1	*Group 2*	*Group 3*	*Group 4*	*Group 5*
9	7	4	10	1
3	10	5	6	2
5	4	4	8	3
9	3	6	12	6
9	6	2	5	5
8	5	9	7	1

3. Carry out the Newman–Keuls procedure for the means from Exercise 2 at the .01 level of significance. Place an asterisk (*) beside all significant mean differences. What is the value of $s_{\bar{t}}$?
4. Carry out a two-way ANOVA for the following data. Use the .05 level of significance and show your work in a two-way ANOVA summary table. The scores in the body of the table are productivity scores.

	Work Group		
Supervisory Style	*Group 1*	*Group 2*	*Group 3*
Close	51	43	39
	38	86	56
	62	28	31
	95	92	62
	41		
	25		
General	112	59	38
	33	77	80
	44	91	19
	56	102	19
	71		75
			33

Construct a two-way ANOVA summary for these data. What are the main effects nominally? What is the significance of the main effects on the scores of workers? What is the significance associated with the interaction effects?

5. Given the following data, determine the values requested.

$$\bar{X}_1 = 28 \quad \bar{X}_2 = 32 \quad \bar{X}_3 = 22 \quad \bar{X}_4 = 33$$

$$s_1^2 = 1.3 \quad s_2^2 = 4.5 \quad s_3^2 = 3.4 \quad s_4^2 = 1.9$$

$$N_1 = 35 \quad N_2 = 27 \quad N_3 = 28 \quad N_4 = 25$$

$$\bar{X}_5 = 26 \quad \bar{X}_6 = 29 \quad \bar{X}_7 = 35 \quad \bar{X}_8 = 25$$

$$s_5^2 = 3.0 \quad s_6^2 = 2.2 \quad s_7^2 = 5.1 \quad s_8^2 = 5.1$$

$$N_5 = 15 \quad N_6 = 19 \quad N_7 = 22 \quad N_8 = 24.$$

Does homogeneity of variance exist for these data? Show your proof by identifying the critical and observed values of either the Hartley F_{max} procedure or Cochran's test. Carry out an ANOVA and determine whether a significant difference exists among these eight means. If a significant difference exists at the 0.5 level, carry out the Newman–Keuls procedure and place an asterisk beside each significant mean difference. What is the value of $s_{\bar{t}}$?

6. What is the significance associated with the following hypothesis test? Use the .01 level of significance.

H_0: $\bar{X}_1 = \bar{X}_2$
H_1: $\bar{X}_1 \neq \bar{X}_2$

$P \leqslant .01$ (two-tailed test).

Information: $\bar{X}_1 = 48.1$ $\bar{X}_2 = 51.9$
$s_1 = 2.2$ $s_2 = 2.6$
$N_1 = 28$ $N_2 = 35.$

Indicate either the t observed and the critical value of t or the Z observed and critical value of Z.

7. Given the following information, carry out the F test and determine (by using either the Newman–Keuls procedure or the Scheffé method) the significance of mean differences in the appropriate summary table.

$\bar{X}_1 = 14.5$ $\bar{X}_2 = 12.1$ $\bar{X}_3 = 10.0$ $\bar{X}_4 = 15.6$ $\bar{X}_5 = 9.8$

$s_1^2 = 6.4$ $s_2^2 = 3.1$ $s_3^2 = 4.5$ $s_4^2 = 3.3$ $s_5^2 = 2.3$

$N_1 = 14$ $N_2 = 12$ $N_3 = 17$ $N_4 = 12$ $N_5 = 15.$

Does homogeneity of variance exist with these data? Show proof to justify your answer (including both critical and observed statistical values associated with either method you select).

8. Given the following information, determine if a significant difference exists between the related samples. Use the Wilcoxon matched pairs–signed ranks test. $P \leqslant .05$, one-tailed test.

Individual	*Time 1*	*Time 2*
1	52	53
2	55	59
3	46	49
4	50	47
5	62	60
6	55	54
7	59	65
8	66	68
9	50	49
10	39	53
11	42	47
12	49	57
13	55	59
14	39	41
15	39	55
16	35	45
17	26	23
18	55	50

9. Given the following information, carry out the randomization test for two independent samples. Assume the .05 level of significance.

Sales Scores	
Group 1	*Group 2*
15	25
18	16
23	29
15	17
18	21

10. With an observed $\overline{X} = 250$, $s = 32$, and $N = 101$, determine the significance associated with the following hypothesis.

$$H_0\colon \mu = 260$$
$$H_1\colon \mu \neq 260$$

$$P \leqslant .01 \text{ (two-tailed test).}$$

Show the critical value and the observed value associated with t.

11. Supply the missing values for each item below given the following information.

$$\overline{X}_1 = 14 \qquad \overline{X}_2 = 12 \qquad \overline{X}_3 = 19$$
$$s_1 = 3.1 \qquad s_2 = 6.8 \qquad s_3 = 1.9$$
$$N_1 = 15 \qquad N_2 = 10 \qquad N_3 = 12$$
$$\overline{X}_4 = 21 \qquad \overline{X}_5 = 16 \qquad \overline{X}_6 = 17$$
$$s_4 = 4.5 \qquad s_5 = 4.1 \qquad s_6 = 5.4$$
$$N_4 = 13 \qquad N_5 = 20 \qquad N_6 = 29.$$
$$\text{MS}_{\text{within}} = 6.93 \qquad \text{SS}_{\text{bet}} = 156 \qquad P \leqslant .05$$

(Construct an ANOVA summary table and enter the information given. Solve for all remaining portions of the table: $\text{SS}_{\text{within}}$, df, SS_{total}, and so on.)

What is the significant value of F shown in Table A16? What is the observed value of F? What is your decision regarding the means?

Carry out the Scheffé procedure for the mean differences shown above. Attach asterisks to the significant mean differences at the .05 level.

12. Test the following hypothesis:

$$H_0\colon \overline{X}_1 = \overline{X}_2$$
$$H_1\colon \overline{X}_1 \neq \overline{X}_2$$

$$P \leqslant .10.$$

where $\overline{X}_1$ observed = 78.9, $\overline{X}_2$ observed = 84.5, $N_1 = 53$, $N_2 = 29$, $s_1 = 4.1$, and $s_2 = 6.3$. Identify the observed t value and the critical value of t. Supply the appropriate degrees of freedom and state your decision regarding H_0.

REFERENCES

Bills, Robert E., *Manual for the Index of Adjustment and Values.* Auburn, Ala.: Alabama Polytechnical Institute, 1958.

Blau, Peter M., "Patterns of Interaction among a Group of Officials in a Government Agency," in R. H. Rubenstein and C. J. Haberstroh, eds., *Some Theories of Organization.* Homewood, Ill., Richard D. Irwin, Inc. and The Dorsey Press, 1966, pp. 397-408.

Downie, N. M., and R. W. Heath, *Basic Statistical Methods* (4th ed.). New York: Harper & Row, Publishers, 1974.

Edwards, A. L., and K. C. Kenney, "A Comparison of the Thurstone and Likert Techniques of Attitude Scale Construction," *Journal of Applied Psychology*, **30**: 72-83, 1946.

Giacquinta, Joseph B., "Status, Risk, and Receptivity to Innovations in Complex Organizations: A Study of the Responses of Four Groups of Educators to the Proposed Introduction of Sex Education in Elementary School," *Sociology of Education*, **48**: 38-58, 1975.

Hildreth, G., et al., *Manual of Direction, Metropolitan Readiness Test*, Forms A and B. New York: Harcourt Brace Jovanovich, Inc., 1964.

Huck, Schuyler W., William H. Cormier, and William G. Bounds, Jr., *Reading Statistics and Research.* New York: Harper & Row, Publishers, 1974.

Ivancevich, John M., "Changes in Performance in a Management by Objectives Program," *Administrative Science Quarterly*, **19**: 563-574, 1974.

Labovitz, Sanford, "Some Observations on Measurement and Statistics," *Social Forces*, **46**: 151-160, 1967.

Minton, J. H., "The Impact of Sesame Street on Readiness," *Sociology of Education*, **48**: 141-151, 1975.

Morse, Nancy C., and E. Reimer, "The Experimental Change of a Major Organizational Variable," *Journal of Abnormal Psychology*, **52**: 120-129, 1956.

Spitzer, Stephen P., J. R. Stratton, J. D. Fitzgerald, and B. K. Mach, "The Self Concept: Test Equivalence and Perceived Validity," *The Sociological Quarterly*, **7**: 265-280, 1966.

Winer, B. J., *Statistical Principles and Experimental Design*, 2nd ed. New York: McGraw-Hill Book Company, 1971.

9 Nominal Tests of Significance

The tests of significance in this chapter and those covered in Chapter 10 have found wide application in the social science literature. Categorical phenomena such as race, religion, ethnic background, sex, political affiliation, and group membership are examined extensively by social scientists in the course of their scientific investigations.

When the measurement associated with such phenomena is restricted to the nominal level, we will be equally restricted in terms of what can be done with the data statistically. Fortunately, a number of statistical tests of significance exist to assist us in our analysis of data measured according to a nominal scale.

This chapter is organized as follows. First, a single-sample test of significance, the chi-square statistic, will be examined. Three tests for determining the significance of difference between two independent samples are included: (1) the Z test for differences between proportions, (2) a chi-square two independent-sample extension of the single-sample case, and (3) Fisher's exact test. The McNemar test will follow as a two-related sample measure of significance of difference. Finally, a third version of the chi-square statistic for k independent samples will be presented. This discussion will be followed by a k-related sample test, the Cochran Q statistic.

Most of the procedures in this chapter are referred to as *goodness-of-fit tests.* The goodness-of-fit label applies to the "fit" between an *observed set of frequencies* (across k categories or in some nominal crosstabulation of variables) and an *expected set of frequencies.* For instance, an equal opportunity employer in a company concerned about sexual equality in employment might strive to achieve a perfect balance of males and females in a variety of non-sex-specific occupations. The "expected" distribution of 100 employees in company X might be as follows:

Company X		
Males	*Females*	
50	50	$N = 100$

In reality, the distribution of males and females might be

Company X		
Males	*Females*	
65	35	$N = 100$

The goodness of fit here would refer to the discrepancy between what is actually observed (i.e., the 65–35 male–female split) and what would be expected if full sexual equality were present (i.e., a 50–50 male–female split). The greater the discrepancy, the less the goodness of fit. The greater the equality, the better the goodness of fit. There are statistical measures that evaluate the significance of difference between what is observed and what is expected according to chance (i.e., expected according to some ideal model or standard). One of these procedures is the chi-square statistic.

□ SINGLE-SAMPLE TESTS: THE CHI-SQUARE STATISTIC

The chi-square test is probably the most popular goodness-of-fit statistic used in the social sciences today. This judgment is based solely on the frequency with which this test is applied in the literature. However, the chi-square test is not the best statistic to use under all circumstances where nominal-level data are encountered. We will examine certain weaknesses and strengths of this procedure after the following example.

Metz (1966) was interested in examining the relationship between certain background variables, such as education, income, sex, age, and numbers of children, and attitude toward fluoridation of public water supplies of various communities. Some information was obtained from data collected by the National Opinion Research Center, representing a cross section of 1862 persons from the general public. As a part of the research, Metz obtained measures of knowledge of fluoridation from these persons. He was able to determine that a portion of the sample had "correct knowledge," a portion had "incorrect knowledge," and a portion were "uncertain" about the effects of fluoridation.

A sample was obtained of 192 persons who indicated that they were unfavorable toward fluoridation of the water supply of their communities. These persons were differentiated from one another across three categories of knowledge of fluoridation: (1) "correct;" (2) "incorrect;" and (3) "uncertain." Metz wanted to know if persons who were unfavorable toward fluoridation differed at all concerning their knowledge about it. The following hypothesis set is suggested by Metz's research:

H_0: Persons who are unfavorable toward fluoridation will not differ in their knowledge of the effects of fluoridation.

H_1: Persons who are unfavorable toward fluoridation will differ in their knowledge of the effects of fluoridation.

$$P \leqslant .001 \text{ (two-tailed test).}$$

Table 9.1 shows 192 persons unfavorably disposed to fluoridation and distributed according to knowledge of fluoridation of the public water supply. To test the hypothesis set above, we must determine an expected distribution of frequencies for the 192 subjects in Table 9.1. To accomplish this, we must divide the total number of persons (N) by the number of categories into which they have been divided,

TABLE 9.1
Unfavorable Disposition Toward Fluoridation and Knowledge of Fluoridation for 192 Subjects.

	Knowledge of Fluoridation (Observed Frequencies)			
	Correct	*Incorrect*	*Uncertain*	
Unfavorable disposition toward fluoridation	121 (63%)	40 (21%)	31 (16%)	$N = 192$ $N = 100\%$

TABLE 9.2
Expected Distribution of Frequencies of Unfavorable Disposition Toward Fluoridation and Knowledge of Fluoridation for 192 Subjects.

	Knowledge of Fluoridation (Expected Frequencies)			
	Correct	*Incorrect*	*Uncertain*	
Unfavorable disposition toward fluoridation	64	64	64	$N = 192$

k, or $N/k = \frac{192}{3} = 64$. This will mean that 64 frequencies will be placed in each of the three categories, as shown in Table 9.2. This distribution of frequencies is based on the assumption that persons unfavorable toward fluoridation are equally divided in their knowledge of the effects of fluoridation. The researcher may actually believe that these persons have incorrect knowledge or are uncertain about the effects of fluoridation. In any case, it has been hypothesized that what has been observed (the observed frequencies in Table 9.1) does not differ from what would be expected according to chance (the expected frequencies in Table 9.2). The wording of H_0 and H_1 does not make this explicit, although goodness of fit is clearly implied.

The following chi-square test is applied:

$$\chi^2 = \sum\left[\frac{(O_k - E_k)^2}{E_k}\right],$$

where

O_k = observed frequencies in the kth cell
E_k = expected frequencies in the kth cell

For the data in Tables 9.1 and 9.2, we carry out our computations as follows:

$$\chi^2 = \frac{(121 - 64)^2}{64} + \frac{(40 - 64)^2}{64} + \frac{(31 - 64)^2}{64}$$

$$= \frac{(57)^2}{64} + \frac{(24)^2}{64} + \frac{(33)^2}{64}$$

$$= \frac{3249}{64} + \frac{576}{64} + \frac{1089}{64}$$

$$= 50.766 + 9.000 + 17.016$$

$$= 76.782.$$

The observed chi-square (χ^2) value = 76.782.

To determine the statistical significance of our observed $\chi^2 = 76.782$, we must turn to Table A4, Appendix A. Across the top of the table are both one- and two-tailed probabilities. Down the left-hand side of the table are degrees of freedom, df. For a single-sample test such as the one we are conducting above, the df are defined as $k - 1$, where k is the number of categories into which our data have been divided. In this case, $k = 3$ and $k - 1 = 2$ df. Entering Table A4 with 2 df at the .001 level of significance with a two-tailed test, we determine where these values intersect in the body of the table. This defines the critical value of χ^2 that we must equal or exceed with our observed χ^2 value. The critical value is 13.815 in this case. It is clearly equaled or exceeded by our observed χ^2 of 76.782. Therefore, H_0 is rejected and H_1 is supported. There is a difference between persons having different knowledge of the effects of fluoridation regarding their unfavorable disposition toward it. This statement is significant at the .001 level.

Assumptions of the Chi-Square Test

For the single-sample chi-square test, the following assumptions apply: (1) the data must be classifiable and fit the nominal level of measurement, (2) the sample size must be 25 or larger, and (3) the sample must be randomly selected.

Advantages and Disadvantages of the Chi-Square Test

One of the primary advantages of the chi-square test is that it is easy to apply to categorical data. It is a goodness-of-fit statistic that reveals the significance associated with the fit between what we observe and what would be expected according to some "chance" distribution of frequencies. The direction of the distribution of frequencies can be determined readily if a one-tailed hypothesis test is made. This can be done by a casual inspection of the arrangement of table frequencies to see if they are consistent with the arrangement predicted under H_1.

A table of critical chi-square values exists for instant interpretation of the significance of any observed χ^2 value for either one- or two-tailed tests.

The major weakness of chi square is that it is quite sensitive to very small or very large sample sizes. If a sample is less than 25, the resulting χ^2 is increasingly distorted and becomes unusually large. This leads the researcher to believe that the data being analyzed may be significant when no real practical significance can be attached to the distribution of frequencies. The same phenomenon occurs whenever samples become large. For instance, if a sample is in excess of

250, the χ^2 value is increasingly distorted, again by becoming unusually large. In order to illustrate the influence of sample size on observed χ^2 values, consider the following hypothetical distribution of frequencies:

k Categories				
A	*B*	*C*	*D*	
25	40	60	15	$N = 140$

The observed χ^2 for these data = 32.857. (The solution is left as an exercise for the reader.) If we were to double the frequencies throughout the four categories above without changing the proportionate distribution of them, the resulting χ^2 would be exactly twice as large as the original observed χ^2 of 32.857. Thus for the new distribution (i.e., the original distribution of frequencies doubled), we would have

k Categories				
A	*B*	*C*	*D*	
50	80	120	30	$N = 280$

The new χ^2 would be (2)(32.857) = 65.714. We have done nothing to influence the proportionate distribution of frequencies except double them. The resulting χ^2 value would lead us to believe that the new distribution is even more significantly distributed throughout the four categories than the original distribution of them. This false sense of significance often leads persons to make unwarranted statements about the data and their theoretical and/or substantive importance. Because of the sensitivity of chi square to sample sizes that are particularly large and small, it is recommended that a reasonable operating range for this statistic be between 25 and 250. Applications of chi square to N's less than 25 or larger than 250 are inappropriate, and resulting statistical values and accompanying probabilities should be viewed and interpreted with caution.

An additional disadvantage of chi square is that whenever expected cell frequencies are less than 5 for any cell, distortion is introduced which yields an unusually large observed χ^2 value. For instance, if we observed 25 persons distributed throughout six categories, our expected frequencies for the six cells would be N/k or $\frac{25}{6} =$ 4.2 frequencies per cell. This condition would result in an unsatisfactory application of chi square because of the misleading χ^2 value obtained. Consider the following hypothetical example of an $N = 25$ distributed according to a range of agreements and disagreements with some attitudinal variable:

Attitude X						
Strongly Agree	*Agree*	*Undecided, Probably Agree*	*Undecided, Probably Disagree*	*Disagree*	*Strongly Disagree*	
6	3	0	5	10	1	$N = 25$

The chi-square test could be applied here, but the results would be quite misleading. One way of overcoming the problem of few expected cell frequencies is to "collapse" the six categories above into fewer cells. This is a way of "beefing up" cell frequencies and making it possible to apply the chi-square test correctly. For example, we could collapse the "strongly agree," "agree," and "undecided, probably agree" categories into one category, the "undecided, probably disagree" into a second category, and the "disagree" and "strongly disagree" into a third category, yielding the following new data arrangement:

Attitude X			
Strongly Agree, Agree, and Undecided, Probably Agree	*Undecided, Probably Disagree*	*Disagree, and Strongly Disagree*	
9	5	11	$N = 25$

Now, our expected cell frequencies would be N/k or $\frac{25}{3} = 8.3$ per cell. Our application of chi square can proceed without the "small-expected-cell-frequency" criticism. It is important to note that collapsing of cell frequencies can be done only when logical cell combinations are possible. For example, it would not be logical to combine "undecided, probably agree" with "disagree" and "undecided, probably disagree," or to combine "strongly agree," "agree," "undecided, probably agree," and "undecided, probably disagree" in the same cell. This would be equivalent to mixing apples and oranges. Therefore, "agree" categories are combined only with other "agree" categories, and "disagree" categories are combined only with other "disagree" categories.

A common misconception associated with the chi-square test concerns the actual or "observed" distribution of cell frequencies. Some persons think that if the observed cell frequencies are less than 5, the chi-square test should not be applied. This is simply not true. The "less-than-5-frequencies-in-any-cell" rule or recommendation applies only to expected cell frequencies. On occasion, however, we would probably collapse cell frequencies in our observed distribution in order to beef up cell numbers and qualify our data for a legitimate chi-square application.

□ TWO-SAMPLE TESTS: INDEPENDENT SAMPLES

In this section we examine three tests for determining the significance of difference between two independent samples of elements. It is assumed that we have nominal or classifiable data. Three tests treated here include (1) the Z test for differences between proportion, (2) Fisher's exact test, and (3) the chi-square test for two independent samples.

The Z Test for Differences Between Proportions

The Z test for proportion differences examines two samples and the proportionate distribution of some nominal dichotomous characteristic between them. As an example, Olsen (1970) conducted a survey of physicians, including questions about their present practice, their social and geographical origins, medical specialties, and motivations for locating their practices in particular communities. Olsen was interested in factors that influenced physicians to locate their medical practices in particular regions.

Physicians from metropolitan and nonmetropolitan areas were randomly selected and included in the survey. In one portion of his investigation, Olsen divided the physicians into "specialists" and "generalists" (general practitioners). These two samples were asked to indicate if "medical facilities to work with" (i.e., the latest medical equipment, modern hospitals, etc.) was a primary reason for causing them to locate where they were at present. The breakdown of responses to this question is shown in Table 9.3.

Table 9.3 represents a cross-tabulation of specialists and generalists according to whether they answered "yes" or "no" to the question about the importance of medical facilities in influencing the location of their medical practice. It is apparent that a greater portion of specialists regarded "facilities to work with" as an important factor in selecting the location of their present practice compared with generalists. But is the difference between proportions significant statistically? This question can be answered by applying the Z test to these data. The Z test takes the general form

$$Z = \frac{p_1 - p_2}{s_{p_1 - p_2}},$$

where

p_1 and p_2 = proportion of "yes" responses for groups 1 and 2
$s_{p_1 - p_2}$ = standard error of the difference between the two proportions

TABLE 9.3
A 2 X 2 Tabular Distribution of Specialists and Generalists and Influence of "Facilities to Work with" in Selecting Their Present Location.

		Type of Physician	
		Specialist ($N_1 = 236$)	*Generalist* ($N_2 = 87$)
"Facilities to Work with Are Important"	Yes	40.7% (.407 = p_1) *a*	28.7% (.287 = p_2) *b*
	No	59.3% (.593 = q_1) *c*	71.3% (.713 = q_2) *b*
		100.0%	100.0%

Source: Donald B. Olsen, "A Comparative Analysis of Metropolitan and Non-Metropolitan Physicians in Southern Appalachia," unpublished master's thesis, University of Tennessee, Knoxville, 1970.

The standard error term is computed as follows:

$$s_{p_1 - p_2} = \sqrt{\frac{p_1 q_1}{N_1} + \frac{p_2 q_2}{N_2}},$$

where

$$q_1 = 1 - p_1$$
$$q_2 = 1 - p_2$$
N_1 and N_2 = sample sizes for groups 1 and 2

It might be argued that specialists would tend to be more concerned with modern facilities and equipment compared with generalists. Areas of the country that have greater access to more specialized equipment and facilities might tend to attract specialists more, compared with regions where facilities are less adequate. The following hypothesis set is suggested by Olsen's research:

H_0: There will be no difference between specialists and generalists concerning the importance they attach to facilities to work with; if there is a difference, generalists will attach more importance to facilities to work with compared with specialists.

H_1: Specialists will attach more importance to facilities to work with compared with generalists.

$$P \leqslant .01 \quad \text{(one-tailed test).}$$

The data in Table 9.3 are obtained as follows. Cells *a* and *b* contain the proportions of specialists and generalists (p_1 and p_2) who answer "yes" to the question: "Did facilities to work with significantly attract you to your present location?" Cells *c* and *d* contain the proportions of specialists and generalists (q_1 and q_2) who answer "no" to the same question. The two samples, $N_1 = 236$ and $N_2 = 87$, are distributed throughout Table 9.3 as shown. These cell frequencies have been converted to proportions for simple transfer to the Z formula. Taking the data in Table 9.3, we may determine the observed Z as follows:

$$Z = \frac{.407 - .287}{\sqrt{\dfrac{(.407)(.593)}{236} + \dfrac{(.287)(.713)}{87}}}$$

$$= \frac{.120}{\sqrt{\dfrac{.241351}{236} + \dfrac{.204631}{87}}}$$

$$= \frac{.120}{\sqrt{.0010 + .0024}}$$

$$= \frac{.120}{\sqrt{.0034}}$$

$$= \frac{.120}{.058}$$

$$= 2.07.$$

We may take our observed Z value of 2.07 to the table of areas of the normal curve, Table A3, Appendix A, and compare it with the critical value of Z for the .01 level of significance for a one-tailed test. This value of $Z = 2.33$. If our observed Z value equals or exceeds 2.33, we may reject H_0 at the .01 level of significance. Since 2.07 fails to equal or exceed the critical value of Z in this instance, we fail to reject H_0 and conclude tentatively that no significant difference exists between specialists and generalists regarding their attraction to "facilities to work with" as a major factor influencing the location of their medical practice.

One "salvaging" feature of Table 9.3 is that the difference between specialists and generalists was in the direction predicted under H_1, in spite of the fact that the difference was not significant statistically. Sometimes directionality can be important even if the statistics computed fail to reflect this. Perhaps the accessibility to facilities to work with combined with additional features such as colleague associations and socioeconomic variables would lend to a more specific prediction of a constellation of factors influencing one's location of medical practice. Of course, a more complex statistical analysis would have to be made. Statistical tests and models that analyze simultaneously several factors and how they jointly impinge on some dependent variable are often called multivariate procedures. Multivariate statistics are treated in Chapter 12.

Assumptions of the Z Test. The primary assumptions of the Z test for differences between proportions are (1) nominal-level data that are amenable to categorization, (2) independent samples, and (3) sample sizes of $N_1 + N_2 > 30$.

Advantages and Disadvantages of the Z Test. The Z test for differences between proportions provides an approximation of a Z value that can be used in conjunction with the unit normal distribution. This does not mean that the Z test requires normality. The formula for the Z test merely provides an approximation of Z that can be interpreted according to the normal-curve table, Table A3. Because of our familiarity with Z values and their utility in statistical decision making, the Z approximation provided by this test is an attractive feature of it.

Another advantage is that the Z test can handle large numbers of elements. Many nonparametric statistical procedures are limited to relatively small sample size applications. There are no sample-size restrictions with the Z test. When $N_1 + N_2 < 30$, the resulting Z value may be treated as a t value, with $N_1 + N_2 - 2$ degrees of freedom and interpreted accordingly.

Fisher's Exact Test

Fisher's exact test is a procedure designed to provide an exact probability associated with an observed distribution of frequencies throughout a 2 X 2 table. A *2 X 2 table* is a simple cross-tabulation of two variables that have been dichotomized. Table 9.4 is a 2 X 2 table with four cells, labeled a, b, c, and d, respectively. The table has two rows and two columns. The row totals are shown as $a + b$ and $c + d$. The column totals are shown as $a + c$, and $b + d$. The N for the entire table is the sum of frequencies in cells a, b, c, and d.

TABLE 9.4
A 2 X 2 Table.

		Variable X		
		Column 1	*Column 2*	*Marginal Totals*
Variable Y	*Row 1*	a	b	$a + b$
	Row 2	c	d	$c + d$
	Row Totals	$a + c$ (N_1)	$b + d$ (N_2)	$N = a + b + c + d$

In the general case, tables are designated as $r \times c$, where r is the number of rows and c is the number of columns.

Fisher's exact test is applied when $N_1 + N_2 < 25$ (where $N_1 = a + c$ and $N_2 = b + d$), and where data have been arranged into a 2 X 2 cross-tabulation. Specifically, Fisher's exact test answers the question, "What is the probability associated with observing the present table of frequencies and any more extreme version of that table?" The following example is provided.

Wood and Zald (1966) examined the impact of racial integration and resistance to changes in church policy in the Methodist Church. The data were gathered from the "Southern State Conference of the Methodist Church," a pseudonym used to preserve the anonymity of the actual conference investigated.

One aspect of the study by Wood and Zald concerned liberal and conservative attitudes of ministers in churches which were predominantly white and nonwhite. These investigators speculated that predominantly white churches would tend to have liberal ministers, whereas predominantly nonwhite churches would tend to have more conservative or moderate ministers. The following hypothesis set is suggested by their research:

H_0: There is no difference between predominantly white and nonwhite churches and the conservativism-liberalism of ministers; if there is a difference, nonwhite churches will tend to have more liberal ministers.

H_1: There will be more conservative ministers in predominantly nonwhite churches and more liberal ministers in predominantly white churches.

$$P \leqslant .10 \quad \text{(one-tailed test).}$$

TABLE 9.5
Conservativism-Liberalism of Methodist Church Ministers in White and Nonwhite Churches.

		Minister's Views		
		Conservative or moderate	*Liberal*	*Totals*
Percent nonwhite	*High*	13 (a)	1 (b)	14
	Low	8 (c)	3 (d)	11
	Totals	21 (N_1)	4 (N_2)	$N = 25$

Source: James R. Wood and Mayer N. Zald, "Aspects of Racial Integration in the Methodist Church: Sources of Resistance to Organizational Policy," *Social Forces*, 45:260, 1966.

Wood and Zald observed the data shown in Table 9.5. A casual inspection of Table 9.5 shows that the data are at least consistent with the direction predicted under H_1. However, are these data significantly in the predicted direction? Fisher's exact test will provide the answer. To carry out this test, we must determine the exact probability associated with the data in Table 9.5. We must also determine the exact probability associated with any more extreme form of Table 9.5. By definition, the most extreme form of any table we examine is one that contains a 0 in one or more of the cells. There are no cells in Table 9.5 containing a 0, so we must focus on the smallest cell frequency (in this case, cell b contains the smallest cell frequency) and reduce this frequency by 1. Maintaining our marginal totals as they exist in the original table, we make appropriate adjustments in the other three cells of the table so that the row and column totals will continue to be the same. Table 9.6 is the new tabular arrangement and represents the most extreme form of the data in Table 9.5, given the existing marginal totals. At least one cell now contains a 0. We may proceed with our exact probability computations for Tables 9.5 and 9.6 as follows:

$$P = \frac{(a+b)!(c+d)!(a+c)!(b+d)!}{N!a!b!c!d!},$$

TABLE 9.6
Most Extreme Version of the Data in Table 9.5.

14 *a*	0 *b*	14
7 *c*	4 *d*	11
21 ($N_1 = a + c$)	4 ($N_2 = b + d$)	$N = 25$

where

$a, b, c,$ and d = respective cell frequencies
N = total number of frequencies in the table

$$P_1 = \frac{14!11!21!4!}{25!13!1!8!3!} = \frac{630}{3450} = .18$$

$$P_2 = \frac{14!11!21!4!}{25!14!0!7!4!} = \frac{45}{1725} = \underline{.03}$$

$$P_c = .21,$$

where P_c is the cumulative probability. With a one-tailed cumulative probability (P_c) = .21, we fail to reject the null hypothesis at the .10 level. The rejection of H_0 meant that we would have to observe a cumulative probability equal to or smaller than .10.[1]

Assumptions of Fisher's Exact Test. The primary assumptions associated with Fisher's exact test are (1) randomness, (2) nominal or categorical data, (3) two independent samples, and (4) combined sample sizes $\leqslant 25$.

[1] We can always determine how many separate probabilities will need to be computed (and how many more extreme tabular arrangements will exist) by using the simple formula, scf + 1, where scf = the smallest cell frequency observed in the original table. If the smallest cell frequency = 4, we will need to compute scf + 1 or 4 + 1 = 5 separate probabilities to derive the final P_c value. If the scf = 1 as it does in the case of Table 9.5, then scf + 1 = 1 + 1 = 2 separate probabilities will need to be computed to derive the final P_c value. A separate probability must be computed for each table and summed.

Advantages and Disadvantages of Fisher's Exact Test. A primary advantage of Fisher's exact test is that it yields an exact probability that can be compared directly with the probability associated with the hypothesis test. The formula for deriving each tabular probability can be made applicable to two-tailed, nondirectional hypothesis tests by simply doubling the probability of the resulting P_c value. Therefore, had we made a two-tailed test of the original hypothesis set, the two-tailed P_c value would have been (2) (.21) = .42.

Fisher's exact test is almost always exclusively used for 2 X 2 tables, although a procedure is available for applying the test to 2 X 3 tabular cases.[2] Because of the complexity associated with the 2 X 3 case of Fisher's exact test, it will not be presented here.

Fisher's exact test handles situations for which the chi-square test is inappropriate. A major limitation of chi square is that it should not be applied to tables where the sample size is less than 25. Fisher's exact test is explicitly designed for such small-N applications, and as such it is an excellent alternative when chi square cannot be used.

On the negative side, Fisher's exact test uses factorials in the derivation of exact probabilities. Although factorials are not difficult to work with, some persons regard them as cumbersome in application. The 2 X 2 tabular restriction is sometimes regarded as a limitation as well. However, since this procedure is intended for small N's of 25 or less, this 2 X 2 "limitation" cannot be taken seriously.

When data are arranged in some *r* X *c table* larger than 2 X 2, a logical *collapsing* of categories would be in order if the researcher wanted to carry out Fisher's exact test. When sample size exceeds 25, Fisher's exact test becomes inappropriate and the chi-square test for two independent samples or the Z test for differences between proportions would be reasonable alternatives to apply for two-independent sample hypothesis tests at the nominal level.

The Chi-Square Test for Two Independent Samples

An extension of the chi-square test for a single-sample case, the two-independent-sample version of the chi-square test is a goodness-of-fit statistic for the analysis of *r* X 2 tabular distributions. In an interesting study of female delinquency, Morris (1964) examined a sample of 128 females ranging in age from 13 to 16. One aspect of Morris's study concerned differences between delinquent and non-

[2] Albert Pierce, *Fundamentals of Non-parametric Statistics: A Sample Space Approach* (Encino, Calif.: Dickenson Publishing Co., Inc., 1969). Computer programs have been developed for applying Fisher's exact test to the general *r* X *c* case. But a discussion of such programs is beyond the scope of this book.

delinquent females and how their mothers resolved differences of opinion between themselves and their husbands.

Morris indicates that "respondents were asked what their mothers did if they wanted something but were not sure the fathers would agree to it. Responses were classified into . . . categories including 'coercive' (domineering) and 'democratic' (implying free and equal discussion." It was believed that democratic parental relations would more likely typify nondelinquent females, whereas coercive parental relations would tend to characterize delinquent females. The following hypothesis set was suggested by Morris's research:

H_0: There is no difference between coercive and democratic resolutions of parental conflicts and whether or not the daughters are delinquent.
H_1: There is a difference between coercive and democratic resolutions of parental conflicts and whether or not the daughters are delinquent.

$$P \leqslant .05 \quad \text{(two-tailed test).}$$

Morris cross-tabulated the 128 female subjects into a 2 X 2 table according to delinquent–nondelinquent and how their mothers dealt with disagreements with their fathers (i.e., coercive or democratic). These data are shown in Table 9.7. These data are referred to as the *observed distribution of frequencies.* Another table must be created containing the *expected distribution of frequencies.* To construct

TABLE 9.7
Delinquency–Nondelinquency of 128 Females by Mother's Resolution of Disagreements with Fathers.

		How Mother Deals with Father		
		Coercively	*Democratically*	*Totals*
Daughters Are:	*Nondelinquents*	29 *a*	34 *b*	63
	Delinquents	43 *c*	22 *d*	65
	Totals	72 (N_1)	56 (N_2)	$N = 128$

Source: Ruth R. Morris, "Female Delinquency and Relational Problems," *Social Forces,* **43**:87, 1964.

this expected frequency table, the researcher must determine the products of the row and column totals for each cell and divide each product by the N for the entire table. For instance, the product of row and column totals for cell a divided by N would be (63) (72)/ 128 = 35.4. Each of the expected cell frequencies is computed as follows and shown below:

$$a = \frac{(63)(72)}{128} = \frac{4536}{128} = 35.4$$

$$b = \frac{(63)(56)}{128} = \frac{3528}{128} = 27.6$$

$$c = \frac{(65)(72)}{128} = \frac{4680}{128} = 36.6$$

$$d = \frac{(65)(56)}{128} = \frac{3640}{128} = 28.4.$$

With these expected cell frequencies, we may compute our observed χ^2 value as follows:

$$\chi^2 = \Sigma\left[\frac{(O_k - E_k)^2}{E_k}\right],$$

where

O_k = observed cell frequency for the kth cell
E_k = expected cell frequency for the kth cell

The computation of our observed χ^2 value is given in Table 9.8. The observed χ^2 value for Table 9.7 is 5.202 as is shown. We may turn to Table A4 with degrees of freedom = $(r - 1)(c - 1)$ or (rows − 1) (columns − 1) = (2 − 1) (2 − 1) = 1 df. Where 1 df intersects with the .05 level of significance for a two-tailed test is the critical value of χ^2 that we must equal or exceed with our observed χ^2 value. The critical value of χ^2 is 3.841. Since our observed value of 5.202 equals or

TABLE 9.8

Cell	O_k	E_k	$(O_k - E_k)^2$	$(O_k - E_k)^2/E_k$
a	29	35.4	40.96	40.96/35.4 = 1.157
b	34	27.6	40.96	40.96/27.6 = 1.484
c	43	36.6	40.96	40.96/36.6 = 1.119
d	22	28.4	40.96	40.96/28.4 = 1.442
				$\chi^2 = \Sigma\left[\frac{(O_k - E_k)^2}{E_k}\right] = 5.202$

exceeds 3.841, we may reject H_0 and support H_1 that there is a difference between coercive and democratic resolutions of parental conflict and whether or not daughters are delinquent.

Further inspection of Table 9.7 reveals that a greater portion of nondelinquents have democratic parental conflict resolution, whereas delinquents tend to have coercive parental conflict resolution. We have determined this on the basis of the diagonal distribution of frequencies in this table. In Table 9.7, cells *b* and *c* contain the majority of frequencies. This enables us to attach directionality to these data. In the general case, *diagonal distributions of frequencies in these tables are desirable*, where cells *a* and *d* or cells *b* and *c* contain the majority of frequencies. Less desirable (and less informative) tabular arrangements are where the majority of frequencies "bunch up" in the following cell combinations: (1) *a* and *b*; (2) *b* and *c*; (3) *a* and *c*; and (4) *b* and *d*. Graphically portrayed next are two hypothetical tabular arrangements that we might define as "desirable":

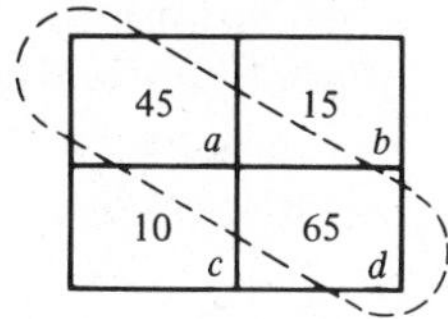

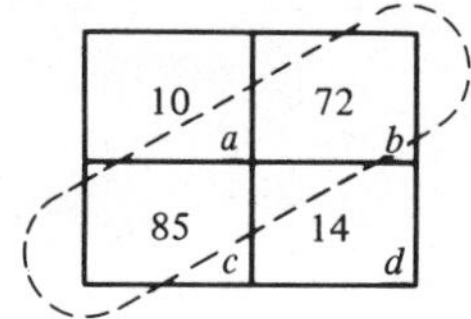

The following four tabular arrangements are less desirable (and somewhat less informative):

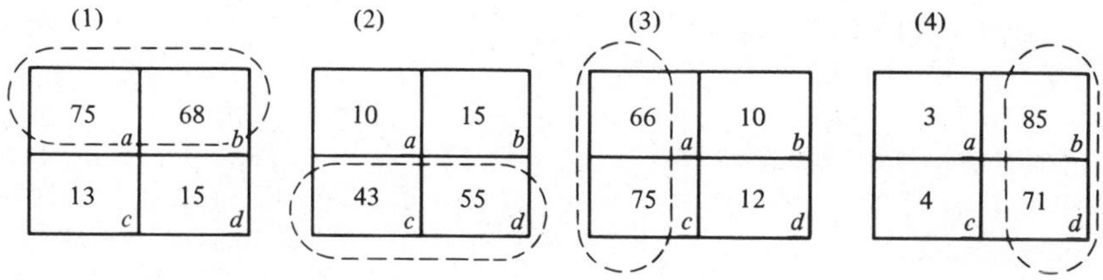

When the researcher encounters tabular distributions where the cell frequencies are diagonally distributed, as is the case in the desirable tables presented above, the direction of goodness-of-fit can be established clearly if a one-tailed hypothesis test is wanted. Regardless of whether a one- or two-tailed hypothesis test is in order, these tabular distributions maximize the information for the researcher's benefit. Later, if a measure of association is applied to these data, we can demonstrate clearly that generally, persons who say "yes" on variable X also say "yes" on variable Y, and those who say "no" on variable X also tend to say "no" on variable Y (or some other similar statement can be made).

Tables (1), (2), (3), and (4) in the preceding figure are less desirable, however, because we cannot make such associational statements. When data bunch up, as has been illustrated hypothetically above, this means that there is a lopsided distribution of frequencies occurring on the independent variable [tables (3) and (4)] or on the dependent variables [tables (1) and (2)]. For instance, if we were examining differences between males and females on some dependent variable, an imbalance or lopsided split of 7 males and 156 females would lead to tabular arrangement (4) (where cells a and c would comprise males, and where cells b and d would comprise females). If sex were an important independent variable, there would be almost no variation on that variable. In this case, a test of significance of difference using sex as a major independent variable would be practically meaningless. In the extreme case, if there were no males in our sample, sex could not be treated as a legitimate independent variable because of the absence of variability. We must observe as close to a 50–50 split on the independent variable as possible to maximize the effectiveness of a goodness-of-fit test such as chi square. It is also desirable that roughly a 50–50 split occurs on the dependent variable as well. This allows for reasonable fluctuations of both variables to occur within different cells of whatever table we examine.

Assumptions of the Chi-Square Test. The assumptions of the chi-square test for two independent samples are (1) randomness, (2) nominal-level data, (3) independent samples, and (4) a sample size ranging from 25 to 250.

Advantages and Disadvantages of the Chi-Square Test. Again, because of the sensitivity of the χ^2 statistic to extremely small N's (i.e., less than 25) or extremely large N's (i.e., more than 250), applications of this test outside these recommended N ranges are not encouraged. If the researcher applies the chi-square test to extremely small samples or extremely large ones, a degree of distortion is introduced that amplifies the magnitude of the resulting χ^2 value. This distortion tends to give the investigator a false sense of statistical significance associated with the observed table of frequencies.

When appropriately applied, the chi-square test is a rapid method of determining goodness of fit for categorical data. It is well known and widely used in the social science literature. There is an interpretive table with critical values of chi square that accompanies all hypothesis tests, thus making this technique increasingly attractive in research work. Of course, whenever the researcher is able to assume a higher level of measurement with the data being analyzed, more appropriate statistical tests would be desirable, which would use more of the information available. In some respects, the chi-square test is a "last resort" if other, more powerful, tests are ruled out as statistical alternatives.

In the event that the researcher encounters tabular distributions such as those described above as being less desirable, and where frequencies tend not to bunch up in a diagonal fashion, the Z test for differences between proportions might be considered as a useful alternative. If two groups of persons predominantly favored some position on a dependent variable (i.e., bunching up in either cells a and b or in cells c and d), we could use the Z test to help answer the question of whether a greater proportion of persons favored the issue compared with another group.

Yates' Correction for Continuity

When sample size ranges from 25 to 75, a correction factor is recommended that is designed to reduce slightly the magnitude of the resulting observed chi-square value. This is called Yates' correction for continuity. It consists simply of reducing the magnitude of difference between each observed and each expected cell frequency by .5. It is applied exclusively to 2×2 tables such as Table 9.7, although the sample size in that table is well beyond the recommended range of application for this procedure. If we were to apply Yates' correction to the data in Table 9.7, we would move each expected cell frequency .5 closer to its observed cell frequency counterpart. For instance, the observed frequency for cell a was 29. The original expected cell frequency for cell a was 35.4. We will apply Yates' correction by moving 35.4 closer to the observed frequency by changing 35.4 to 34.9 (a difference of .5 points). Yates' correction applied to the data in Table 9.7 results in the modification for all cells shown in Table 9.9. The resulting chi-square observed value is now 4.422, a reduction from the original value (without Yates' correction applied) of 5.202. This is not a substantial reduction in observed chi-square values, and the 4.422 value continues to equal or exceed the original critical chi-square value of 3.841 for the .05 level of significance (two-tailed test). But the correction illustrates the general effect of Yates' procedure on the reduction of the overall magnitude of the observed chi-square value.

Yates' correction is recommended only for sample sizes ranging from 25 to 75. The correction applied to samples of size 200, for instance, would make the difference in the observed chi-square values

TABLE 9.9

Cell	O_k	E_k	$(O_k - E_k)^2$	$(O_k - E_k)^2/E_k$
a	29	34.9	34.81	34.81/34.9 = .997
b	34	28.1	34.81	34.81/28.1 = 1.239
c	43	37.1	34.81	34.81/37.1 = .938
d	22	27.9	34.81	34.81/27.9 = 1.248
				$\chi^2 = 4.422$

(with or without the correction applied) negligible. This correction is a conservative step to offset the distorting impact of relatively small sample sizes. Reducing the size of the observed chi-square value makes it slightly more difficult to reject H_0's in hypothesis tests. Yates' correction for continuity should never be applied to tables larger than 2 × 2.

□ TWO-SAMPLE TESTS: RELATED SAMPLES

The McNemar Test

When the researcher has nominal-level information and is interested in determining whether a significant distributional change occurs for the data from one time period to the next, the McNemar test for significance of change is a useful option. The following example is provided.

Marcum and Bean (1976) were interested in examining Mexican-Americans as a minority group and their degree of mobility and integration into the larger society. A sample of Mexican-American couples were interviewed as a part of an Austin, Texas, family survey. A portion of the survey requested information about the husband's father's socioeconomic status. This would provide Marcum and Bean with a fairly accurate estimate of the family's social-class origins. Additional information was obtained that included the husband's current socioeconomic status. Socioeconomic statuses for husband's fathers and for husbands were measured by a Socioeconomic Index (SEI) developed by Reiss (1961). Resulting SEI scores enabled Marcum and Bean to classify husbands (and couples) according to "class of origin" and "class of destination." Presumably, husbands whose class of destination was higher than their original class of origin would be examples of upwardly mobile Mexican-Americans and potentially indicate their gradual acceptance into the "larger" society.

The following hypothesis set is suggested by the work of Marcum and Bean:

H_0: There will be no change from class of origin to class of destination for a sample of Mexican-Americans.
H_1: There will be a change from class of origin to class of destination for a sample of Mexican-Americans.

$$P \leqslant .01 \text{ (two-tailed test).}$$

Table 9.10 shows before (i.e., class of origin) and after (i.e., class of destination) classifications for 186 Mexican-American subjects. The row totals indicate that 102 subjects were of "high"-class origin, while 84 subjects were of "low"-class origin (i.e., according to their respective SEI scores). The column totals indicate that 117 subjects were of "high"-class origin, and that 69 were of "low"-class origin in the "after" period (i.e., the class of destination).

The McNemar test for significance of change will answer the question: Did a significant change take place from one time period to the next from class of origin to class of destination? The formula for the McNemar test is

$$\chi_m^2 = \frac{(|c_1 - c_2| - 1)^2}{c_1 + c_2},$$

TABLE 9.10
Class of Origin and Class of Destination Cross-Tabulation for 186 Mexican-Americans.

		Class of Destination (After)		
		High	*Low*	*Totals*
Class of Origin (Before)	*High*	72 *a*	30 *b*	102
	Low	45 *c*	39 *d*	84
Totals		117	69	$N = 186$

Source: John P. Marcum and Frank D. Bean. "Minority Group Status as a Factor in the Relationship Between Mobility and Fertility: The Mexican-American Case," *Social Forces*, 55: 144, 1976.

where c_1 and c_2 are general labels applied to those cells containing persons who changed from one status condition to the next. (In the present example, the cells containing those persons who change are cells *b* and *c*.) Using the values from Table 9.10, we have

$$\chi_m^2 = \frac{(|30 - 45| - 1)^2}{30 + 45}$$

$$= \frac{(14)^2}{75}$$

$$= \frac{196}{75}$$

$$= 2.613.$$

With an observed $\chi_m^2 = 2.613$, we may turn to Table A4, with 1 degree of freedom. Where 1 df intersects with the .01 level of significance for a two-tailed test defines the critical value of χ_m^2 we must equal or exceed in order to reject H_0. The critical value of $\chi_m^2 = 6.635$, and therefore we are unable to reject H_0 at the .01 level. There is no significant difference between Mexican-Americans in their classes of origin and their classes of destination.

An inspection of Table 9.10 will reveal that somewhat more Mexican-American subjects had changed from low to high socioeconomic status. Had a directional prediction been made, our examination of Table 9.10 would have shown directional consistency, although statistical significance was not achieved. Had a one-tailed test of the hypothesis been made, Marcum and Bean may have hypothesized under H_1 that more Mexican-Americans would change from low to high socioeconomic status (i.e., from the origin condition to the destination condition). Specifically, the following hypothesis set would indicate a one-tailed test:

H_0: Mexican-Americans will not change from social class of origin to social class of destination; if there is a change, more Mexican-Americans will change from high social class of origin to low social class of destination.

H_1: Mexican-Americans will tend to change from low social class of origin to high social class of destination.

$$P \leqslant .01 \text{ (one-tailed test).}$$

Entering Table A4 with 1 df, we would find the new critical value of $\chi_m^2 = 5.412$ for the .01 level (one-tailed test). Since our observed χ_m^2 fails to equal or exceed this new one-tailed critical value, we again fail to reject H_0 at the .01 level of significance.

Assumptions of the McNemar Test. The primary assumptions of the McNemar test are (1) randomness, (2) nominal or classifiable information, and (3) related samples through persons used as their own controls in a before–after experiment or investigation.

Advantages and Disadvantages of the McNemar Test. Few tests exist for analyzing nominal-level categorical changes from one time period to the next for related samples. Therefore, the McNemar test is to some extent "one of a kind." It is easy to compute and approximates the chi-square distribution with 1 degree of freedom. [One degree of freedom is always used for χ_m^2 interpretations because this test is always applied to a 2 × 2 tabular situation—$df = (r - 1)(c - 1) = (2 - 1)(2 - 1) = 1$ df.]

Since the McNemar test is a chi-square-based statistical procedure, the same sensitivity to sample-size fluctuations would apply here as would pertain to any chi-square test for two samples. A reasonable operating range for the McNemar test would be $c_1 + c_2$ from 25 to 250. This applies only to the sums of frequencies in the two cells containing persons who change from one type of condition to the other. Whenever $(c_1 + c_2)/2$ is less than 5 (i.e., when the sum of persons who change divided by 2 falls below 5 frequencies), the McNemar test is inappropriate. Under conditions such as these, no statistical test would be recommended. As an alternative, a simple directional statement from the researcher would be in order.

The McNemar test cannot be applied to matched sets of individuals. It is impossible to contrive a situation using matched pairs of subjects where the McNemar test would be appropriate. This limitation is strictly a function of the formula design. If the researcher has matched individuals and wishes to determine the significance of difference between them on some nominal-level characteristic, Cochran's Q test, described in the following section, would be applied conservatively to the two-sample case (even though it is designed for k related samples).

□ *k* INDEPENDENT SAMPLE TESTS: CHI SQUARE FOR *k* SAMPLES

An extension of the chi-square test is appropriate for situations where the investigator has independent samples across k nominal variable subclasses. The computational procedure for the chi-square test for k independent samples is identical to the two-sample chi-square test. A brief example will be provided below.

Greenwald (1978) was interested in examining the attitudes and beliefs of a large number of scientists and engineers in the San Francisco Bay area. One aspect of his research focused on the perceived economic insecurity of these professional persons and the degree to which they blamed other individuals for their own personal misfortune (in the form of economic insecurity).

Greenwald speculated that those persons who had a low degree of economic insecurity would tend not to blame "circumstances beyond the individual's control" for contributing to economic insecurity. Also, Greenwald reasoned that persons with a high degree of perceived economic insecurity would tend to blame "circumstances beyond the individual's control" for such perceived feelings. The following hypothesis set was suggested by the work of Greenwald:

H_0: There is no difference between persons of varying degrees of subjective insecurity and whether or not they blame circumstances beyond their control for such subjective insecurity; if there is a difference, persons with high subjective insecurity will tend not to blame circumstances beyond their control for their subjective insecurity.

H_1: Persons with high subjective insecurity will tend to blame circumstances beyond their control for this insecurity; persons with low subjective insecurity will not blame circumstances beyond their control for this insecurity.

$P \leqslant .01$ (one-tailed test).

The data in Table 9.11 represent a cross-tabulation of subjective insecurity (according to "high," "medium," and "low" categories) and whether subjective insecurity is blamed on circumstances beyond the individual's control (dichotomized into "yes" and "no" responses).

The formula for chi square is

$$\chi^2 = \sum \left[\frac{(O_k - E_k)^2}{E_k}\right],$$

where O_k and E_k are the observed and expected cell frequencies for the kth cell.

The expected cell frequencies for the data in Table 9.11 have been determined by obtaining the product of marginal row and column totals, where each cell is found and dividing the product by the total table N. The computational work for the expected cell frequencies is as follows:

$$a = \frac{(63)(70)}{140} = 31.5$$

$$b = \frac{(32)(70)}{140} = 16.0$$

TABLE 9.11
Cross-Tabulation of Subjective Insecurity and Whether or Not Persons Blame Others for Insecurity.

		Subjective Insecurity			
		High	*Medium*	*Low*	*Row Totals*
Blames Factors Beyond Control for Subjective Insecurity	*Yes*	42 *a*	18 *b*	10 *c*	70
	No	21 *d*	14 *e*	35 *f*	70
Column Totals		63	32	45	$N = 140$

Source: Data suggested by research conducted by Howard P. Greenwald, "Politics and the New Insecurity: Ideological Changes of Professionals in a Recession," *Social Forces*, **57**: 103–118, 1978.

$$c = \frac{(45)(70)}{140} = 22.5$$

$$d = \frac{(63)(70)}{140} = 31.5$$

$$e = \frac{(32)(70)}{140} = 16.0$$

$$f = \frac{(45)(70)}{140} = 22.5.$$

Once these expected cell frequencies have been determined, we may carry out the chi-square test for *k* samples as shown in Table 9.12. Carrying out these computations yields an observed $\chi^2 = 21.163$. We take this observed value to the chi-square table, Table A4, with $(r - 1)(c - 1)$ or $(2 - 1)(3 - 1) = 2$ degrees of freedom. We identify the critical value that must be equaled or exceeded by our observed chi square where the .01 level of significance (one-tailed probability) intersects with 2 df, or 7.824, as shown. Since our observed χ^2 of 21.163 equals or exceeds the critical value shown, we may reject H_0 and support H_1 that our data do differ from what would be expected according to chance.

An inspection of the distribution of cell frequencies throughout

TABLE 9.12

Cell	O_k	E_k	$(O_k - E_k)^2$	$(O_k - E_k)^2/E_k$
a	42	31.5	110.25	(110.25)/31.5 = 3.500
b	18	16	4.00	(4.00)/16 = .250
c	10	22.5	156.25	(156.25)/22.5 = 6.944
d	21	31.5	110.25	(110.25)/31.5 = 3.500
e	14	16	4.00	(4.00)/16 = .250
f	35	22.5	156.25	(156.25)/22.5 = 6.944
				$\chi^2 = 21.163$

the table provides convincing evidence that the direction is consistent with what has been predicted under H_1, that those persons with high subjective insecurity blame circumstances beyond an individual's control, whereas those persons with low subjective insecurity tend not to blame circumstances beyond an individual's control.

Assumptions of the Chi-Square Test for *k* Samples

The primary assumptions are (1) randomness, (2) nominal data that can be classified into *k* discrete categories, (3) independent samples, and (4) a reasonable sample-size range from 25 to 250. Again, applications of chi square to *N*'s smaller or larger than this recommended range should be interpreted with caution.

Advantages and Disadvantages of the Chi-Square Test

The advantages and disadvantages of this test are identical to those in the two-sample case. The test is easy to use, and tables exist for ready interpretation of the significance of goodness of fit. For tables larger than 2 × 2, it is somewhat more difficult to determine directionality by observing distributions of cell frequencies. The chi-square test is quite sensitive to extremely large and extremely small sample sizes. Under conditions when chi square is applied to *N*'s smaller than 25 or larger than 250, a type of distortion occurs that renders the observed chi-square value unusually large. Cautious interpretations of chi-square values are encouraged if the test is used in these situations.

□ *k*-SAMPLE TESTS—RELATED SAMPLES: THE COCHRAN *Q* TEST

When the researcher has data at the nominal level of measurement and *k* related samples (either through persons used as their own controls over *k* time periods or through matching), the *Cochran Q test* can be applied. One initial requirement is that the nominal variable under investigation can logically be *dichotomized* into "yes–no," "agree–disagree," "favorable–unfavorable," "high–low," "strong–mild," and so on. The following example is provided.

Weinstein (1979) was concerned with mental hospital patient attitudes toward hospitalization. Weinstein noted in a literature review that generally, patients' perceptions of their own hospitalization become increasingly favorable from the date of their original admission to the time of their discharge. Based on Weinstein's ideas about patient attitude changes toward hospitalization over time, 38 patients in a large mental hospital facility in the Southeast were examined over a 6-month period. Attendant interviewers recorded favorable–unfavorable responses of all patients during four different time periods. These time periods included (1) the initial attitude of patients at the time of their admission to the hospital, (2) their attitudes at the end of the first 2-month period, (3) their attitudes at the end of the next 2-month period, and (4) their attitudes at the end of 6 months.

"Attitude toward hospitalization" was dichotomized into "favorable–unfavorable." Attendant interviewers judged patient responses according to the particular mode of satisfaction expressed by patients toward benefits derived from treatment, quality of patient care, and satisfaction with the ward and general hospital services.

Unfavorable responses were coded with a 0, favorable responses with a 1. The following hypothesis set was subjected to test:

H_0: There is no change in patient attitudes toward hospitalization over a 6-month treatment period; if there is a change, it will be toward more unfavorable responses.

H_1: There will be a change in patient attitudes toward more favorable responses to hospitalization during a 6-month treatment period.

$$P \leqslant .01 \text{ (one-tailed test).}$$

The responses of 38 mental patients are shown for the four different time periods in Table 9.13. Table 9.13 is constructed as follows. Favorable or unfavorable responses by patients are entered in each time period column as shown. Favorable responses are indicated by a 1, whereas unfavorable responses are indicated by a 0. We must sum the 1 responses for each of the four columns (i.e., time periods). These sums are shown as the various S_i values at the bottom of each column.

For each patient, we must sum the 1 values across the four time periods and enter each sum in the column labeled *F*. Once this has been done for each patient, all of these *F* sums are summed as shown

TABLE 9.13
Mental Patient Favorable-Unfavorable Responses to Hospitalization over Four Time Periods.

Patient	*Time 1*	*Time 2*	*Time 3*	*Time 4*	*F*	F^2
1	0	0	0	1	1	1
2	0	1	1	1	3	9
3	1	1	1	1	4	16
4	0	0	0	0	0	0
5	0	0	0	1	1	1
6	1	1	1	1	4	16
7	1	0	1	1	3	9
8	0	1	1	1	3	9
9	0	1	1	1	3	9
10	0	0	0	0	0	0
11	1	0	1	1	3	9
12	0	1	1	1	3	9
13	0	1	1	1	3	9
14	0	1	0	0	1	1
15	0	0	1	1	2	4
16	1	1	1	1	4	16
17	0	0	0	0	0	0
18	1	1	1	1	4	16
19	0	0	0	0	0	0
20	0	1	1	1	3	9
21	1	1	1	1	4	16
22	0	0	1	1	2	4
23	0	0	0	0	0	0
24	0	0	1	1	2	4
25	0	1	1	1	3	9
26	1	1	1	1	4	16
27	0	1	1	1	3	9
28	0	0	0	1	1	1
29	0	0	1	1	2	4
30	0	1	1	0	2	4
31	1	0	0	1	2	4
32	0	0	0	0	0	0
33	0	0	1	1	2	4
34	0	0	1	1	2	4
35	1	1	1	1	4	16
36	1	1	1	1	4	16
37	1	1	0	1	3	9
38	0	0	0	0	0	0
$N = 38$	$S_1 = 12$	$S_2 = 19$	$S_3 = 25$	$S_4 = 29$	$\Sigma F = 85$	$\Sigma F^2 = 263$

Source: Dean J. Champion, "Patient's Attitudes Toward Hospitalization," unpublished paper, Department of Sociology, University of Tennessee, Knoxville, 1979.

(ΣF). Finally, each patient's F sum is squared and placed in the last column, F^2. These squares of F are then summed (ΣF^2). With these values we can carry out Cochran's Q test by using the following formula:

$$Q = \frac{(k-1)\left[k \sum S_i^2 - \left(\sum F\right)^2\right]}{k\left(\sum F\right) - \sum F^2},$$

where

k = number of samples (in this case, the number of time periods)
S_i = total number of favorable responses for each sample
$\sum F$ = total number of favorable responses across all samples
$\sum F^2$ = sum of the squared total of favorable responses for each individual across the k time periods

Substituting symbols in the formula for values from Table 9.13, we can carry out our computation to obtain the observed value of Q:

$$Q = \frac{(4-1)\,[(4)(12^2 + 19^2 + 25^2 + 29^2) - (85)^2]}{(4)(85) - 263}$$

$$= \frac{(3)\,[(4)(144 + 361 + 625 + 841) - 7225]}{340 - 263}$$

$$= \frac{(3)\,[(4)(1971) - 7225]}{77}$$

$$= \frac{(3)(7884 - 7225)}{77}$$

$$= \frac{(3)(659)}{77}$$

$$= \frac{1977}{77}$$

$$= 25.675.$$

Our observed Q value is 25.675. Since the Q statistic approximates the chi-square distribution, we may enter Table A4 with $k - 1$ or $4 - 1$ degrees of freedom (where k = the number of time periods). Where our df intersects with the .01 probability level (for a one-tailed test) defines the critical value of Q that we must equal or exceed with our observed Q value. The critical value of $Q = 9.837$ (with 3 df) and is equaled or exceeded by our observed $Q = 25.675$. We may reject H_0 and support H_1, tentatively concluding that patients will tend to have more favorable responses toward hospitalization during the time of their treatment period.

Since our hypothesis test was one-tailed or directional, we must examine closely the various S_i values rather than to rely completely on the observed Q value. Are there more favorable responses among the patients from one time period to the next? The sums of favorable responses from the first through the fourth time periods are 12, 19, 25, and 29, respectively. These S_i's do indicate an increase in favorable responses across the four time periods.

Whenever the Q statistic is applied and a one-tailed hypothesis test is made, the researcher must examine the various S_i values to make sure that the data are in the predicted direction under H_1. Had we observed S_i values across the four time periods that tended to decrease (i.e., 29, 25, 19, and 12, respectively), this trend would not be in the direction predicted under H_1 and H_0 could not have been rejected. This would be true in spite of the fact that the observed Q value was statistically significant. Directional tests of significance must correctly predict direction of differences across k groups in order for H_0's to be rejected. In the present instance, our directional prediction was supported by the direction of the data observed in Table 9.13. H_0 was rejected and H_1 was supported.

Assumptions of the Cochran Q Test

The primary assumptions of this test are (1) randomness; (2) the nominal level of measurement, where a variable can be dichotomized logically; and (3) related samples of elements, either matched in some way or used as their own controls over k different time periods.

Advantages and Disadvantages of the Cochran Q Test

The primary advantage of the Q test is that it is one of the few tests that exist for assessing differences between k related samples for the nominal level of measurement. Since it approximates the chi-square distribution and utilizes Table A4, this provides an additional advantage.

A third feature of this test is that it lends itself to applications where persons are matched as well as used as their own controls in before–after experiments. This means that the Q test can function with greater versatility compared with the McNemar test, which is restricted to persons used as their own controls. Under matching conditions involving two samples of elements, the Cochran Q test can be applied instead of the McNemar test. If we were to compare the complexity of the two formulas (i.e., the McNemar and Cochran Q formulas), the Q formula is by far the more laborious to compute. But considering the fact that the McNemar test cannot be applied to matched subjects, the use of the Cochran Q test in such instances would more than offset the disadvantage of the greater complexity of its formula compared with the McNemar test.

The Q statistic is a conservative goodness-of-fit procedure. It is approximately 80 to 85 percent powerful in rejecting false H_0's. It should never be applied if the number of sets of individuals is below 5, however. This is partially a function of the fact that Q is a chi-square-based statistic.

The Q test provides an overall assessment of the significance of difference between k groups and answers the general question: Does a significant difference exist between the groups *somewhere?* This is the same question answered by the parametric F test for k independent samples at the interval measurement level. Unfortunately, we do not have equivalent techniques such as the Newman–Keuls procedure or the Scheffé method to determine where significant differences between groups occur when the Q test is applied. Therefore, if the researcher wishes to know specifically which time periods differ the most concerning favorableness of patient's views toward hospitalization, a test must be made of each pair of time periods.

The Cochran Q test can function as its own "probe" and the researcher may simply apply the test to each pair of time period differences. Of course, if the persons are used as their own controls, the McNemar test can be applied to each pair of time periods as another alternative. A third and less desirable alternative is to use the sign test (to be treated in Chapter 10) to evaluate each pair of time periods. Although the ordinal-level-of-measurement assumption underlies the proper application of the sign test, it can be applied as a "probe" for differences between pairs of time periods if the results are conservatively and cautiously interpreted. The recommendation would be to select the McNemar test as a "probe" if possible, then the Q test applied to pairs of time periods. The sign test could be applied as a last resort.

□ SUMMARY

This chapter has presented an array of tests of significance appropriate for the analysis of data measured according to a nominal scale. Most tests that have been presented are categorically termed goodness-of-fit procedures, because an assessment is made of the significance of difference between what the researcher observes and what might be expected according to chance.

The most popular goodness-of-fit procedure is the chi-square test. It is useful for analyses of single samples as well as for two- and k-

sample cases. It is somewhat sensitive to fluctuations in sample size, however. Therefore, a recommended sample-size "operating range" would be between N's of 25 to 250, regardless of whether a single-sample, two-sample, or k-sample hypothesis test were being made.

For the two-sample application of chi square, Yates' correction for continuity was presented. This correction factor is applied when sample size ranges from 25 to 75 and is appropriate for data arranged into 2×2 tables only. The effect of Yates' correction is to reduce the magnitude of the resulting observed chi-square value and render a more conservative chi-square result.

When the researcher has two independent samples for investigation, either Fisher's exact test or the Z test for differences between proportions could be applied. Which test is selected would depend on the combined sample sizes of the two samples. When the combined sample sizes are 25 or fewer, Fisher's exact test would be appropriate. Obviously, this would be one alternative to using the chi-square test because of the small N involved. When the researcher has combined sample sizes in excess of 250, the Z test would be an appropriate alternative compared with chi square.

All three tests in the two-independent sample category provide different kinds of information about the observed data. Fisher's exact test gives an exact probability associated with observing an original data arrangement in a 2×2 table or any more extreme arrangement of the same data. The chi-square test renders a statistical evaluation of goodness of fit between some observed distribution of frequencies and some "expected" or "chance" distribution of them. The Z test is perhaps the most flexible of the three, providing the researcher with an evaluation of the significance of proportionate differences between categories. The Z test also functions well with either very small or very large N's, whereas the chi-square test and Fisher's exact test are relatively restricted.

For the analysis of related samples, the McNemar test for significance of change is available. It can only be used when persons are used as their own controls in a before–after experimental arrangement, however. The results of the McNemar test approximate the chi-square distribution and Table A4 can be used.

When k independent samples are encountered, the k-sample version of the chi-square test may be employed. The researcher must again consider the sensitivity of chi square to very small or very large samples, however. When k related samples are available for analysis, Cochran's Q test can be applied. This also approximates the chi-square distribution and gives the researcher a conservative statistical result that evaluates the significance of difference between groups across k time periods or k groups of matched individuals.

The procedures to follow in Chapter 10 are designed for situations where ordinal-level data are obtained for analysis.

SELECTED STUDY TERMS

Goodness of fit
Observed and expected frequencies
Chi square
Fisher's exact test
2 X 2 table
Collapsing $r \times c$ tables
Desirable tabular distributions
Yates' correction for continuity
McNemar test
Cochran Q test
Dichotomy

EXERCISES

1. Test the following hypothesis set:

   H_0: There is no difference between what is observed and what is expected according to chance.
   H_1: There is a difference between what is observed and what is expected according to chance.

   $$P \leqslant .05 \quad \text{(two-tailed test).}$$

   (a) The data for Exercise 1 are as follows:

		Variable X: *Yes*	Variable X: *No*	*Row Totals*
Variable y	*High*	25	17	42
	Low	12	43	55
	Column Totals	37	60	$N = 97$

   (b) What is the observed chi square for this table?
   (c) How many degrees of freedom are associated with it?
   (d) What is the critical value of chi square?
   (e) What is your decision regarding H_0?
2. A researcher observes the following table, reflecting changes in attitudes of psychiatric social workers toward an experimental therapy program. These persons are asked to indicate their feelings toward the therapy program before they actually see it in operation. Next, they are asked to evaluate it after a 6-month exposure to it in an actual hospital setting. Use the McNemar test for significance of change to determine whether or not any change in

attitude occurred. Assume a nondirectional, two-tailed hypothesis test made at the .01 level of significance.

		After Program		
		Approve	*Disapprove*	*Totals*
Before Program	*Approve*	12	6	18
	Disapprove	26	3	29
	Totals	38	9	$N = 47$

(a) What is the observed chi-square value?
(b) What is the critical value of chi square?
(c) How many degrees of freedom are there associated with this table?
(d) What is your decision about the change in attitude, if any? Describe your findings in a brief paragraph.

3. Two samples of elements have been randomly selected. One sample consists of 120 Catholics, and the other sample consists of 200 Protestants. These persons have been asked to indicate their attitude toward voluntary birth control. The data are

		Sample		
		Catholics	*Protestants*	*Totals*
Attitude Toward Voluntary Birth Control	*Favor*	70	120	190
	Oppose	50	80	130
	Totals	120	200	$N = 320$

Use the Z test for difference between proportions and determine the significance of difference between Catholics and Protestants who favor voluntary birth control. Assume a two-tailed test at the .01 level of significance.
(a) Does a statistically significant difference exist between Protestants and Catholics on the birth control issue?
(b) Present your evidence in the form of an observed Z value and the critical value of Z for the .01 level.

4. A researcher has four ethnic groups selected randomly. Each ethnic group has been labeled A, B, C, and D, respectively. Each person is asked to indicate his or her political preference. The following 3×4 table is generated:

		Ethnic Group				
		A	B	C	D	Totals
Political Preference	Party A	21	11	8	4	44
	Party B	10	22	14	3	49
	Party C	2	15	15	19	51
	Totals	33	48	37	26	$N = 144$

(a) If you were to test an hypothesis of goodness of fit for these data, what would you obtain as an observed chi-square value?
(b) What would be the critical value of chi square for the .05 level of significance, assuming a two-tailed test?
(c) Would you reject or fail to reject H_0 at the .05 level?
(d) Can Yates' correction for continuity be applied to the table above? Why or why not? Explain.
(e) What are the degrees of freedom for this table?
(f) Which version of the chi-square test did you apply in this instance (i.e., single-sample, two-sample, k-sample)?

5. A researcher observes the following information for five groups of 10 individuals each, matched according to a large number of social and personal characteristics.

	Group			
Person	1	2	3	4
1	0	0	1	1
2	1	1	1	1
3	0	1	0	1
4	0	0	0	1
5	1	0	1	1
6	0	0	1	0
7	0	0	1	1
8	1	1	1	1
9	0	0	1	0
10	1	1	0	1

(a) Carry out Cochran's Q test for these data and determine the observed Q value.
(b) Assuming a nondirectional, two-tailed test of some H_0 that no difference exists between the k sets of matched individuals, what conclusion would you reach at the .01 level of significance?
(c) What is the critical value of Q?
(d) How many degrees of freedom are associated with these data?
(e) What distribution is approximated by the Q statistic?

6. Write a brief essay on the weaknesses and strengths of chi square for two samples. What two alternative statistical procedures can be selected when-

ever chi square is inappropriate? Under what conditions would you apply each of the two tests you mentioned? Explain.

7. A researcher observes the following information for a sample of mail clerks regarding their satisfaction with work:

Satisfaction with Work

High	*Low*	*Total*
25	45	70

Using the chi-square test, do these data differ from what would be expected according to chance? Assume a two-tailed test at the .01 level of significance.
   (a) Briefly describe your conclusions and supporting evidence (i.e., your observed chi-square value and the critical value of chi square).
   (b) How many degrees of freedom are associated with these data?

8. Apply Yates' correction for continuity to the data in Exercise 1.
   (a) What is the nature of the change in the resulting chi-square value?
   (b) What is the recommended sample-size range for applying Yates' correction for continuity? Why is this so?
   (c) What is the general effect of applying Yates' correction to 2 × 2 tables? What is meant by the fact that applying Yates' correction to these data is a conservative step on the researcher's part? Explain.

9. A researcher has obtained two small samples of elements. These two groups represent consultants for two large firms. On the basis of a problem-solving test taken by all members of both groups, the group members have been cross-tabulated according to "solves problems slowly" and "solves problems quickly." Use Fisher's exact test and determine the probability associated with observing the accompanying table and any more extreme version of that table.

	Group 1	*Group 2*	*Totals*
Solves Problems Slowly	11	4	15
Solves Problems Quickly	2	8	10
Totals	13	12	$N = 25$

   (a) What is P_c associated with these data?
   (b) How many separate probabilities did you need to compute to obtain P_c? Why? Explain.
   (c) What would you regard as the primary limitation of Fisher's exact test? Explain.
   (d) On the basis of your results and an inspection of the data in the table, can anything be said about the two groups of consultants and how they solve problems? Write a short paragraph summarizing your response.

REFERENCES

Champion, Dean J., "Patients' Attitudes Toward Hospitalization," unpublished paper, Department of Sociology, University of Tennessee, Knoxville, 1979.

Greenwald, Howard P., "Politics and the New Insecurity: Ideological Changes of Professionals in a Recession," *Social Forces*, **57**:103-118, 1978.

Marcum, John P., and Frank D. Bean, "Minority Group Status as a Factor in the Relationship Between Mobility and Fertility: The Mexican-American Case," *Social Forces*, **55**:135-148, 1976.

Metz, A. Stafford, "An Analysis of Some Determinants of Attitude Toward Fluoridation," *Social Forces*, **44**:477-484, 1966.

Morris, Ruth R., "Female Delinquency and Relational Problems," *Social Forces*, **43**:82-89, 1964.

Olsen, Donald B., "A Comparative Analysis of Metropolitan and Non-Metropolitan Physicians in Southern Appalachia," unpublished master's thesis, University of Tennessee, Knoxville, 1970.

Reiss, Albert J., Jr., *Occupations and Social Status.* New York: The Free Press, 1961.

Siegel, Sidney, *Nonparametric Statistics for the Behavioral Sciences.* New York: McGraw-Hill Book Company, 1956.

Weinstein, Raymond M., "Patient Attitudes Toward Mental Hospitalization: A Review of Quantitative Research," *Journal of Health and Social Behavior*, **20**:237-258, 1979.

Wood, James R., and Mayer N. Zald, "Aspects of Racial Integration in the Methodist Church: Sources of Resistance to Organizational Policy," *Social Forces*, **45**:255-265, 1966.

10

Ordinal-Level Tests of Significance

This chapter presents an array of tests of significance of difference for data measured according to an ordinal scale. Compared with the tests of significance discussed in Chapter 9, these procedures utilize ordinality and are most appropriate for analysis of attitudinal data. A researcher has usually achieved the ordinal level of measurement whenever Likert, Thurstone, or Guttman scaling procedures have been used to derive attitudinal scores. Some additional measurement scales include Osgood's Semantic Differential, Coombs' "unfolding technique," and the *Q*-sort.

The chapter organization is as follows. A single-sample technique, the Kolmogorov–Smirnov test, will be discussed. Three two-independent sample tests will follow: (1) the Wald–Wolfowitz runs test, (2) the two-sample version of the Kolmogorov–Smirnov test, and (3) the Mann–Whitney *U* test. For situations when the researcher has two related samples, the sign test will be presented as a conservative option. Two k-independent sample procedures will follow, including the Kruskal–Wallis H test, and the median test. Finally, the Friedman two-way ANOVA test will be presented as a k-related-sample ordinal test of significance.

□ A SINGLE-SAMPLE TEST: THE KOLMOGOROV–SMIRNOV TEST

The Kolmogorov–Smirnov (K–S) test is a goodness-of-fit procedure in a sense. A distribution of frequencies is arranged throughout k ranked or *gradated categories.* This observed distribution of frequencies is compared with an hypothetical distribution that is presumed to be equally distributed throughout the k categories. The actual comparison is made between cumulative frequencies from one category to the next. If there is substantial variation between the two cumulative frequency distributions (i.e., between what is observed and what would be expected if the data were equally divided across the k categories), the observed frequency distribution would be considered significantly different from what would be expected according to chance. The following example is provided.

Harvey and Slatin (1975) conducted a study of the relationship between children's socioeconomic status (SES) and their teacher's expectations. These researchers assumed that "teacher's expectations of a child's school performance . . . [would] . . . vary directly with the teacher's perception of the child's social class" (Harvey and Slatin, 1975, p. 141). In the initial phase of their study, photographs were obtained of nine white school children ranging in age from 8 to 12. The photographs were touched up to present a studio photo effect, eliminating the potential bias of background scenery or other clues to each child's SES.

Subsequently, a sample of 96 teachers was obtained. The teachers were asked to examine each of the children's photographs and make judgments of the child's SES. The children were unknown to the teachers. Furthermore, there was no way to ascertain the children's true SES from their appearance in the photo. Included in the questionnaire administered to the teachers were items relating to the "success" or "failure" behaviors of children in school such as "reading books independently" (a success behavior) and being "in trouble" (a failure behavior). Therefore, all 96 teachers could conceivably select all 9 children as being ones who "probably read independently" (or "have trouble in school"). Of course, the teachers were at liberty to refuse to evaluate any or all of the 9 children.

A total of 312 selections of children were made by the 96 teachers on "reads independently" as one of several categories. (A possible 96 X 9 = 864 selections could have been made had the teachers assigned all children observed to this particular category.) Table 10.1 shows the teacher's perceived SES of the children across three SES categories: lower, middle, and upper. The following hypothesis set is suggested by the work of Harvey and Slatin:

H_0: There is no difference in assignments of the children to three SES categories by the teachers.
H_1: There is a difference in assignments of children to three SES categories by teachers.

$$P \leqslant .01 \quad \text{(two-tailed test).}$$

Using the K–S one-sample procedure to test this hypothesis set, we must proceed as follows. Table 10.1 consists of five rows. The first row (R_1) is the observed distribution of 312 selections across the three SES categories. Row 2 (R_2) is the expected distribution of these same children through the three categories. Expected frequencies in each category are determined by N/k, where N is the number

TABLE 10.1
Teacher's Assignment of Children to Three SES Categories.

	SES Categories			
	Lower	*Middle*	*Upper*	*Totals*
Number of Children Perceived as Fitting This Category (R_1)	18	120	174	312
Expected Number of Children in Each Category (R_2)	104	104	104	312
Cumulative Observed Frequencies for Row 1 (R_3)	$\frac{18}{312}$	$\frac{138}{312}$	$\frac{312}{312}$	100%
Cumulative Expected Frequencies for Row 2 (R_4)	$\frac{104}{312}$	$\frac{208}{312}$	$\frac{312}{312}$	100%
Absolute Difference Between Cumulative Distributions in Row 3 and Row 4 (R_5)	$\frac{86}{312}$	$\frac{70}{312}$	–	
(Proportions)	(.28)	(.22)	(–)	

Source: Dale G. Harvey and Gerald T. Slatin, "The Relationship Between Child's SES and Teacher Expectations: A Test of the Middle-Class Bias Hypothesis," *Social Forces*, **54:** 145, 1975.

of selections and k the number of categories. In this case, $N/k = 312/3 = 104$. Therefore, 104 selections would be expected in each of the three categories.

Row 3 (R_3) is a cumulative frequency distribution of row 1. The first cell contains 18 frequencies out of 312 of them. These are added to those in the second cell to yield 138 frequencies (i.e., 18 + 120 = 138). These are added to those in the third cell to yield 312 (i.e., 138 + 174 = 312). The fourth row (R_4) is a cumulative frequency distribution of row 2. The expected frequencies in the first cell, 104, are added to those of the second cell to yield 208 frequencies (i.e., 104 + 104 = 208). These 208 frequencies are added to those in the third cell, or 208 + 104 = 312 frequencies.

The fifth row (R_5) consists of the absolute differences between the fractions in row 3 and row 4, respectively. In other words, for the first cell we would have (104/312) - (18/312) = 86/312. In the second cell, (208/312) - (138/312) = 70/312. The third cell is (312/312) - (312/312) = 0. We focus upon the largest observed difference between the two cumulative frequency distributions. This difference is 86/312 and is designated D. We must now translate this observed D into a proportion, or 86/312 = .28.

We are now ready to evaluate the significance of this largest proportionate difference, $D = .28$. Table A.9 contains critical values of D for various levels of significance. Probabilities are found across the top of the table, and sample sizes are found down the left-hand column. Our $N = 312$ in the present case. Therefore, we must use the "over 35" line in the table to obtain the critical value of D. Since the .01 level of significance is being used, we will use the formula shown in the table as $1.63/\sqrt{N}$ to determine the critical D value. This is $1.63/\sqrt{312} = 1.63/17.66 = .09$. We must equal or exceed .09 with our observed D value from Table 10.1 in order to reject H_0. Clearly, the observed $D = .28$ exceeds .09, and we may reject H_0 at the .01 level of significance. Tentatively, we may conclude that teachers do differ in their assignments of the children to the three categories.

Had we wished to make a one-tailed hypothesis test, an examination of the distribution of frequencies throughout Table 10.1 would be required to ensure that the data were consistent with the directional prediction under H_1. For instance, had Harvey and Slatin predicted that more teachers would assign the children to the "upper" SES category, the distribution of frequencies in Table 10.1 would be consistent with this prediction. Had the distribution of frequencies in Table 10.1 turned out to be 174 lower SES, 120 middle SES, and 18 upper SES, the data would be arranged in a direction opposite to that predicted under H_1. In that event, it would not be appropriate to conduct the K–S test. Again, this reflects the risk a researcher takes in making one-tailed, directional hypothesis tests. Although there is less risk associated with a two-tailed or nondirectional hypothesis test, two-tailed tests are generally less informative compared with one-tailed ones. Whichever type of test is conducted by the researcher (i.e., a one- or a two-tailed test) will depend on the amount of information possessed beforehand about the sample selected.

Assumptions of the Kolmogorov–Smirnov Test

The primary assumptions of the K–S one-sample test are (1) randomness, and (2) the ordinal level of measurement underlying the variable studied. Sometimes an assumption is made that the variable under investigation be continuous. In any event, the researcher will create k discrete, graded categories across which N individuals will be distributed.

Advantages and Disadvantages of the K–S Test

One apparent advantage of the K–S one-sample test is that it can be applied to a sample divided into any number of graded categories. Compared with the chi-square test, which could be applied to the same data in Table 10.1 to answer the same question, the K–S test utilizes more information. It takes advantage of the ordinality that exists between the k categories.

The K–S test has a power of 85 to 90 percent in relation to rejecting false null hypotheses. Use of Table A9 permits rapid determination of critical D values so that hypothesis tests can be made easily.

There are no difficult or complex calculations involved in the derivation of the observed D or the critical D value with which it is compared. There are virtually no sample-size restrictions. There are no serious disadvantages of the K–S one-sample test for research applications and hypothesis testing.

□ TWO-SAMPLE TESTS: INDEPENDENT SAMPLES

In this section we examine three procedures for evaluating *differences between two independent samples* according to some characteristic measured at the ordinal level. These tests include (1) the Wald–Wolfowitz runs test, (2) the Kolmogorov–Smirnov two-sample test, and (3) the Mann–Whitney U test.

The Wald-Wolfowitz Runs Test

A conservative and rather direct method for determining the significance of difference between two independent samples on some ordinal characteristic is the Wald–Wolfowitz runs test. Perhaps an attitudinal variable is measured for two samples. Raw scores on the attitudinal scale are arranged from low to high or from high to low, and the resulting distribution is examined for the degree of heterogeneity present. The following example is provided.

Rubenstein (1976) was interested in studying the visual and motor behaviors of infants. From a private pediatric practice, Rubenstein observed 20 six-month-old infants, 10 boys and 10 girls. One aspect of Rubenstein's research examined differences in the amount of time the infants would spend playing with familiar objects (i.e., toys from their homes) and novel or unfamiliar objects (i.e., toys provided by the researcher and not available to the infants in their homes). It was subsequently determined that both male and female infants tended to play longer with novel or unfamiliar objects. The amount of time spent manipulating objects was measured in terms of seconds. One question suggested by Rubenstein's research was whether male infants spend more time with novel objects compared with their female counterparts. The following hypothesis set is suggested:

H_0: There is no difference between male and female infants and the amount of time spent manipulating novel or unfamiliar objects.
H_1: Male and female infants differ in the amount of time spent manipulating novel or unfamiliar objects.

$$P \leqslant .05 \quad \text{(two-tailed test).}$$

Amounts of time spent manipulating novel or unfamiliar objects by male and female infants are shown in Table 10.2. Do the two groups of infants "come from the same population" in terms of time spent playing with new and unfamiliar objects? Or is there a significant difference between male and female infants in this regard? The Wald–Wolfowitz runs test may be applied to answer these questions.

First, the data in Table 10.2 are arranged from low to high (based on the magnitude of each score relative to the others) as follows:

$$\overline{199\quad 202\quad 203\quad 215}^{\,1}\quad \underline{221\quad 229}_{\,2}\quad \overline{237\quad 245\quad 249}^{\,3}$$

$$\underline{253\quad 257\quad 259\quad 275\quad 285\quad 288\quad 296\quad 304}_{\,4}\quad \overline{308\quad 310\quad 322}^{\,5}$$

Next, a line is drawn over each female infant score and under each male infant score, as shown. It will be observed that several scores for the females (and for the males) are immediately adjacent to one another. These consecutive scores from the same sample constitute a

TABLE 10.2
Amount of Time Spent by Male and Female Infants Manipulating Novel or Unfamiliar Objects.

Amount of Time (seconds)	
Males (N_1 = 10)	*Females* (N_2 = 10)
253	308
221	237
229	245
257	249
259	202
296	203
285	310
288	215
275	322
304	199

run. One or more scores from the group of males which "run together" constitute another run; and so on. Our results reveal a total of five runs of scores between the two samples. The total observed number of runs is designated R. Therefore, $R = 5$. The fewer the number of runs or R, the more different the two groups of infants will be.

We must turn to Table A13, which contains various critical values of R. This will aid us in assessing the significance of the $R = 5$ that we have observed. Table A13 is designed for small samples of elements, where N_1 and N_2 are both no larger than 20. Where our $N_1 = 10$ and $N_2 = 10$ intersect in the body of the table identifies the critical number of runs. Our observed number of runs, R, must be equal to or less than the critical R shown in the table in order to reject H_0 at the .05 level of significance. The critical $R = 6$, and since our observed $R = 5$, we may reject H_0 and support H_1 at the .05 level. We may conclude tentatively that male and female infants differ significantly in the amount of time spent manipulating novel or unfamiliar objects.

If either N_1 or N_2 exceed 20, Table A13 cannot be used. In that event, an approximation of a Z value may be obtained by using the following formula:

$$Z = \frac{\left| R - \left(\dfrac{2N_1N_2}{N_1 + N_2} + 1 \right) \right| - .5}{\sqrt{\dfrac{2N_1N_2(2N_1N_2 - N_1 - N_2)}{(N_1 + N_2)^2(N_1 + N_2 - 1)}}},$$

where

R = observed number of runs
N_1 and N_2 = number of elements in each sample

The resulting Z value is interpreted as any other Z value. Table A3 would be used to determine the critical value of Z for various significance levels. The larger the Z value, the greater the significance of difference between two distributions of scores.

Assumptions of the Wald–Wolfowitz Runs Test. The primary assumptions of the runs test are (1) randomness, (2) independent samples, and (3) the ordinal level of measurement.

Advantages and Disadvantages of the Runs Test. The primary advantage of the runs test compared with the other two tests in this section is that the raw scores may be dealt with directly rather than transformed into ranks or categorized. The runs test is quick and easy to apply, and there are no sample-size restrictions. It provides the researcher with the most conservative evaluation of differences between two distributions of scores. Compared with the parametric t test, the runs test is approximately 75 to 80 percent as powerful for rejecting false null hypotheses.

The main drawback of the runs test is that the presence of a considerable number of *tied scores* interferes with the effectiveness of the test results. Tied scores present the researcher with a special problem. Suppose that two groups of 10 persons each have the following scores, arranged from low to high:

$$\underbrace{1\ 2\ 3}_{A}\ \overbrace{4\ 5\ 6}^{B}\ \underbrace{7}_{A}\ 8\ 8\ 8\ 8\ \underbrace{9\ 10\ 11\ 12}_{A}\ \overbrace{13\ 14\ 15\ 16\ 17}^{B}.$$

If we designate scores belonging to one group as A scores and the scores belonging to the other group as B scores as has been done above, we can determine the number of runs readily. But there are four tied scores of 8. If all of these scores belonged to group A, we would have the following arrangement:

$$\underbrace{1\ 2\ 3}_{A}\ \overbrace{4\ 5\ 6}^{B}\ \underbrace{7\ 8\ 8\ 8\ 8\ 9\ 10\ 11\ 12}_{A}\ \overbrace{13\ 14\ 15\ 16\ 17}^{B}.$$

Or if all of the four scores of 8 belonged to group B, we would have the following arrangement:

B B B
1 2 3 4 5 6 7 8 8 8 8 9 10 11 12 13 14 15 16 17.
A A A

These two situations are not problematic for the researcher, because the scores of 8 can be blended in with other scores belonging to the group possessing them. But if the tied scores are distributed between the two groups (i.e., suppose that each group has two scores of 8), any number of runs arrangements could be determined. The number of runs could be minimized as follows:

B B B
1 2 3 4 5 6 7 8 8 8 8 9 10 11 12 13 14 15 16 17.
A A A

Or the number of runs could be maximized as follows:

B B B B
1 2 3 4 5 6 7 8 8 8 8 9 10 11 12 13 14 15 16 17.
A A A A

Whenever the researcher is confronted with this situation, the recommendation is to maximize the number of runs possible. This is a conservative step and reduces the likelihood of rejecting H_0. If the investigator were to minimize the number of runs and increase the likelihood of rejecting H_0, a charge of researcher bias or "data juggling" could be made. If there are any tied scores belonging to two groups, the safe alternative would be to select another test. The Mann–Whitney U test would be the best alternative, although the researcher would need to spend considerably more time carrying out the necessary computations.

The Kolmogorov–Smirnov Two-Sample Test

The Kolmogorov–Smirnov (K–S) two-sample test is an extension of the K–S test for a single sample. In the single-sample case, the K–S test evaluated the significance of difference between an observed and an expected cumulative frequency distribution. The present version of the K–S test evaluates the significance of difference between two independent samples, where the samples have both been arranged into a cumulative frequency distribution throughout k categories. The greatest proportionate difference between the two samples in any given category is used for hypothesis test purposes. Consider the following example.

Haug and Lavin (1978) conducted a study that examined patient attitudes toward physician authority. These researchers wanted to know if variations in the method of payment for medical services would influence patients' reactions toward the physician's authority in prescribing certain kinds of treatment or therapy. For instance, would patients who pay directly for medical services value the physician's advice more compared with those patients who belong to some sort of medical prepayment plan? Haug and Lavin noted that "[it has been suggested] that persons who pay directly for medical advice value it more, and accept it more readily, whereas those in a prepayment system, lacking the immediate connection between amount of care and cost, begin to feel that services are 'free,' and therefore of lesser value and more subject to challenge." (Haug and Lavin, p. 280.)

Using a measure of "questioning physician authority" (QPA), Haug and Lavin examined two independent samples of patients. The first sample of 188 patients consisted of those persons who participated in a prepayment system and were labeled "prepaid." The second sample of 226 persons were those who paid for services as the services were performed. These were labeled the "fee-for-service" group. Table 10.3 shows the two samples of patients cross-tabulated according to the degree to which they questioned physician authority (QPA, ranging from "high," "moderately high," "moderately low," and "low."). The following hypothesis set is suggested by the work of Haug and Lavin:

H_0: There is no difference between prepaid and fee-for-service patients and the degree to which they question physician authority.

H_1: The prepaid and fee-for-service patient groups differ in the degree to which they question physician authority.

$$P \leqslant .001 \quad \text{(two-tailed test).}$$

Table 10.3 is constructed as follows. Based on the QPA scale, four categories of gradated responses are created from "high" to "low," as shown across the top of the table. Both groups of patients (prepaid and fee-for-service) are assigned one of the four categories, depending on their respective QPA scores. Rows 1 and 2 (R_1 and R_2) contain the two distributions of frequencies throughout the four categories created.

Row 3 (R_3) is a cumulative frequency distribution of the frequencies in row 1. The frequencies from the first cell in row 3 are added to those in the second cell, and so on. (These have also been transformed into cumulative proportions as well. For instance, 42/188, or 42 persons out of 188, becomes .223; 119/188 = .633; and so on.) Row 4 (R_4) consists of a cumulative frequency distribution of the

TABLE 10.3
Prepaid and Fee-for-Service Patients Cross-Tabulated by "Questioning Physician Authority."

	Questioning Physician Authority				
	High	*Moderately high*	*Moderately low*	*Low*	*Totals*
Prepaid (R_1)	42	77	50	19	$N_1 = 188$
Fee-for-Service (R_2)	47	90	53	36	$N_2 = 226$
Cumulative Prepaid (R_3) *(cumulative proportion)*	$\frac{42}{188}$ (.223)	$\frac{119}{188}$ (.633)	$\frac{169}{188}$ (.899)	$\frac{188}{188}$ (1.000)	
Cumulative Fee-for-Service (R_4) *(cumulative proportion)*	$\frac{47}{226}$ (.208)	$\frac{137}{226}$ (.606)	$\frac{190}{226}$ (.841)	$\frac{226}{226}$ (1.000)	
Absolute Difference (R_5) *Between* R_3 *and* R_4	.015	0.27	.058	–	

Source: Marie Haug and Bebe Lavin, "Method of Payment for Medical Care and Public Attitudes Toward Physician Authority," *Journal of Health and Social Behavior*, **19**:282, 1978.

data in row 2. This has been determined in the same manner as the data in row 3.

Finally, row 5 (R_5) consists of the absolute proportionate differences between each pair of cells in rows 3 and 4. For instance, the absolute difference between the pair of cells in rows 3 and 4 for high QPA scores would be .223 – .208 = .015. The absolute difference for the second pair of cells would be .633 – .606 = .027, and so on. The absolute differences in the two cumulative frequency distributions (expressed in proportion terms) have been entered in row 5. Focusing on the largest proportionate difference, which is .058, we are now ready to evaluate the statistical significance of it.

We now turn to Table A11. In the left-hand column are one- and two-tailed probabilities. The body of the table to the right of these probabilities contains formulas that will yield critical values. Since our hypothesis test is being made at the .001 level of significance, we use the formula, $1.95\sqrt{N_1 + N_2/N_1N_2}$ to obtain the critical D value.

The critical D values that are obtained by using the formulas in Table A11 are actually *critical proportions* that our largest observed proportionate difference must equal or exceed in order to be significant statistically. We will refer to the largest difference between the two cumulative proportion distributions in Table 10.3 as our observed D value. The critical value of D that we must equal or exceed is determined as follows:

$$\text{Critical value of } D = 1.95\sqrt{\frac{188 + 226}{(188)(226)}}$$

$$= 1.95\sqrt{\frac{414}{42{,}488}}$$

$$= 1.95\sqrt{.0097}$$

$$= (1.95)(.098)$$

$$= .191.$$

The resulting critical value of $D = .191$. We must obtain a D equal to or larger than .191 with our observed D in order to reject the null hypothesis. With an observed D of only .058, we fail to reject H_0. We may conclude that there is no significant difference between the method of payment for physician services and the degree to which persons challenge a physician's authority. This decision has been made at the .001 level of significance (two-tailed test).

Had a one-tailed test of the hypothesis been made, the researcher would have used the one-tailed probability column shown in Table A11 to obtain the critical value of D. In the one-tailed hypothesis test situation, however, the researcher would be obligated to examine the two distributions of frequencies in order to determine if the direction predicted under H_1 was consistent with the two frequency distributions. If Haug and Lavin had predicted that the prepaid group would be more likely to challenge physician authority compared with the fee-for-service group, a distributional arrangement should have been observed such as that shown in Table 10.4. Note that a greater number of prepaid patients would fall in the first two categories (high and moderately high) compared with the fee-for-service patients. A majority of the fee-for-service patients would probably be found in the latter categories (i.e., moderately low and low). Had the opposite arrangement been observed, the K–S test would not be

TABLE 10.4

	QPA				
	High	*Mod. High*	*Mod. Low*	*Low*	*Totals*
Prepaid	77	50	42	19	$N_1 = 188$
Fee-for-Service	36	47	53	90	$N_2 = 226$

appropriate. This is because the direction of the distribution of frequencies would not be consistent with that predicted under H_1. Table 10.5 is an example of a distributional arrangement that would nullify the use of the K–S test where an incorrect directional prediction had been made.

Assumptions of the K–S Two-Sample Test. The primary assumptions of the K–S test are (1) randomness, (2) two independent samples, and (3) the ordinal level of measurement.

Advantages and Disadvantages of the K–S Test. Compared with the Wald–Wolfowitz runs test, the K–S test is approximately 85 to 90 percent as powerful as the parametric *t* test for rejecting false null hypotheses. The greater power differential of the K–S test makes it a more desirable alternative compared with the runs test.

The K–S test deals with tied scores effectively. Any cell containing more than one frequency constitutes a tied-score situation. In Table 10.3, for instance, there are 42 tied scores in the first cell in row 1,

TABLE 10.5

	QPA				
	High	*Mod. High*	*Mod. Low*	*Low*	*Totals*
Prepaid	19	42	50	77	$N_1 = 188$
Fee-for-Service	90	53	47	36	$N_2 = 226$

77 tied scores in the second cell in row 1, 90 tied scores in the second cell in row 2, and so on. The researcher must create k categories into which the data for the two samples can be distributed. The raw scores cannot be dealt with directly as was the case with the runs test.

The K–S test is particularly useful for comparing two distributions of elements on some ordinal characteristic. The researcher simply identifies an attitudinal or behavioral variable, divides the variable logically into k graded subclasses or categories, and compares the resulting cumulative frequency distributions according to the proportionate differences between them.

A table is available (Table A11) for determining critical D values for hypothesis-test purposes. The K–S test is easy to compute and is subject to no sample-size restrictions. It has no restrictive distributional assumptions such as normality, and it is properly regarded as one of the better nonparametric two-sample tests at the ordinal level of measurement. There are no serious disadvantages associated with the K–S test.

The Mann-Whitney *U* Test

The Mann-Whitney U test (referred to as the *U test*) is the best known of the nonparametric tests of significance of difference between two independent samples of elements on some ordinal characteristic. Compared with the runs test and the K–S two-sample test, it is the most powerful at rejecting false null hypotheses. Compared with the t test, the U test is about 95 percent as powerful. Appropriate for a wide variety of sample sizes and research applications, the U test is frequently cited in the professional social science literature. An application of the U test is illustrated by the following example.

Wellisch et al. (1978) were interested in factors associated with increasing the effectiveness of elementary schools. One part of their investigation focused upon the nature of school management and organization: To what extent is administrative leadership important in contributing to the success of an elementary school teaching program? How are achievement levels of students affected by different administrative leadership orientations?

These researchers obtained data from 26 schools. Using national criteria (i.e., national norms for student achievement, nationally administered achievement tests, etc.), some of the schools were designated as "successful," and other schools were designated as "unsuccessful." The successfulness of any particular school was determined by whether or not it was above or below national norms on student achievement. Observers and interviewers entered each school and questionnaires were administered to various school officials, including members of the administration and the faculty.

One part of their study examined how strongly administrators felt about coordinated instructional programs and the importance of communication of their ideas about instruction to the teachers. Measures were obtained on the variable "concern for instruction," and raw scores were forthcoming. Wellisch et al. believed that the more successful schools would have more aggressive administrators who would take the lead by promoting improvements in instruction quality. The following hypothesis set is suggested by the research of Wellisch et al.:

H_0: Successful schools will not differ from unsuccessful schools on administrative concern for instruction quality; if there is a difference, unsuccessful schools will have greater administrative concern for instruction quality.

H_1: Successful schools will exhibit greater administrative concern for instructional quality compared with unsuccessful schools.

$P \leqslant .05$ (one-tailed test).

Table 10.6 contains two samples of schools. The first sample, $N_1 = 14$, consists of those schools labeled successful. The second sample, $N_2 = 12$, consists of those schools labeled unsuccessful. Raw scores are shown for both samples of schools which reflect varying degrees of administrative concern for instructional quality. The larger the score, the greater the administrative concern. In a second column adjacent to each of the columns of raw scores, various ranks have been assigned. The ranks have been assigned according to the magnitude of the raw scores shown for both groups. For example, the largest raw score for either group is assigned the rank of 1. The next largest score for either group is assigned the rank of 2; and so on. We must rank all the schools from 1 to N or from 1 to 26 in this case.

Where we encounter two or more raw scores that are identical, they are simply assigned the average of the ranks they would occupy if different. For instance, if the largest score happened to be 85, and if 85 occurred three times, we would assign all three raw scores of 85 the average of the first three ranks, or $(1 + 2 + 3)/3 = 2$. All scores have been ranked across the two groups in Table 10.4 as shown.

Once ranks have been assigned, we must sum the two columns of ranks (R_1 and R_2). These sums are shown in Table 10.6 as ΣR_1 and ΣR_2, respectively. With these sums of ranks and our respective N's, we may proceed with the U test. The formula for the U statistic is

$$U = N_1 N_2 + \frac{(N_1)(N_1 + 1)}{2} - \sum R_1,$$

TABLE 10.6
Successful and Unsuccessful Schools and Degree of Administrative Concern for Instructional Quality.

Administrative Concern for Instructional Quality (raw scores)			
Successful Schools		*Unsuccessful Schools*	
$N_1 = 14$	R_1	$N_2 = 12$	R_2
51	1	41	10
47	4	44	6
43	7	32	17.5
29	20.5	37	15
40	12	30	19
28	22.5	22	26
46	5	25	25
41	10	28	22.5
33	16	26	24
32	17.5	48	3
29	20.5	42	8
39	13	41	10
49	2		
38	14		
	$\Sigma R_1 = 165$		$\Sigma R_2 = 186$

Source: Table format and idea suggested by the research of Jean B. Wellisch, A. H. MacQueen, R. A. Carriere, and G. A. Duck, "School Management and Organization in Successful Schools," *Sociology of Education*, **51**: 211–226, 1978.

where

N_1 and N_2 = two sample sizes
$\sum R_1$ = sum of ranks for group 1

Using the values from Table 10.6, we may compute the U statistic as follows:

$$U = (14)(12) + \frac{(14)(14+1)}{2} - 165$$

$$= 168 + \frac{210}{2} - 165$$

$$= 168 + 105 - 165$$

$$= 273 - 165$$

$$= 108.$$

Once we have determined this U value, we must determine a second U value (designated U') as follows:

$$\begin{aligned} U' &= N_1 N_2 - U \\ &= (14)(12) - 108 \\ &= 168 - 108 \\ &= 60. \end{aligned}$$

We are interested only in the smaller of the two U values we have obtained. Since the smaller U value is 60, this becomes our observed U value. To evaluate the statistical significance of our observed $U = 60$, we must turn to the Mann–Whitney U test tables, Tables A8.1 through A8.10. The first six tables (A8.1 to A8.6) are for situations where the larger of the two sample sizes is 8 or smaller. The last set of four tables (A8.7 to A8.10) are for situations where the larger of the two sample sizes ranges from 9 to 20. The heading of each of these tables defines the probability associated with the hypothesis test and whether a one- or two-tailed interpretation is desired.

The table of interest to us in the present example is Table A8.10. The larger of the two sample N's is found across the top of the table, and the smaller of the two N's is found down the left-hand column. The body of the table contains critical values of U. Where our $N_1 = 14$ and $N_2 = 12$ intersect in the body of the table identifies the critical value of U, which is 51 in this case. We must observe a U value equal to or smaller than the critical U value of 51 in order to reject H_0 at the .05 level of significance (one-tailed test). Since our observed U value is larger than the critical U value of 51, we fail to reject H_0. We must conclude that for the data in Table 10.6, there is no significant difference between the two samples of schools regarding administrative concern for instructional quality.

Where extremely small samples are encountered (i.e., where the larger of the two sample N's is 8 or smaller), the first six tables (Tables A8.1 to A8.6) can be used. We would simply find the table with the heading bearing the larger sample-size designation. Next, we would find the smaller N across the top of the table. Finally, we would locate our observed U value down the left-hand column. Where the smaller N intersects the observed U value defines the probability at which our observed U value is significant statistically. Suppose that we had two samples, $N_1 = 5$ and $N_2 = 7$. We would turn to Table A8.5 (with the larger $N = 7$) and locate the smaller N across the top of the table.[1] Further suppose that in carrying out the U

[1] It makes no difference whether the first or second sample is larger; the larger of the two N's will constitute the table heading as shown.

test, our smaller observed U value happened to be 6. Where $U = 6$ intersects $N = 5$ in the body of the table defines the probability at which the $U = 6$ is significant. In this case, the probability is .037. Had a hypothesis test been made at the .05 level of significance, the U value observed would have been significant at .037 (which is less than .05), and H_0 probably would have been rejected.

When either of our two sample N's exceeds 20, none of the tables (Tables A8.1 to A8.10) can be used. An approximation of a Z value can be obtained by applying the following formula:

$$Z = \frac{U - \left(\frac{N_1 N_2}{2}\right)}{\sqrt{\frac{(N_1 N_2)(N_1 + N_2 + 1)}{12}}},$$

where

N_1 and N_2 = respective sample sizes
U = smaller of the two observed U values

The resulting Z value is interpreted as we would interpret any Z value using Table A3. Again, this does not mean that we must assume normality to apply the U test. We merely obtain an approximation of a Z value that permits us to evaluate the statistical significance of our observed U value. The smaller the U value, the larger the Z value observed will become. Accordingly, the larger the Z value becomes, the more significant the difference between the two samples observed.

Assumptions of the Mann–Whitney U Test. The primary assumptions of the U test include (1) randomness, (2) independent samples, and (3) the ordinal level of measurement.

Advantages and Disadvantages of the U Test. Compared with the other tests in this section (the runs test and the K–S test), the U test is the most powerful nonparametric equivalent to the parametric t test. Tables are available for interpreting the statistical significance of observed U values for N's ranging from 3 to 20, and an approximation of Z is possible with an alternative formula when sample sizes exceed 20.

The only possible limitation of the U test pertains to tied scores. When tied scores are present, the average of the ranks otherwise occupied by the tied scores is assigned each of the scores. Siegel (1956) provides a "correction factor" to apply whenever excessive numbers of scores are tied.[2] The elaborate correction suggested by Siegel affects the statistical outcome of the U test by making it easier to reject the null hypothesis. Given the fact that it is a time-consuming process to correct for tied scores with a result that yields a less conservative test, it is recommended that the correction for tied scores not be made. Where excessive numbers of scores are tied, it would be better to apply the K–S two-sample test instead. The K–S test does deal with ties well and would therefore be the more promising alternative.

The U test is easy to apply and is perhaps the most popular nonparametric test alternative used in the research literature compared with the t test. A conversion of raw scores to ranks makes the application of the U test more cumbersome compared with the runs test. All in all, little fault is found with the Mann–Whitney U test for appropriate research applications.

□ A TEST FOR TWO RELATED SAMPLES: THE SIGN TEST

When the researcher has two matched sets of subjects or when persons have been used as their own controls in a before–after experimental design, the sign test may be used to determine the significance of difference between two sets of scores derived from an ordinal scale. The sign test is a straightforward technique that examines the directionality associated with score differences. It performs a function similar to the Wilcoxon matched pairs–signed ranks test, although the sign test does not examine the magnitude of score changes or score differences. The application of the sign test can be illustrated as follows.

Campbell (1958) investigated some social psychological correlates of attitude change in a school system undergoing racial desegregation. A large number of students were examined over a 1-year period. Questionnaires were administered to students both before and after a desegregation order had been received from the federal courts. Campbell determined that the white students in the schools studied could be divided according to the nature and degree of contact they had previously had with black students. It was reasoned that the more contact the white students had with black students prior to the

[2] Although the figure is purely arbitrary, an "excessive" number of tied scores might be operationally defined as 25 percent or more.

desegregation order, the more favorable white students' attitudes would be toward black students entering formerly all-white schools.

Based on Campbell's notions concerning white student attitude change, the following hypothesis set is suggested:

H_0: There is no difference in the degree of favorable response toward black students by white students before and after school desegregation; if there is a difference, white student attitudes will be unfavorable.
H_1: White student's attitudes toward black students will become increasingly favorable after school desegregation.

$$P \leqslant .05 \text{ (one-tailed test).}$$

Focusing upon an hypothetical sample of 18 white students who have had previous extensive contacts with black students, before and after raw scores on a racial tolerance measure are presented in Table 10.7. The larger the score, the greater the racial tolerance and the

TABLE 10.7
Before-and-After Racial Tolerance Scores for 18 White Students in a Desegregated School.

Racial Tolerance Scores		
Before Desegregation	*After Desegregation*	*Sign Associated with Change in Score*
25	29	+
27	28	+
16	21	+
29	28	–
19	29	+
15	25	+
19	20	+
28	26	–
32	31	–
32	33	+
29	26	–
30	33	+
23	26	+
29	31	+
19	17	–
20	30	+
19	21	+
23	26	+
$N = 18$		Sum of fewer signs = m = 5

Note: Hypothetical scores based on research conducted by Ernest Q. Campbell, "Some Social Psychological Correlates of Direction in Attitude Change," *Social Forces*, **36:** 336, 1958.

greater the favorableness of the white students toward the black students.

Table 10.7 is easily constructed as follows. The first two columns present raw racial tolerance scores for the 18 white students before and after school desegregation. The final column contains the signs (either + or −) associated with the score changes from one time period to the next. The less frequently occurring signs are summed and designated m.

From the data in Table 10.7 we can determine that a majority of white student's scores increased from one time period to the next. Five scores decreased over the two time periods, however. Therefore, $m = 5$. We may evaluate the significance of our observed m value by turning to Table A18. This table contains one-tailed probabilities for various breakdowns of + and − score changes. We find the sample size, $N = 18$, down the left-hand column. Across the top of the table, we can find the m value. Where $N = 18$ intersects the observed $m = 5$ defines the probability associated with our particular distribution of signs. This probability is shown as .048. Since this probability is equal to or less than the .05 level of significance at which the hypothesis set was being tested, we may reject H_0 and support H_1—white student attitudes will become increasingly favorable toward black students after desegregation.

For two-tailed test applications where $N \leqslant 25$, the probabilities in Table A18 must be doubled. Had we made the hypothesis test above at the .05 level of significance with a two-tailed instead of a one-tailed test, the probability associated with the 13–5 split for our sample of 18 students would have been .048(2) = .096. With a probability this large, we could not reject H_0 at the .05 level.

When we exceed a sample size of 25 (i.e., where we have 26 or more matched pairs or when we have 26 or more persons used as their own controls in a before–after experimental situation), Table A18 cannot be used. An approximation of a Z value may be obtained by using the following formula:

$$Z = \frac{2m - N}{\sqrt{N}},$$

where

m = sum of the less frequently occurring signs
N = number of pairs of untied scores

Had we examined a sample of 35 students and observed a 27–8 split in the positive (+) and negative (−) signs, our observed m would equal 8. The observed Z value would be computed as follows:

$$Z = \frac{(2)(8) - 35}{\sqrt{35}}$$
$$= \frac{-19}{5.9}$$
$$= -3.22.$$

The resulting Z value is -3.22 and would be interpreted as any other Z value by using Table A3. Again, a normal distribution is not assumed as a precondition associated with the application of the sign test. The Z value is merely an approximation. For example, the critical value of Z for the .05 level of significance with a two-tailed test would be ± 1.96. Clearly, any hypothesis we would have tested would be rejected at the .05 level with an observed Z value as large as -3.22.

Assumptions of the Sign Test

The primary assumptions of the sign test are (1) randomness, (2) the ordinal level of measurement, and (3) two related samples of elements.

Advantages and Disadvantages of the Sign Test

Beside being a rapid method of determining the significance of difference between two related samples, the sign test gives us a conservative appraisal of differences between groups. Compared with the Wilcoxon matched pairs–signed ranks test, which is sometimes used conventionally to perform the same function, the sign test has power equivalent to 75 percent for rejecting false null hypotheses.

One drawback of the sign test is that all elements are eliminated from a sample where no differences in scores exist from one time period to the next. For instance, if we observed 50 pairs of scores and 10 pairs of scores were the same from one time period to the next (reflecting no attitudinal change), these pairs of scores would be dropped from the sample, yielding a resulting $N = 40$. There were no tied scores in Table 10.7 for the 18 students. Had there been several pairs of scores that were tied, these score pairs would have been dropped, and our resulting N would be something less than 18.

If a substantial number of scores happen to be tied, this condition could seriously impair our analysis of data using the sign test. If we ignore those persons who do not experience score changes from one time period to the next and focus only on those persons who do change, we run the risk of making a misleading interpretation of our study results. Sometimes, observing no change in scores is as important as observing score changes. In any case, the researcher should accompany any discussion of findings where the sign test is used with a statement concerning tied scores, if any. This is often a valuable bit of information for the reader.

A table of probabilities exists for samples up to 25, and an approximation of Z can be obtained by a special formula for assessing the significance of m, the sum of the less frequently occurring signs.

□ k-SAMPLE TESTS: INDEPENDENT SAMPLES

Two tests are presented in this section which are designed to determine the significance of difference among k independent samples where the ordinal level of measurement has been achieved. Respectively, these tests are (1) the median test for k samples; and (2) the Kruskal–Wallis H test.

The Median Test

The median test is designed to determine if k distributions of scores differ according to whether the scores are above or below the median score for all groups combined. Some research conducted by Trigg (1972) will illustrate the usefulness and simplicity of the median test.

Trigg was interested in factors that influenced physicians to locate their medical practice in particular geographical areas. She had an opportunity to obtain responses from physicians in both rural and urban regions in the Southeast. In one phase of her study, Trigg asked physicians to indicate the importance of colleague relationships and modern hospital facilities in influencing their decision to locate in a given area. The "degree of importance of colleague associations and hospital facilities" was measured according to a Likert scale and ordinal scores were achieved.

Trigg reasoned that physicians who located their medical practice in rural areas would be less inclined to cite colleague relations and hospital facilities as prime motivating factors compared with urban physicians. Presumably, physicians who valued such factors would tend to seek out these things in areas more likely to supply them, such as the larger metropolitan or urban regions. Physicians in more rural locales would be less likely to enjoy extensive colleague associations, and the hospital facilities would probably not be as modern.

Five samples of physicians were compared. These physicians were located in geographical areas ranging from rural (5000 or under in population) to urban (100,000 or more in population). For Trigg, the five physician samples represented five differing degrees of urbanization from low to high. A median score was computed for the measure of degree of importance of colleague associations and hospital facilities for all physicians in the study. Trigg was able to place physicians in each sample either above or below the overall median for all physicians on this attitudinal variable. These data are presented in Table 10.8.

Trigg developed the following hypothesis set:

H_0: There will be no difference among five groups of physicians in the degree of importance of colleague relationships and hospital facilities.
H_1: There will be a difference among the five physician groups in the degree of importance of colleague relationships and hospital facilities.

$$P \leqslant .05 \text{ (two-tailed test).}$$

The instrument used by Trigg to measure degree of importance of colleague relationships and hospital facilities consisted of 10 items with a six-point response pattern (i.e., "strongly agree," "agree," "undecided, but probably agree," "undecided, but probably disagree," "disagree," and "strongly disagree"). Possible scores on this scale ranged from 10 (the smallest score) to 60 (the largest score). The median for all physicians combined was 35. Each physician sample in Table 10.8 has been dichotomized on this variable according to whether each score is at the median or above it or below it as shown.

To test the hypothesis set above, the k-sample version of the chi-square test was employed for the data in Table 10.8. The procedures to follow are treated in Chapter 9. The resulting χ^2 value is 15.872. We can determine the significance of this observed chi-square value by turning to Table A4 with $k - 1$ degrees of freedom (where k = the number of physician samples in this case). The df for the data in Table 10.6 are $k - 1$ or $5 - 1$ or 4 df. With 4 df at the .05 level of significance (a two-tailed test), we must equal or exceed the critical value of chi square of 9.488 with our observed chi-square value. It is clear that 15.872 is statistically significant at the .05 level and that H_0 can be rejected. We may tentatively conclude that physicians from different geographical areas differ in the degree of importance they attach to colleague relationships and hospital facilities in influencing the location of their medical practice.

Assumptions of the Median Test. The primary assumptions of the median test are (1) randomness, (2) the ordinal level of measurement, and (3) k independent samples.

TABLE 10.8
Size of Geographical Area (Population) and Degree of Importance of Colleague Relations and Hospital Facilities for 188 Physicians.

Degree of Importance of Colleague Relationships and Hospital Facilities		Population Size					
		5000 or less	*5000–25,000*	*25,000–50,000*	*50,000–100,000*	*100,000+*	*N*
	High (raw score ⩾ median)[a]	3 (9)	12 (16.5)	14 (14)	25 (23.5)	40 (31)	94
	Low (raw score < median)[a]	15 (9)	21 (16.5)	14 (14)	22 (23.5)	22 (31)	94
	Totals	18	33	28	47	62	$N = 188$

Source: Data based on information compiled by Martelle D. Trigg, "Differential Mobility Among Black and White Physicians in the State of Tennessee," unpublished Ph.D. dissertation, University of Tennessee, Knoxville, 1972.

[a]Median = 35. Values in parentheses are the expected values for each cell.

Advantages and Disadvantages of the Median Test. A chi-square-based, goodness-of-fit statistic, the median test is quick and easy to apply. Compared with the Kruskal–Wallis *H* test to follow, the median test is considerably more conservative. It has a power equivalent of about 80 percent for rejecting false null hypotheses.

If the researcher desires a rapid indication of whether *k* samples differ on some ordinal characteristic, the median test could be applied quite rapidly. Later, if more information is required about the nature of differences between groups, the more powerful Kruskal–Wallis *H* test could be applied as a less conservative procedure.

There are no serious disadvantages associated with the median test. It approximates the chi-square distribution and is therefore familiar in principle to most researchers. We can inspect the data in Table 10.8, for instance, and determine which physician samples are predominantly above or below the overall group median. Directionality is easy to ascertain by a simple inspection of the distribution of frequencies throughout the table.

If the researcher wants to know which groups of physicians differ from one another, the median test can also be applied to two samples at a time. Since the median test approximates the chi-square distribution, the reader is cautioned to observe the same operating range of sample size associated with chi square. In short, the median test should be restricted to samples no larger than 250. Beyond that, the researcher must exercise increasing caution in interpreting test results because of the increasingly distorted observed chi square value.

The Kruskal-Wallis *H* Test

The Kruskal–Wallis *H* test is an extension of the Mann–Whitney *U* test in a sense. It is designed to evaluate differences between *k* independent samples according to some variable measured according to an ordinal scale. Raw scores for *k* groups are *ranked across the groups*, and an *H* test is performed to determine the significance of difference between the *k* sets of ranks. The following example from the literature illustrates the application of the *H* test.

Schmitt (1966) was interested in studying changes in self-concept as a function of the socialization process. His research focused upon three samples of women at various stages of becoming Catholic nuns. According to Schmitt, "the girl goes through three major periods, the postulancy, the novitiate, and the juniorate. The duration of the first phase is one year, the second, two years, and the third, two years. The postulancy is a preparatory stage. The novitiate, in several respects, is the central stage, in that the girl experiences the fundamentals of religious life. It is at this juncture that the girl receives her initial white habit. During the juniorate, the temporary vows are taken. This period solidifies the whole religious training of the novitiate" (Schmitt, 1966: 315).

Schmitt wanted to know if any differences existed between girls at these different stages concerning their expression of ideological statements. Ideological statements are "statements of a religious, philosophical, or moral nature." (Schmitt, 1966, p. 320.) It might be argued that as girls become increasingly committed to becoming nuns in that particular socialization process, their ideological views and statements might become more pronounced. The following hypothesis set is suggested by the research of Schmitt:

H_0: There is no difference among postulants, novitiates, and juniorates regarding ideological scores.

H_1: There is a difference among postulants, novitiates, and juniorates regarding their ideological scores.

$$P \leqslant .01 \text{ (two-tailed test).}$$

Raw ideological scores for three groups of girls at three different socialization stages are shown in Table 10.9. In Table 10.9, the larger the score, the stronger the ideological views of the girls.

TABLE 10.9
Ideological Scores for Three Groups of Girls at Various Stages in Becoming Catholic Nuns.

Postulants		*Novitiates*		*Juniorates*	
$N_1 = 10$	R_1	$N_2 = 12$	R_2	$N_3 = 15$	R_3
32	37	48	15	64	1
50	14	46	17.5	56	8.5
38	32.5	59	5	45	19
41	25	42	22	62	3
43	20	41	25	59	5
38	32.5	40	28.5	47	16
35	36	55	10	41	25
36	35	46	17.5	63	2
38	32.5	42	22	42	22
40	28.5	38	32.5	58	7
		40	28.5	56	8.5
		40	28.5	51	13
				54	11.5
				54	11.5
				59	5
	$\Sigma R_1 = 293$		$\Sigma R_2 = 252$		$\Sigma R_3 = 158$

Source: Data based on idea provided by Raymond L. Schmitt, "Major Role Change and Self Change," *Sociological Quarterly*, 7: 311–322, 1966.

Table 10.9 is constructed as follows. In columns labeled R_1, R_2, and R_3, ranks are assigned to each girl's raw ideological score. Beginning with the largest score of 64 in the postulant group, a rank of 1 is assigned as shown. A rank of 2 is assigned the next largest score of 63. A rank of 3 is assigned the next largest score of 62. There are three scores of 59 (the next largest score), and the *average of the ranks* otherwise assigned to each score will be given to each. These three scores would take up ranks 4, 5, and 6, respectively. Therefore, the average of these ranks, 5, is assigned to each of the scores of 59, as shown. The researcher continues to rank all scores across all groups.

Once the ranking has been completed, the ranks in each R_i column are summed. The sums of ranks, ΣR_i, are then used in the following formula to determine the observed H value:

$$H = \frac{12}{N(N+1)} \Sigma \left(\frac{\sum R_i^2}{N_i} \right) - [3(N+1)],$$

where

N = total number of people in the k samples
N_i = number of people in the ith sample
R_i = sum of ranks for the ith sample

Using the information derived from Table 10.9, we carry out our H computation as follows:

$$\begin{aligned} H &= \frac{12}{(37)(37+1)} \left[\frac{(293)^2}{10} + \frac{(252)^2}{12} + \frac{(158)^2}{15} \right] - [(3)(37+1)] \\ &= \frac{12}{1406} \left[\frac{85{,}849}{10} + \frac{63{,}504}{12} + \frac{24{,}964}{15} \right] - 114 \\ &= .008(8584.9 + 5292 + 1664.27) - 114 \\ &= (.008)(15541.17) - 114 \\ &= 124.33 - 114 \\ &= 10.33. \end{aligned}$$

The resulting H value is 10.33. To determine the statistical significance associated with this observed H value, we must turn to Table A4 with $k - 1$ degrees of freedom (where k = the number of groups). Since there are three groups of girls (postulants, novitiates, and juniorates), $k = 3$ and $k - 1 = 3 - 1 = 2$ df. Where 2 df intersects with the .01 level of significance (two-tailed test) across the top of the table defines the critical H value we must equal or exceed in order to reject H_0 and support H_1. The critical value from Table A4 is 9.210. Since our observed $H = 10.33$ and exceeds 9.210, we may reject H_0 and conclude that there is a difference among the three groups regarding their ideological views.

Had we elected to conduct a one-tailed, directional hypothesis test, we would have to inspect Table 10.9 and see whether or not the differences in the sums of ranks were consistent with the direction of score differences predicted under H_1. For instance, had Schmitt predicted that postulates would have the lowest ideological scores and juniorates the highest scores, the sums of ranks in Table 10.9 would be consistent with this prediction. The smallest rank sum (ΣR_i) would be associated with the largest ideological scores,whereas the largest rank sum would be associated with the smallest ideological scores. Table A4 would again be used. With direction of difference predicted, however, the one-tailed probability line in the table would be used in this instance.

Assumptions of the Kruskal–Wallis H Test. The primary assumptions of the H test are (1) randomness, (2) the ordinal level of measurement, and (3) k independent samples.

Advantages and Disadvantages of the H Test. The Kruskal–Wallis H test is the most powerful nonparametric equivalent to the parametric F test for analysis of variance. When certain assumptions of the F test are not met (such as normality or homogeneity of variance), the Kruskal-Wallis H test would be an excellent alternative, in spite of the fact that we would only be using the ordinality rather than the interval properties of the variable. The H test has power of approximately 95 percent compared with the F test. But like the F test, the H test merely answers the question: Does a difference exist somewhere among the k samples? To determine where significant differences between k groups occur, a two-sample test must be applied to probe for these differences. The test of choice in this instance is the Mann–Whitney U test. There is no nonparametric equivalent to the Newman–Keuls or Scheffé procedures that would permit the researcher to make a single test of all significant group differences. Therefore, the samples must be compared, two at a time, by means of the U test.

The H test approximates the chi-square distribution, and H is equivalent to a chi-square value with $k - 1$ degrees of freedom. Since the chi-square distribution is involved, the researcher is cautioned to apply the H test when sample sizes combined range at least from 25 to 250. Beyond 250, the H value becomes increasingly distorted and could yield misleading results.

The H test handles tied scores well both within and across groups.

H is easy to apply and interpret. It has few restrictive assumptions and is a popular k-sample measure of significance of difference in the social science literature.

□ A TEST FOR *k* RELATED SAMPLES

The Friedman Two-Way ANOVA

The Friedman two-way analysis-of-variance test is designed for situations where the researcher has three or more groups of subjects who have been matched on a number of salient characteristics or have been used as their own controls over k different time periods. It is one of the only tests available for k related samples where ordinal data are involved. The following example is provided.

Berlew and Hall (1966) were interested in the relationship between company expectations of new employees and subsequent employee performance levels. A division of the Bell Telephone Company was selected by these researchers as the study site. The subjects for the investigation were recent college graduates who enrolled in managerial training programs conducted by the Bell System. Basing their theoretical scheme in organizational socialization theory, these researchers believed that newly hired managers who were given challenging jobs initially would achieve higher performance effectiveness ratings over the next few years compared with those managers hired to perform routine and considerably less challenging tasks. According to Berlew and Hall (1966, p. 212), "The company expectations were coded in 18 categories which were empirically formulated to reflect the variety of expectations the companies had for managerial employees." Therefore, these researchers were able to differentiate employees according to the degree of challenge associated with any job assigned them.

The Bell Telephone Company conducted yearly appraisals of each employee's effectiveness of job performance, and Berlew and Hall were able to chart each employee's effectiveness accordingly. A random sample of 23 employees was selected for investigation over a 5-year period. Based on interviews with company officials each year, these researchers were able to determine raw performance scores for each of the 23 employees ranging from 1 (completely unsatisfactory performance) to 10 (outstanding performance).

For purposes of illustrating the Friedman two-way analysis-of-variance test, the 23 managers selected for study have been hypothetically divided into two groups. The first group of 13 managers consists of those persons given challenging job assignments with the company initially. The second group of 10 subjects consists of those managers given unchallenging assignments initially. Two Friedman tests will be performed on the data to follow. The first Friedman test will examine differences between the challenging assignment group of 13 subjects over five yearly time periods. The second Friedman test will examine those persons given unchallenging jobs and their variations in job performance over the same five yearly time periods. Table 10.10 presents two sets of information for the two managerial groups over five different time periods. In this instance, each manager functions as his or her own control from one time period to the next. This procedure yields k related samples (i.e., five related samples for each of the managerial groups).

Table 10.10 is constructed as follows. Each employee's job performance score (on a scale from 1 to 10) is indicated in each of the five

TABLE 10.10
Performance Scores for Two Managerial Groups Given Challenging and Unchallenging Initial Job Assignments.

Manager Number	*Job Performance Levels* Year 1	R_1	Year 2	R_2	Year 3	R_3	Year 4	R_4	Year 5	R_5
					Challenging Job Assignment Group					
1	6	5	7	4	8	2.5	8	2.5	9	1
2	5	5	7	4	8	3	9	2	10	1
3	7	4.5	7	4.5	8	2.5	8	2.5	9	1
4	6	4.5	6	4.5	8	3	9	2	10	1
5	7	5	8	3.5	8	3.5	9	1.5	9	1.5
6	7	5	8	4	9	3	10	1.5	10	1.5
7	6	5	8	4	9	3	10	1.5	10	1.5
8	6	4.5	7	2.5	6	4.5	7	2.5	9	1
9	3	5	5	3	6	2	4	4	7	1
10	7	3	6	4	5	5	9	1	8	2
11	5	4.5	5	4.5	6	3	7	1.5	7	1.5
12	6	4	7	3	5	5	8	2	9	1
13	6	4	6	4	6	4	7	2	8	1
$N_1 = 13$	$\Sigma R_1 = 59$		$\Sigma R_2 = 49.5$		$\Sigma R_3 = 44$		$\Sigma R_4 = 26.5$		$\Sigma R_5 = 16$	
					Unchallenging Job Assignment Group					
1	5	1.5	4	3	3	4.5	5	1.5	3	4.5
2	4	1.5	4	1.5	3	3	2	4.5	2	4.5
3	6	3	7	1.5	7	1.5	5	4.5	5	4.5
4	4	1	3	2	2	3.5	2	3.5	1	5
5	3	1.5	3	1.5	2	4	2	4	2	4
6	4	2.5	5	1	4	2.5	3	4.5	3	4.5
7	6	1	5	2.5	5	2.5	4	4	3	5
8	3	2.5	3	2.5	4	1	2	4.5	2	4.5
9	7	1	5	2	4	3	3	4.5	3	4.5
10	4	1	3	3	3	3	2	5	3	3
$N_2 = 10$	$\Sigma R_1 = 16.5$		$\Sigma R_2 = 20.5$		$\Sigma R_3 = 28.5$		$\Sigma R_4 = 40.5$		$\Sigma R_5 = 44$	

time periods as shown. For example, for the "challenging job assignment group, manager 1 has performance scores of 6, 7, 8, 8, and 9 across the five time periods. Manager 2 has performance scores of 5, 7, 8, 9, and 10 over the five time periods; and so on. We focus upon each set of performance scores for each manager and rank them from the highest to the lowest performance score. Beginning with the first manager, we assign the rank of 1 to the largest score of the five, which is 9. We assign the average of the next two ranks (i.e., ranks 2 and 3) or 2.5 each to the next two largest performance scores of 8. The rank of 4 is assigned the score of 7, and the rank of 5 is assigned the smallest performance score of 6. We proceed in this fashion until all managers' scores have been ranked from 1 to 5.

Finally, we sum the ranks assigned the managers' scores for each of the five time periods. Because we are dealing with two different groups of elements over five time periods, two sets of hypotheses will be tested. Based on the research of Berlew and Hall, the following hypothesis sets are suggested:

SET 1

H_0: Managers who receive challenging job assignments initially will not change in their job performance level over five different time periods.
H_1: Managers who receive challenging job assignments initially will change in their job performance level over five different time periods.

$$P \leqslant .001 \quad \text{(two-tailed test).}$$

SET 2

H_0: Managers who receive unchallenging job assignments initially will not change in their job performance level over five different time periods.
H_1: Managers who receive unchallenging job assignments initially will change in their job performance level over five different time periods.

$$P \leqslant .001 \quad \text{(two-tailed test).}$$

Both sets of hypotheses can be tested by using the Friedman formula:

$$\chi_r^2 = \left[\frac{12}{Nk(k+1)} \sum \left(\sum R_i\right)^2\right] - [3N(k+1)],$$

where

k = number of groups or time periods

$\left(\sum R_i\right)^2$ = square of the sum of ranks under each of the experimental conditions or time periods (i)

N = number of individuals under each of the different time periods

Using the information from Table 10.10 for the first hypothesis set, the Friedman test is computed as follows:

$$\chi_r^2 = \frac{12}{(13)(5)(5+1)} [(59)^2 + (49.5)^2 + (44)^2 + (26.5)^2 + (16)^2] - [(3)(13)(5+1)]$$

$$= \frac{12}{390} (3481 + 2450.25 + 1936 + 702.25 + 256) - 234$$

$$= (.030)(8825.5) - 234$$

$$= 264.765 - 234$$

$$= 30.765.$$

The first observed $\chi_r^2 = 30.765$.

Using the information from Table 10.10 for the second set of hypotheses, the Friedman test is computed as follows:

$$\chi_r^2 = \frac{12}{(10)(5)(5+1)} [(16.5)^2 + (20.5)^2 + (28.5)^2 + (40.5)^2 + (44)^2] - [(3)(10)(5+1)]$$

$$= \frac{12}{300} (272.25 + 420.25 + 812.25 + 1640.25 + 1936) - 180$$

$$= (.040)(5081) - 180$$

$$= 203.24 - 180$$

$$= 23.24.$$

The second observed $\chi_r^2 = 23.24$.

Both of these χ_r^2 values may be taken to Table A4 with $k - 1$ degrees of freedom (where k is defined as the number of time periods). In each case, there are five different time periods. Therefore, $k = 5$, and $k - 1 = 5 - 1 = 4$ df. Where 4 df intersects the .001 level of significance (two-tailed test) across the top of the table defines the critical value of χ_r^2 that we must equal or exceed in order to reject H_0 for both hypothesis sets. The critical value of $\chi_r^2 = 18.465$. In both instances, we can reject H_0 and conclude that managers in both groups (i.e., those given challenging and unchallenging initial job assignments) differ across the five time periods according to their job performance scores.

It was necessary to carry out two separate Friedman tests here because two separate samples of elements were involved over k different time periods. Had all 23 subjects been considered a single sample at the outset (i.e., suppose that all 23 managers had been assigned challenging jobs initially), only one Friedman test would have sufficed for the 23 persons. But Berlew and Hall were concerned about the implications of being assigned challenging and unchallenging jobs for job performance. It was necessary to examine two different groups of managers over the time periods indicated.

While two-tailed hypothesis tests were conducted for the data in Table 10.10, one-tailed tests could have been conducted easily as well. But making a directional prediction would involve examining the data in Table 10.10 to make sure that the job performance scores were generally in the direction predicted under H_1. For instance, Berlew and Hall believed that those persons who had challenging job assignments initially would tend to have higher job performance ratings over time. An examination of the rank sums trend (ΣR_i's) for the first group of 13 managers over the five time periods would indicate that performance scores tended to increase over the 5-year period (i.e., 59, 49.4, 44, 26.5, and 16). The smaller the rank sum, the larger the performance scores for each of the yearly evaluation periods. The same type of evaluation could be made for those persons assigned less challenging jobs. Over the 5-year period, we observe in Table 10.10 that the second manager group experienced a general decline in job performance ratings. Again, we can pay attention to the trend of the rank sums (i.e., 16.5, 20.5, 28.5, 40.5, and 44).

It should be noted that the two samples of managers could also be compared within each time period. Since the two samples of subjects would be independent and not related, some appropriate two-independent sample technique such as the Kolmogorov–Smirnov test of significance or the Mann–Whitney U test could be applied if the researcher so desired. Such a test would be applied to the two samples for year 1, again for year 2, again for year 3, and so on. Such two-sample comparisons would tell these researchers if the two groups of managers differed on job performance levels initially and at any other time throughout the duration of the study.

Assumptions of the Friedman Test. The primary assumptions of the Friedman test are (1) randomness, (2) the ordinal level of measurement, and (3) k related samples through matching or by using persons as their own controls over k time periods.

Advantages and Disadvantages of the Friedman Test. The Friedman test is also a chi-square-based statistical procedure with $k - 1$ degrees of freedom. It is somewhat cumbersome to apply for situations where sample sizes are quite large, although the results of the test are easily interpreted for both one- and two-tailed hypothesis tests.

The Friedman test is one of a very few procedures that can be applied to ordinal data for k related samples. This is one of its key advantages. It has a power equivalent to 85 to 90 percent for rejecting false null hypotheses. Since the Friedman test utilizes the chi-square distribution for its interpretation, the researcher should observe the usual caution that the test is somewhat sensitive to extremely small samples.

Like the Kruskal–Wallis H test, the Friedman test answers the basic question: Does a difference exist somewhere between k related samples? To determine which time periods differ significantly from one another, a two-sample probe would be necessary. The sign test might be one appropriate alternative, although it should be remembered that tied scores are eliminated from one's sample when the test is applied. For the data in Table 10.10, there are not many tied scores for each individual manager over the five different time periods. For other data, however, numerous tied scores could yield misleading results if the researcher were to apply the sign test.

One additional alternative is to use the Friedman test itself as a two-sample probe. Any k-sample test can function as its own probe in a two-sample test capacity. Although the operations would be tedious, the Friedman test could be applied to each pair of time periods. For the first set of managers in Table 10.10, a total of $k(k-1)/2$ or $5(5-1)/2 = 20/2 = 10$ different Friedman tests would need to be conducted for all pairs of samples. Ten additional Friedman tests would need to be conducted for analyzing differences between all sample pairs for the second set of managers as well. This is tantamount to carrying out a large number of t tests once the researcher has observed a significant F value in the parametric analysis of variance test. There is no Newman–Keuls procedure that can be applied to k related samples at the ordinal level of measurement. Therefore, if the researcher wants more specific information, the tediousness of multiple Friedman tests or sign tests must be anticipated.

□ SUMMARY

In this chapter we have examined a fairly broad assortment of tests of significance for data measured according to an ordinal scale. The Kolmogorov–Smirnov (K–S) single-sample test performs a function similar to the chi-square test. However, the K–S test takes advantage of the ordinality that exists across k categories. To this extent, at least, the K–S test makes use of more information compared with its nominal-level significance test counterpart. There are few restrictions governing the appropriate application of the K–S test in either the single-sample or two-sample cases.

Three tests were presented for analyzing differences between two independent samples. The Wald–Wolfowitz runs test, the least powerful of the three tests discussed, is appropriate when the researcher is interested in a rapid appraisal of differences in scores between two samples. This test deals with raw scores directly. The runs test is quite sensitive to tied scores, however. In cases where a considerable number of tied scores exists, the K–S two-sample test should be selected as an alternative. The K–S two-sample test is moderately powerful and permits the researcher to compare two cumulative frequency distributions according to k graded categories. The K–S test adapts well to tied-score situations and has no serious sample-size restrictions. The Mann–Whitney U test is the most powerful nonparametric equivalent to the parametric t test. Compared with the runs test and the K–S test, it obligates the researcher to rank scores across groups and then compare the distributions of ranks. Although the U test is not particularly sensitive to tied scores, it would probably be appropriate to apply the K–S test to data where more than 25 percent of the scores are tied. The U test has no serious sample-size restrictions.

When the researcher has two related samples, the sign test can be used. This test is simple to apply and interpret. It has no sample-size restrictions, and a table exists for interpreting the significance of score changes or differences in scores. When the table cannot be used because of larger sample sizes, a Z approximation is available.

Two tests were presented for analyzing differences between k independent samples. The median test, the more conservative of the two procedures, examines k samples according to whether persons are above or below the grand median. The Kruskal–Wallis H test, an extension of the Mann–Whitney U test, again utilizes ranking across all groups as a means of determining the significance of difference in ordinal score arrangements. Both of these procedures are based on the chi-square distribution.

The final test presented was the Friedman two-way analysis-of-variance procedure. This test evaluates the significance of difference between k matched sets of individuals or between scores from the same persons used as their own controls over k time periods. The Friedman test is one of the few of its kind to perform such a function.

In the case of k-sample tests, the researcher may want to know where significant differences between groups occur. Appropriate two-sample "probes" for the median test would be the median test itself applied to all two-sample combinations of scores. The Mann–Whitney *U* test would be preferred as the two-sample probe for the Kruskal–Wallis *H* test. Finally, either the sign test or the Friedman test itself could function as the two-sample probe effectively applied to all pairs of samples to determine where significant differences occur between groups.

In Chapter 11 we examine a variety of measures of association appropriate for evaluating the relationships between two variables.

SELECTED STUDY TERMS

Gradated categories
Cumulative proportion distribution
Two-sample probes
Runs test
Tied scores
Critical proportion
U test
Sign test
H test
Averaging of ranks assigned tied scores
Ranking across groups

EXERCISES

1. Carry out the sign test for the following information, using the .05 level of significance.

Group Member	*Time 1*	*Time 2*
1	225	229
2	215	214
3	235	250
4	210	211
5	216	213
6	200	210
7	245	245
8	247	250
9	221	220
10	214	219
11	221	225
12	230	220
13	215	219
14	244	240
15	223	226
16	220	223
17	231	233
18	216	218

Group Member	*Time 1*	*Time 2*
19	214	213
20	218	215
21	210	220
22	229	230

(a) What is your decision regarding the application of the sign test? Is there a significant difference between the two time periods at the .05 level of significance with a one-tailed test (assuming that a directional hypothesis test had been made originally, where scores were predicted to increase in value over time)? What is your proof for the conclusion you have reached?

(b) Could the Mann–Whitney U test be applied to these data? Why or why not? Explain briefly.

2. For the following data, determine if any significant difference exists using the Wald–Wolfowitz runs test.

Group 1 Raw Scores	*Group 2 Raw Scores*
23	29
28	28
18	32
17	15
19	21
25	27
13	22
30	35
12	41
	43
	39

(a) What is the significance of difference between the two groups of scores, using the .05 level of significance?

(b) Can the Mann–Whitney U test be used for these data? Why or why not? Explain. In what respects would the Mann–Whitney U test be superior to the runs test, if at all? Explain.

3. For the data below, carry out the single-sample Kolmogorov–Smirnov test, using the .05 level of significance (two-tailed):

Categories

Very Unfavorable	*Unfavorable*	*Favorable*	*Very Favorable*	
29	16	43	71	$N = 159$

(a) What is your decision? Do these data differ from what would be expected according to chance? Why or why not?

(b) Could chi square be applied to these data? Why or why not?

4. Carry out the Mann–Whitney U test for the following data. Assume a hypothesis test at the .01 level of significance (two-tailed).

Attitude Scores	
Group 1	*Group 2*
45	53
47	59
52	40
44	41
43	51
51	55
43	57
33	62
45	50
51	58
56	63
	47
	56

(a) What is your decision about rejecting (or failing to reject) the null hypothesis of no difference between the two groups of scores above? Explain.
(b) Could the runs test be applied to the two sets of scores above? Why or why not? What criticisms would you offer for applying the runs test to these data? Explain.

5. Four groups of employees are examined below. These employees have been matched with one another on a number of salient characteristics. Does a significant difference exist between these four groups on a measure of job satisfaction? Assume that each employee group has a different type of supervision. Also assume that the Friedman test will be used at the .05 level of significance (two-tailed test).

Job Satisfaction Scores			
Group 1	*Group 2*	*Group 3*	*Group 4*
18	21	23	29
15	14	17	19
10	18	14	21
11	10	15	22
16	21	20	23
19	18	19	25
20	19	20	21
22	22	23	25
16	14	19	28

(a) Define k and N. How many degrees of freedom are associated with these data? What distribution is approximated by the Friedman test results?
(b) What two-sample probe could be used to determine the significance of difference between each pair of groups above? Explain the rationale underlying your choice of two-sample test.

6. Two groups are given an attitudinal measure. Later, the researcher creates five gradated categories into which the attitudinal scores are divided. Using the Kolmogorov–Smirnov two-sample test, does a significant difference exist between the two groups on the attitudinal characteristic? Use a two-tailed test at the .05 level of significance.

Gradated Attitudinal Categories

	High	*Moderately High*	*Moderately Low*	*Low*	
Group 1	10	23	25	35	$N_1 = 93$
Group 2	22	15	10	5	$N_2 = 52$

(a) What decision do you reach as a result of carrying out the K–S two-sample test? Is there a significant difference between the two groups?
(b) What is the *critical proportion* used in reaching your decision?

7. Three samples have been selected and measures have been obtained on some attitudinal characteristic. Raw scores for the three samples are shown below. Carry out the Kruskal-Wallis H test, using the .01 level of significance (two-tailed test), and determine whether or not a difference exists somewhere among them.

Attitudinal Scores

Group 1	*Group 2*	*Group 3*
35	42	41
28	43	37
27	55	49
19	57	43
29	41	46
31	63	44
32	56	47
29	49	43
22	51	46
19	39	33
20	57	42
17	58	
16		

(a) What conclusion do you reach about differences among the three groups? Support your conclusions by providing the critical value of H and the observed value of H.
(b) Could the Friedman test be applied to these data? Why or why not? Explain.
(c) How many degrees of freedom are associated with the data above?
(d) What distribution is approximated by the H value?
(e) What two-sample test would be preferred as a probe for differences between each pair of groups? Explain your choice.

8. Attitudinal scores have been obtained for four groups of individuals. An overall median has been determined, and the groups have been placed into the following arrangement, either above or below the median. Using the

median test at the .05 level of significance, does a significant difference exist between these four groups? Assume a two-tailed test.

	Group 1	*Group 2*	*Group 3*	*Group 4*	*Totals*
Above Median	19	22	36	41	118
Below Median	35	23	14	46	118

(a) What conclusion do you reach about differences between these four groups?

(b) What distribution is approximated by the median test results? How many degrees of freedom are there for the table?

9. Carry out the sign test for the following data. A sample of parents was selected to participate in a family seminar designed to educate parents in open communication with their children. The sample of parents was divided into those possessing traditional views and those possessing equalitarian views. The researcher is interested to know whether the seminar had any effect on parent's views. The data for before and after the seminar are as follows:

		After Seminar	
		Traditional Views	*Equalitarian Views*
Before Seminar	*Traditional Views*	14	29
	Equalitarian Views	7	13

Use the .05 level of significance (two-tailed test) to determine if a significant change took place.

REFERENCES

Berlew, David E., and Douglas T. Hall, "The Socialization of Managers: Effects of Expectations on Performance," *Administrative Science Quarterly*, 2:207-223, 1966.

Campbell, Ernest Q., "Some Social Psychological Correlates of Direction in Attitude Change," *Social Forces*, **36**:335-340, 1958.

Harvey, Dale G., and Gerald T. Slatin, "The Relationship Between Child's SES and Teacher Expectations: A Test of the Middle-Class Bias Hypothesis," *Social Forces*, **54**:140-159, 1975.

Haug, Marie, and Bebe Lavin, "Method of Payment for Medical Care and Public Attitudes Toward Physician Authority," *Journal of Health and Social Behavior*, **19**:279-291, 1978.

Rubenstein, Judith, "Concordance of Visual and Manipulative Responsiveness to Novel and Familiar Stimuli: A Function of Test Procedures or of Prior Experience?" *Child Development*, **47**:1197-1199, 1976.

Schmitt, Raymond L., "Major Role Change and Self Change," *Sociological Quarterly*, 7:311-322, 1966.

Siegel, Sidney, *Nonparametric Statistics for the Behavioral Sciences.* New York: McGraw-Hill Book Company, 1956.

Trigg, Martelle D., "Differential Mobility Among Black and White Physicians in the State of Tennessee," unpublished doctoral dissertation, University of Tennessee, Knoxville, 1972.

Wellisch, Jean B., et al., "School Management and Organization in Successful Schools," *Sociology of Education*, **51**:211-226, 1978.

Winer, B. J., *Statistical Principles and Experimental Design*, 2nd ed. New York: McGraw-Hill Book Company, 1971.

11 Measures of Association for Two Variables

Thus far we have considered an array of tests of significance that assist us in making decisions about differences between groups. In previous chapters our attention was directed toward contrasting a single group of elements against an expected or "chance" distribution or toward observed differences between two or more groups on any number of variables. This chapter departs from such tests of significance of difference. We focus on a variety of procedures that are designed to measure the *degree of association between variables.*

Numerical expressions of the degree to which two variables are "in step" or fluctuate predictably in relation to one another are referred to as *coefficients of association.* Procedures that yield coefficients of association are called *measures of association.* Tests of theory or theoretical schemes often involve measures of association. To what extent do two variables vary one from the other? To what extent does a relationship exist between one variable and another? For instance, it might be believed that an association exists between pay and motivation to work. It may appear that as employees are paid more money, their motivation to work harder increases accordingly. An association would be said to exist between pay and motivation to work.

In another instance, it might be believed that increasing the number of street lights in a given section of a city will decrease the amount of crime in that section. Subsequently, if a researcher observes that well-lighted sections of the city have appreciably fewer crimes committed compared with poorly lit sections, one conclusion drawn might be that an association exists between the incidence of crime and the amount of city lighting.

A third example might be that graduate schools believe that graduate students in their institutions will do better in their thesis and dissertation writing if their Graduate Record Examination (GRE) verbal scores are high. Later, if students with high verbal scores on the GRE do better in their thesis and paper writing compared with students who did poorly on the same test, it may be suspected that an association exists between GRE performance and success in the completion of written work in graduate school.

In each of these instances, two variables were seen as being "in step" with one another, or "correlated," "related," or "associated."[1]

□ ON THE MEANING OF ASSOCIATION

There are various ways of describing the association between variables. One way of discussing variable associations is in terms of the *strength of the association.* A strong association between two vari-

[1] The terms *correlation* and *relationship* will be used infrequently in discussions in this chapter. This is because they tend to imply more strongly (compared with the term *association*) that a causal relation exists between variables. Cause–effect relationships are often difficult to establish. The simple appearance of an association between variables is insufficient justification for assuming that a causal relation exists between them. Of course, we are interested ultimately in establishing cause–effect relations between variables. This is largely what scientific inquiry is about. We must observe associations between variables initially as we move toward the development of a causal relation between them. Through replications of research projects conducted by others and repetitive tests of theory, we hope to build sound, causal schemes that explain and predict relations between variables. Our theoretical schemes are designed to accomplish these objectives. But causal models take time to build. Our knowledge of which factors influence others predictably is incomplete. Therefore, we approach the task of observing associations between variables with a certain degree of caution and conservatism. It is in this conservative context that the present chapter is couched.

ables is gauged according to how closely we approach +1.00 (a perfect positive association) or −1.00 (a perfect negative association). No association is indicated by 0. Association coefficients are either positive or negative and are typically expressed to the nearest hundredth. From a conventional standpoint, association coefficients of ±.30 or larger are considered as good in the social science research literature. The following crude guide may be used to assess the general strength of association coefficients:

±0.00– .25 = no association or low association (weak association)

±.26– .50 = moderately low association (moderately weak association)

±.51– .75 = moderately high association (moderately strong association)

±.76–1.00 = high association (strong association) up to perfect association.

Figures 11.1 and 11.2 illustrate (1) a perfect positive association between variables and (2) a perfect negative association between two variables, respectively. In Figure 11.1, a unit increase in variable X is followed by a unit increase in variable Y. Plotting the intersection points enables us to draw a straight line representing the perfect positive association between the two variables, as shown. The association between variables X and Y in Figure 11.1 is said to be *linear*. In Figure 11.2, a unit increase in variable Y is followed by a unit decrease in variable X. If variable X decreases 1 unit each and every time variable Y increases 1 unit, a perfect negative association will be established, as shown. The points of intersection between the two

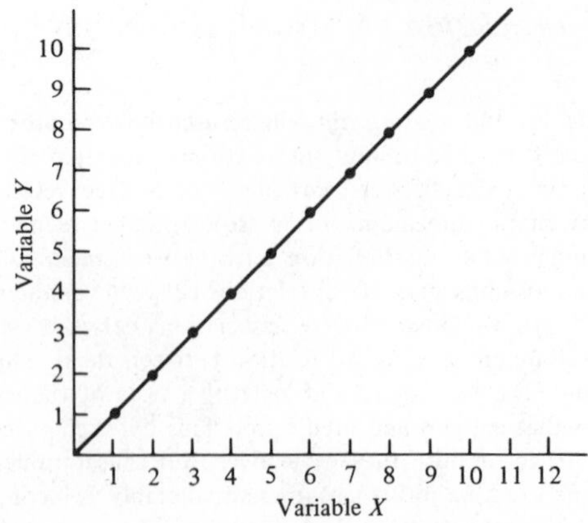

FIGURE 11.1. Perfect Positive Association Between Variables X and Y.

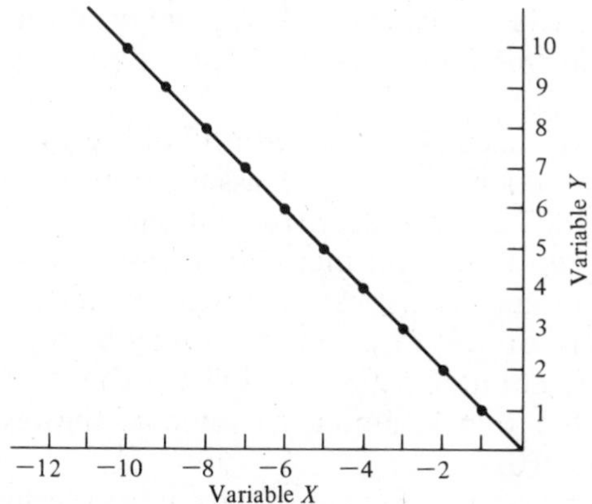

FIGURE 11.2. Perfect Negative (Inverse) Association Between Variables X and Y.

variables permit us to draw a line representing the perfect degree of association between them. The association between variables X and Y in Figure 11.2 is also linear, although it is a perfect negative or *inverse association.*

Nonlinear associations between variables are represented by lines drawn from intersection points that are not aligned in a straight-line fashion. Figure 11.3 represents a *curvilinear association* between variables X and Y. Some measures of association to be discussed in this chapter require that a linear association exists between the two variables before the measure can be applied legitimately. Most of the measures included here do not require this stringent assumption, however.

If we were to discuss association in terms of the direction and strength of it, an association coefficient of .32 would be a "mod-

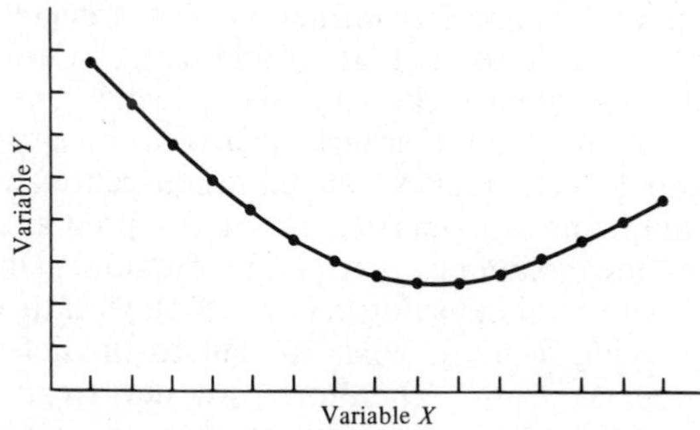

FIGURE 11.3. Curvilinear Association Between Variables X and Y. Values on variable Y tend to decrease for a time as the values on variable X increase. While X continues to increase, the values on Y begin to increase after a time as well.

erately low positive association." An association coefficient of −.55 would be a "moderately strong (or moderately high) negative association.

Another way of discussing association is in terms of the *statistical significance* of it. Each measure of association can be evaluated in terms of how significant the departure of the observed coefficient is from 0. Therefore, almost all measures of association are accompanied by tests of their statistical significance. If the researcher observes a coefficient of .83, for instance, it may be that the association observed is significant at the .05 level of probability. A test of significance is conducted that is similar to some of the tests presented in Chapters 8, 9, and 10.

Yet another way of discussing association is in terms of *prediction.* Of course, we are interested in whether an observed coefficient of association is positive or negative, strong or weak, or significant or nonsignificant statistically. But we are also interested in the *predictive utility* of certain variables in relation to others. If we are concerned about factors that contribute to juvenile delinquency, for instance, what good will it do for us to know how socioeconomic status or peer-group pressure, respectively, contribute to delinquency? What kind of association exists between delinquency and broken homes?

In the area of job performance, for example, how will managers benefit from knowing the effect of certain types of supervision on employee job satisfaction or work motivation or esprit de corps? To what extent can school counselors anticipate or predict how students will do in certain courses requiring mathematical skills if the counselors have a knowledge of these student's prior mathematical aptitude scores on a national examination?

All of these prediction situations involve associations between variables. But our interest is in forecasting accurately anticipated behaviors of persons based on previous knowledge of other crucial variables that we have designated as influential to one degree or another. We would like to be able to say that "if X, then Y." Certainly, an employment counselor would like to make effective and perfect job placements based on certain criteria provided by prospective employees. A juvenile delinquency rehabilitation center would like to "cure" all delinquents who participate in the program. Of course, these examples are assuming "perfect prediction." Unfortunately, our predictions of social behaviors and psychological dispositions are imperfect to varying degrees. What we fail to predict accurately is often designated as *error.* Therefore, we devote a considerable amount of time to identifying, measuring, and utilizing variables that will minimize errors in our prediction schemes.

Utilizing certain measures of association in our research will often

TABLE 11.1

	Children Under Continuous Adult Supervision	
	Yes	*No*
Delinquent	0	50
Nondelinquent	50	0

serve the function of telling us how much error we have accounted for in predicting particular behavioral outcomes. Suppose that we are interested in the association between delinquency and whether children are or are not under continuous adult supervision. We may believe that children who are under the continuous supervision by adults will have little or no opportunity to commit delinquent acts. Those children who do not have continuous adult supervision may be in a better position to act in a delinquent manner if they desire to do so. Therefore, we predict initially that delinquency will depend on whether or not children are under continuous adult supervision. We expect to find the association between these two variables shown in Table 11.1, provided that a perfect relation exists between them (assume that we have a sample of 50 delinquents and a sample of 50 nondelinquents). There are no errors in this cross-tabulation. But if we observe the "less-than-perfect" cross-tabulation of the association between these two variables (Table 11.2), the exceptions to our per-

TABLE 11.2

	Children Under Continuous Adult Supervision	
	Yes	*No*
Delinquent	5	45
Nondelinquent	40	10

fect predictions become errors. There are 15 errors in this cross-tabulation. Five of the delinquents are under continuous adult supervision and 10 nondelinquents are not under continuous adult supervision. Although the knowledge we have of whether or not children are under continuous adult supervision did not result in a perfect prediction, we did manage to account for a large amount of the error we would otherwise have without this knowledge. In other words, we accounted for 85 of the cases of delinquents and nondelinquents, and we failed to account for the remaining 15 cases.

We are now in a position to appreciate the importance of knowing whether children are or are not under continuous adult supervision and if they are delinquent or nondelinquent. If we had predicted that all children in our sample of 100 were delinquent, we would have been wrong 50 times (because 50 persons in our sample are nondelinquent). By the same token, had we predicted that all persons in our sample were nondelinquent, we still would have made 50 errors (because 50 persons would be delinquent). With a knowledge of continuous or noncontinuous adult supervision, we have minimized our prediction error as follows:

$$\frac{\text{original error} - \text{error with continuous adult supervision variable}}{\text{original error}}(100)$$

$$= \frac{50 - 15}{50}(100)$$

$$= \frac{35}{50}(100)$$

$$= 70 \text{ percent.}$$

We have reduced the error in predicting delinquency by 70 percent as the result of using the adult supervision variable as a predictor of delinquency. In other words, instead of committing 50 errors originally, we only commit 15 errors using a predictor variable such as adult supervision. We have reduced the actual number of errors we would have originally committed from 50 to 35, a 70 percent error reduction. This *proportional reduction in error* is conventionally designated PRE. Some measures of association have PRE interpretations, whereas others do not. Generally, measures of association that have PRE interpretations are preferred over measures of association that do not have them. Therefore, PRE becomes one of the important criteria for determining which measures of association we will use in our research and data analysis.

This chapter is organized as follows. Measures of association that are useful for determining the degree of association between two nominal variables will be discussed. These measures include (1) Pearson's coefficient of contingency, *C*; (2) Cramer's *V*; (3) Tschuprow's *T*; (4) the phi coefficient; (5) the tetrachoric *r*; and (6) Guttman's coefficient of predictability, lambda. Following this discussion will be a presentation of three measures of association when the researcher has two ordinal variables for analysis. These measures include (1) Kendall's tau, (2) Somers' *d*, and (3) Goodman's and Kruskal's gamma coefficient of ordinal association. Two tests for two interval variables will follow: (1) the Spearman's rho, and (2) the Pearson *r*.

The remainder of the chapter examines different combinations of variables that meet different level-of-measurement requirements. A measure of association will be presented for situations when the researcher has one nominal and one ordinal variable for analysis. This procedure is Wilcoxon's theta, the coefficient of differentiation. Following this measure will be a presentation of the correlation ratio, eta, which is specifically designed to measure the association between one nominal and one interval level variable. Finally, a measure of association for one ordinal and one interval variable will be presented. This measure is Jaspen's *M*, or coefficient of multiserial correlation.

□ MEASURES OF ASSOCIATION FOR TWO NOMINAL VARIABLES

This section contains the largest variety of measures for determining associations between two variables at any measurement level. One reason for this is the fact that many variables in the social sciences are classifiable or categorical. Religion, ethnic background, race, political party, sex, school major, and cultural background (i.e., rural or urban) are some of the many variables that are best measured according to a nominal scale. Therefore, much work has been done to devise measures that can reflect the degree of association between two nominally measured variables.

The fact that so many measures of association for two nominal variables are presented here does not mean that they are necessarily the best measures. Each one has strengths and weaknesses relative to the others. The primary reasons for their inclusion are that (1) they are frequently computed and presented as a portion of a computer printout in statistical programs, and (2) they have differential utility for the researcher, depending on the project undertaken and the variables being analyzed. Researchers should be familiar with them in order to make informed choices at the point of data analysis.

Pearson's *C*, the Coefficient of Contingency

The coefficient of contingency, C, is an index of the degree of association between two variables that have been cross-tabulated in an $r \times c$ table. Usually, but not always, a chi-square value has been computed first as a measure of the goodness of fit for the distribution of tabular frequencies. Once the chi-square value has been computed, however, it still is imperative that the researcher determines the degree of association between variables for the table. Pearson's C is derived directly from the observed chi-square value by the following formula:

$$C = \sqrt{\frac{\chi^2}{N + \chi^2}},$$

where

χ^2 = observed chi-square value for an $r \times c$ table
N = sample size for the table

The following example of the application of C is provided. Nixon (1975) investigated the association between a faculty member's status and attitudinal support of traditional labor tactics on college campuses. Labor tactics included attempts by faculty organizations at collective bargaining for higher salaries and better working conditions. A faculty member's status was indicated by junior or senior rank (junior ranks were defined as "untenured faculty," senior ranks as "tenured faculty."). As a part of his research, Nixon found the distribution of high and low support for labor tactics among junior and senior faculty interviewed shown in Table 11.3.

An observed $\chi^2 = 6.227$ was determined to be significant statistically at the .05 level of probability (two-tailed test, 1 degree of freedom). With this observed chi-square value and the table $N = 91$, the following Pearson's C was computed:

$$C = \sqrt{\frac{6.227}{91 + 6.227}}$$

$$= \sqrt{.0640}$$

$$= .25.$$

The resulting C observed = .25. Using the interpretation scheme suggested at the beginning of the chapter for assessing the strength of the association, we might say that the $C = .25$ is a low association. There are some problems associated with making this sort of interpretation of C, however. These will be discussed shortly. For the

TABLE 11.3
Degree of Faculty Support for Labor Tactics Among Junior and Senior Faculty.

	Faculty Status		
	Junior	*Senior*	*Totals*
Support for Labor Tactics	17	31	48
Support Against Labor Tactics	26	17	43
Totals	43	48	$N = 91$

Source: Howard L. Nixon II, "Faculty Support of Traditional Labor Tactics on Campus," *Sociology of Education*, **48:** 280, 1975.

Note: $\chi^2 = 6.227$ ($P < .05$, two-tailed test). $C = .25$; $\overline{C} = .35$.

time being, we may say that a low degree of association exists between a faculty member's status and support for the use of traditional labor tactics on campus.

Assumptions of C. The primary assumptions of the C coefficient are that (1) the data can be arranged into an $r \times c$ table; (2) the sample is randomly drawn; and (3) the sample size should be in excess of 25. This stems from the fact that C is based on a χ^2 value and is therefore subject to its limitations as well.

Advantages and Disadvantages of C. The only advantages of Pearson's C are that (1) it can be computed for tables of any $r \times c$ size, (2) it can be computed directly from a chi-square value, and (3) it is easy to compute.

On the negative side, C is merely an index number. It can be demonstrated that no matter how "perfect" the association is between two variables, C can never achieve 1.00. In fact, for the data in Table 11.3, the largest C value that could possibly be computed would be approximately .71. For this reason, a correction factor must be applied to bolster the magnitude of the observed C value to make it comparable to 1.00. In short, we must divide the observed C value by a correction factor (which is actually the largest value it could possibly achieve for a table of any specified $r \times c$ size) in order to give a result that could be compared with 1.00. Table 11.4 contains various correction factors associated with C for tables ranging in size from

TABLE 11.4
Corrections for Pearson's C for $r \times c$ Tables.

Table Size	(Divisor) Correction	Table Size	(Divisor) Correction	Table Size	(Divisor) Correction
2 × 2	.707	3 × 9	.843	6 × 6	.913
2 × 3	.685	3 × 10	.846	6 × 7	.930
2 × 4	.730	4 × 4	.866	6 × 8	.936
2 × 5	.752	4 × 5	.863	6 × 9	.941
2 × 6	.765	4 × 6	.877	6 × 10	.945
2 × 7	.774	4 × 7	.888	7 × 7	.926
2 × 8	.779	4 × 8	.893	7 × 8	.947
2 × 9	.783	4 × 9	.898	7 × 9	.952
2 × 10	.786	4 × 10	.901	7 × 10	.955
3 × 3	.816	5 × 5	.894	8 × 8	.935
3 × 4	.786	5 × 6	.904	8 × 9	.957
3 × 5	.810	5 × 7	.915	8 × 10	.961
3 × 6	.824	5 × 8	.920	9 × 9	.943
3 × 7	.833	5 × 9	.925	9 × 10	.966
3 × 8	.838	5 × 10	.929	10 × 10	.949

Note: All correction factors for tables where $r \neq c$ have been determined by a procedure described in Charles C. Peters and Walter R. Van Voorhis, *Statistical Procedures and Their Mathematical Bases* (New York: McGraw-Hill Book Company, 1940) pp. 393–399, and Thomas C. McCormick, *Elementary Social Statistics* (New York: McGraw-Hill Book Company, 1941), pp. 207–208.

2 × 2 to 10 × 10. Depending on the table size we are dealing with, the appropriate correction factor should be selected from Table 11.4 and divided into our observed C value. The result of this division will be to inflate the value of C to bring it more into line with other measures of association, which can achieve 1.00. The correction factor shown in Table 11.4 for a 2 × 2 table is .707. Dividing our observed C value by .707, we have .25/.707 = .35. We refer to this C value as a *corrected* C or $\overline{C}$ (read: C bar). For many researchers, this additional step to correct for C is an annoyance and a disadvantage of the test.

Another problem is that uncorrected C values cannot be compared with one another directly unless they are computed for tables that (1) are the same size, and (2) have identical marginal totals. Corrected C values, $\overline{C}$ values, may be compared with one another directly, however. But rapid comparisons of uncorrected C values must be delayed in order for such corrections to be made. Perhaps the best thing to be said of C is that it does provide us with an initial clue about the potential association existing between the two variables that have been cross-tabulated.

The Significance of C. The statistical significance of a C value is the chi-square value that has been computed for the table. If the observed chi-square value is significant, by definition the C value is significant at the same level of probability. For the data in Table 11.3, the C value of .25 (corrected to .35) is significant at the .05 level, although it continues to remain a moderately low degree of association between the two variables.

Cramer's V

An improvement over the coefficient of contingency, C, is Cramer's V. This measure of association can achieve 1.00 without the aid of a correction factor. It is computed as follows:

$$V = \sqrt{\frac{\chi^2}{(N)(a-1)}},$$

where

χ^2 = observed chi-square value for some $r \times c$ table
N = sample size for the table
a = smaller number associated with the rows and columns

To furnish the reader with some comparative figures, Cramer's V has been computed for the data in Table 11.3 as follows:

$$V = \sqrt{\frac{6.227}{(91)(2-1)}}$$
$$= \sqrt{\frac{6.227}{91}}$$
$$= \sqrt{.0684}$$
$$= .26.$$

Notice that the observed $V = .26$ is only slightly larger compared with the original uncorrected $C = .25$. When degrees of freedom are larger than 1, the general effect on V is to decrease it considerably compared with the C coefficient.

Assumptions, Advantages, and Disadvantages of Cramer's V. Cramer's V may be computed for any data where a chi-square value has been determined. Like Pearson's C, Cramer's V is what is sometimes known as a *chi-square-based measure of association.* It is easy to compute and interpret. Although it does not have a PRE interpretation, it provides us with a more reliable measure of the degree of association between two nominal variables compared with Pearson's

C. Its value can range from 0 (no association) to +1.00 (perfect association). No correction factor is involved.

It should be noted that both *C* and *V* are always positive. If the researcher needs to determine the *direction of the association* between variables, this can be accomplished easily by inspecting the arrangement of frequencies throughout the table.

The primary assumptions of Cramer's *V* include randomness and the nominal level of measurement. There are no sample size restrictions. The significance of Cramer's *V* is measured by the significance associated with the observed χ^2 for the table. If the χ^2 is significant statistically, so is Cramer's *V*.

Tschuprow's *T*

A third chi-square-based measure of association is known as Tschuprow's *T*. When tables have an identical number of rows and columns (i.e., when $r = c$), Tschuprow's *T* is identical in computation to Cramer's *V*. However, when $r \neq c$, the general result is to decrease the value of *T* compared with *V*. The formula for Tschuprow's *T* is as follows:

$$T = \sqrt{\frac{\chi^2}{(N)\sqrt{(r-1)(c-1)}}},$$

where

χ^2 = observed chi square for the table
r and c = number of rows and columns in the table
N = sample size for the table

Suppose that a researcher observed a $\chi^2 = 25.2$ with a 4×3 table (assuming that $N = 154$). The probability associated with this χ^2 value would be .001. If we were to apply both Cramer's *V* and Tschuprow's *T* to these data, we would have the following:

$$V = \sqrt{\frac{25.2}{(154)(3-1)}}$$

$$= \sqrt{\frac{25.2}{308}}$$

$$= \sqrt{.0818}$$

$$= .29.$$

$$T = \sqrt{\frac{25.2}{(154)\sqrt{(4-1)(3-1)}}}$$

$$= \sqrt{\frac{25.2}{(154)\sqrt{6}}}$$

$$= \sqrt{\frac{25.2}{(154)(2.449)}}$$

$$= \sqrt{\frac{25.2}{377.46}}$$

$$= \sqrt{.0668}$$

$$= .26.$$

The Cramer's $V = .29$ and $T = .26$. Had the table size involved been 4×4, 5×5, or any other size where $r = c$, the values of V and T would have been identical. (The proof of this similarity is left as an exercise for the reader.)

One limitation of Tschuprow's T is that whenever $r \neq c$, T can never achieve +1.00. Also, like C and V, T is always a positive coefficient of association. To determine the direction of an association between variables, an inspection of tabular frequencies is in order. Tschuprow's T has no PRE interpretation and is like C and V in this respect. This is a major limitation compared with other measures of association to be discussed in this section. The assumptions for applying T are that the data must be measured according to a nominal scale and that the sample must be random.

Pearson's *C*, Cramer's *V*, and Tschuprow's *T* Compared

Clearly, the most inferior measure of the three presented thus far is Pearson's C. It must be corrected in order to yield +1.00. Also, we cannot compare C's with one another when they are based on tables of different $r \times c$ sizes. Cramer's V values may be directly compared with one another, regardless of the different table sizes involved.

Tschuprow's T is also an improvement over C, although we have seen that for instances where $r \neq c$, T cannot achieve +1.00. Cramer's V is the best measure of the three presented so far. It is easily computed and can achieve +1.00 under any $r \times c$ condition. Since all three measures are provided the researcher in computer printouts and one frequently encounters them in research articles, it seems reasonable to have a general idea of the differential utility of each measure and how each functions in relation to the others.

The Phi Coefficient, ϕ

When the researcher has nominal data arranged into a 2 X 2 table, it is possible to obtain a PRE evaluation of the variables by using the phi coefficient, ϕ. As an example, let us examine the work of Katz and Martin (1962). These researchers were interested in early career-choice patterns of persons who subsequently became nurses. At what point in one's life was a definite decision made to pursue nursing as a career and seek admission to nursing school?

As a part of their study, Katz and Martin questioned 66 persons enrolled in a school of nursing at a "southern university." One question pertained to the age at which the career decision to enter nursing was made. Some students who were asked this question at the beginning of their schooling did not remain in the program through graduation. For various reasons, they dropped out of school. Table 11.5 shows the different ages at which a definite decision to enter nursing was made and whether or not the students graduated. The original χ^2 for this table was 3.835, which was significant statistically at the .05 level (one-tailed test). If we were to use phi as our coefficient of association for these data, we would use the formula

$$\phi = \frac{ad - bc}{\sqrt{(a+b)(c+d)(a+c)(b+d)}},$$

TABLE 11.5
Relation Between Graduating from Nursing School and Age When the Student Definitely Decided to Study Nursing.

	Age at the Time of Definite Decision		
	Under 16	*16 or over*	*Totals*
Graduated	12 a	24 b	36 $(a+b)$
Not Graduated	3 c	27 d	30 $(c+d)$
Totals	15 $(a+c)$	51 $(b+d)$	$N = 66$

Source: Fred E. Katz and Harry W. Martin, "Career Choice Processes," *Social Forces*, **41**:152, 1962.

Note: $\chi^2 = 3.835$ ($P < .05$, 1 df, one-tailed test); $\phi = .28$.

where

$$a, b, c, \text{ and } d = \text{cells of the } 2 \times 2 \text{ table}$$
$$(a+b), (c+d), (a+c), (b+d) = \text{marginal totals of the } 2 \times 2 \text{ table}$$

Carrying out our calculations based on the information provided in Table 11.5, we have

$$\phi = \frac{(12)(27) - (24)(3)}{\sqrt{(36)(30)(51)(15)}}$$
$$= \frac{324 - 72}{\sqrt{826{,}200}}$$
$$= \frac{252}{908.955}$$
$$= .28.$$

The resulting phi value = .28. Using the crude guide at the beginning of the chapter to evaluate the strength of the association, we would conclude that a moderately low degree of association exists between age at the time of making the definite decision to enter nursing and whether or not these persons stayed in school to complete their program and graduate.

To obtain a PRE interpretation of the observed ϕ value, we must square it. Therefore, PRE = $\phi^2 = (.28)^2 = .08$. We would say that 8 percent of the error in predicting graduating or not graduating has been accounted for by using "age at which definite decision was made" as a predictor of it. Of course, $1 - \phi^2$ indicates the amount of error we would fail to account for by using "age at which the definite decision was made" as a predictor of it. In this case, $1 - \phi^2 = 1 - .08 = .92$, or 92 percent of the error would be unexplained. It would seem, therefore, that the age at which the definite decision was made to enter nursing was of little consequence insofar as graduating or not graduating from nursing school was concerned.

Assumptions of Phi. To compute the phi coefficient, the data must be arranged into a 2 X 2 table. The data must be naturally dichotomous and measured at the nominal level.

Advantages and Disadvantages of Phi. The principal disadvantage of phi is that it can only be applied to 2 X 2 tables. Also, when large samples are encountered (i.e., when $N > 250$), the phi coefficient becomes increasingly cumbersome to apply. On the positive side of the ledger, phi is interpretable as a PRE measure through ϕ^2. Compared with Pearson's C, Cramer's V, and Tschuprow's T, this is a distinct advantage of phi. Another advantage is that phi can achieve 0 when no association exists and 1.00 when a perfect association exists.

Phi may achieve both positive and negative values, again differing from the other measures presented so far in this section. One additional limitation of phi is that the frequencies for both the independent and dependent variables must be divided equally in order for the resulting phi value to potentially achieve ± 1.00. Any uneven split of marginal totals will yield a phi value that would be less than ± 1.00. Therefore, the researcher should strive to achieve as close to a 50–50 split on both variables as possible. This dichotomization should not be forced to the extent that the resulting variable subdivisions are illogical, however. Phi is maximized in value and meaning whenever 50–50 splits are achieved or closely approximated for both independent and dependent variable frequencies.

The Significance of Phi. The statistical significance of the phi coefficient is determined by a chi-square test:

$$\chi^2 = N\phi^2 \quad \text{(with 1 degree of freedom).}$$

For the data in Table 11.5, we would evaluate the significance of the phi as follows:

$$\chi^2 = (66)(.08) = 5.28.$$

Turning to Table A4 with 1 df, we find that an observed $\chi^2 = 5.28$ would be significant at $P < .05$.

The Tetrachoric r, r_{tet}

An alternative to the phi coefficient will be mentioned here briefly. The tetrachoric r, r_{tet}, is sometimes used in research work for analyzing data presented in 2×2 tables. Under proper conditions where all assumptions have been met, r_{tet} provides a close approximation of the Pearson r (described later in this chapter). Data for both independent and dependent variables are assumed to be continuous, but these are "forced" into dichotomies for purposes of constructing a 2×2 table. The r_{tet} formula is quite complex, but Davidoff and Goheen (1953) have determined estimates for r_{tet} based on the results of the simple formula

$$\frac{bc}{ad},$$

where

a, b, c, d = frequencies in the four cells of a 2 × 2 table
ad or bc = larger of the two products that would be placed in the formula numerator

For instance, if we were to apply r_{tet} to the data in Table 11.5, we would have $bc/ad = (12)(27)/(24)(3) = 324/72 = 4.5$. Turning to Table A21, we find this value in the column labeled bc/ad and the equivalent r_{tet} would be shown adjacent to it. In this case, our observed bc/ad of 4.5 has an $r_{tet} = .54$ associated with it.

Although an $r_{tet} = .54$ is considerably larger than the phi coefficient for the same data in Table 11.5 ($\phi = .28$), r_{tet} would more accurately reflect the strength of the association between variables, provided that certain assumptions were met. First, r_{tet} assumes that both variables are normally distributed. Second, r_{tet} assumes that a linear relation exists between the two variables. Other assumptions include a continuum underlying the traits measured, randomness, and the nominal level of measurement. The first two assumptions are the most rigorous to achieve, however.[2]

If a PRE interpretation is desired for a 2 × 2 table, r_{tet} would be unacceptable because it lacks such an interpretation. If a measure of the strength of the association between variables is desired, r_{tet} would probably be superior to phi. However, r_{tet} is restricted in its application far beyond the normality and linearity assumptions. For one thing, it is assumed that r_{tet} will be inappropriate if radical splits occur on either the independent or dependent variables. If a 90–10 or a 98–2 split occurs on either variable, r_{tet} becomes an unreliable measure of association. If any given cell contains no frequencies, r_{tet} should not be used under any circumstances. Zeros in cells cause gross distortions to occur (e.g., coefficients of +1.00 would be observed under conditions where something other than perfect association exists between the two variables). This disturbing property of r_{tet}, coupled with the restrictive assumptions associated with it, make the measure considerably less desirable compared than the phi coefficient. It is mentioned here primarily because it is sometimes provided in computer printouts together with V, T, phi, and other nominal measures of association. Today it is used relatively infrequently in research work. This is probably due to the fact that such stringent assumptions must be met before it can be properly applied.

[2] An excellent discussion of a defense of normality and linearity for dichotomous characteristics is provided by Guilford and Fruchter (1978, pp. 311–313).

Guttman's Coefficient of Predictability, Lambda, λ

Perhaps the best and most flexible measure of association between two nominal variables is lambda, λ. Lambda may be applied to tables of any size and can achieve +1.00. There are other features of lambda that make it a desirable alternative as well. Before discussing these, however, an example of the application of lambda is in order.

Alsikafi and Hughes (1973) were interested in examining the occupational orientations of persons in a variety of labor unions. One portion of their study was devoted to an examination of participation levels of members of two different types of unions—craft and industrial. What was the association between type of union and level of participation in union activity? These researchers cross-tabulated "type of union" with "level of participation" for union members sampled. Table 11.6 presents a hypothetical distribution of their findings. One way of answering the question of whether an association exists between these two variables is to apply the lambda coefficient to the data in Table 11.6. The lambda formula is as follows:

$$\lambda = \frac{\sum f_r + \sum f_c - (F_r + F_c)}{2N - (F_r - F_c)},$$

where

f_r = largest frequency occurring in a row
f_c = largest frequency occurring in a column
F_r = largest marginal frequency occurring among the rows
F_c = largest marginal frequency occurring among the columns
N = number of observations for the table

Using the information supplied in Table 11.6, we may compute the lambda value as follows:

$$\lambda = \frac{(32 + 47) + (32 + 26 + 47) - (71 + 58)}{(2)(140) - (71 + 58)}$$

$$= \frac{(79 + 105) - (129)}{280 - 129}$$

$$= \frac{55}{151}$$

$$= .36.$$

The resulting λ = .36. We may interpret this coefficient in terms of its strength by stating that a moderately low association exists be-

TABLE 11.6
Union Membership and Level of Participation in Union Activities.

	Level of Participation			
Type of Union	*High*	*Medium*	*Low*	*Totals*
Craft	32	26	11	69
Industrial	10	14	47	71
Totals	42	40	58	$N = 140$

Source: Hypothetical data based on research by M. Alsikafi and Michael Hughes, "Craft and Industrial Labor Unions: A Study in Occupational Orientations," *LSU Journal of Sociology*, 3:38–60, 1973.

tween type of union and level of participation in the union organization. Or we may interpret lambda directly as a PRE measure. A PRE interpretation would be that 36 percent of the error in predicting the two variables (i.e., type of union and level of participation) has been accounted for by using each as a predictor of the other. This statement is *symmetrical.* This means that regardless of whether type of union or level of participation is used as the independent variable, the same coefficient of .36 will be observed.

If the researcher is interested in determining which variable, type of union or level of participation, is the better predictor, an alternative formula for lambda must be used. This formula is *asymmetrical* and is designated lambda *a* or λ_a. The asymmetrical formula for lambda is

$$\lambda_a = \frac{\sum f_i - F_d}{N - F_d},$$

where

f_i = largest frequency occurring within each subclass of the independent variable
F_d = largest frequency found within the dependent variable subtotals
N = total number of observations for the table

Applying this formula to the data in Table 11.6, using level of participation as independent and the predictor of type of union membership, we have

$$\lambda_a = \frac{(32 + 26 + 47) - 71}{140 - 71}$$

$$= \frac{105 - 71}{69}$$

$$= \frac{34}{69}$$

$$= .49.$$

The first $\lambda_a = .49$. The PRE interpretation of this association is that 49 percent of the error in predicting the type of union has been accounted for by using level of participation as the predictor of it.

Now, let us rearrange the data in Table 11.6 so that type of union is the independent variable and predictor of level of participation in the union. Table 11.7 shows this rearrangement. Applying the asymmetrical formula for lambda again to the data in Table 11.7, we have

$$\lambda_a = \frac{(32 + 47) - 58}{140 - 58}$$

$$= \frac{79 - 58}{82}$$

$$= \frac{21}{82}$$

$$= .26.$$

The resulting $\lambda_a = .26$. In PRE terms, this means that we have accounted for 26 percent of the error in predicting the level of participation in unions by using type of union as a predictor of it. It would appear that level of participation in a union is a better predictor of union type than type of union is of level of participation in a union. This is one of the most valuable benefits of the asymmetrical lambda formula.

Assumptions of Lambda. Lambda does not have many restrictive assumptions. We must have nominal data that can be cross-tabulated into some $r \times c$ tabular form. Also, we must have randomness.

TABLE 11.7
Union Type as a Predictor of Level of Participation in the Union.

	Type of Union		
Level of Participation	*Craft*	*Industrial*	*Totals*
High	32	10	42
Medium	26	14	40
Low	11	47	58
Totals	69	71	$N = 140$

Advantages and Disadvantages of Lambda. The primary advantages of lambda are that it can yield a PRE interpretation that is both symmetric and asymmetric, and it can also reflect the degree or strength of association between variables. For any kind of directional statement to be made, an inspection of the distribution of cell frequencies is in order.

Lambda requires no correction factor and can achieve +1.00. Lambda is applicable to tables of virtually any size, and lambda values from different table sizes may be compared directly.

One disadvantage of lambda which occurs infrequently is that a lambda coefficient may equal 0 or indicate no association when association between variables actually exists. This is because of certain peculiar distributions of frequencies throughout the cells. When lambda is applied to a table where visual inspection reveals that an association likely exists, a lambda value of 0 should be viewed with skepticism.[3]

[3] Costner (1965) recommends the use of an alternative measure of association when lambda yields a 0 and the researcher suspects that association actually exists. The alternative procedure is Goodman's and Kruskal's tau_b, which is discussed at length in Goodman and Kruskal (1954). This procedure will yield a nonzero under circumstances where lambda yields a 0. To this extent, there is some degree of improvement in predictability.

□ MEASURES OF ASSOCIATION FOR TWO ORDINAL VARIABLES

When the researcher has two variables measured according to an ordinal scale, the three tests presented in this section might be applicable. The tests to be discussed include (1) Kendall's tau, τ; (2) Somers' d; and (3) Goodman's and Kruskal's gamma coefficient of ordinal association, γ.

Kendall's Tau, τ

Kendall's tau, τ, is a useful measure of association between two sets of scores that have been measured according to ordinal scales. This procedure is appropriate for data arranged into ranks and not in cross-tabulated form such as in some $r \times c$ table. The following example is provided.

Hanson (1975) was interested in determining the association between the IQ of children and the degree of stability of their home environment. A sample of children was obtained and given the Stanford Binet IQ test. Also, a measure of home stability was administered to these children. The children were ages 9 to 10. Hanson was convinced that a positive association between IQ and the stability of the home environment would be found, based on previous investigations of the relationships between these phenomena. The following data shown in Table 11.8 represent some hypothetical IQ and home stability scores for 25 children. IQ scores for the 25 children range from 90 (lower scores) to 135 (higher scores). The home stability scores range from 39 (low stability) to 74 (high stability).

Table 11.8 is constructed as follows. IQ scores for the 25 children are ranked from high to low as shown in the IQ column. Their corresponding home stability raw scores are placed adjacent to their IQ scores in the "home stability" column. Next, in a column R_1, the IQ scores are ranked directly from 1 to 25, as shown. Column R_2 consists of the ranks assigned to the home stability scores from 1 to 25 also. Column R_2 becomes the object of our attention for determining values in the final two columns.

In the column "number of higher ranks," we focus upon the first rank of the first child, which is 2. We count the number of ranks below 2 that are higher than 2. Twenty-three ranks are higher, and we place this value adjacent to the rank of 2, as shown. The next rank of 1 also has 23 ranks below it which are higher. We continue down this column until we have entered all values as shown in the "number of higher ranks" column.

TOTAL 11.8
Association Between IQ and Home Stability for 25 Children.

Child Number	*IQ*	*Home Stability*	R_1	R_2	*Number of Higher Ranks*	*Number of Lower Ranks*
1	135	72	1	2	23	1
2	134	74	2	1	23	0
3	133	69	3	4	21	1
4	132	71	4	3	21	0
5	128	65	5	7	18	2
6	127	64	6	8	17	2
7	126	63	7	9	16	2
8	125	62	8	10	15	2
9	124	49	9	16	9	7
10	123	68	10	5	15	0
11	122	66	11	6	14	0
12	121	55	12	11	13	0
13	120	51	13	14	10	2
14	119	54	14	12	11	0
15	116	50	15	15	9	1
16	114	42	16	23	2	7
17	113	47	17	18	6	2
18	110	48	18	17	6	1
19	108	46	19	19	5	1
20	106	45	20	20	4	1
21	100	53	21	13	4	0
22	99	39	22	25	0	3
23	96	43	23	22	1	1
24	92	44	24	21	1	0
25	90	41	25	24	0	0
					$\Sigma H = 264$	$\Sigma L = 36$

Note: Hypothetical scores based on research by Ralph A. Hanson, "Consistency and Stability of Home Environment Measures Related to IQ," *Child Development*, **46**:470–480, 1975.

The final column, "number of lower ranks," represents the number of ranks below each rank in column R_2 which are lower than that rank. For instance, the first rank of 2 has one rank below it that is lower than 2 (i.e., 1). The rank of 16 (farther down the column) has seven ranks below it that are lower than 16 (i.e., 5, 6, 11, 14, 12, 15, and 13). We carry out this procedure until all values have been determined for the final column. We sum these values. With these sums we may carry out the formula for Kendall's tau. The formula is

$$\tau = \frac{\Sigma H - \Sigma L}{\frac{N(N-1)}{2}},$$

where

$\sum H$ and $\sum L$ = sums of the number of higher and lower ranks respectively
N = number of children in our sample

With the data from Table 11.8, we may compute τ as follows:

$$\tau = \frac{264 - 36}{\frac{(25)(25 - 1)}{2}}$$

$$= \frac{228}{300}$$

$$= .76.$$

Our observed $\tau = .76$. We would interpret this value as being a strong association between IQ and home stability.

Assumptions of Kendall's Tau. The primary assumptions underlying Kendall's tau are that we must have randomness and scores measured according to an ordinal scale. There are no distributional requirements associated with this coefficient. An additional assumption is that N should be greater than 10 for proper application.

Advantages and Disadvantages of Kendall's Tau. Kendall's tau is specifically designed for scores in the format shown in Table 11.8. When data are cross-tabulated such as those shown in Table 11.7, Kendall's tau would be inappropriate (even assuming that the ordinal level of measurement had been achieved). Tau values also range from -1.00 to +1.00.

One flaw associated with tau is that it is not suitable for situations where tied scores exist. Several authors have provided corrections for tau values whenever tied scores are present (see Downie and Heath, 1974, or Siegel, 1956). However, since a better measure exists for two ordinal variables that does handle ties well (gamma), the recommendation is not to apply Kendall's tau whenever tied scores are present. The tediousness of the correction procedure and the small change in the resulting tau value provides little reward for applying the correction.

The Significance of Tau. Kendall's tau may be assessed in terms of its statistical significance by using the following formula, which results in an approximation of a Z value:

$$Z = \frac{\tau}{\sigma_\tau},$$

where

τ = observed Kendall's tau value
σ_τ = standard error of tau, defined as

$$\sqrt{\frac{2(2N+5)}{9N(N-1)}}$$

With our observed tau = .76, the test of the significance of it becomes

$$Z = \frac{.76}{\sqrt{\frac{(2)(50+5)}{(9)(25)(25-1)}}}$$

$$= \frac{.76}{\sqrt{\frac{110}{5400}}}$$

$$= \frac{.76}{\sqrt{.0204}}$$

$$= \frac{.76}{.143}$$

$$= 5.31.$$

Our observed $Z = 5.31$. Using Table A3, we can determine the significance associated with this value. For instance, we would need to equal or exceed a $Z = 2.58$ in order for the observed tau value to be significant statistically at the .01 level (with a two-tailed test). Obviously, our observed $Z = 5.31$ is far in excess of this critical Z value, and we can conclude that the tau is significant.

Somers' d_{yx}

A measure of association designed for cross-tabulated data measured according to an ordinal scale, Somers' d_{yx} provides the researcher with a relatively simple method for determining which variable is the better predictor. It is strictly an asymmetric PRE measure. Therefore, it is necessary to utilize each of the two variables studied as independent in relation to the other in order to evaluate the predictive utility of each. The following example is provided.

Segal (1969) investigated the association between work satisfaction and perceived powerlessness among a sample of Chilean physicians in a large hospital in Santiago. He believed that work satisfactions would vary according to the perceived powerlessness of physicians. Powerlessness was defined by Segal as "the feeling that one does not have control over the way his work is defined and organized." (Segal, 1969, p. 196.) A Guttman scale was used to render an ordinal measure of this variable. Work satisfactions were measured similarly by appropriate items revealing one's degree of contentment with the type of work performed. A specific relationship was believed to exist between these variables as follows. As one's perceived powerlessness tended to increase, one's satisfaction with work would tend to decrease. Therefore, if Segal's theorizing were sound, we would expect to find a fairly strong, inverse association between these variables. Based on Segal's ideas, some hypothetical data have been arranged into a cross-tabulated form and presented in Table 11.9.

Each cell in Table 11.9 has been lettered to make the computational work easier to follow. Since Somers' d_{yx} is asymmetric, two d values must be computed. One value, d_{yx}, will yield a coefficient that will indicate how much variation in variable Y will occur as a function of variable X as a predictor of it. The other coefficient, d_{xy}, will indicate the amount of error in predicting variable X that is accounted for by using variable Y as a predictor of it. These formulas

TABLE 11.9
Perceived Powerlessness and Work Satisfactions for 150 Chilean Physicians.

Work Satisfaction (variable Y)	*Physician's Perceived Powerlessness (variable X)*			
	Low	*Medium*	*High*	*Totals*
High	25 *a*	18 *b*	10 *c*	53
Medium	12 *d*	13 *e*	15 *f*	40
Low	8 *g*	17 *h*	32 *i*	57
Totals	45	48	57	$N = 150$

are as follows. Where X is a predictor of Y,

$$d_{yx} = \frac{\sum f_a - \sum f_i}{\sum f_a + \sum f_i + T_y}.$$

When Y is the predictor of X,

$$d_{xy} = \frac{\sum f_a - \sum f_i}{\sum f_a + \sum f_i + T_x},$$

where

f_a = frequency of agreements
f_i = frequency of inversions
T_y and T_x = pairs of scores tied on Y and on X

Operationally defined, these values are determined as follows for the cells in Table 11.9:

$$\sum f_a = (a)(e+f+h+i) + (b)(f+i) + (d)(h+i) + (e)(i).$$

$$\sum f_i = (c)(d+e+g+h) + (b)(d+g) + (f)(g+h) + (e)(g).$$

$$T_x = (a)(d+g) + (d)(g) + (b)(e+h) + (e)(h) + (c)(f+i) + (f)(i).$$

$$T_y = (a)(b+c) + (b)(c) + (d)(e+f) + (e)(f) + (g)(h+i) + (h)(i).$$

These terms are determined from the data in Table 11.9 as follows:

$$\begin{aligned}\sum f_a &= (25)(13+15+17+32) + (18)(15+32) \\ &\quad + (12)(17+32) + (13)(32) \\ &= 1925 + 846 + 588 + 416 \\ &= 3775.\end{aligned}$$

$$\begin{aligned}\sum f_i &= (10)(12+13+8+17) + (18)(12+8) \\ &\quad + (15)(8+17) + (13)(8) \\ &= 500 + 360 + 375 + 104 \\ &= 1339.\end{aligned}$$

$$\begin{aligned}T_y &= (25)(18+10) + (18)(10) + (12)(13+15) \\ &\quad + (13)(15) + (8)(17+32) + (17)(32) \\ &= 700 + 180 + 336 + 195 + 392 + 544 \\ &= 2347.\end{aligned}$$

$$T_x = (25)(12 + 8) + (12)(8) + (18)(13 + 17) + (13)(17) + (10)(15 + 32) + (15)(32)$$
$$= 500 + 96 + 540 + 221 + 470 + 480$$
$$= 2307.$$

Summarizing these values, we have

$$\sum f_a = 3775$$
$$\sum f_i = 1339$$
$$T_y = 2347$$
$$T_x = 2307.$$

We may now determine our first d_{yx} value:

$$d_{yx} = \frac{3775 - 1339}{3775 + 1339 + 2347}$$
$$= \frac{2436}{7461}$$
$$= .326 = .33.$$

$$d_{xy} = \frac{3775 - 1339}{3775 + 1339 + 2307}$$
$$= \frac{2436}{7421}$$
$$= .328 = .33.$$

Based on these d values, it seems that neither variable is the better predictor. This is probably attributable to the distribution of frequencies in Table 11.9. Usually, Somers' d yields different values when the independent variable is rearranged to be dependent. (Had we carried out these d coefficients to three places instead of to the nearest hundredth, d_{yx} would have been .326, and d_{xy} would have been .328.) Variable Y has an almost imperceptible edge in predictive utility over variable X. Powerlessness influences work satisfaction levels slightly more than work satisfaction influences powerlessness.

Assumptions of Somers' d. The primary assumptions for Somers' d are two variables measured according to an ordinal scale and randomness.

Advantages and Disadvantages of Somers' d. Somers' d can achieve perfect negative and perfect positive association, ranging from -1.00 to $+1.00$, depending on the distribution of table frequencies. The asymmetric PRE interpretation feature of Somers' d also makes it attractive to use in research.[4] The strength of the association between variables can be assessed by examining the absolute value of d.

Compared with other measures of association we have treated thus far, Somers' d is a bit more laborious to compute. But computer programs are available that yield asymmetric values of d for both variables examined, and the asymmetric property of d gives it a strength that other measures in this section lack. An additional advantage of d is that it can be computed for any $r \times c$ table.

Goodman's and Kruskal's Gamma, γ

A measure of association for two ordinal variables that is almost computationally identical with Somers' d is Goodman's and Kruskal's gamma, γ. Gamma is a symmetrical PRE measure, however, and regardless of which variable is utilized as the independent one, the same gamma value will result. The formula for gamma is as follows:

$$\gamma = \frac{\sum f_a - \sum f_i}{\sum f_a + \sum f_i},$$

where

f_a = frequency of agreements
f_i = frequency of inversions

The data provided in Table 11.9 will suffice for illustrating the computation of gamma. It was shown in the discussion of Somers' d that $\Sigma f_a = 3775$ and $\Sigma f_i = 1339$. With these values, gamma is computed as follows:

$$\gamma = \frac{3775 - 1339}{3775 + 1339}$$

$$= \frac{2436}{5114}$$

$$= .48.$$

[4] There is a continuing controversy over whether Somers' d constitutes a valid measure of PRE. The reader is referred to Costner (1965), Morris (1970), and Somers (1962, 1968) for detailed commentary on the relative merits of d_{yx} and d_{xy} as PRE measures.

We would interpret a gamma of this magnitude as a moderately strong association between perceived powerlessness and work satisfaction. An inspection of the arrangement of frequencies in Table 11.9 will show that the association is actually a negative one, despite the positive coefficient of .48. The absolute value of gamma, $|.48|$, would be directly interpreted as a PRE measure.

Assumptions of Gamma. To properly apply gamma, we must have two variables measured according to an ordinal scale. We must also have randomness.

Advantages and Disadvantages of Gamma. The absolute value of gamma is directly interpretable as a PRE measure. The range of values gamma may assume is from -1.00 to $+1.00$. Gamma may be applied to data cross-tabulated in any $r \times c$ table. It does not need a correction for direct interpretation. In fact, of all measures available for two ordinal variable associations, Costner (1965) recommends gamma.

One weakness of gamma is that under certain conditions, a perfect association between variables of $+1.00$ or -1.00 will result when, in fact, perfect association does not exist. In some respects, this is a limitation similar to that of lambda. Perfect or near-perfect association between variables can be detected fairly easily. In a 3×3 tabular arrangement, for instance, perfect positive and perfect negative associations[5] would appear as shown in Table 11.10.

The Significance of Gamma. The statistical significance of gamma for sample sizes ranging from 4 to 40 may be evaluated by examining

TABLE 11.10

		Variable X		
		High	*Med.*	*Low*
Variable Y	*High*	100	0	0
	Med.	0	100	0
	Low	0	0	100

Perfect Positive Association

		Variable X		
		High	*Med.*	*Low*
Variable Y	*High*	0	0	100
	Med.	0	100	0
	Low	100	0	0

Perfect Negative Association

[5] For a more elaborate discussion of tabular conditions where gamma would fail to function properly, see Mueller et al. (1977, pp. 217–219).

Table A12. This table contains critical gamma values for the .05 and .01 significance levels for one- and two-tailed tests. For situations where $N > 40$, an approximation of a Z value may be obtained. The method for approximating Z and determining the statistical significance associated with an observed gamma is

$$Z = (\gamma)\sqrt{\frac{\sum f_a - \sum f_i}{N(1 - \gamma^2)}}.$$

Using our observed gamma = .48, $\Sigma f_a = 3775$, $\Sigma f_i = 1339$, and $N =$ 150, we would have

$$\begin{aligned} Z &= (.48)\sqrt{\frac{3775 - 1339}{(150)(1 - .48^2)}} \\ &= (.48)\sqrt{21.09} \\ &= (.48)(4.592) \\ &= 2.20. \end{aligned}$$

With a Z this large, we could conclude that our observed gamma of .48 is significant at the .05 level with a two-tailed test (the critical Z value would be ± 1.96).

□ MEASURES OF ASSOCIATION FOR TWO INTERVAL VARIABLES

When the researcher has two interval-level variables available for analysis, it may be possible to use one of the two procedures discussed in this section. These are (1) the Spearman's rho, r_s; and (2) the Pearson r.

Spearman's Rho, r_s

A measure of association for two interval-level variables that is extremely limited in its application is Spearman's rho, r_s. This procedure has conventionally been applied to ordinal data in the past, although the arithmetic operations technically require that the data be measured according to an interval scale. Also, Spearman's rho has a sensitivity to tied scores that prohibits its effective use whenever any noticeable number of tied scores are present. The following example will illustrate the application of r_s.

Shichor (1973) was interested in determining the degree of association between regional prestige of graduate departments of sociology and the general ability of those departments to attract and hire recent Ph.D. graduates from equally prestigious schools. Data were obtained from a national study of the quality of graduate departments and university prestige. Nine regions for the American Sociological Association were identified and ranked from high to low (1 to 9) according to the prestige norms established in the national study. Aggregate prestige scores were obtained for newly hired faculty based on these same national norms. Some hypothetical data relating to the prestige of faculty hired by these ranked regional schools are shown in Table 11.11.

The formula for Spearman's rho is

$$r_s = 1 - \left[\frac{6 \sum D^2}{N(N^2 - 1)}\right],$$

where

D^2 = squared differences between the two sets of ranks
N = sample size

In Table 11.11, two rankings have been created for the prestige levels of the regions and the newly hired faculty. In a column labeled "D," simple differences in ranks are entered. The East North Central region, for example, has a rank of 1 in one column and a rank of 2 in the other column. We would enter a difference between the two ranks of 1 in the D column as shown. The D^2 column consists of each of these differences between ranks squared. These squared rank

TABLE 11.11
National Prestige Rankings for ASA Regions and Prestige Ranks of Hired Faculty.

Region (ranked by prestige of faculty)		*Prestige Rankings of Hired Faculty*	*D*	D^2
East North Central	(1)	2	1	1
Pacific	(2)	3	1	1
West North Central	(3)	1	2	4
Mid Atlantic	(4)	5	1	1
South Atlantic	(5)	7	2	4
West South Central	(6)	6	0	0
East South Central	(7)	8	1	1
New England	(8)	4	4	16
Mountain	(9)	9	0	0
				$\Sigma D^2 = 28$

Source: Based on an idea provided by David Shichor, "Prestige and Regional Mobility of New Ph.D.'s in Sociology," *The American Sociologist*, 8: 180–186, 1973.

differences are summed to yield $\Sigma D^2 = 28$, as shown. This information is used in the formula for rho as follows:

$$r_s = 1 - \left[\frac{(6)(28)}{(9)(81 - 1)}\right]$$

$$= 1 - \frac{168}{720}$$

$$= 1 - .23$$

$$= .77.$$

An observed $r_s = .77$ may be interpreted as a strong positive association between the region ranked by prestige and the ranked prestige of faculty hired.

Assumptions of Spearman's Rho. The primary assumptions of rho are that the researcher has two variables measured according to an interval scale and that the sample is randomly drawn.[6]

Advantages and Disadvantages of Spearman's Rho. When tied scores exist, the computation of rho is simply inappropriate. An elaborate procedure for correcting for tied scores is outlined in Siegel (1956). But the general result of this correction is to yield an almost imperceptible change in the original rho value. Rather than correct for tied scores, the general recommendation is to utilize an alternative procedure such as Kendall's tau. Even though tau is not particularly suited for tied scores, it handles tied scores better than Spearman's rho. If the number of tied scores is excessive (i.e., more than 25 percent of the scores are tied), gamma is suggested as an alternative. This will necessarily involve a loss of information (moving from the interval measurement level to the ordinal level), but the gain in handling the data properly more than offsets this minor data loss.

On the positive side, rho can deal effectively with small numbers of untied scores without making stringent distributional assumptions associated with Pearson's r. Spearman's rho is well known to researchers, and computer programs exist for its computation. It is easy to apply and interpret. Under the appropriate conditions, it provides a reasonable measure of the strength of an association between

[6] Some investigators claim that Spearman's rho would be appropriate for "ordered metric data" or "successive interval data" or "equal-appearing interval data," which some attitudinal measures purportedly achieve. At present, the controversy is unresolved.

variables. It is important to visually inspect the data to verify directionality, however. Rho values can range from −1.00 to +1.00, reflecting perfect negative or positive association. Rho also has a PRE interpretation. We must square rho, r_s^2, in order to determine the amount of error reduced in one variable by using the other as a predictor of it.

The Significance of Spearman's Rho. A simple test of the significance of Spearman's rho exists. Our observed rho value is used in the following formula, which results in an approximation of Z:

$$Z = \frac{r_s}{s},$$

where s is the standard error of rho $(1/\sqrt{N-1})$, or

$$Z = \frac{r_s}{\frac{1}{\sqrt{N-1}}}.$$

If we happened to observe a rho value $r_s = .75$, with an $N = 50$,

$$Z = \frac{.75}{\frac{1}{\sqrt{50-1}}}$$

$$= \frac{.75}{.143}$$

$$= 5.24.$$

A Z this large would be significant at the .01 level, two-tailed test (the critical value of $Z = \pm 2.58$). When $N < 30$, Table A14 may be used.

The Pearson *r*

One of the best-known measures of association in any research field is the Pearson *r*. For many persons receiving statistical training, the Pearson *r* was the primary measure of association used for years. When all assumptions associated with the Pearson *r* are satisfied, it becomes perhaps the best measure of association available. However, the assumptions underlying this procedure are quite severe. Often, we find that because of our failure to satisfy one or more of its assumptions, we cannot apply it properly in our research work. But precisely because of its popularity and the fact that most persons are familiar with it, the Pearson r has been both used and misused in social scientific research. We examine an application of the Pearson r in the following example.

Indik (1964) investigated the relation between organizational size and the proportionate size of the administrative component. Basing his research, in part, on previous literature and study findings, Indik proposed that as organizations grow larger, their administrative components tend to decrease. In short, proportionally fewer supervisors and administrators will be required to manage large organizations compared with smaller organizations.

One way of defining organizational size was to identify the number of full-time employees of the organization. To measure the supervisory ratio, the number of persons in supervisory or administrative roles was taken in proportion to the total number of full-time personnel. Therefore, in an organization consisting of 100 persons, 10 administrators would yield an administrative component of 10 to 100 or .10 or 10 percent. In an organization of 1000 persons, an administrative component of 130 persons would yield 130 to 1000 or .13 or 13 percent, and so on. Table 11.12 contains some hypothetical figures relating to a sample of 15 organizations.

Table 11.12 is constructed as follows. The first column, variable X, contains various values of organizational size (i.e., the number of full-time personnel in each organization). The second column, variable Y, contains percentage figures of the A/P ratio (i.e., the percentage of persons who perform administrative functions in relation to the total number of full-time personnel). The third column, X^2, contains the squares of the values of organizational size in the first column. The fourth column, Y^2, contains the squares of the percentage A/P ratios from the second column. Finally, in the column, XY, the products of columns X and Y are found. All values in each column are summed to yield the values shown at the bottom of the table. These values are then used in the following formula for r:

$$r = \frac{N\sum XY - (\sum X)(\sum Y)}{\sqrt{[N\sum X^2 - (\sum X)^2][N\sum Y^2 - (\sum Y)^2]}},$$

where

N = sample size
X and Y = values on variables X and Y
X^2 and Y^2 = squared values on variables X and Y
XY = products of scores on variables X and Y

TABLE 11.12
Association Between Organizational Size and Proportionate Size of the Administrative Component.

Organizational Size (Variable X)	A/P Ratio[a] (percent) (Variable Y)	X^2	Y^2	XY
1. 125	20	15,625	400	2,500
2. 128	18	16,384	324	2,304
3. 130	16	16,900	256	2,080
4. 95	22	9,025	484	2,090
5. 82	24	6,724	576	1,968
6. 140	15	19,600	225	2,100
7. 65	22	4,225	484	1,430
8. 59	21	3,481	441	1,239
9. 75	25	5,625	625	1,875
10. 88	23	7,744	529	2,024
11. 100	15	10,000	225	1,500
12. 120	14	14,400	196	1,680
13. 110	18	12,100	324	1,980
14. 105	20	11,025	400	2,100
15. 99	23	9,801	529	2,277
$\Sigma X = 1{,}521$	$\Sigma Y = 296$	$\Sigma X^2 = 162{,}659$	$\Sigma Y^2 = 6{,}018$	$\Sigma XY = 29{,}147$

[a]A/P ratio = number of administrators to number of full-time personnel in organization.

Supplying values in this formula taken from Table 11.12 we compute r as follows:

$$r = \frac{(15)(29{,}147) - (1{,}521)(296)}{\sqrt{[(15)(162{,}659) - (1{,}521)^2][(15)(6{,}018) - (296)^2]}}$$

$$= \frac{437{,}205 - 450{,}216}{\sqrt{(126{,}444)(2654)}}$$

$$= \frac{-13{,}011}{18{,}318.9}$$

$$= -.71.$$

The resulting $r = -.71$. Since Indik's original contention was that an inverse (or negative) association would obtain between the two variables, organizational size and administrative component, the observed $r = -.71$ is consistent with this prediction. There does appear to be a negative association between these two variables.

We may obtain a PRE interpretation for r by squaring it. Therefore, PRE $= r^2 = (-.71)^2 = .50$. Fifty percent of the error in predicting one variable with a knowledge of the other has been accounted for.

The Significance of a Pearson r. The statistical significance of a Pearson r can be determined quite easily. Table A.7 in the Appendix may be used with $N - 2$ degrees of freedom, where df ranges from 1 to 100. The body at the table contains various r values to four places for different df. Any observed r value that equals or exceeds the critical r value shown in the table for a given df is significant at the probability level at the top of the table. Two other methods for determining the significance of r are also possible. When the sample size is less than 50, an approximation of the t statistic is derived by the following formula:

$$t = \frac{r}{\sqrt{1 - r^2}} \sqrt{N - 2},$$

where

r = observed Pearson r
N = sample size

For our original observed $r = -.71$, we would have

$$\begin{aligned} t &= \frac{-.71}{\sqrt{1 - (-.71)^2}} \sqrt{15 - 2} \\ &= (-1)(3.606) \\ &= -3.606. \end{aligned}$$

The resulting $t = -3.606$, which we may interpret by turning to Table A5, with $N - 2$ degrees of freedom. With 13 df in this case, we can determine that our observed $r = -.71$ is significant at $P < .005$ (with a one-tailed test, since we had predicted the direction of the association earlier). The critical value that we equaled or exceeded in the t table for 13 df was -3.012. Our observed $t = -3.606$ clearly exceeded this value for the level of significance indicated.

Whenever our sample size exceeds 50, an approximation of the Z statistic may be determined by the following formula:

$$Z = \frac{r}{s_r},$$

where s_r is the standard error of an r, or $1/\sqrt{N - 1}$. Had our sample size been 65, for instance, we would have

$$Z = \frac{-.71}{\frac{1}{\sqrt{65 - 1}}}$$

$$= \frac{-.71}{.125}$$

$$= -5.68.$$

A Z value as large as -5.68 would be significant statistically at any conventional level of significance we wished to use. For example, a two-tailed critical value of Z for the .01 level of significance would be ± 2.58. Clearly, -5.68 equals or exceeds this critical value.

The Significance of Difference Between Two r's. Sometimes a researcher may wish to determine if two observed r values differ. Suppose that a researcher is investigating the relation between height and weight for two different samples participating in two different diet programs. Let us call the different programs A and B, respectively. Pearson r's for the two groups are computed. The following hypothetical data are available as follows:

Diet Program A		*Diet Program B*	
$r_{xy_1} = .83$	$N_1 = 55$	$r_{xy_2} = .72$	$N_2 = 75$

The formula for evaluating the significance of difference between the two r values is

$$Z = \frac{Z_{F_1} - Z_{F_2}}{s_{D_z}},$$

where

Z_{F_1} and Z_{F_2} = Fisher Z values
s_{D_z} = standard error of the difference between the two Z_F values

$$s_{D_z} = \sqrt{\frac{1}{(N_1 - 1)} + \frac{1}{(N_2 - 1)}}.$$

Observe that we cannot compare r coefficients directly in the numerator term. We must transform these coefficients to *Fisher Z values* (Z_F). To do this, we must turn to Table A.6. We simply find our various r values in the left-hand column of the table and a Fisher Z value will be found immediately to the right of it. The Fisher Z for the first $r = .83$ is 1.1870. (This is an $r = .830$ in the table.) Our second $r = .72$ has associated with it a Fisher $Z = .9076$. With these Fisher Z values obtained, we may now carry out our computational work as follows:

$$Z = \frac{1.1870 - .9076}{\sqrt{\frac{1}{55 - 3} + \frac{1}{75 - 3}}}$$

$$= \frac{.2794}{\sqrt{.0331}}$$

$$= \frac{.2794}{.18}$$

$$= 1.55.$$

Therefore, $Z = 1.55$. Had we been interested in testing the significance of difference between the two r values at the .05 probability level with a two-tailed, nondirectional test, a critical value of $Z = \pm 1.96$ would have been required. Our observed $Z = 1.55$ would fail to equal or exceed 1.96, and therefore we would conclude that a significant difference does not exist between the two r values.

Assumptions of the Pearson r. There are five assumptions associated with Pearson's r. First, we must have randomness. Second, we must have the two variables measured according to an interval scale. Third, we must have linearity between the two variables. This means that we must observe a straight line associated with the intersection points of variables X and Y. A curvilinear relation between the two variables will blur any r value computed. We would be led to believe that no association exists between the two variables, when, in fact, a curvilinear relation does exist.

A fourth assumption of r is that the distributions of scores for both variables are approximately normally distributed. This is referred to as a *bivariate normal distribution.* Skewed distributions of scores for either variable will adversely affect the resulting r value. Finally, the intersection points of variables X and Y should form an ellipse around the line drawn for the slope of the association. This property is known as *homoscedasticity* and is illustrated in Figure 11.4.

To apply r properly, all of these assumptions should be met as fully as possible. Whenever any one or more of these assumptions are not met by the researcher, there is an increasing likelihood that re-

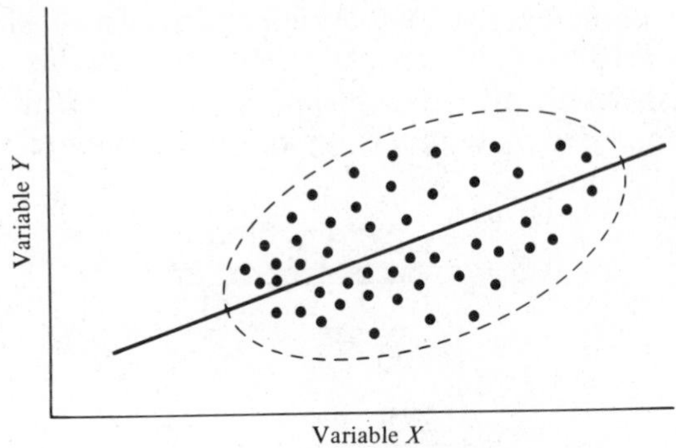

FIGURE 11.4. Ellipse Around the Slope of the Association.

sulting r values will be grossly misleading. Other measures of association that do not have such restrictive assumptions should be selected as alternatives. Some measures at the ordinal level of measurement might be selected such as gamma. In spite of the fact that some data loss would occur (i.e., moving from the interval to the ordinal level of measurement), the researcher would be able to rely on resulting gamma values in contrast to the unreliable results of an improperly applied r value.

Advantages and Disadvantages of the Pearson r. The Pearson r is the best-known measure of association available. The fact that it is popular does not necessarily mean that it is the best measure to use in most social research situations, however. We have already examined a number of alternative measures that provide excellent indicators of association between variables, but without the restrictive assumptions of r.

The value of r^2 is interpretable as a PRE measure. In this instance, the interpretation is a symmetrical one. It makes no difference which variable is designated as independent or dependent. The same r value will be obtained in either event.

Computer programs exist for the computation of r for larger sample applications and for grouped-data situations. For small-sample applications, the Pearson r is fairly easy to compute and understand. It is the measure of association that is most consistent with the crude strength-of-association guide presented at the beginning of the chapter.

On the negative side, the stringent assumptions that precede the proper application of r make it very difficult for this measure to be applied legitimately in research. More often than not, misapplications of the Pearson r will be found in the research literature of most social science fields. This is primarily a function of the popularity of r and the lack of familiarity researchers have with the assumptions underlying it.

□ MEASURES OF ASSOCIATION FOR VARIABLES OF DIFFERENT MEASUREMENT LEVELS

The last section of this chapter examines several useful measures of association that are properly applied to situations when the researcher has one nominal and one ordinal variable, one nominal and one interval variable, and/or one ordinal and one interval variable. These different variable combinations were formerly treated in the following manner.

Suppose that a researcher had a measure of religious affiliation and another measure for political conservativism–liberalism. Religious categorization would yield a nominal scale at best. A continuum of political conservativism–liberalism would possibly yield an ordinal scale. To determine the degree of association between these two variables, the researcher would often treat the variable measured according to an ordinal scale as though it were nominal only. In short, the ordinal variable would be reduced to the nominal level, and an appropriate nominal-level measure of association would be applied. It should be apparent that the researcher would be discarding needlessly the ordinality associated with the political conservativism–liberalism measure. It would be ideal if the ordinality inherent in the measure of this variable could be preserved. Fortunately, a number of specialized procedures have been developed that enable investigators to retain variables in their original measurement form, and we no longer have to throw away data by reducing it to the lowest common denominator.

Three measures will be presented that allow the researcher to preserve the different scale properties of each variable examined. These include (1) Wilcoxon's theta for measuring the association between one nominal and one ordinal variable; (2) eta, the correlation ratio, for measuring the association between one nominal and one interval variable; and (3) Jaspen's M for measuring the association between one ordinal and one interval variable.

Wilcoxon's Theta, θ

When the investigator has two variables, one of which is measured according to an ordinal scale and the other according to a nominal scale, Wilcoxon's theta would be a useful association measure to ap-

TABLE 11.13
Sexual Permissiveness for Males and Females.

	(Low)		*Sexual Permissiveness*			*(High)*	
Sex	*0*	*1*	*2*	*3*	*4*	*5*	*Totals*
Males	12	16	18	22	28	35	131
Females	29	22	24	15	12	9	111
Totals	41	38	42	37	40	44	$N = 242$

Source: Idea for table based on Ira L. Reiss, "Sexual Permissiveness Among Negroes and Whites," *American Sociological Review*, **29**: 688–698, 1964.

ply. Theta preserves the level-of-measurement properties of both variables and provides an excellent coefficient of association. The following research is presented to illustrate the application of theta.

Reiss (1964) was interested in studying premarital sexual permissiveness differences between males and females. Using a Guttman scale to measure sexual permissiveness, Reiss obtained permissiveness scale types ranging from 0 (low permissiveness) to 5 (high permissiveness). The sexual permissiveness scale was defined as ordinal. The nominal variable was sex with two subclasses, male and female. Some hypothetical data have been arranged in Table 11.13 to show the association between sexual permissiveness and sex classification. What is the degree of association between these two variables? This question can be answered by applying Wilcoxon's theta. The formula for theta is

$$\theta = \frac{\sum D_i}{T_2},$$

where

$\sum D_i$ = absolute difference between the total frequencies above each rank and below each rank for pairs of nominal subclass variables, or $|f_a - f_b|$

T_2 = each total frequency on the nominal subclasses multiplied by every other total frequency; these products are summed to give T_2

The formula for theta is applied as follows. We begin with the first category (0) for males and multiply the frequency, 12, by the sum of all frequencies below and to the left of it on the female subclass. Since there are no frequencies below and to the left of 12, we move to the next cell to the right, (1), and multiply the frequencies, 16, by the sum of all frequencies below and to the left of it on the female subclass. This is (16)(29). We proceed to the right until we have done this for all male categories [the last category is (35)(29 + 22 + 24 +

15 + 12]. The sum of all of these products yields our first value in the formula for D_i. The value we obtain is the f_a value.

Next, we move back to the first cell on the male subclass (0) and multiply the frequencies in that cell by the sum of all frequencies below and to the right of it on the female subclass. This becomes (12)(22 + 24 + 15 + 12 + 9). We continue moving to the right, one cell at a time, carrying out this procedure until we have determined all products. The sum of these products will yield our f_b value. This procedure is illustrated fully below:

$$\begin{aligned} f_a &= (12)(0) + (16)(29) + (18)(29 + 22) + (22)(29 + 22 + 24) \\ &\quad + (28)(29 + 22 + 24 + 15) + (35)(29 + 22 + 24 + 15 + 12) \\ &= 464 + 918 + 1650 + 2520 + 3570 \\ &= 9122. \end{aligned}$$

$$\begin{aligned} f_b &= (12)(22 + 24 + 15 + 12 + 9) + (16)(24 + 15 + 12 + 9) \\ &\quad + (18)(15 + 12 + 9) + (22)(12 + 9) + (28)(9) + (35)(0) \\ &= 984 + 960 + 648 + 462 + 252 \\ &= 3306. \end{aligned}$$

Once we have determined our f_a and f_b values, we must determine the absolute difference between them. With these values, our ΣD_i becomes

$$\begin{aligned} \sum D_i &= |9122 - 3306| \\ &= 5816. \end{aligned}$$

With a difference of 5816 as shown, we divide this numerator term by T_2. T_2 refers to the product of all different category sums on the nominal variable. Since there are only two nominal categories in this instance (i.e., male and female), we only have one product, or (131)(111) = 14,541. Theta is determined as follows:

$$\begin{aligned} \theta &= \frac{5.816}{14{,}541} \\ &= .40. \end{aligned}$$

According to our guide for assessing the strength of the association, it would appear that there is a moderately low association between sexual permissiveness and sex of respondents. A PRE interpretation would be that we have reduced the error in predicting each variable with a knowledge of the other by 40 percent.

Assumptions of Theta. The primary assumptions for theta are randomness and a pair of variables where one is measured according to an ordinal scale, while the other is measured according to a nominal scale.

Advantages and Disadvantages of Theta. The major advantage of theta is that it allows us to exploit the ordinal-level variable fully without reducing it to its nominal properties. It is one of the few tests available for assessing associations between variables where one is measured according to an ordinal scale and the other is measured according to a nominal scale.

Theta is easy to compute and interpret. It has a PRE interpretation that is symmetrical. Given the fact that so many variables in the social sciences are measured according to nominal and ordinal scales, a measure of association that permits us to compute a coefficient without modifying the variables is a definite advantage. There are no serious disadvantages associated with theta.

Eta, the Correlation Ratio, η

If the researcher wants to determine the degree of association between one nominal and one interval variable, *eta*, the correlation ratio (η), may be used. Some instances of the utility of the correlation ratio might include examining the association between race and income, group membership and age, religious affiliation and church attendance, and occupational category and amount of leisure time.

One option available to the researcher is to reduce the interval-level variable to the ordinal measurement level and compute theta. This would result in some data loss, however. The correlation ratio will preserve the properties of the variable measured according to an interval scale. It will permit the researcher to compute the degree of association between k categories on a nominal variable and the selected interval variable. The following illustration will demonstrate.

Ladinsky (1967) was interested in the relation between educational attainment and occupational achievement of a sample of Detroit lawyers. Many lawyers are associated with law firms, whereas others are in private practice.

Ladinsky designated a portion of the sample of lawyers selected for study as "solo" (i.e., lawyers who practice law privately). Another sample of lawyers was designated as "firm" (i.e., lawyers who are associated with medium to large law firms). Based on previous research, Ladinsky believed that solo lawyers would tend to have less undergraduate training and training of poorer quality compared with firm lawyers. Also, it was believed that the income levels of the

TABLE 11.14
Type of Lawyer and Income Level.

Type of Lawyer (variable X)				
Solo ($N_1 = 13$)			Firm ($N_2 = 14$)	
Income Level (thousands of dollars per year) (variable Y)				
Y_1	Y_1^2		Y_2	Y_2^2
27	729		28	784
40	1600		35	1225
19	361		42	1764
35	1225		39	1521
37	1369		41	1681
41	1681		47	2209
33	1089		62	3844
28	784		58	3364
26	676		41	1681
22	484		33	1089
27	729		29	841
26	676		47	2209
42	1764		49	2401
			42	1764
$\Sigma Y_1 = 403$	$\Sigma Y_1^2 = 13{,}167$		$\Sigma Y_2 = 593$	$\Sigma Y_2^2 = 26{,}377$
$\overline{Y}_1 = 31.0$ (group 1 mean)		$\overline{Y}_T = 36.9$ (grand mean)	$\overline{Y}_2 = 42.4$ (group 2 mean)	

$$\Sigma Y_1^2 + \Sigma Y_2^2 = \Sigma Y_T^2 = 13{,}167 + 26{,}377 = 39{,}544$$

Source: Table based on idea by Jack Ladinsky, "Higher Education and Work Achievement Among Lawyers," *Sociological Quarterly*, 8:222–232, 1967.

groups would differ accordingly. One question generated by Ladinsky's research is whether income level is related to type of lawyer. Using as our measure of income level yearly salary figures (reported in thousands of dollars), some hypothetical data are presented in Table 11.14.

The nominal variable in this case is type of lawyer. It is used as a predictor variable in this instance. To what extent can we predict income levels of lawyers by knowing the type of lawyer? The degree of association between these two variables will provide a tentative answer to this question.

Table 11.14 is constructed as follows. The yearly incomes of both types of lawyers are placed in columns Y_1 and Y_2, respectively. These incomes are then summed, yielding ΣY_1 and ΣY_2, respectively. Next, each income in columns Y_1 and Y_2 is squared and placed in columns Y_1^2 and Y_2^2, as shown. These squares of incomes are then summed (ΣY_1^2 and ΣY_2^2).

Means are computed for both groups and designated as $\overline{Y}_1$ and $\overline{Y}_2$ as shown. Next, a grand mean for both groups is computed by summing all incomes across both groups and dividing by the total number of lawyers in the table [i.e., (403 + 593)/(13 + 14) = 996/27 = 36.9]. Finally, the sums of the squared incomes for both groups are summed, or $\Sigma Y_1^2 + \Sigma Y_2^2 = 13{,}167 + 26{,}377 = 39{,}544$. With these values, we may determine eta, the correlation ratio, using the following formula:

$$\eta = \sqrt{1 - \frac{\sum Y_T^2 - (N_1)(\overline{Y}_1)^2 - (N_2)(\overline{Y}_2)^2}{\sum Y_T^2 - (N_1 + N_2)(\overline{Y}_T)^2}},$$

where

N_1 and N_2 = two sample sizes
$\overline{Y}_T$ = grand mean for groups 1 and 2 combined
$\overline{Y}_1$ and $\overline{Y}_2$ = mean scores for groups 1 and 2
$\sum Y_T^2$ = sum of squared scores across both samples

Using the information from Table 11.14, we have

$$\eta = \sqrt{1 - \frac{39{,}544 - (13)(31)^2 - (14)(42.4)^2}{39{,}544 - (13 + 14)(36.9)^2}}$$

$$= \sqrt{1 - \frac{39{,}544 - 12{,}493 - 25{,}168.64}{39{,}544 - 36{,}763.47}}$$

$$= \sqrt{1 - \frac{1882.36}{2780.53}}$$

$$= \sqrt{1 - .68}$$

$$= \sqrt{.32}$$

$$= .57.$$

The resulting eta value = .57. This would indicate that a moderately high association exists between type of lawyer and income level. If we wished to have a PRE interpretation for eta, we must square this value. Therefore, $\eta^2 = (.57)^2 = .32$. We may say that 32 percent of the error in predicting income level has been accounted for by using type of lawyer as a predictor of it. These findings would seem to provide some support for Ladinsky's notions about solo and firm lawyers and income differentials.

The Significance of Eta. The statistical significance of an observed eta value is tested by the following F formula:

$$F = \frac{\eta^2 (N - k)}{(1 - \eta^2)(k - 1)},$$

where

N = total number of persons in both samples
k = number of subclasses on the nominal variable

Using our observed eta = .57, we test its significance as follows:

$$F = \frac{(.32)(27 - 2)}{(1 - .32)(2 - 1)}$$

$$= \frac{8}{.68}$$

$$= 11.764.$$

With an observed $F = 11.764$, we enter Table A16, with $k - 1$ degrees of freedom (across the top of the table) and $N - k$ degrees of freedom (down the left-hand side of the table). These df are 2 - 1 = 1 df and 27 - 2 = 25 df, respectively. Where these values intersect in the body of the table defines the critical value of F that we must equal or exceed for either the .05 level (lightface type) or the .01 level (boldface type). The critical value of F for the .01 level of significance is 7.77 in this instance. We would be able to say that our observed eta = .32 is significantly different from 0 (no association) at the .01 probability level.

Assumptions of Eta. The primary assumptions underlying the correlation ratio are (1) randomness, (2) one variable measured according to a nominal scale and one variable measured according to an interval scale, (3) a continuous distribution for the interval variable, and (4) curvilinearity. Some researchers recommend that the sample size be fairly large (i.e., $N > 30$). The small samples used in Table 11.14 were intended for illustration purposes. There is a possibility that smaller sample sizes will contribute to a certain amount of distortion in the magnitude of eta. The larger the sample, the less the likelihood of such distortion.

Advantages and Disadvantages of Eta. The correlation ratio is often suggested as an alternative measure of association to the Pearson r whenever the bivariate normal distribution or linearity assumptions are not met. The correlation ratio has no such distributional restrictions. In fact, this measure will reflect accurately an association between variables that is curvilinear. This is one of its major strengths contrasted with Pearson's r.

The correlation ratio has a PRE interpretation. It is one of the only measures available for measuring association between a qualitative (nominal) variable and a variable measured according to an interval scale. It is fairly easy to compute. In Table 11.14, the application of eta was illustrated for two groups only. This measure can be extended to any number of groups.

If we were examining income levels for four groups of lawyers, for instance, the computational formula for eta would be

$$\eta = \sqrt{1 - \frac{\sum Y_T^2 - (N_1)(\overline{Y}_1)^2 - (N_2)(\overline{Y}_2)^2 - (N_3)(\overline{Y}_3)^2 - (N_4)(\overline{Y}_4)^2}{\sum Y_T^2 - (N_1 + N_2 + N_3 + N_4)(\overline{Y}_T)^2}},$$

where

N_1 through N_4 = four sample sizes
$\overline{Y}_1$ through $\overline{Y}_4$ = mean scores for the four groups
$\overline{Y}_T$ = grand mean for the four groups
$\sum Y_T^2$ = sum of squared scores across the four samples

This procedure is merely an extension of what was done in the case of two subclasses on the nominal variable (Table 11.14 had two subclasses–solo and firm–on the type of lawyer nominal variable).

Jaspen's *M*

Under certain conditions where a researcher is examining one variable measured according to an ordinal scale and another according to an interval scale, a measure of association known as Jaspen's M (or Jaspen's *coefficient of multiserial association*) may be applied. One alternative to this procedure that is considerably easier to manage is to reduce the interval-level variable to the ordinal level and carry out the gamma coefficient. However, this results in a needless data loss. Jaspen's M, the coefficient of multiserial correlation, is one of the more complicated procedures presented in this chapter. But under the appropriate conditions described above, it permits the researcher to maximize the level of measurement achieved for both variables. The following example of the application of Jaspen's M is provided.

Ehrlich (1967) examined the relationship between community leaders and such variables as income, age, education, and social position. On the basis of interviews conducted with a large sample of Prince George's County, Maryland residents, various community leaders were identified. Subsequently, a sample of these leaders was

TABLE 11.15
Sample of Prince George's County, Maryland, Residents According to Length of Residence and Degree of Community Involvement.

Degree of Community Involvement (Variable X)				
(High)				*(Low)*
5	*4*	*3*	*2*	*1*
Years in the Community (Variable Y)				
15	16	5	10	2
17	12	10	12	5
19	8	12	10	11
23	3	4	8	4
14	20	10	2	6
28	14	9	7	4
22	13	8	5	7
12	12		5	9
9	10		5	6
15	10			
22				
21				
$\Sigma Y_1 = 217$	$\Sigma Y_2 = 118$	$\Sigma Y_3 = 58$	$\Sigma Y_4 = 64$	$\Sigma Y_5 = 54$
$\overline{Y}_1 = 18.1$	$\overline{Y}_2 = 11.8$	$\overline{Y}_3 = 8.3$	$\overline{Y}_4 = 7.1$	$\overline{Y}_5 = 6.0$
$N_1 = 12$	$N_2 = 10$	$N_3 = 7$	$N_4 = 9$	$N_5 = 9$

$\Sigma Y = 511$ $\Sigma Y^2 = 7275$ $s_y = 6.05$
$N_T = 47$ (i.e., $N_1 + N_2 + N_3 + N_4 + N_5$)

Source: Idea for table based on research by Howard J. Ehrlich, "The Social Psychology of Reputations for Community Leadership," *Sociological Quarterly*, 8:514–580, 1967.

selected for more intensive examination by Ehrlich. One dimension of interest to Ehrlich was the degree of community involvement by these leaders. On the basis of an index of membership and participation, five groups of leaders were identified, ranging from high to low community involvement. Table 11.15 shows some hypothetical data relating to length of residence in the community of community leaders manifesting differing degrees of community involvement.

Degree of community involvement is identified as the ordinal variable with five subclasses, ranging from 5 (high involvement) to 1 (low involvement). Length of residence in the community (measured by years) is the variable measured according to an interval scale. To what extent does an association exist between these two variables?

Table 11.15 has been constructed as follows. Across the top of the table are degrees of community involvement. In each column are years of residence in the community for each sample of community leaders. Degree of community involvement has been designated as variable X, and years in the community has been labeled as variable Y. The scores (years of residence) for each group are summed as shown for various ΣY_i values. Means are also computed for each group as shown. In the lower left-hand corner of the table, the sum of all scores across the five groups has been indicated (i.e., $217 + 118 + 58 + 64 + 54 = 511 = \Sigma Y$). Also, a ΣY^2 value has been computed. This is the sum of all of the squared scores (i.e., $15^2 + 17^2 + 19^2 + \cdots + 7^2 + 9^2 + 6^2 = 7275 = \Sigma Y^2$). With these values, an s_y (the standard error of Y) has been computed as follows:

$$s_y = \sqrt{\frac{\Sigma Y^2 - \frac{(\Sigma Y)^2}{N_T}}{N_T}},$$

where N_T is the sum of all samples. With the values from Table 11.15, s_y is computed as follows:

$$s_y = \sqrt{\frac{7275 - \frac{(511)^2}{47}}{47}}$$

$$= \sqrt{\frac{1719.234}{47}}$$

$$= \sqrt{36.579}$$

$$= 6.05.$$

Our observed $s_y = 6.05$, as shown in Table 11.15.

It is now necessary to create an additional table. In Table 11.16, the ranks of degree of community involvement have been arranged from high to low in the far left column. The next column contains the means ($\bar{Y}_i$'s) for each sample as shown. The third column contains the proportion of each sample to the total number of persons across all samples. For instance, there are 12 persons in the first group. Therefore, $12/47 = .26$. There are 10 persons in the second sample. Therefore, $10/47 = .21$, and so on.

The next column, cp, contains cumulative proportions from the previous column. In short, $.26 + .21 = .47$. Then $.47 + .15 = .62$; and so on.

The next column, *Cp*, contains cumulative proportions from the these cumulative proportions. We must turn to Table A15 to determine each ordinate to be placed in the o_b column. Table A15 is arranged so that various proportions are found in either the far left or far right columns. Although these are reported to three places, we need to find the proportion matching each cumulative proportion in

TABLE 11.16
Summary Table for the Jaspen's *M* Computation.

Ranks	$\overline{Y}_i$	p	Cp	o_b	o_a	$o_b - o_a$	$(o_b - o_a)^2$	$\frac{(o_b - o_a)^2}{p}$	$(\overline{Y}_i)(o_b - o_a)$
5	18.1	.26	.26	.3244	0	.3244	.1052	.4046	5.8716
4	11.8	.21	.47	.3978	.3244	.0734	.0054	.0257	.8661
3	8.3	.15	.62	.3808	.3978	–.0170	.0003	.0020	–.1411
2	7.1	.19	.81	.2714	.3808	–.1094	.0120	.0632	–.7767
1	6.0	.19	1.00	0	.2714	–.2714	.0737	.3879	–1.6284
						0		.8834	4.1915

$$\Sigma\left[\frac{(o_b - o_a)^2}{p}\right] = .8834 \qquad \Sigma(\overline{Y}_i)(o_b - o_a) = 4.1915$$

the p column of Table 11.16. The first proportion, .26, has an ordinate value associated with it equal to .3244. (The ordinate column is the center column in each page of Table A15.) We proceed until we have entered all ordinates associated with the cumulative proportions in Table 11.16.

The identification of ordinates is for the purpose of "normalizing" the ordinal variable. Some of the rationale for doing this will be treated in subsequent discussion.

In the column o_a, we simply identify ordinates that are above any ordinate in column o_b. Since there are no ordinates above .26 (from column Cp), we enter a 0. Moving down the o_a column, the first ordinate above .47 (from column Cp) is .3244 (from column o_b). We enter this in column o_a as shown. Notice that column o_a is a repeat of column o_b down to and including the last ordinate of .2714.

The next column, $o_b - o_a$, is simply the difference between the ordinates placed in column o_b and in column o_a. These values are squared for the next column, $(o_b - o_a)^2$. The values in this column are then divided by the corresponding proportion from column p. In other words, .1052/.26 = .4046; .0054/.21 = .0257; and so on.

The final column is the product of each mean $(\overline{Y}_i)$ with the value adjacent to it in the $(o_b - o_a)$ column. As an example, the first product would be (18.1) (.3244) = 5.8716. Our primary interest is in the last two columns. The sums of these columns are shown in Table 11.16. With this information and with the information from Table 11.15, we may compute Jaspen's M as follows:

$$M = \frac{\sum(\overline{Y}_i)\,(o_b - o_a)}{(s_y)\sum\left[\dfrac{(o_b - o_a)^2}{p}\right]}.$$

Using the information from Tables 11.15 and 11.16 in the formula for M, we have

$$\begin{aligned} M &= \frac{4.1915}{(6.05)\,(.8834)} \\ &= \frac{4.1915}{5.344} \\ &= .78. \end{aligned}$$

Our observed $M = .78$. This would be interpreted as a strong association between degree of community involvement and length of time in the community. If a PRE interpretation is desired, we must square the M value. Therefore, $M^2 = (.78)^2 = .61$. We may say that 61 percent of the error in predicting one variable with a knowledge of the other has been accounted for.

The Significance of Jaspen's M. In order to determine the statistical significance of Jaspen's M, we must convert the M value to an equivalent Pearson r value by the following formula:

$$r = (M)\sqrt{\Sigma\left[\frac{(o_b - o_a)^2}{p}\right]}.$$

Using the information we have determined from Table 11.13, we compute the r as follows:

$$r = (.78)\sqrt{.8834}$$
$$= (.78)(.9399)$$
$$= .73.$$

Our observed r value = .73. We must turn to Table A7 with $N_T - 2$ degrees of freedom. This table contains critical values of r for various levels of significance. For our example, with df = 47 − 2 = 45, we would need to observe an r equal to or greater than .372 to achieve statistical significance at the .01 level of probability. Our observed r = .73 is clearly statistically significant.

Assumptions of Jaspen's M. Included among the assumptions underlying the appropriate application of Jaspen's M are randomness and two variables, measured according to an ordinal and an interval scale, respectively. An additional assumption is that the ordinal variable can be "standardized" or "normalized" in such a way that we may assume equal spacing between units on the ordinal scale. This was the reason for determining ordinates for the ranks in Table 11.16.

It is also assumed that the interval-level variable is normally distributed. The ordinal variable is forced, in a sense, into an approximation of a normal distribution for purposes of carrying out the test.

Advantages and Disadvantages of Jaspen's M. The major advantages associated with Jaspen's M are that it is one of the few tests available for determining association between an ordinal–interval variable combination, and it has a PRE interpretation. It is closely related to the Pearson r in its interpretation as well.

On the negative side, it is extremely cumbersome to apply. It is likely that many students will have to repeat the operations involved in its computation several times before gaining an understanding of it. It has several restrictive assumptions, including normality for both variables. To an extent, this is unrealistic. But since we are extremely limited in our choice of statistical tests for associations between such variable combinations, we may tolerate minor departures from meeting all assumptions fully. Freeman (1965) discusses Jaspen's *M* at great length, covering to some degree the normalization of the ordinal variable and other assumptions crucial to its appropriate application.

□ SUMMARY

This chapter has covered a wide variety of measures of association appropriate for assessing two-variable relationships. The following summary table will be helpful in deciding which measures to choose from whenever data analyses calling for measures of association are in order. Table 11.17 is a cross-tabulation of levels of measurement. In each cell of the table are various measures of association for different level-of-measurement variable combinations.

Although we have covered numerous measures of association in the present chapter, the subject has by no means been exhausted. There are literally dozens of measures of association available to the researcher. An attempt has been made to include some of the

TABLE 11.17
Measures of Association for Different Variable Combinations.

	Nominal	*Ordinal*	*Interval*
Nominal	Pearson's *C* Lambda Cramer's *V* Tschuprow's *T* Phi Tetrachoric *r*	Theta	Eta, the correlation ratio
Ordinal		Gamma Kendall's tau Somer's d_{yx}	Jaspen's *M*
Interval			Spearman's rho Pearson's *r*

more popular and easy-to-understand procedures that are used conventionally in social science literature.

For nominal–nominal variable combinations, the lambda coefficient is perhaps the most versatile of those presented. It has a PRE interpretation that is both symmetric and asymmetric. It is easy to compute, can be applied to any $r \times c$ table, and is an integral part of many computer programs. Some of the chi-square-based measures of association, such as Pearson's C and the phi coefficient, serve useful functions as well. Their frequency of use in the research literature would indicate a need to be familiar with their weaknesses and strengths and specific applications.

At the level of assessing relationships between two ordinal variables, Goodman's and Kruskal's gamma would be preferred. It is easy to compute, can be applied to many $r \times c$ tables, and has a symmetric PRE interpretation. The fact that it has few restrictive assumptions also contributes to its usefulness for researchers. Somers' d_{yx} is also a strong contender. It is exclusively an asymmetric measure of PRE, but it suffers from none of the distributional problems that sometimes interfere with the sound application of gamma or Kendall's tau.

When the researcher has two interval-level variables, the Pearson r is by far the preferred measure of choice. But the fact that it places such restrictive requirements on the data to be analyzed makes it difficult to apply properly. When all the assumptions associated with this measure have been met, however, it is an excellent measure of association. It has a straightforward computational format, is easy to interpret, and has a symmetric PRE interpretation through r^2.

The Spearman's rho, r_s, was included in the two-interval variable section, although it is conventionally applied to two ordinal-variable associations. It is less useful compared with Pearson's r. It is too sensitive to tied scores. But it, too, has received a strong amount of attention over the years. It is still used in many research situations.

Of course, when the researcher is confronted with nominal–ordinal, nominal–interval, or ordinal–interval variable combinations, few choices are offered. Theta is appropriate for nominal–ordinal variable associations. It has a PRE interpretation and is easy to use. Eta, the correlation ratio, is appropriate for nominal–interval variable combinations. Eta squared is a measure of PRE that adds to its value as a research tool.

Finally, Jaspen's M is appropriate for ordinal–interval variable associations. It is perhaps the most tedious measure of association to compute. But it has a PRE interpretation through M^2 and is analogous to the Pearson r in its meaning. It is hoped that the material presented here will enable the reader to make appropriate selections of measures whenever data analysis is undertaken in the future.

SELECTED STUDY TERMS

Measure of association
Strength of association
Linearity
Curvilinear association
Proportional reduction in error
Chi-square-based measure of association
Direction of association
Symmetric and asymmetric PRE interpretation
Pearson *r*
Fisher *Z* transformation
Bivariate normal distribution
Homoscedasticity

EXERCISES

1. Carry out gamma for the following information.

		Variable X		
		High	Medium	Low
	High	46	21	10
Variable Y	Medium	22	28	15
	Low	14	33	55

   (a) What can you say about the association between variables X and Y in terms of the strength of the association?
   (b) What can be said about these variables in terms of PRE? Explain.
2. For the following scores, determine Spearman's rho.

Variable X	Variable Y
21	58
32	45
26	51
29	55
19	44
15	43
12	40
20	50
33	65
31	28

Variable X	Variable Y
35	45
34	68
14	36

(a) Briefly summarize the major limitations of Spearman's rho compared with gamma.
(b) Is Spearman's rho appropriate for situations where the researcher has numerous tied scores? Why or why not?

3. For the following data, carry out Somers' d_{yx} and determine which variable, X or Y, is the better predictor.

		Variable X		
		High	Medium	Low
Variable Y	High	56	41	34
	Medium	20	25	20
	Low	22	35	65

(a) Which variable is the better predictor?
(b) Can lambda be computed for these data? Why or why not?
(c) What advantages would Somers' d have over lambda for the data in the table? What advantage would lambda have over Somers' d? Explain.

4. Given the following scores, determine the Pearson r.

Variable X	Variable Y
115	29
122	35
139	41
120	30
117	31
114	35
122	24
119	28
122	31
125	33
131	32
148	26
159	21
142	19
146	29
141	27

Variable X	*Variable Y*
138	26
128	28
129	22
150	21
129	19
120	22
116	29
147	28
151	25
148	15
139	30
136	29
135	33
122	35
120	37
123	39
125	42
145	36
157	29
162	30

(a) What r value have you computed? Does it have a PRE interpretation? Explain.
(b) Would Spearman's rho be a suitable alternative for determining the degree of association for these data? Why or why not? Explain.
(c) What are some critical assumptions associated with the Pearson r? Discuss these assumptions briefly.

5. Given the following 2 X 2 table, determine the coefficients of association requested.

		Variable X	
		High	*Low*
Variable Y	*Yes*	75	22
	No	14	83

(a) Determine phi. What PRE interpretation can be given in this instance? Explain.
(b) Determine Pearson's coefficient of contingency, C, for these data. What must be done first to compute C?
(c) Can C values be compared directly with one another? Why or why not? Explain.
(d) What is lambda for this table? What PRE interpretation can be given to the lambda computed? Explain.

6. For the following data, provide the coefficients requested:

Religion	Social Class Upper-upper	Lower-upper	Upper-middle	Lower-middle
A	15	22	28	35
B	21	26	22	28
C	52	38	17	10

(a) Determine theta for these data. What kind of PRE interpretation can be given the theta value you have computed? Explain.
(b) Can lambda be computed for these same data? Why or why not? What advantage(s) would lambda have in relation to theta? Explain.
(c) Can gamma be computed for these data? Why or why not? Explain.

7. Below are various income values and sex classifications. Determine eta, the correlation ratio, for these data.

Income	Sex
$15,000	Male
12,500	Female
22,000	Female
18,500	Male
12,500	Female
13,000	Male
14,000	Male
17,500	Male
11,200	Female
9,500	Female
12,500	Male
23,200	Male
15,500	Male
22,900	Male
18,600	Female
19,000	Male
14,200	Female
12,000	Female
21,000	Male
20,000	Male
29,500	Male
21,200	Female
12,600	Female
11,300	Female
15,600	Male
16,500	Male
16,600	Female
22,800	Female
17,100	Male

(a) What is the observed eta value for these data?
(b) Does eta have a PRE interpretation? Why or why not?

(c) Could lambda be computed for these data? What would have to be done for lambda to be computed? Explain.
(d) Could the phi coefficient be computed for these data? What would have to be done for phi to be computed? Explain.
(e) What is the strength of the association between these two variables? Provide a brief statement.

8. For the following scores, determine Kendall's tau.

Individual	*Variable X*	*Variable Y*
1	9	7
2	17	10
3	16	5
4	10	6
5	8	9
6	14	11
7	18	15
8	7	4
9	15	8
10	6	3

(a) What is the observed tau value?
(b) Does tau have a PRE interpretation? If so, what can be said in terms of PRE for the two variables? Explain.

9. For the following data, determine the coefficients requested.

		Variable X	
		Agree	*Disagree*
Variable Y	*Yes*	75	25
	No	82	16

(a) What is phi for these data?
(b) What is r_{tet} for these data?
(c) Is there anything unusual about this table that would limit your choice of association measure used? Explain.

REFERENCES

Alsikafi, M., and Michael Hughes, "Craft and Industrial Labor Unions: A Study in Occupational Orientations," *LSU Journal of Sociology*, **3**:38–60, 1973.

Costner, Herbert L., "Criteria for Measures of Association," *American Sociological Review*, **30**:341–353, 1965.

Davidoff, M. D., and H. W. Goheen, "A Table for the Rapid Determination of the Tetrachoric Correlation Coefficient," *Psychometrika*, **18**:115-121, 1953.

Downie, N. M., and R. W. Heath, *Basic Statistical Methods*, 4th ed. New York: Harper & Row, Publishers, 1974.

Ehrlich, Howard J., "The Social Psychology of Reputations for Community Leadership," *Sociological Quarterly*, **8**:514-530, 1967.

Freeman, Linton C., *Elementary Applied Statistics: For Students in Behavioral Science.* New York: John Wiley & Sons, Inc., 1965.

Goodman, Leo A., and William H. Kruskal, "Measures of Association for Cross Classifications," *Journal of the American Statistical Association*, **49**:732-764, 1954.

Guilford, J. P., and Benjamin Fruchter, *Fundamental Statistics in Psychology and Education.* New York: McGraw-Hill Book Company, 1978.

Hanson, Ralph A., "Consistency and Stability of Home Environment Measures Related to IQ," *Child Development*, **46**:470-480, 1975.

Indik, Bernard P., "The Relationship Between Organization Size and Supervision Ratio," *Administrative Science Quarterly*, **9**:301-312, 1964.

Katz, Fred E., and Harry W. Martin, "Career Choice Processes," *Social Forces*, **41**:149-154, 1962.

Ladinsky, Jack, "Higher Education and Work Achievement Among Lawyers," *Sociological Quarterly*, **8**:222-232, 1967.

McCormick, Thomas C., *Elementary Social Statistics.* New York: McGraw-Hill Book Company, 1941.

Morris, Raymond N., "Multiple Correlation and Ordinally Scaled Data," *Social Forces*, **48**:299-311, 1970.

Nixon, Howard L., II, "Faculty Support of Traditional Labor Tactics on Campus," *Sociology of Education*, **48**:276-286, 1975.

Peters, Charles C., and Walter R. Van Voorhis, *Statistical Procedures and Their Mathematical Bases.* New York: McGraw-Hill Book Company, 1940.

Reiss, Ira L., "Sexual Permissiveness Among Negroes and Whites," *American Sociological Review*, **29**:688-698, 1964.

Shichor, David, "Prestige and Regional Mobility of New Ph.D.'s in Sociology," *The American Sociologist*, **8**:180-186, 1973.

Segal, Bernard E., "Hierarchy and Work Dissatisfaction in a Chilean Hospital," *Social Forces*, **48**:193-202, 1969.

Siegel, Sidney, *Nonparametric Statistics for the Behavioral Sciences.* New York: McGraw-Hill Book Company, 1956.

Somers, R. H., "A New Asymmetric Measure of Association for Ordinal Variables," *American Sociological Review*, **27**:799-811, 1962.

Somers, R. H., "On the Measurement of Association," *American Sociological Review*, **33**:291-292, 1968.

12

k-Variable Measures of Association

In Chapter 11 we examined associations between two variables for different measurement levels. When a researcher wishes to determine the degree of association between more than two variables, the computations involved become increasingly cumbersome. Several measures of association for k variables will be presented here. These are sometimes referred to as *measures of multiple correlation*, and the results are multiple correlation coefficients.

Perhaps a researcher wants to know the extent to which such factors as age and socioeconomic status will influence voting patterns. One way of approaching this problem is to examine the degree of association among age, socioeconomic status, and voting behavior. If we designate voting behavior as variable 1, socioeconomic status as variable 2, and age as variable 3, we would obtain a *multiple correlation coefficient* that would appear symbolically as

$$R_{1.23} \qquad \text{(read: } R \text{ one-dot-two-three.)}$$

R stands for the relation between the three variables. In this case, we are using variables 2 and 3 as independent, variable 1 as dependent. The relation R shows the strength of association among variables 1, 2, and 3. The subscript, 1.23, refers to the fact that variable 1 is the dependent variable and that variables 2 and 3 are the independent variables functioning in a sense as "predictors." (If we had five variables, four of which were independent, we would have $R_{1.2345}$, where variable 1 is the dependent variable and variables 2, 3, 4, and 5 are the independent variables.)

Most of the examples in this chapter will be limited to three-variable situations. When we extend our computational work beyond three variables, the solutions call for mathematical strategies that are beyond the scope of this text. Several excellent advanced references that have relatively simplified presentations of k-variable multiple correlation problems are listed at the end of the chapter.

The chapter organization is as follows. First, we examine a procedure for determining the degree of agreement between k variables that are measured according to an ordinal scale. This procedure is called Kendall's coefficient of concordance, W. Following this discussion is the presentation of a multiple correlation problem with two predictor or independent variables. Finally, we examine a special situation in which the researcher wants to evaluate the association between two variables with a third variable held constant. This is referred to as *partial correlation.* We might wish to examine the association between voting behavior and age, for instance, while controlling for or *partialing out* socioeconomic status. Or we may wish to examine the association between voting behavior and socioeconomic status while controlling for age. We discuss partial correlation in greater detail in that section.

□ KENDALL'S COEFFICIENT OF CONCORDANCE, *W*, FOR *k* ORDINAL VARIABLES

Kendall's coefficient of concordance, W, is a method of determining the degree of agreement between k variables where each has been measured according to an ordinal scale. For example, the art work of several artists may be evaluated by 25 judges. We might want to determine the degree of agreement among the judges according to how closely they ranked the artists from high to low. Or we may be interested in how closely related several variables are for a sample of persons in a given work setting. To what extent are salary, prestige of the job, and job satisfaction related for an employee sample? Converting scores on these different variables to ranks will enable us to determine Kendall's coefficient of concordance, W, as the measure of the degree of agreement between these variables. The following example is provided to illustrate the application of W to social data.

Cates (1965) was interested in the prestige rankings of various health professions. In her review of the literature, Cates determined that several earlier studies had been conducted that ranked various categories of health professionals differently. In her own research, which included questionnaires administered to a large sample of introductory sociology students, a ranking of health professionals from high to low was determined. At this point, Cates wanted to know how in step the results of her study were compared with the other studies that had been conducted. Therefore, she arranged the rankings assigned different health professionals by the students adjacent to the rankings reported in the previous studies. Table 12.1 shows six classifications of health professionals and the degree of agreement evidenced by the results of the three studies.

For purposes of establishing a degree of consistency in labeling from one study to the next, health professionals were categorized as follows: physicians, pharmacists, dentists, optometrists, chiropractors, and osteopaths. Table 12.1 shows these different health professional categories ranked by Cates and by two other researchers in independent investigations (James, 1957; Hartman, 1936).

Table 12.1 is constructed as follows. Rankings from the three studies are assigned each of the six health professional categories from 1 to 6 (high to low). In the case of a tie between ranks, the average of the ranks otherwise assigned would be given both professional categories. In the study by James, for instance, physicians and dentists were both ranked highest by the sample studied. Therefore, the average of the first two ranks, $(1 + 2)/2 = 1.5$, was assigned each category as shown.

TABLE 12.1
Rankings of Health Occupations in Three Studies.

Health Professional Category	*Rankings by:* Cates	James	Hartman	*Rank Sum*
Physicians	1	1.5	1	3.5
Pharmacists	2	5	3	10
Dentists	3	1.5	2	6.5
Optometrists	4	3	5	12
Chiropractors	5	6	6	17
Osteopaths	6	4	4	14
			ΣRS = Sum of rank sum =	63

Source: Judith Cates, "Images of the Health Professions," *Sociological Quarterly*, **6**: 391–397, 1965.

Next, the ranks assigned each health professional category by each of the three studies are summed across each category. For physicians, the sum of ranks assigned is $1 + 1.5 + 1 = 3.5$. This is done for each and every health professional category. Once these sums have been determined, these sums are summed as well. We will label this value as the sum of the rank sums or Σ RS.

The next step is to determine a distribution of rank sums based on the idea that all categories received equal rankings. This distribution is equivalent to an "expected" set of cell frequencies that we might determine if we were to compute the chi-square test. In this case we must take the Σ RS and divide it by N, the number of health professional categories that are being ranked. The sum of rank sums, Σ RS, divided by $N = \frac{63}{6} = 10.5$. If there were perfect "disagreement," and all categories were ranked so that each rank sum were identical, 10.5 would be the "expected" rank sum for each health professional category. We would expect rank sums for each category as shown in Table 12.2.

Next, we determine an S value, which is the sum of all squared differences between expected and observed rank sums. The value, S, is defined as follows:

$$\begin{aligned} S &= (10.5 - 3.5)^2 + (10.5 - 10)^2 + (10.5 - 6.5)^2 + (10.5 - 12)^2 \\ &\quad + (10.5 - 17)^2 + (10.5 - 14)^2 \\ &= 49 + .25 + 16 + 2.25 + 42.25 + 12.25 \\ &= 122. \end{aligned}$$

The resulting $S = 122$. Once we have completed these operations, we may apply the following formula for W, the coefficient of concordance:

$$W = \frac{S}{(\frac{1}{12})\, k^2 (N^3 - N)},$$

TABLE 12.2
"Expected" Rank Sums for the Data in Table 12.1.

Health Professional Category	*Rank Sums*
Physicians	10.5
Pharmacists	10.5
Dentists	10.5
Optometrists	10.5
Chiropractors	10.5
Osteopaths	10.5
	$\Sigma RS = 63.0$

where

S = sum of the squares of the observed deviations from the expected sum of ranks
k = number of variables ranked
N = number of individuals in the sample being ranked

Using the information from Table 12.1 and our $S = 122$, we determine W as follows:

$$W = \frac{122}{(\frac{1}{12})(3)^2(6^3 - 6)}$$

$$= \frac{122}{(.075)(216 - 6)}$$

$$= \frac{122}{157.5}$$

$$= .77.$$

The resulting $W = .77$. We might interpret this W to mean that a strong association exists between the rankings of the three studies investigating prestige among health professionals.

Another example might provide additional application potential of W. Suppose that we observed eight individuals in an organization. These persons completed questionnaires which purportedly measured the following variables: satisfaction with one's pay, working hours, work associates, and supervision. Assuming that we were able to obtain raw scores for each of these variables for the eight persons examined and rank them, we might observe some hypothetical data, such as those shown in Table 12.3.

TABLE 12.3
Rankings of Eight Employees for Satisfaction with Pay, Working Hours, Work Associates, and Supervision.

	Satisfaction with:				*Rank Sums*	
Individual	*Pay*	*Working Hours*	*Work Associates*	*Supervision*	*Observed*	*Expected*
1	2	1	1	3	7	18
2	1	3	3	2	9	18
3	3	2	2	1	8	18
4	5	4	6	4	19	18
5	4	8	5	5	22	18
6	8	7	4	6	25	18
7	7	6	8	8	29	18
8	6	5	7	7	25	18
					$\Sigma RS = 144$	$\Sigma RS = 144$

In Table 12.3, each individual has been ranked according to the intensity of his or her score on each of the four variables. Each person's ranks are summed, and the resulting sum of rank sums = 144 as shown. Next, we determine the expected rank sum for each individual if all individuals were distributed equally for each of the four variables. This would be $\Sigma\ \text{RS}/N = \frac{144}{8} = 18$. If there were equal rank sums for all eight individuals, these rank sums would be 18. Note that these values have been placed conveniently in an expected column of rank sums.

Our next step is to determine the value of S. This is the sum of the squared differences between each expected rank sum and the adjacent observed rank sum, or

$$\begin{aligned} S &= (18-7)^2 + (18-9)^2 + (18-8)^2 + (18-19)^2 + (18-22)^2 \\ &\quad + (18-25)^2 + (18-29)^2 + (18-25)^2 \\ &= 121 + 81 + 100 + 1 + 16 + 49 + 121 + 49 \\ &= 538. \end{aligned}$$

The resulting $S = 538$. With this information and with the information in Table 12.3, we may compute W as follows:

$$\begin{aligned} W &= \frac{538}{(\frac{1}{12})(4)^2(8^3 - 8)} \\ &= \frac{538}{(1.333)(512 - 8)} \\ &= \frac{538}{(1.333)(504)} \\ &= \frac{538}{671.8} \\ &= .80. \end{aligned}$$

An observed $W = .80$ is again a strong degree of association among the four variables: satisfaction with pay, working hours, work associates, and supervision. It would appear that persons who are highly satisfied with pay are also highly satisfied with the other work specifications indicated. Also, those persons who are less satisfied with one variable are also less satisfied with the others.

The Significance of W

A test of the statistical significance of W may be conducted by applying an approximation of the chi-square test as follows:

$$\chi^2 = \frac{S}{(\frac{1}{12})\,kN(N+1)},$$

where

N = number of individuals being ranked
k = number of variables

The result is a χ^2 value with $N - 1$ degrees of freedom (where N is the number of persons ranked).

With an observed $W = .77$ from Table 12.1, we would compute the chi-square value as follows (assume that $k = 3, N = 6$):

$$\begin{aligned}\chi^2 &= \frac{122}{(\frac{1}{12})(3)(6)(6+1)}\\ &= \frac{122}{(.25)(42)}\\ &= \frac{122}{10.5}\\ &= 11.619.\end{aligned}$$

Our first $W = .77$ has a chi square observed = 11.619. We take this value to the chi-square table, Table A4, with $N - 1$ or $6 - 1$ df. With 5 df we determine that our observed W is significant at the .05 level of probability. Associated with the .05 level of significance is a critical value of chi square = 11.070, which we are able to equal or exceed with our observed value of 11.619.

For the second $W = .80$ from Table 12.3, we may apply the chi-square test again as follows (assume that $k = 4$ and $N = 8$):

$$\begin{aligned}\chi^2 &= \frac{538}{(\frac{1}{12})(4)(8)(8+1)}\\ &= \frac{538}{(.333)(72)}\\ &= \frac{538}{23.976}\\ &= 22.439.\end{aligned}$$

The resulting chi square observed = 22.439, which equals or exceeds the .01 critical value of chi square (18.475 with $N - 1$ or $8 - 1$ or 7 degrees of freedom).

Assumptions of W

Kendall's coefficient of concordance, W, assumes ordinal-level or rankable data for each and every variable correlated. Random sampling is also assumed.

Advantages and Disadvantages of W

When the investigator is interested in determining the degree of agreement between k variables measured according to an ordinal scale, W is one of the only procedures that can be used to provide a fairly easy solution. There is no limit to the number of variables that can be correlated. There are no sample-size restrictions or distributional requirements underlying the application of W.

The coefficient W is interpreted in much the same way as any other measure of association for a two-variable situation. It does not have a PRE interpretation, however. Behavioral scientists should find W a useful tool for k-variable ordinal associations.

□ MULTIPLE CORRELATION, R

If we are fortunate enough to have at our disposal a variety of variables measured according to an interval scale, it is possible to determine the degree of agreement or multiple correlation between several of these variables simultaneously.

Usually, one of the variables is designated as dependent and the others as independent. The identification of dependent and independent variables has usually preceded the computation of a multiple correlation in the theoretical scheme developed by the investigator. In the theoretical scheme upon which the researcher's work is based, tentative causal relations between variables are set forth as assumptions or in propositional form. A preliminary examination of the theory will indicate which variables are to be used in which capacity.

The multiple R that we eventually obtain indicates the degree of association among the k variables. When we square R, R^2 becomes a PRE measure as well. Then R^2 will tell us about the amount of error we can account for on the dependent variable as a result of correlating it with several independent variables.

A prior step that facilitates the R computation is to compute all two-variable associations for k variables. Literally, this means that for four variables, Pearson r's need to be computed for the relation between variables 1 and 2, 1 and 3, 1 and 4, 2 and 3, 2 and 4, and 3 and 4. Computer programs are available to generate what is called a *matrix of intercorrelations*. This matrix is a table representing every

TABLE 12.4
Matrix of Intercorrelations.[a]

	X_1	X_2	X_3	X_4	X_5	X_6	X_7	X_8	X_9	X_{10}	X_{11}
X_1	1.00	.22	–.59	.49	–.18	.66	–.43	.15	.43	–.28	.50
X_2		1.00	–.45	.27	–.11	–.42	.35	.30	–.33	.21	.35
X_3			1.00	–.63	–.19	.84	–.64	–.52	.44	.55	–.43
X_4				1.00	.10	–.70	.62	.20	–.55	–.28	.40
X_5					1.00	.16	.66	.67	.05	–.67	–.41
X_6						1.00	.36	–.27	.35	.33	–.61
X_7							1.00	.71	–.47	–.79	–.10
X_8								1.00	–.19	–.94	–.39
X_9									1.00	.25	–.35
X_{10}										1.00	.03
X_{11}											1.00

Source: John D. Photiadis, "Corollaries of Migration," *Sociological Quarterly*, **6**: 339–348, 1965.

[a] X_1 = net migration; X_2 = total population; X_3 = percentage of total population that is rural–farm; X_4 = percentage employed in manufacturing; X_5 = percentage of unemployed; X_6 = percentage of low-income families; X_7 = percentage of part-time farmers; X_8 = percentage of decrease in number of farms (1950–1960); X_9 = average acres per farm; percentage of commercial farms; X_{11} = percentage of dwellings that are sound and have all plumbing facilities.

variable correlated with every other variable. Table 12.4 is a matrix of intercorrelations computed for migration data collected by Photiadis (1965).

From the matrix of intercorrelations shown in Table 12.4, it is possible to compute multiple correlations between any number of variables. To illustrate the computation of a multiple R, we focus upon three variables from Table 12.4: (1) net migration, (2) total population, and (3) percentage of total population that is rural–farm. The smaller matrix of intercorrelations is reproduced below:

	X_1	X_2	X_3
X_1	1.00	.22	–.59
X_2		1.00	–.45
X_3			1.00

Using these values, we may apply the following formula for R:

$$R_{1.23} = \sqrt{\frac{r_{12}^2 + r_{13}^2 = 2r_{12}r_{13}r_{23}}{1 - r_{23}^2}},$$

where

$$r_{12}^2 = (.22)^2 \qquad r_{12} = .22$$
$$r_{13}^2 = (-.59)^2 \qquad r_{13} = -.59$$
$$r_{23}^2 = (-.45)^2 \qquad r_{23} = -.45.$$

Computing $R_{1.23}$, we have

$$R_{1.23} = \sqrt{\frac{(.22)^2 + (-.59)^2 - (2)(.22)(-.59)(-.45)}{1 - (-.45)^2}}$$
$$= \sqrt{\frac{.048 + .348 - (2)(.058)}{1 - .202}}$$
$$= \sqrt{\frac{.396 - .116}{.798}}$$
$$= \sqrt{\frac{.280}{.798}}$$
$$= \sqrt{.351}$$
$$= .59.$$

$R_{1.23} = .59$. This might be interpreted as a moderately high degree of association between the three variables. If we square R, $R^2 = (.59)^2 = .35$. This would mean that 35 percent of the error in predicting net migration has been accounted for by using as predictors the variables "total population" and "percentage of total population that is rural farm."

Assumptions of R

Technically, all the assumptions that apply to the Pearson r for two interval-level variable associations also apply to multiple association measures that are comprised of many r values. Linearity, homoscedasticity, randomness, bivariate normal distribution, and the interval level of measurement are key assumptions underlying the proper application of the Pearson r. However, as we increase the number of variables to be correlated, we also increase the likelihood that certain relationships between additional variables may not be linear. Or homoscedasticity may not prevail under all conditions. Or the bivariate normal distributional assumption may not be met with certain variable combinations. We increase the likelihood of errors in interpretation of multiple R values as we increase the number of variables to be correlated.

One quite common source of errors in interpretation stems from the fact that a matrix of intercorrelations may combine variables that are not theoretically connected. Also, the variables correlated may be measured at levels of measurement other than the interval level. Suppose that a researcher were to gather data from a survey. A questionnaire containing 40 or 50 measures of different variables may be administered.

Sex, years of education, political affiliation, religious preference, socioeconomic status, job satisfaction, level of information, anxiety, style of supervision, organizational size, frequency of church attendance, race, ethnic background, size of work group, levels of supervision, and other such variables may be included in the questionnaire. A matrix of intercorrelations will correlate all of these variables with one another. In short, Pearson *r*'s will be computed for the association between sex and organization size, size of work group and political affiliation, church attendance and job satisfaction, years of education and levels of supervision, and any other number of nonsensical associations. Multiple correlations indiscriminately computed for these variables will be virtually meaningless. It is necessary, therefore, that the researcher develop a consistent theoretical scheme that sets forth certain logical variable associations to be examined in detail. Multiple correlations are meaningfully interpreted only when they are generated from a coherent theoretical scheme. All too often, students accept as valid all information provided in computer printouts. Computers are not programmed to discern one variable or measurement level from another. It is up to the researcher to apply such discrimination to interpretations of computer printout information.

□ PARTIAL CORRELATION

Partial correlation is a measure of the association between two or more variables where one or more variables have been held constant or partialed out of the original association. Suppose that we observe an association between grades and membership in sororities and fraternities. We will obtain a random sample of Greeks (sorority and fraternity members) and non-Greeks (persons not affiliated with such organizations). We may observe an association between grades and Greek/non-Greek membership as shown in Table 12.5. This association may be spurious, however. *Spuriousness* is defined as an observed association between two variables that is really attributable to a third, usually unknown, variable. If we decide to take into account the amount of time students study for their examinations, this may alter the original association observed between grades and Greek/non-

TABLE 12.5
A Two-Variable Cross-Tabulation of Grades and Fraternity/Sorority Membership–Nonmembership.

		Greeks	*Non-Greeks*
Grades	*High*	100	75
	Low	50	90

TABLE 12.6
The Relation Between Grades and Fraternity/Sorority Membership, Controlling for Amount of Study.

		Student Studies a Lot		*Student Studies Little*	
		Greeks	*Non-Greeks*	*Greeks*	*Non-Greeks*
Grades	*High*	100	75	0	0
	Low	0	0	50	90

Greek membership. We may observe the hypothetical breakdown, controlling for "amount of study," in Table 12.6. Now we can see that the amount of study rather than Greek/non-Greek membership appears to be more of an influence on grades. The original association between Greek/non-Greek membership and grades was spurious.

Partial correlation will enable us to evaluate the influence of other variables on any two-variable association. We may wish to see the relation between variables 1 and 2 with variable 3 partialed out. This would be symbolically portrayed as

$r_{12.3}$ (the relation between variables 1 and 2 with variable 3 partialed out).

An illustration of the application of a partial r is provided by Ross (1976).

Ross investigated the relation between the size and growth of educational institutions, faculty productivity, and the degree to which innovative academic programs were instituted. Some hypothetical associations between three variables are provided below:

where

variable 1 = institutionalization of innovative academic programs
variable 2 = organizational size
variable 3 = organizational growth

Subsequently, Pearson r's were computed for each of these variable combinations. These are

$$r_{12} = .64$$

$$r_{13} = .85$$

$$r_{23} = .55.$$

It would appear that strong associations exist for all the two-variable combinations. But what if we were to examine just the association between the institutionalization of innovative academic programs and organizational size while partialing out the effects of organizational growth? We would determine this partial r by the following formula:

$$r_{12.3} = \frac{r_{12} - r_{13}r_{23}}{\sqrt{(1 - r_{13}^2)(1 - r_{23}^2)}}.$$

Applying the hypothetical data to this formula, we have

$$\begin{aligned} r_{12.3} &= \frac{.64 - (.85)(.55)}{\sqrt{(1 - .85^2)(1 - .55^2)}} \\ &= \frac{.64 - .47}{\sqrt{(1 - .72)(1 - .30)}} \\ &= \frac{.17}{\sqrt{.196}} \\ &= \frac{.17}{.44} \\ &= .38. \end{aligned}$$

The resulting partial $r_{12.3} = .38$. When we examine the relation between organization size and institutionalization of innovative academic programs while controlling for organizational growth, the original association between the two variables (innovation of academic programs and organizational size) drops from .64 to .38.

Partial correlation formulas can also be applied to any other pair of variables, controlling for a third. For instance, if we want to know the relation between variables 1 and 3 while partialing out variable 2, our formula would be

$$r_{13.2} = \frac{r_{13} - r_{12}r_{23}}{\sqrt{(1 - r_{12}^2)(1 - r_{23}^2)}}.$$

Assumptions of the Partial *r*

Again, since Pearson's *r* values are applied in the computation of partial *r*'s, the same assumptions prevail. Pearson *r*'s are properly computed when the researcher can assume randomness, interval-level data, a bivariate normal distribution, homoscedasticity, and linearity.

Advantages and Disadvantages of Partial *r*

There are no disadvantages associated with partial *r* coefficients when properly applied. The primary advantage is that partial *r*'s permit the researcher to examine relations between any pair of variables while controlling for a third variable. Of course, there are additional formulas to handle situations where more than one variable is partialed out. But such instances are rare, and the procedures involved in the computational work are beyond the scope of this book.

□ SUMMARY

This chapter has examined three major techniques for determining associations between *k* variables. Kendall's coefficient of concordance is designed to determine the degree of agreement between *k* variables measured according to an ordinal scale. The resulting coefficient, *W*, does not have a PRE interpretation. However, *W* gives a rather reliable account of the strength of the association that exists between *k* variables, and the crude interpretive table at the beginning of Chapter 11 can be used for *W* interpretations.

Multiple *R* or a measure of multiple correlation for three variables was presented. This procedure assists the researcher in determining the degree of association between three variables. One of these variables is considered dependent, and an R^2 gives a PRE account of the degree of variation on the dependent variable that is attributable to two other independent variables. Partial correlation is a method of determining the degree of association between a pair of variables with one or more variables partialed out or controlled for. This technique is useful for determining the presence of spuriousness between variables. It also helps in establishing the influence or lack of influence of additional variables on an original observed association.

Beyond this book are advanced procedures that help the researcher examine complex interrelations between variables. Not only are association measures treated in more advanced form, but more complex tests of significance of difference will be encountered. As our theory building becomes increasingly complex and sophisticated, our tests and statistical procedures used for analyzing such schemes increase in complexity as well. Some useful texts covering advanced statistical tests and measures of association are cited in the references for this chapter and are recommended. The reader is now at a point where such tests can be encountered and understood with adequate study. The principles upon which such tests have been based have been presented in this book and can enhance one's understanding of more difficult material presented in more advanced courses.

In a sense, we have only scratched the surface of statistical tests and procedures here. We hope that the reader will find many of the tests presented in this and previous chapters useful for data analysis when research is conducted. Also, reading professional journals and understanding the procedures of analysis should be somewhat easier now. There is considerably more to learn, but a foundation has been provided upon which new learning can be based.

SELECTED STUDY TERMS

Partial correlation
Multiple R
Partialing out a variable
Matrix of intercorrelations
Spuriousness

EXERCISES

1. Given the following information, "partial out" variable 3 and determine the partial r.

$$r_{12} = .46$$

$$r_{13} = .65$$

$$r_{23} = .26.$$

2. Determine Kendall's coefficient of concordance for the following data:

	Variable			
	W	*X*	*Y*	*Z*
Judge's Rankings	1	3	2	7
	2	2	1	6
	3	1	3	5
	4	7	4	3
	5	6	6	1
	6	5	5	2
	7	4	8	3
	8	9	7	4
	9	8	9	9

(a) What is W? Is W significant at the .05 level? Show proof of your answer.

3. Given the following matrix of intercorrelations, determine the multiple R.

		Variable		
		1	*2*	*3*
Variable	*1*	1.00	.23	.48
	2		1.00	.62
	3			1.00

$R_{1.23} = ?$

Does the resulting R value by itself have a PRE interpretation? Why or why not? What must be done to yield a PRE interpretation? What is your PRE interpretation in this instance?

4. Determine the degree of agreement for five employees on the three variables listed in the table.

	Variable		
Employee	*Job Interest*	*Morale*	*Group Cohesion*
1	2	1	4
2	1	3	5
3	3	4	3
4	4	5	2
5	5	2	1

What is the observed W? Is it significant at the .01 level? Show proof of answer.

REFERENCES

Blalock, Hubert M., *Social Statistics*, 2nd ed. New York: McGraw-Hill Book Company, 1972.

Cates, Judith, "Images of the Health Professions," *Sociological Quarterly*, **6**:391-397, 1965.

Downie, N. M., and R. W. Heath, *Basic Statistical Methods*, 4th ed. New York: Harper & Row Publishers, 1974.

Edwards, Allen L., *Statistical Methods*, 2nd ed. New York: Holt, Rinehart and Winston, 1967.

Guilford, J. P., and Benjamin Fruchter, *Fundamental Statistics in Psychology and Education.* New York: McGraw-Hill Book Company, 1978.

Hartman, George, "The Relative Social Prestige of Representative Medical Specialties," *Journal of Applied Psychology*, **20**:659-663, 1936.

James, Warren, "Differential Acceptance of Occupations as Professions," unpublished Ph.D. thesis, Ohio State University, 1957.

Photiadis, John D., "Corollaries of Migration," *Sociological Quarterly*, **6**:339-348, 1965.

Ross, R. Danforth, "The Institutionalization of Academic Innovation: Two Models," *Sociology of Education*, **49**: 146-155, 1976.

Walker, Helen, and Joseph Lev, *Statistical Inference.* New York: Holt, Rinehart and Winston, 1953.

Winer, B. J., *Statistical Principles and Experimental Design*, 2nd ed. New York: McGraw-Hill Book Company, 1971.

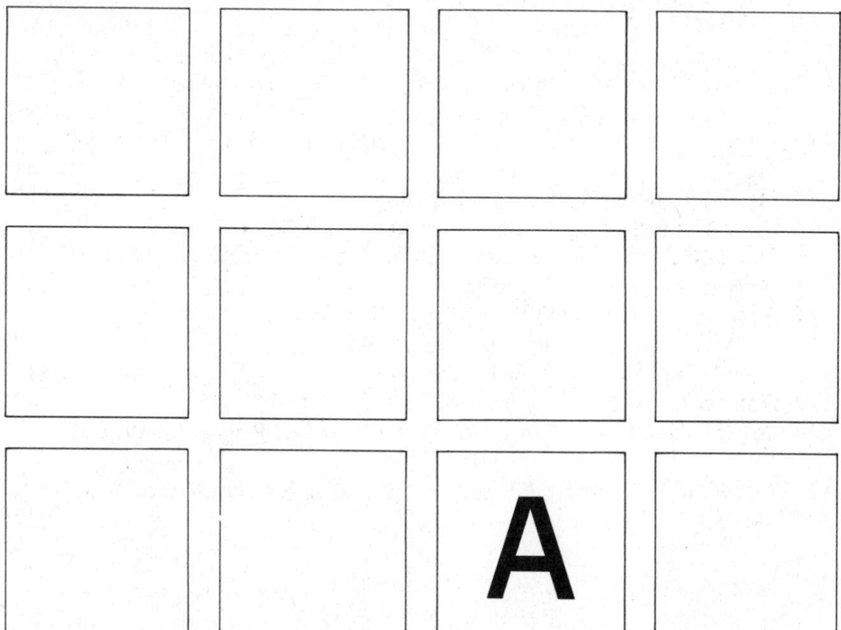

Tables

TABLE A1

Squares, Square Roots, and Reciprocals of Integers from 1 to 1000.

n	n^2	$\sqrt{n}$	$\frac{1}{n}$	$\frac{1}{\sqrt{n}}$
1	1	1.0000	1.000000	1.0000
2	4	1.4142	.500000	.7071
3	9	1.7321	.333333	.5774
4	16	2.0000	.250000	.5000
5	25	2.2361	.200000	.4472
6	36	2.4495	.166667	.4082
7	49	2.6458	.142857	.3780
8	64	2.8284	.125000	.3536
9	81	3.0000	.111111	.3333
10	100	3.1623	.100000	.3162
11	121	3.3166	.090909	.3015
12	144	3.4641	.083333	.2887
13	169	3.6056	.076923	.2774
14	196	3.7417	.071429	.2673
15	225	3.8730	.066667	.2582
16	256	4.0000	.062500	.2500
17	289	4.1231	.058824	.2425
18	324	4.2426	.055556	.2357
19	361	4.3589	.052632	.2294
20	400	4.4721	.050000	.2236
21	441	4.5826	.047619	.2182
22	484	4.6904	.045455	.2132
23	529	4.7958	.043478	.2085
24	576	4.8990	.041667	.2041
25	625	5.0000	.040000	.2000
26	676	5.0990	.038462	.1961
27	729	5.1962	.037037	.1925
28	784	5.2915	.035714	.1890
29	841	5.3852	.034483	.1857
30	900	5.4772	.033333	.1826
31	961	5.5678	.032258	.1796
32	1024	5.6569	.031250	.1768
33	1089	5.7446	.030303	.1741
34	1156	5.8310	.029412	.1715
35	1225	5.9161	.028571	.1690
36	1296	6.0000	.027778	.1667
37	1369	6.0828	.027027	.1644
38	1444	6.1644	.026316	.1622
39	1521	6.2450	.025641	.1601
40	1600	6.3246	.025000	.1581
41	1681	6.4031	.024390	.1562
42	1764	6.4807	.023810	.1543
43	1849	6.5574	.023256	.1525
44	1936	6.6332	.022727	.1508
45	2025	6.7082	.022222	.1491
46	2116	6.7823	.021739	.1474
47	2209	6.8557	.021277	.1459
48	2304	6.9282	.020833	.1443
49	2401	7.0000	.020408	.1429
50	2500	7.0711	.020000	.1414

Source: "Table M" Squares, Square Roots and Reciprocals of Integers from 1-1000 from *Introduction to Applied Statistics* by J. G. Peatman. Copyright © 1963 by John G. Peatman. Reprinted by permission of Harper & Row, Publishers, Inc.

TABLE A1 *(continued)*

n	n^2	$\sqrt{n}$	$\frac{1}{n}$	$\frac{1}{\sqrt{n}}$
51	2601	7.1414	.019608	.1400
52	2704	7.2111	.019231	.1387
53	2809	7.2801	.018868	.1374
54	2916	7.3485	.018519	.1361
55	3025	7.4162	.018182	.1348
56	3136	7.4833	.017857	.1336
57	3249	7.5498	.017544	.1325
58	3364	7.6158	.017241	.1313
59	3481	7.6811	.016949	.1302
60	3600	7.7460	.016667	.1291
61	3721	7.8102	.016393	.1280
62	3844	7.8740	.016129	.1270
63	3969	7.9373	.015873	.1260
64	4096	8.0000	.015625	.1250
65	4225	8.0623	.015385	.1240
66	4356	8.1240	.015152	.1231
67	4489	8.1854	.014925	.1222
68	4624	8.2462	.014706	.1213
69	4761	8.3066	.014493	.1204
70	4900	8.3666	.014286	.1195
71	5041	8.4261	.014085	.1187
72	5184	8.4853	.013889	.1179
73	5329	8.5440	.013699	.1170
74	5476	8.6023	.013514	.1162
75	5625	8.6603	.013333	.1155
76	5776	8.7178	.013158	.1147
77	5929	8.7750	.018987	.1140
78	6084	8.8318	.012821	.1132
79	6241	8.8882	.012658	.1125
80	6400	8.9443	.012500	.1118
81	6561	9.0000	.012346	.1111
82	6724	9.0554	.012195	.1104
83	6889	9.1104	.012048	.1098
84	7056	9.1652	.011905	.1091
85	7225	9.2195	.011765	.1085
86	7396	9.2736	.011628	.1078
87	7569	9.3274	.011494	.1072
88	7744	9.3808	.011364	.1066
89	7921	9.4340	.011236	.1060
90	8100	9.4868	.011111	.1054
91	8281	9.5394	.010989	.1048
92	8464	9.5917	.010870	.1043
93	8649	9.6437	.010753	.1037
94	8836	9.6954	.010638	.1031
95	9025	9.7468	.010526	.1026
96	9216	9.7980	.010417	.1021
97	9409	9.8489	.010309	.1015
98	9604	9.8995	.010204	.1010
99	9801	9.9499	.010101	.1005
100	10000	10.0000	.010000	.1000

TABLE A1 (continued)

n	n^2	$\sqrt{n}$	$\frac{1}{n}$	$\frac{1}{\sqrt{n}}$
101	10201	10.0499	.009901	.0995
102	10404	10.0995	.009804	.0990
103	10609	10.1489	.009709	.0985
104	10816	10.1980	.009615	.0981
105	11025	10.2470	.009524	.0976
106	11236	10.2956	.009434	.0971
107	11449	10.3441	.009346	.0967
108	11664	10.3923	.009259	.0962
109	11881	10.4403	.009174	.0958
110	12100	10.4881	.009091	.0953
111	12321	10.5357	.009009	.0949
112	12544	10,5830	.008929	.0945
113	12769	10.6301	.008850	.0941
114	12996	10.6771	.008772	.0937
115	13225	10.7238	.008696	.0933
116	13456	10.7703	.008621	.0928
117	13689	10.8167	.008547	.0925
118	13924	10.8628	.008475	.0921
119	14161	10.9087	.008403	.0917
120	14400	10.9545	.008333	.0913
121	14641	11.0000	.008264	.0909
122	14884	11.0454	.008197	.0905
123	15129	11.0905	.008130	.0902
124	15376	11.1355	.008065	.0898
125	15625	11.1803	.008000	.0894
126	15876	11.2250	.007937	.0891
127	16129	11.2694	.007874	.0887
128	16384	11.3137	.007813	.0884
129	16641	11.3578	.007752	.0880
130	16900	11.4018	.007692	.0877
131	17161	11.4455	.007634	.0874
132	17424	11.4891	.007576	.0870
133	17689	11.5326	.007519	.0867
134	17956	11.5758	.007463	.0864
135	18225	11.6190	.007407	.0861
136	18496	11.6619	.007353	.0857
137	18769	11.7047	.007299	.0854
138	19044	11.7473	.007246	.0851
139	19321	11.7898	.007194	.0848
140	19600	11.8322	.007143	.0845
141	19881	11.8743	.007092	.0842
142	20164	11.9164	.007042	.0839
143	20449	11.9583	.006993	.0836
144	20736	12.0000	.006944	.0833
145	21025	12.0416	.006897	.0830
146	21316	12.0830	.006849	.0828
147	21609	12.1244	.006803	.0825
148	21904	12.1655	.006757	.0822
149	22201	12.2066	.006711	.0819
150	22500	12.2474	.006667	.0816

TABLE A1 (*continued*)

n	n^2	$\sqrt{n}$	$\frac{1}{n}$	$\frac{1}{\sqrt{n}}$
151	22801	12.2882	.006623	.0814
152	23104	12.3288	.006579	.0811
153	23409	12.3693	.006536	.0808
154	23716	12.4097	.006494	.0806
155	24025	12.4499	.006452	.0803
156	24336	12.4900	.006410	.0301
157	24649	12.5300	.006369	.0798
158	24964	12.5698	.006329	.0796
159	25281	12.6095	.006289	.0793
160	25600	12.6491	.006250	.0791
161	25921	12.6886	.006211	.0788
162	26244	12.7279	.006173	.0786
163	26569	12.7671	.006135	.0783
164	26896	12.8062	.006098	.0781
165	27225	12.8452	.006061	.0778
166	27556	12.8841	.006024	.0776
167	27889	12.9228	.005988	.0774
168	28224	12.9615	.005952	.0772
169	28561	13.0000	.005917	.0769
170	28900	13.0384	.005882	.0767
171	29241	13.0767	.005848	.0765
172	29584	13.1149	.005814	.0762
173	29929	13.1529	.005780	.0760
174	30276	13.1909	.005747	.0758
175	30625	13.2288	.005714	.0756
176	30976	13.2665	.005682	.0754
177	31329	13.3041	.005650	.0752
178	31684	13.3417	.005618	.0750
179	32041	13.3791	.005587	.0747
180	32400	13.4164	.005556	.0745
181	32761	13.4536	.005525	.0743
182	33124	13.4907	.005495	.0741
183	33489	13.5277	.005464	.0739
184	33856	13.5647	.005435	.0737
185	34225	13.6015	.005405	.0735
186	34596	13.6382	.005376	.0733
187	34969	13.6748	.005348	.0731
188	35344	13.7113	.005319	.0729
189	35721	13.7477	.005291	.0727
190	36100	13.7840	.005263	.0725
191	36481	13.8203	.005236	.0724
192	36864	13.8564	.005208	.0722
193	37249	13.8924	.005181	.0720
194	37636	13.9284	.005155	.0718
195	38025	13.9642	.005128	.0716
196	38416	14.0000	.005102	.0714
197	38809	14.0357	.005076	.0712
198	39204	14.0712	.005051	.0711
199	39601	14.1067	.005025	.0709
200	40000	14.1421	.005000	.0707

TABLE A1 (continued)

n	n^2	$\sqrt{n}$	$\frac{1}{n}$	$\frac{1}{\sqrt{n}}$
201	40401	14.1774	.004975	.0705
202	40804	14.2127	.004950	.0704
203	41209	14.2478	.004926	.0702
204	41616	14.2829	.004902	.0700
205	42025	14.3178	.004878	.0698
206	42436	14.3527	.004854	.0697
207	42849	14.3875	.004831	.0695
208	43264	14.4222	.004808	.0693
209	43681	14.4568	.004785	.0692
210	44100	14.4914	.004762	.0690
211	44521	14.5258	.004739	.0688
212	44944	14.5602	.004717	.0687
213	45369	14.5945	.004695	.0685
214	45796	14.6287	.004673	.0684
215	46225	14.6629	.004651	.0682
216	46656	14.6969	.004630	.0680
217	47089	14.7309	.004608	.0679
218	47524	14.7648	.004587	.0677
219	47961	14.7986	.004566	.0676
220	48400	14.8324	.004545	.0674
221	48841	14.8661	.004525	.0673
222	49284	14.8997	.004505	.0671
223	49729	14.9332	.004484	.0670
224	50176	14.9666	.004464	.0668
225	50625	15.0000	.004444	.0667
226	51076	15.0333	.004425	.0665
227	51529	15.0665	.004405	.0664
228	51984	15.0997	.004386	.0662
229	52441	15.1327	.004367	.0661
230	52900	15.1658	.004348	.0659
231	53361	15.1987	.004329	.0658
232	53824	15.2315	.004310	.0657
233	54289	15.2643	.004292	.0655
234	54756	15.2971	.004274	.0654
235	55225	15.3297	.004255	.0652
236	55696	15.3623	.004237	.0651
237	56169	15.3948	.004219	.0650
238	56644	15.4272	.004202	.0648
239	57121	15.4596	.004184	.0647
240	57600	15.4919	.004167	.0645
241	58081	15.5242	.004149	.0644
242	58564	15.5563	.004132	.0643
243	59049	15.5885	.004115	.0642
244	59536	15.6205	.004098	.0640
245	60025	15.6525	.004082	.0639
246	60516	15.6844	.004065	.0638
247	61009	15.7162	.004049	.0636
248	61504	15.7480	.004032	.0635
249	62001	15.7797	.004016	.0634
250	62500	15.8114	.004000	.0632

TABLE A1 *(continued)*

n	n^2	$\sqrt{n}$	$\frac{1}{n}$	$\frac{1}{\sqrt{n}}$
251	63001	15.8430	.003984	.0631
252	63504	15.8745	.003968	.0630
253	64009	15.9060	.003953	.0629
254	64516	15.9374	.003937	.0627
255	65025	15.9687	.003922	.0626
256	65536	16.0000	.003906	.0625
257	66049	16.0312	.003891	.0624
258	66564	16.0624	.003876	.0623
259	67081	16.0935	.003861	.0621
260	67600	16.1245	.003846	.0620
261	68121	16.1555	.003831	.0619
262	68644	16.1864	.003817	.0618
263	69169	16.2173	.003802	.0617
264	69696	16.2481	.003788	.0615
265	70225	16.2788	.003774	.0614
266	70756	16.3095	.003759	.0613
267	71289	16.3401	.003745	.0612
268	71824	16.3707	.003731	.0611
269	72361	16.4012	.003717	.0610
270	72900	16.4317	.003704	.0609
271	73441	16.4621	.003690	.0607
272	73984	16.4924	.003676	.0606
273	74529	16.5227	.003663	.0605
274	75076	16.5529	.003650	.0604
275	75625	16.5831	.003636	.0603
276	76176	16.6132	.003623	.0602
277	76729	16.6433	.003610	.0601
278	77284	16.6733	.003597	.0600
279	77841	16.7033	.003584	.0599
280	78400	16.7332	.003571	.0598
281	78961	16.7631	.003559	.0597
282	79524	16.7929	.003546	.0595
283	80089	16.8226	.003534	.0594
284	80656	16.8523	.003521	.0593
285	81225	16.8819	.003509	.0592
286	81796	16.9115	.003497	.0591
287	82369	16.9411	.003484	.0590
288	82944	16.9706	.003472	.0589
289	83521	17.0000	.003460	.0588
290	84100	17.0294	.003448	.0587
291	84681	17.0587	.003436	.0586
292	85264	17.0880	.003425	.0585
293	85849	17.1172	.003413	.0584
294	86436	17.1464	.003401	.0583
295	87025	17.1756	.003390	.0582
296	87616	17.2047	.003378	.0581
297	88209	17.2337	.003367	.0580
298	88804	17.2627	.003356	.0579
299	89401	17.2916	.003344	.0578
300	90000	17.3205	.003333	.0577

TABLE A1 (*continued*)

n	n^2	$\sqrt{n}$	$\frac{1}{n}$	$\frac{1}{\sqrt{n}}$
301	90601	17.3494	.003322	.0576
302	91204	17.3781	.003311	.0575
303	91809	17.4069	.003300	.0574
304	92416	17.4356	.003289	.0574
305	93025	17.4642	.003279	.0573
306	93636	17.4929	.003268	.0572
307	94249	17.5214	.003257	.0571
308	94864	17.5499	.003247	.0570
309	95481	17.5784	.003236	.0569
310	96100	17.6068	.003226	.0568
311	96721	17.6352	.003215	.0567
312	97344	17.6635	.003205	.0566
313	97969	17.6918	.003195	.0565
314	98596	17.7200	.003185	.0564
315	99225	17.7482	.003175	.0563
316	99856	17.7764	.003165	.0563
317	100489	17.8045	.003155	.0562
318	101124	17.8326	.003145	.0561
319	101761	17.8606	.003135	.0560
320	102400	17.8885	.003125	.0559
321	103041	17.9165	.003115	.0558
322	103684	17.9444	.003106	.0557
323	104329	17.9722	.003096	.0556
324	104976	18.0000	.003086	.0556
325	105625	18.0278	.003077	.0555
326	106276	18.0555	.003067	.0554
327	106929	18.0831	.003058	.0553
328	107584	18.1108	.003049	.0552
329	108241	18.1384	.003040	.0551
330	108900	18.1659	.003030	.0550
331	109561	18.1934	.003021	.0550
332	110224	18.2209	.003012	.0549
333	110889	18.2483	.003003	.0548
334	111556	18.2757	.002994	.0547
335	112225	18.3030	.002985	.0546
336	112896	18.3303	.002976	.0546
337	113569	18.3576	.002967	.0545
338	114244	18.3848	.002959	.0544
339	114921	18.4120	.002950	.0543
340	115600	18.4391	.002941	.0542
341	116281	18.4662	.002933	.0542
342	116964	18.4932	.002924	.0541
343	117649	18.5203	.002915	.0540
344	118336	18.5472	.002907	.0539
345	119025	18.5742	.002899	.0538
346	119716	18.6011	.002890	.0538
347	120409	18.6279	.002882	.0537
348	121104	18.6548	.002874	.0536
349	121801	18.6815	.002865	.0535
350	122500	18.7083	.002857	.0535

TABLE A1 *(continued)*

n	n^2	$\sqrt{n}$	$\frac{1}{n}$	$\frac{1}{\sqrt{n}}$
351	123201	18.7350	.002849	.0534
352	123904	18.7617	.002841	.0533
353	124609	18.7883	.002833	.0532
354	125316	18.8149	.002825	.0531
355	126025	18.8414	.002817	.0531
356	126736	18.8680	.002809	.0530
357	127449	18.8944	.002801	.0529
358	128164	18.9209	.002793	.0529
359	128881	18.9473	.002786	.0528
360	129600	18.9737	.002778	.0527
361	130321	19.0000	.002770	.0526
362	131044	19.0263	.002762	.0526
363	131769	19.0526	.002755	.0525
364	132496	19.0788	.002747	.0524
365	133225	19.1050	.002740	.0523
366	133956	19.1311	.002732	.0523
367	134689	19.1572	.002725	.0522
368	135424	19.1833	.002717	.0521
369	136161	19.2094	.002710	.0521
370	136900	19.2354	.002703	.0520
371	137641	19.2614	.002695	.0519
372	138384	19.2873	.002688	.0518
373	139129	19.3132	.002681	.0518
374	139876	19.3391	.002674	.0517
375	140625	19.3649	.002667	.0516
376	141376	19.3907	.002660	.0516
377	142129	19.4165	.002653	.0515
378	142884	19.4422	.002646	.0514
379	143641	19.4679	.002639	.0514
380	144400	19.4936	.002632	.0513
381	145161	19.5192	.002625	.0512
382	145924	19.5448	.002618	.0512
383	146689	19.5704	.002611	.0511
384	147456	19.5959	.002604	.0510
385	148225	19.6214	.002597	.0510
386	148996	19.6469	.002591	.0509
387	149769	19.6723	.002584	.0508
388	150544	19.6977	.002577	.0508
389	151321	19.7231	.002571	.0507
390	152100	19.7484	.002564	.0506
391	152881	19.7737	.002558	.0506
392	153664	19.7990	.002551	.0505
393	154449	19.8242	.002545	.0504
394	155236	19.8494	.002538	.0504
395	156025	19.8746	.002532	.0503
396	156816	19.8997	.002525	.0503
397	157609	19.9249	.002519	.0502
398	158404	19.9499	.002513	.0501
399	159210	19.9750	.002506	.0501
400	160000	20.0000	.002500	.0500

TABLE A1 (continued)

n	n^2	$\sqrt{n}$	$\frac{1}{n}$	$\frac{1}{\sqrt{n}}$
401	160801	20.0250	.002494	.0499
402	161604	20.0499	.002488	.0499
403	162409	20.0749	.002481	.0498
404	163216	20.0998	.002475	.0498
405	164025	20.1246	.002469	.0497
406	164836	20.1494	.002463	.0496
407	165649	20.1742	.002457	.0496
408	166464	20.1990	.002451	.0495
409	167281	20.2237	.002445	.0494
410	168100	20.2485	.002439	.0494
411	168921	20.2731	.002433	.0493
412	169744	20.2978	.002427	.0493
413	170569	20.3224	.002421	.0492
414	171396	20.3470	.002415	.0491
415	172225	20.3715	.002410	.0491
416	173056	20.3961	.002404	.0490
417	173889	20.4206	.002398	.0490
418	174724	20.4450	.002392	.0489
419	175561	20.4695	.002387	.0489
420	176400	20.4939	.002381	.0488
421	177241	20.5183	.002375	.0487
422	178084	20.5426	.002370	.0487
423	178929	20.5670	.002364	.0486
424	179776	20.5913	.002358	.0486
425	180625	20.6155	.002353	.0485
426	181476	20.6398	.002347	.0485
427	182329	20.6640	.002342	.0484
428	183184	20.6882	.002336	.0483
429	184041	20.7123	.002331	.0483
430	184900	20.7364	.002326	.0482
431	185761	20.7605	.002320	.0482
432	186624	20.7846	.002315	.0481
433	187489	20.8087	.002309	.0481
434	188356	20.8327	.002304	.0480
435	189225	20.8567	.002299	.0479
436	190096	20.8806	.002294	.0479
437	190969	20.9045	.002288	.0478
438	191844	20.9284	.002283	.0478
439	192721	20.9523	.002278	.0477
440	193600	20.9762	.002273	.0477
441	194481	21.0000	.002268	.0476
442	195364	21.0238	.002262	.0476
443	196249	21.0476	.002257	.0475
444	197136	21.0713	.002252	.0475
445	198025	21.0950	.002247	.0474
446	198916	21.1187	.002242	.0474
447	199809	21.1424	.002237	.0473
448	200704	21.1660	.002232	.0472
449	201601	21.1896	.002227	.0472
450	202500	21.2132	.002222	.0471

TABLE A1 *(continued)*

n	n^2	$\sqrt{n}$	$\frac{1}{n}$	$\frac{1}{\sqrt{n}}$
451	203401	21.2368	.002217	.0471
452	204304	21.2603	.002212	.0470
453	205209	21.2838	.002208	.0470
454	206116	21.3073	.002203	.0469
455	207025	21.3307	.002198	.0469
456	207936	21.3542	.002193	.0468
457	208849	21.3776	.002188	.0468
458	209764	21.4009	.002183	.0467
459	210681	21.4243	.002179	.0467
460	211600	21.4476	.002174	.0466
461	212521	21.4709	.002169	.0466
462	213444	21.4942	.002165	.0465
463	214369	21.5174	.002160	.0465
464	215296	21.5407	.002155	.0464
465	216225	21.5639	.002151	.0464
466	217156	21.5870	.002146	.0463
467	218089	21.6102	.002141	.0463
468	219024	21.6333	.002137	.0462
469	219961	21.6564	.002132	.0462
470	220900	21.6795	.002128	.0461
471	221841	21.7025	.002123	.0461
472	222784	21.7256	.002119	.0460
473	223729	21.7486	.002114	.0460
474	224676	21.7715	.002110	.0459
475	225625	21.7945	.002105	.0459
476	226576	21.8174	.002101	.0458
477	227529	21.8403	.002096	.0458
478	228484	21.8632	.002092	.0457
479	229441	21.8861	.002088	.0457
480	230400	21.9089	.002083	.0456
481	231361	21.9317	.002079	.0456
482	232324	21.9545	.002075	.0455
483	233289	21.9773	.002070	.0455
484	234256	22.0000	.002066	.0455
485	235225	22.0227	.002062	.0454
486	236196	22.0454	.002058	.0454
487	237169	22.0681	.002053	.0453
488	238144	22.0907	.002049	.0453
489	239121	22.1133	.002045	.0452
490	240100	22.1359	.002041	.0452
491	241081	22.1585	.002037	.0451
492	242064	22.1811	.002033	.0451
493	243049	22.2036	.002028	.0450
494	244036	22.2261	.002024	.0450
495	245025	22.2486	.002020	.0449
496	246016	22.2711	.002016	.0448
497	247009	22.2935	.002012	.0449
498	248004	22.3159	.002008	.0449
499	249001	22.3383	.002004	.0448
500	250000	22.3607	.002000	.0447

TABLE A1 *(continued)*

n	n^2	$\sqrt{n}$	$\frac{1}{n}$	$\frac{1}{\sqrt{n}}$
501	251001	22.3830	.001996	.0447
502	252004	22.4054	.001992	.0446
503	253009	22.4277	.001988	.0446
504	254016	22.4499	.001984	.0445
505	255025	22.4722	.001980	.0445
506	256036	22.4944	.001976	.0445
507	257049	22.5167	.001972	.0444
508	258064	22.5389	.001969	.0444
509	259081	22.5610	.001965	.0443
510	260100	22.5832	.001961	.0443
511	261121	22.6053	.001957	.0442
512	262144	22.6274	.001953	.0442
513	263169	22.6495	.001949	.0442
514	264196	22.6716	.001946	.0441
515	265225	22.6936	.001942	.0441
516	266256	22.7156	.001938	.0440
517	267289	22.7376	.001934	.0440
518	268324	22.7596	.001931	.0439
519	269361	22.7816	.001927	.0439
520	270400	22.8035	.001923	.0439
521	271441	22.8254	.001919	.0438
522	272484	22.8473	.001916	.0438
523	273529	22.8692	.001912	.0437
524	274576	22.8910	.001908	.0437
525	275625	22.9129	.001905	.0436
526	276676	22.9347	.001901	.0436
527	277729	22.9565	.001898	.0436
528	278784	22.9783	.001894	.0435
529	279841	23.0000	.001890	.0435
530	280900	23.0217	.001887	.0434
531	281961	23.0434	.001883	.0434
532	283024	23.0651	.001880	.0434
533	284089	23.0868	.001876	.0433
534	285156	23.1084	.001873	.0433
535	286225	23.1301	.001869	.0432
536	287296	23.1517	.001866	.0432
536	288369	23.1733	.001862	.0432
538	289444	23.1948	.001859	.0431
539	290521	23.2164	.001855	.0431
540	291600	23.2379	.001852	.0430
541	292681	23.2594	.001848	.0430
542	293764	23.2809	.001845	.0430
543	294849	23.3024	.001842	.0429
544	295936	23.3238	.001838	.0429
545	297025	23.3452	.001835	.0428
546	298116	23.3666	.001832	.0428
547	299209	23.3880	.001828	.0428
548	300304	23.4094	.001825	.0427
549	301401	23.4307	.001821	.0427
550	302500	23.4521	.001818	.0426

TABLE A1 *(continued)*

n	n^2	$\sqrt{n}$	$\frac{1}{n}$	$\frac{1}{\sqrt{n}}$
551	303601	23.4734	.001815	.0426
552	304704	23.4947	.001812	.0426
553	305809	23.5160	.001808	.0425
554	306916	23.5372	.001805	.0425
555	308025	23.5584	.001802	.0424
556	309136	23.5797	.001799	.0424
557	310249	23.6008	.001795	.0424
558	311364	23.6220	.001792	.0423
559	312481	23.6432	.001789	.0423
560	313600	23.6643	.001786	.0423
561	314721	23.6854	.001783	.0422
562	315844	23.7065	.001779	.0422
563	316969	23.7276	.001776	.0421
564	318096	23.7487	.001773	.0421
565	319225	23.7697	.001770	.0421
566	320356	23.7908	.001767	.0420
567	321489	23.8118	.001764	.0420
568	322624	23.8328	.001761	.0420
569	323761	23.8537	.001757	.0419
570	324900	23.8747	.001754	.0419
571	326041	23.8956	.001751	.0418
572	327184	23.9165	.001748	.0418
573	328329	23.9374	.001745	.0418
574	329476	23.9583	.001742	.0417
575	330625	23.9792	.001739	.0417
576	331776	24.0000	.001736	.0417
577	332929	24.0208	.001733	.0416
578	334084	24.0416	.001730	.0416
579	335241	24.0624	.001727	.0416
580	336400	24.0832	.001724	.0415
581	337561	24.1039	.001721	.0415
582	338724	24.1247	.001718	.0415
583	339889	24.1454	.001715	.0414
584	341056	24.1661	.001712	.0414
585	342225	24.1868	.001709	.0413
586	343396	24.2074	.001706	.0413
587	344569	24.2281	.001704	.0413
588	345744	24.2487	.001701	.0412
589	346921	24.2693	.001698	.0412
590	348100	24.2899	.001695	.0412
591	349281	24.3105	.001692	.0411
592	350464	24.3311	.001689	.0411
593	351649	24.3516	.001686	.0411
594	352836	24.3721	.001684	.0410
595	354025	24.3926	.001681	.0410
596	355216	24.4131	.001678	.0410
597	356409	24.4336	.001675	.0409
598	357604	24.4540	.001672	.0409
599	358801	24.4745	.001669	.0409
600	360000	24.4949	.001667	.0408

TABLE A1 (*continued*)

n	n^2	$\sqrt{n}$	$\frac{1}{n}$	$\frac{1}{\sqrt{n}}$
601	361201	24.5153	.001664	.0408
602	362404	24.5357	.001661	.0408
603	363609	24.5561	.001658	.0407
604	364816	24.5764	.001656	.0407
605	366025	24.5967	.001653	.0407
606	367236	24.6171	.001650	.0406
607	368449	24.6374	.001647	.0406
608	369664	24.6577	.001645	.0406
609	370881	24.6779	.001642	.0405
610	372100	24.6982	.001639	.0405
611	373321	24.7184	.001637	.0405
612	374544	24.7386	.001634	.0404
613	375769	24.7588	.001631	.0404
614	376996	24.7790	.001629	.0404
615	378225	24.7992	.001626	.0403
616	379456	24.8193	.001623	.0403
617	380689	24.8395	.001621	.0403
618	381924	24.8596	.001618	.0402
619	383161	24.8797	.001616	.0402
620	384400	24.8998	.001613	.0402
621	385641	24.9199	.001610	.0401
622	386884	24.9399	.001608	.0401
623	388129	24.9600	.001605	.0401
624	389376	24.9800	.001603	.0400
625	390625	25.0000	.001600	.0400
626	391876	25.0200	.001597	.0400
627	393129	25.0400	.001595	.0399
628	394384	25.0599	.001592	.0399
629	395641	25.0799	.001590	.0399
630	396900	25.0998	.001587	.0398
631	398161	25.1197	.001585	.0398
632	399424	25.1396	.001582	.0398
633	400689	25.1595	.001580	.0397
634	401956	25.1794	.001577	.0397
635	403225	25.1992	.001575	.0397
636	404496	25.2190	.001572	.0397
637	405769	25.2389	.001570	.0396
638	407044	25.2587	.001567	.0396
639	408321	25.2784	.001565	.0396
640	409600	25.2982	.001563	.0395
641	410881	25.3180	.001560	.0395
642	412164	25.3377	.001558	.0395
643	413449	25.3574	.001555	.0394
644	414736	25.3772	.001553	.0394
645	416025	25.3969	.001550	.0394
646	417316	25.4165	.001548	.0393
647	418609	25.4362	.001546	.0393
648	419904	25.4558	.001543	.0393
649	421201	25.4755	.001541	.0393
650	422500	25.4951	.001538	.0392

TABLE A1 *(continued)*

n	n^2	$\sqrt{n}$	$\frac{1}{n}$	$\frac{1}{\sqrt{n}}$
651	423801	25.5147	.001536	.0392
652	425104	25.5343	.001534	.0392
653	426409	25.5539	.001531	.0391
654	427716	25.5734	.001529	.0391
655	429025	25.5930	.001527	.0391
656	430336	25.6125	.001524	.0390
657	431649	25.6320	.001522	.0390
658	432964	25.6515	.001520	.0390
659	434281	25.6710	.001517	.0390
660	435600	25.6905	.001515	.0389
661	436921	25.7099	.001513	.0389
662	438244	25.7294	.001511	.0389
663	439569	25.7488	.001508	.0388
664	440896	25.7682	.001506	.0388
665	442225	25.7876	.001504	.0388
666	443556	25.8070	.001502	.0387
667	444889	25.8263	.001499	.0387
668	446224	25.8457	.001497	.0387
669	447561	25.8650	.001495	.0387
670	448900	25.8844	.001493	.0386
671	450241	25.9037	.001490	.0386
672	451584	25.9230	.001488	.0386
673	452929	25.9422	.001486	.0385
674	454276	25.9615	.001484	.0385
675	455625	25.9808	.001481	.0385
676	456976	26.0000	.001479	.0385
677	458329	26.0192	.001477	.0384
678	459684	26.0384	.001475	.0384
679	461041	26.0576	.001473	.0384
680	462400	26.0768	.001471	.0383
681	463761	26.0960	.001468	.0383
682	465124	26.1151	.001466	.0383
683	466489	26.1343	.001464	.0383
684	467856	26.1534	.001462	.0382
685	469225	26.1725	.001460	.0382
686	470596	26.1916	.001458	.0382
687	471969	26.2107	.001456	.0382
688	473344	26.2298	.001453	.0381
689	474721	26.2488	.001451	.0381
690	476100	26.2679	.001449	.0381
691	477481	26.2869	.001447	.0380
692	478864	26.3059	.001445	.0380
693	480249	26.3249	.001443	.0380
694	481636	26.3439	.001441	.0380
695	483025	26.3629	.001439	.0379
696	484416	26.3818	.001437	.0379
697	485809	26.4008	.001435	.0379
698	487204	26.4197	.001433	.0379
699	488601	26.4386	.001431	.0378
700	490000	26.4575	.001429	.0378

TABLE A1 (*continued*)

n	n^2	$\sqrt{n}$	$\frac{1}{n}$	$\frac{1}{\sqrt{n}}$
701	491401	26.4764	.001427	.0378
702	492804	26.4953	.001425	.0377
703	494209	26.5141	.001422	.0377
704	495616	26.5330	.001420	.0377
705	497025	26.5518	.001418	.0377
706	498436	26.5707	.001416	.0376
707	499849	26.5895	.001414	.0376
708	501264	26.6083	.001412	.0376
709	502681	26.6271	.001410	.0376
710	504100	26.6458	.001408	.0375
711	505521	26.6646	.001406	.0375
712	506944	26.6833	.001404	.0375
713	508369	26.7021	.001403	.0375
714	509796	26.7208	.001401	.0374
715	511225	26.7395	.001399	.0374
716	512656	26.7582	.001397	.0374
717	514089	26.7769	.001395	.0373
718	515524	26.7955	.001393	.0373
719	516961	26.8142	.001391	.0373
720	518400	26.8328	.001389	.0373
721	519841	26.8514	.001387	.0372
722	521284	26.8701	.001385	.0372
723	522729	26.8887	.001383	.0372
724	524176	26.9072	.001381	.0372
725	525625	26.9258	.001379	.0371
726	527076	26.9444	.001377	.0371
727	528529	26.9629	.001376	.0371
728	529984	26.9815	.001374	.0371
729	531441	27.0000	.001372	.0370
730	532900	27.0185	.001370	.0370
731	534361	27.0370	.001368	.0370
732	535824	27.0555	.001366	.0370
733	537289	27.0740	.001364	.0369
734	538756	27.0924	.001362	.0369
735	540225	27.1109	.001361	.0369
736	541696	26.1293	.001359	.0369
737	543169	27.1477	.001357	.0368
738	544644	27.1662	.001355	.0368
739	546121	27.1846	.001353	.0368
740	547600	27.2029	.001351	.0368
741	549081	27.2213	.001350	.0367
742	550564	27.2397	.001348	.0367
743	552049	27.2580	.001346	.0367
744	553536	27.2764	.001344	.0367
745	555025	27.2947	.001342	.0366
746	556516	27.3130	.001340	.0366
747	558009	27.3313	.001339	.0366
748	559504	27.3496	.001337	.0366
749	561001	27.3679	.001335	.0365
750	562500	27.3861	.001333	.0365

TABLE A1 (continued)

n	n^2	$\sqrt{n}$	$\frac{1}{n}$	$\frac{1}{\sqrt{n}}$
751	564001	27.4044	.001332	.0365
752	565504	27.4226	.001330	.0365
753	567009	27.4408	.001328	.0364
754	568516	27.4591	.001326	.0364
755	570025	27.4773	.001325	.0364
756	571536	27.4955	.001323	.0364
757	573049	27.5136	.001321	.0363
758	574564	27.5318	.001319	.0363
759	576081	27.5500	.001318	.0363
760	577600	27.5681	.001316	.0363
761	579121	27.5862	.001314	.0363
762	580644	27.6043	.001312	.0362
763	582169	27.6225	.001311	.0362
764	583696	27.6405	.001309	.0362
765	585225	27.6586	.001307	.0362
766	586756	27.6767	.001305	.0361
767	588289	27.6948	.001304	.0361
768	589824	27.7128	.001302	.0361
769	591361	27.7308	.001300	.0361
770	592900	27.7489	.001299	.0360
771	594441	27.7669	.001297	.0360
772	595984	27.7849	.001295	.0360
773	597529	27.8029	.001294	.0360
774	599076	27.8209	.001292	.0359
775	600625	27.8388	.001290	.0359
776	602176	27.8568	.001289	.0359
777	603729	27.8747	.001287	.0359
778	605284	27.8927	.001285	.0359
779	606841	27.9106	.001284	.0358
780	608400	27.9285	.001282	.0358
781	609961	27.9464	.001280	.0358
782	611524	27.9643	.001279	.0358
783	613089	27.9821	.001277	.0357
784	614656	28.0000	.001276	.0357
785	616225	28.0179	.001274	.0357
786	617796	28.0357	.001272	.0357
787	619369	28.0535	.001271	.0356
788	620944	28.0713	.001269	.0356
789	622521	28.0891	.001267	.0356
790	624100	28.1069	.001266	.0356
791	625681	28.1247	.001264	.0356
792	627264	28.1425	.001263	.0355
793	628849	28.1603	.001261	.0355
794	630436	28.1780	.001259	.0355
795	632025	28.1957	.001258	.0355
796	633616	28.2135	.001256	.0354
797	635209	28.2312	.001255	.0354
798	636804	28.2489	.001253	.0354
799	638401	28.2666	.001252	.0354
800	640000	28.2843	.001250	.0354

TABLE A1 *(continued)*

n	n^2	$\sqrt{n}$	$\frac{1}{n}$	$\frac{1}{\sqrt{n}}$
801	641601	28.3019	.001248	.0353
802	643204	28.3196	.001247	.0353
803	644809	28.3373	.001245	.0353
804	646416	28.3549	.001244	.0353
805	648025	28.3725	.001242	.0352
806	649636	28.3901	.001241	.0352
807	651249	28.4077	.001239	.0352
808	652864	28.4253	.001248	.0352
809	654481	28.4429	.001236	.0352
810	656100	28.4605	.001235	.0351
811	657721	28.4781	.001233	.0351
812	659344	28.4956	.001232	.0351
813	660969	28.5132	.001230	.0351
814	662596	28.5307	.001229	.0351
815	664225	28.5482	.001227	.0350
816	665856	28.5657	.001225	.0350
817	667489	28.5832	.001224	.0350
818	669124	28.6007	.001222	.0350
819	670761	28.6182	.001221	.0349
820	672400	28.6356	.001220	.0349
821	674041	28.6531	.001218	.0349
822	675684	28.6705	.001217	.0349
823	677329	28.6880	.001215	.0349
824	678976	28.7054	.001214	.0348
825	680625	28.7228	.001212	.0348
826	682276	28.7402	.001211	.0348
827	683929	28.7576	.001209	.0348
828	685584	28.7750	.001208	.0348
829	687241	28.7924	.001206	.0347
830	688900	28.8097	.001205	.0347
831	690561	28.8271	.001203	.0347
832	692224	28.8444	.001202	.0347
833	693889	28.8617	.001200	.0346
834	695556	28.8791	.001199	.0346
835	697225	28.8964	.001198	.0346
836	698896	28.9137	.001196	.0346
837	700569	28.9310	.001195	.0346
838	702244	28.9482	.001193	.0345
839	703921	28.9655	.001192	.0345
840	705600	28.9828	.001190	.0345
841	707281	29.0000	.001189	.0345
842	708964	29.0172	.001188	.0345
843	710649	29.0345	.001186	.0344
844	712336	29.0517	.001185	.0344
845	714025	29.0689	.001183	.0344
846	715716	29.0861	.001182	.0344
847	717409	29.1033	.001181	.0344
848	719104	29.1204	.001179	.0343
849	720801	29.1376	.001178	.0343
850	722500	29.1548	.001176	.0343

TABLE A1 *(continued)*

n	n^2	$\sqrt{n}$	$\frac{1}{n}$	$\frac{1}{\sqrt{n}}$
851	724201	29.1719	.001175	.0343
852	725904	29.1890	.001174	.0343
853	727609	29.2062	.001172	.0342
854	729316	29.2233	.001171	.0342
855	731025	29.2404	.001170	.0342
856	732736	29.2575	.001168	.0342
857	734449	29.2746	.001167	.0342
858	736164	29.2916	.001166	.0341
859	737881	29.3087	.001164	.0341
860	739600	29.3258	.001163	.0341
861	741321	29.3428	.001161	.0341
862	743044	29.3598	.001160	.0341
863	744769	29.3769	.001159	.0340
864	746496	29.3939	.001157	.0340
865	748225	29.4109	.001156	.0340
866	749956	29.4279	.001155	.0340
867	751689	29.4449	.001153	.0340
868	753424	29.4618	.001152	.0339
869	755161	29.4788	.001151	.0339
870	756900	29.4958	.001149	.0339
871	758641	29.5127	.001148	.0339
872	760384	29.5296	.001147	.0339
873	762129	29.5466	.001145	.0338
874	763876	29.5635	.001144	.0338
875	765625	29.5804	.001143	.0338
876	767376	29.5973	.001142	.0338
877	769129	29.6142	.001140	.0338
878	770884	29.6311	.001139	.0337
879	772641	29.6479	.001138	.0337
880	774400	29.6648	.001136	.0337
881	776161	29.6816	.001135	.0337
882	777924	29.6985	.001134	.0337
883	779689	29.7153	.001133	.0337
884	781456	29.7321	.001131	.0336
885	783225	29.7489	.001130	.0336
886	784996	29.7658	.001129	.0336
887	786769	29.7825	.001127	.0336
888	788544	29.7993	.001126	.0336
889	790321	29.8161	.001125	.0335
890	792100	29.8329	.001124	.0335
891	793881	29.8496	.001122	.0335
892	795664	29.8664	.001121	.0335
893	797449	29.8831	.001120	.0335
894	799236	29.8998	.001119	.0334
895	801025	29.9166	.001117	.0334
896	802816	29.9333	.001116	.0334
897	804609	29.9500	.001115	.0334
898	806404	29.9666	.001114	.0334
899	808201	29.9833	.001112	.0334
900	810000	30.0000	.001111	.0333

TABLE A1 *(continued)*

n	n^2	$\sqrt{n}$	$\frac{1}{n}$	$\frac{1}{\sqrt{n}}$
901	811801	30.0167	.001110	.0333
902	813604	30.0333	.001109	.0333
903	815409	30.0500	.001107	.0333
904	817216	30.0666	.001106	.0333
905	819025	30.0832	.001105	.0332
906	820836	30.0998	.001104	.0332
907	822649	30.1164	.001103	.0332
908	824464	30.1330	.001101	.0332
909	826281	30.1496	.001100	.0332
910	828100	30.1662	.001099	.0331
911	829921	30.1828	.001098	.0331
912	831744	30.1993	.001096	.0331
913	833569	30.2159	.001095	.0331
914	835396	30.2324	.001094	.0331
915	837225	30.2490	.001093	.0331
916	839056	30.2655	.001092	.0330
917	840889	30.2820	.001091	.0330
918	842724	30.2985	.001089	.0330
919	844561	30.3150	.001088	.0330
920	846400	30.3315	.001087	.0330
921	848241	30.3480	.001086	.0330
922	850084	30.3645	.001085	.0329
923	851929	30.3809	.001083	.0329
924	853776	30.3974	.001082	.0329
925	855625	30.4138	.001081	.0329
926	857476	30.4302	.001080	.0329
927	859329	30.4467	.001079	.0238
928	861184	30.4631	.001078	.0328
929	863041	30.4795	.001076	.0328
930	864900	30.4959	.001075	.0328
931	866761	30.5123	.001074	.0328
932	868624	30.5287	.001073	.0328
933	870489	30.5450	.001072	.0327
934	872356	30.5614	.001071	.0327
935	874225	30.5778	.001070	.0327
936	876096	30.5941	.001068	.0327
937	877969	30.6105	.001067	.0327
938	879844	30.6268	.001066	.0327
939	881721	30.6431	.001065	.0326
940	883600	30.6594	.001064	.0326
941	885481	30.6757	.001063	.0326
942	887364	30.6920	.001062	.0326
943	889249	30.7083	.001060	.0326
944	891136	30.7246	.001059	.0325
945	893025	30.7409	.001058	.0325
946	894916	30.7571	.001057	.0325
947	896809	30.7734	.001056	.0325
948	898704	30.7896	.001055	.0325
949	900601	30.8058	.001054	.0325
950	902500	30.8221	.001053	.0324

TABLE A1 (*continued*)

n	n^2	$\sqrt{n}$	$\frac{1}{n}$	$\frac{1}{\sqrt{n}}$
951	904401	30.8383	.001052	.0324
952	906304	30.8545	.001050	.0324
953	908209	30.8707	.001049	.0324
954	910116	30.8869	.001048	.0324
955	912025	30.9031	.001047	.0324
956	913936	30.9192	.001046	.0323
957	915849	30.9354	.001045	.0323
958	917764	30.9516	.001044	.0323
959	919681	30.9677	.001043	.0323
960	921600	30.9839	.001042	.0323
961	923521	31.0000	.001041	.0323
962	925444	31.0161	.001040	.0322
963	927369	31.0322	.001038	.0322
964	929296	31.0483	.001037	.0322
965	931225	31.0644	.001036	.0322
966	933156	31.0805	.001035	.0322
967	935089	31.0966	.001034	.0322
968	937024	31.1127	.001033	.0321
969	938961	31.1288	.001032	.0321
970	940900	31.1448	.001031	.0321
971	942841	31.1609	.001030	.0321
972	944784	31.1769	.001029	.0321
973	946729	31.1929	.001028	.0321
974	948676	31.2090	.001027	.0320
975	950625	31.2250	.001026	.0320
976	952576	31.2410	.001025	.0320
977	954529	31.2570	.001024	.0320
978	956484	31.2730	.001022	.0320
979	958441	31.2890	.001021	.0320
980	960400	31.3050	.001020	.0319
981	962361	31.3209	.001019	.0319
982	964324	31.3369	.001018	.0319
983	966289	31.3528	.001017	.0319
984	968256	31.3688	.001016	.0319
985	970225	31.3847	.001015	.0319
986	972196	31.4006	.001014	.0318
987	974169	31.4166	.001013	.0318
988	976144	31.4325	.001012	.0318
989	978121	31.4484	.001011	.0318
990	980100	31.4643	.001010	.0318
991	982081	31.4802	.001009	.0318
992	984064	31.4960	.001008	.0318
993	986049	31.5119	.001007	.0317
994	988036	31.5278	.001006	.0317
995	990025	31.5436	.001005	.0317
996	992016	31.5595	.001004	.0317
997	994009	31.5753	.001003	.0317
998	996004	31.5911	.001002	.0317
999	998001	31.6070	.001001	.0316
1000	1000000	31.6228	.001000	.0316

TABLE A2
Random Numbers.

10097	32533	76520	13586	34673	54876	80959	09117	39292	74945
37542	04805	64894	74296	24805	24037	20636	10402	00822	91665
08422	68953	19645	09303	23209	02560	15953	34764	35080	33606
99019	02529	09376	70715	38311	31165	88676	74397	04436	27659
12807	99970	80157	36147	64032	36653	98951	16877	12171	76833
66065	74717	34072	76850	36697	36170	65813	39885	11199	29170
31060	10805	45571	82406	35303	42614	86799	07439	23403	09732
85269	77602	02051	65692	68665	74818	73053	85247	18623	88579
63573	32135	05325	47048	90553	57548	28468	28709	83491	25624
73796	45753	03529	64778	35808	34282	60935	20344	35273	88435
98520	17767	14905	68607	22109	40558	60970	93433	50500	73998
11805	05431	39808	27732	50725	68248	29405	24201	52775	67851
83452	99634	06288	98083	13746	70078	18475	40610	68711	77817
88685	40200	86507	58401	36766	67951	90364	76493	29609	11062
99594	67348	87517	64969	91826	08928	93785	61368	23478	34113
65481	17674	17468	50950	58047	76974	73039	57186	40218	16544
80124	35635	17727	08015	45318	22374	21115	78253	14385	53763
74350	99817	77402	77214	43236	00210	45521	64237	96286	02655
69916	26803	66252	29148	36936	87203	76621	13990	94400	56418
09893	20505	14225	68514	46427	56788	96297	78822	54382	14598
91499	14523	68479	27686	46162	83554	94750	89923	37089	20048
80336	94598	26940	36858	70297	34135	53140	33340	42050	82341
44104	81949	85157	47954	32979	26575	57600	40881	22222	06413
12550	73742	11100	02040	12860	74697	96644	89439	28707	25815
63606	49329	16505	34484	40219	52563	43651	77082	07207	31790
61196	90446	26457	47774	51924	33729	65394	59593	42582	60527
15474	45266	95270	79953	59367	83848	82396	10118	33211	59466
94557	28573	67897	54387	54622	44431	91190	42592	92927	45973
42481	16213	97344	08721	16868	48767	03071	12059	25701	46670
23523	78317	73208	89837	68935	91416	26252	29663	05522	82562
04493	52494	75246	33824	45862	51025	61962	79335	65337	12472
00549	97654	64051	88159	96119	63896	54692	82391	23287	29529
35963	15307	26898	09354	33351	35462	77974	50024	90103	39333
59808	08391	45427	26842	83609	49700	13021	24892	78565	20106
46058	85236	01390	92286	77281	44077	93910	83647	70617	42941
32179	00597	87379	25241	05567	07007	86743	17157	85394	11838
69234	61406	20117	45204	15956	60000	18743	92423	97118	96338
19565	41430	01758	75379	40419	21585	66674	36806	84962	85207
45155	14938	19476	07246	43667	94543	59047	90033	20826	69541
94864	31994	36168	10851	34888	81553	01540	35456	05014	51176
98086	24826	45240	28404	44999	08896	39094	73407	35441	31880
33185	16232	41941	50949	89435	48581	88695	41994	37548	73043
80951	00406	96382	70774	20151	23387	25016	25298	94624	61171
79752	49140	71961	28296	69861	02591	74852	20539	00387	59579
18633	32537	98145	06571	31010	24674	05455	61427	77938	91936
74029	43902	77557	32270	97790	17119	52527	58021	80814	51748
54178	45611	80993	37143	05335	12969	56127	19255	36040	90324
11664	49883	52079	84827	59381	71539	09973	33440	88461	23356
48324	77928	31249	64710	02295	36870	32307	57546	15020	09994
69074	94138	87637	91976	35584	04401	10518	21615	01848	76938

Source: The Rand Corporation, *A Million Random Digits* (New York: The Free Press, 1955). By permission of the publishers.

TABLE A2 *(continued)*

09188	20097	32825	39527	04220	86304	83389	87374	64278	58044
90045	85497	51981	50654	94938	81997	91870	76150	68476	64659
73189	50207	47677	26269	62290	64464	27124	67018	41361	82760
75768	76490	20971	87749	90429	12272	95375	05871	93823	43178
54016	44056	66281	31003	00682	27398	20714	53295	07706	17813
08358	69910	78542	42785	13661	58873	04618	97553	31223	08420
28306	03264	81333	10591	40510	07893	32604	60475	94119	01840
53840	86233	81594	13628	51215	90290	28466	68795	77762	20791
91757	53741	61613	62269	50263	90212	55781	76514	83483	47055
89415	92694	00397	58391	12607	17646	48949	72306	94541	37408
77513	03820	86864	29901	68414	82774	51908	13980	72893	55507
19502	37174	69979	20288	55210	29773	74287	75251	65344	67415
21818	59313	93278	81757	05686	73156	07082	85046	31853	38452
51474	66499	68107	23621	94049	91345	42836	09191	08007	45449
99559	68331	62535	24170	69777	12830	74819	78142	43860	72834
33713	48007	93584	72869	51926	64721	58303	29822	93174	93972
85274	86893	11303	22970	28834	34137	73515	90400	71148	43643
84133	89640	44035	52166	73852	70091	61222	60561	62327	18423
56732	16234	17395	96131	10123	91622	85496	57560	81604	18880
65138	56806	87648	85261	34313	65861	45875	21069	85644	47277
38001	02176	81719	11711	71602	92937	74219	64049	65584	49698
37402	96397	01304	77586	56271	10086	47324	62605	40030	37438
97125	40348	87083	31417	21815	39250	75237	62047	15501	29578
21826	41134	47143	34072	64638	85902	49139	06441	03856	54552
73135	42742	95719	09035	85794	74296	08789	88156	64691	19202
07638	77929	03061	18072	96207	44156	23821	99538	04713	66994
60528	83441	07954	19814	59175	20695	05533	52139	61212	06455
83596	35655	06958	92983	05128	09719	77433	53783	92301	50498
10850	62746	99599	10507	13499	06319	53075	71839	06410	19362
39820	98952	43622	63147	64421	80814	43800	09351	31024	73167
59580	06478	75569	78800	88835	54486	23768	06156	04111	08408
38508	07341	23793	48763	90822	97022	17719	04207	95954	49953
30692	70668	94688	16127	56196	80091	82067	63400	05462	69200
65443	95659	18288	27437	49632	24041	08337	65676	96299	90836
27267	50264	13192	72294	07477	44606	17985	48911	97341	30358
91307	06991	19072	24210	36699	53728	28825	35793	28976	66252
68434	94688	84473	13622	62126	98408	12843	82590	09815	93146
48908	15877	54745	24591	35700	04754	83824	52692	54130	55160
06913	45197	42672	78601	11883	09528	63011	98901	14974	40344
10455	16019	14210	33712	91342	37821	88325	80851	43667	70883
12883	97343	65027	61184	04285	01392	17974	15077	90712	26769
21778	30976	38807	36961	31649	42096	63281	02023	08816	47449
19523	59515	65122	59659	86283	68258	69572	13798	16435	91529
67245	52670	35583	16563	79246	86686	76463	34222	26655	90802
60584	47377	07500	37992	45134	26529	26760	83637	41326	44344
53853	41377	36066	94850	58838	73859	49364	73331	96240	43642
24637	38736	74384	89342	52623	07992	12369	18601	03742	83873
83080	12451	38992	22815	07759	51777	97377	27585	51972	37867
16444	24334	36151	99073	27493	70939	85130	32552	54846	54759
60790	18157	57178	65762	11161	78576	45819	52979	65130	04860

TABLE A2 *(continued)*

03991	10461	93716	16894	66083	24653	84609	58232	88618	19161
38555	95554	32886	59780	08355	60860	29735	47762	71299	23853
17546	73704	92052	46215	55121	29281	59076	07936	27954	58909
32643	52861	95819	06831	00911	98936	76355	93779	80863	00514
69572	68777	39510	35905	14060	40619	29549	69616	33564	60780
24122	66591	27699	06494	14845	46672	61958	77100	90899	75754
61196	30231	92962	61773	41839	55382	17267	70943	78038	70267
30532	21704	10274	12202	39685	23309	10061	68829	55986	66485
03788	97599	75867	20717	74416	53166	35208	33374	87539	08823
48228	63379	85783	47619	53152	67433	35663	52972	16818	60311
60365	94653	35075	33949	42614	29297	01918	28316	98953	73231
83799	42402	56623	34442	34994	41374	70071	14736	09958	18065
32960	07405	36409	83232	99385	41600	11133	07586	15917	06253
19322	53845	57620	52606	66497	68646	78138	66559	19640	99413
11220	94747	07399	37408	48509	23929	27482	45476	85244	35159
31751	57260	68980	05339	15470	48355	88651	22596	03152	19121
88492	99382	14454	04504	20094	98977	74843	93413	22109	78508
30934	47744	07481	83828	73788	06533	28597	20405	94205	20380
22888	48893	27499	98748	60530	45128	74022	84617	82037	10268
78212	16993	35902	91386	44372	15486	65741	14014	87481	37220
41849	84547	46850	52326	34677	58300	74910	64345	19325	81549
46352	33049	69248	93460	45305	07521	61318	31855	14413	70951
11087	96294	14013	31792	59747	67277	76503	34513	39663	77544
52701	08337	56303	87315	16520	69676	11654	99893	02181	68161
57275	36898	81304	48585	68652	27376	92852	55866	88448	03584
20857	73156	70284	24326	79375	95220	01159	63267	10622	48391
15633	84924	90415	93614	33521	26665	55823	47641	86225	31704
92694	48297	39904	02115	59589	49067	66821	41575	49767	04037
77613	19019	88152	00080	20554	91409	96277	48257	50816	97616
38688	32486	45134	63545	59404	72059	43947	51680	43852	59693
25163	01889	70014	15021	41290	67312	71857	15957	68971	11403
65251	07629	37239	33295	05870	01119	92784	26340	18477	65622
36815	43625	18637	37509	82444	99005	04921	73701	14707	93997
64397	11692	05327	82162	20247	81759	45197	25332	83745	22567
04515	25624	95096	67946	48460	85558	15191	18782	16930	33361
83761	60873	43253	84145	60833	25983	01291	41349	20368	07126
14387	06345	80854	09279	43529	06318	38384	74761	41196	37480
51321	92246	80088	77074	88722	56736	66164	49431	66919	31678
72472	00008	80890	18002	94813	31900	54155	83436	35352	54131
05466	55306	93128	18464	74457	90561	72848	11834	79982	68416
39528	72484	82474	25593	48545	35247	18619	13674	18611	19241
81616	18711	53342	44276	75122	11724	74627	73707	58319	15997
07586	16120	82641	22820	92904	13141	32392	19763	61199	67940
90767	04235	13574	17200	69902	63742	78464	22501	18627	90872
40188	28193	29593	88627	94972	11598	62095	36787	00441	58997
34414	82157	86887	55087	19152	00023	12302	80783	32624	68691
63439	75363	44989	16822	36024	00867	76378	41605	65961	73488
67049	09070	93399	45547	94458	74284	05041	49807	20288	34060
79495	04146	52162	90286	54158	34243	46978	35482	59362	95938
91704	30552	04737	21031	75051	93029	47665	64382	99782	93478

TABLE A3

Areas Under the Normal Curve: Fractions of Unit Area from 0 to Z.

The Z values are expressed to the nearest hundredth. The left-hand column contains the first two digits of the Z value. The values across the top of the table are third digits. To determine the proportion of curve area from the mean to a $Z = 1.45$, find 1.4 down the left-hand column. Next, find .05 across the top of the table. Where these values intersect in the body of the table defines the proportion of curve area. In the case of a $Z = 1.45$, the proportion of curve area is .4265.

Z	0.00	0.01	0.02	0.03	0.04	0.05	0.06	0.07	0.08	0.09
0.0	0.0000	0.0040	0.0080	0.0120	0.0160	0.0199	0.0239	0.0279	0.0319	0.0359
0.1	.0398	.0438	.0478	.0517	.0557	.0596	.0636	.0675	.0714	.0753
0.2	.0793	.0832	.0871	.0910	.0948	.0987	.1026	.1064	.1103	.1141
0.3	.1179	.1217	.1255	.1293	.1331	.1368	.1406	.1443	.1480	.1517
0.4	.1554	.1591	.1628	.1664	.1700	.1736	.1772	.1808	.1844	.1879
0.5	.1915	.1950	.1985	.2019	.2054	.2088	.2123	.2157	.2190	.2224
0.6	.2257	.2291	.2324	.2357	.2389	.2422	.2454	.2486	.2517	.2549
0.7	.2580	.2611	.2642	.2673	.2704	.2734	.2764	.2794	.2823	.2852
0.8	.2881	.2910	.2939	.2967	.2995	.3023	.3051	.3078	.3106	.3133
0.9	.3159	.3186	.3212	.3238	.3264	.3289	.3315	.3340	.3365	.3389
1.0	.3413	.3438	.3461	.3485	.3508	.3531	.3554	.3577	.3599	.3621
1.1	.3643	.3665	.3686	.3708	.3729	.3749	.3770	.3790	.3810	.3830
1.2	.3849	.3869	.3888	.3907	.3925	.3944	.3962	.3980	.3997	.4015
1.3	.4032	.4049	.4066	.4082	.4099	.4115	.4131	.4147	.4162	.4177
1.4	.4192	.4207	.4222	.4236	.4251	.4265	.4279	.4292	.4306	.4319
1.5	.4332	.4345	.4357	.4370	.4382	.4394	.4406	.4418	.4429	.4441
1.6	.4452	.4463	.4474	.4484	.4495	.4505	.4515	.4525	.4535	.4545
1.7	.4554	.4564	.4573	.4582	.4591	.4599	.4608	.4616	.4625	.4633
1.8	.4641	.4649	.4656	.4664	.4671	.4678	.4686	.4693	.4699	.4706
1.9	.4713	.4719	.4726	.4732	.4738	.4744	.4750	.4756	.4761	.4767
2.0	.4772	.4778	.4783	.4788	.4793	.4798	.4803	.4808	.4812	.4817
2.1	.4821	.4826	.4830	.4834	.4838	.4842	.4846	.4850	.4854	.4857
2.2	.4861	.4864	.4868	.4871	.4875	.4878	.4881	.4884	.4887	.4890
2.3	.4893	.4896	.4898	.4901	.4904	.4906	.4909	.4911	.4913	.4916
2.4	.4918	.4920	.4922	.4925	.4927	.4929	.4931	.4932	.4934	.4936
2.5	.4938	.4940	.4941	.4943	.4945	.4946	.4948	.4949	.4951	.4952
2.6	.4953	.4955	.4956	.4957	.4959	.4960	.4961	.4962	.4963	.4964
2.7	.4965	.4966	.4967	.4968	.4969	.4970	.4971	.4972	.4973	.4974
2.8	.4974	.4975	.4976	.4977	.4977	.4978	.4979	.4979	.4980	.4981
2.9	.4981	.4982	.4982	.4983	.4984	.4984	.4985	.4985	.4986	.4986
3.0	.4987	.4987	.4987	.4988	.4988	.4989	.4989	.4989	.4990	.4990
3.1	.4990	.4991	.4991	.4991	.4992	.4992	.4992	.4992	.4993	.4993
3.2	.4993	.4993	.4994	.4994	.4994	.4994	.4994	.4995	.4995	.4995
3.3	.4995	.4995	.4995	.4996	.4996	.4996	.4996	.4996	.4996	.4997
3.4	.4997	.4997	.4997	.4997	.4997	.4997	.4997	.4997	.4997	.4998
3.6	.4998	.4998	.4999	.4999	.4999	.4999	.4999	.4999	.4999	.4999
3.9	.5000									

Source: Harold O. Rugg, *Statistical Methods Applied to Education* (Boston: Houghton Mifflin Company, 1917), Table III, pp. 389–390. With the permission of the publishers. Reprinted by permission from *Statistical Methods*, 6th edition, by George W. Snedecor and William G. Cochran. © 1967 by the Iowa State University Press, Ames, Iowa.

TABLE A4

Distribution of χ^2.

Degrees of freedom are defined as $k - 1$ for single samples, where k = the number of categories into which the data are divided. For 2 × 2 tables or larger, df = (rows − 1) (columns − 1). Probabilities for a two-tailed test are shown across the top of the table. For one-tailed test interpretations, simply halve the probability shown; i.e., .10 (two-tailed) becomes .10/2 = .05 for a one-tailed probability.

	Probability													
df	.99	.98	.95	.90	.80	.70	.50	.30	.20	.10	.05	.02	.01	.001
1	$.0^3157$	$.0^3628$	.00393	.0158	.0642	.148	.455	1.074	1.642	2.706	3.841	5.412	6.635	10.827
2	.0201	.0404	.103	.211	.446	.713	1.386	2.408	3.219	4.605	5.991	7.824	9.210	13.815
3	.115	.185	.352	.584	1.005	1.424	2.366	3.665	4.642	6.251	7.815	9.837	11.345	16.268
4	.297	.429	.711	1.064	1.649	2.195	3.357	4.878	5.989	7.779	9.488	11.668	13.277	18.465
5	.554	.752	1.145	1.610	2.343	3.000	4.351	6.064	7.289	9.236	11.070	13.388	15.086	20.517
6	.872	1.134	1.635	2.204	3.070	3.828	5.348	7.231	8.558	10.645	12.592	15.033	16.812	22.457
7	1.239	1.564	2.167	2.833	3.822	4.671	6.346	8.383	9.803	12.017	14.067	16.622	18.475	24.322
8	1.646	2.032	2.733	3.490	4.594	5.527	7.344	9.524	11.030	13.362	15.507	18.168	20.090	26.125
9	2.088	2.532	3.325	4.168	5.380	6.393	8.343	10.656	12.242	14.684	16.919	19.679	21.666	27.877
10	2.558	3.059	3.940	4.865	6.179	7.267	9.342	11.781	13.442	15.987	18.307	21.161	23.209	29.588
11	3.053	3.609	4.575	5.578	6.989	8.148	10.341	12.899	14.631	17.275	19.675	22.618	24.725	31.264
12	3.571	4.178	5.226	6.304	7.807	9.034	11.340	14.011	15.812	18.549	21.026	24.054	26.217	32.909
13	4.107	4.765	5.892	7.042	8.634	9.926	12.340	15.119	16.985	19.812	22.362	25.472	27.688	34.528
14	4.660	5.368	6.571	7.790	9.467	10.821	13.339	16.222	18.151	21.064	23.685	26.873	29.141	36.123
15	5.229	5.985	7.261	8.547	10.307	11.721	14.339	17.322	19.311	22.307	24.996	28.259	30.578	37.697
16	5.812	6.614	7.962	9.312	11.152	12.624	15.338	18.418	20.465	23.542	26.296	29.633	32.000	39.252
17	6.408	7.255	8.672	10.085	12.002	13.531	16.338	19.511	21.615	24.769	27.587	30.995	33.409	40.790
18	7.015	7.906	9.390	10.865	12.857	14.440	17.338	20.601	22.760	25.989	28.869	32.346	34.805	42.312
19	7.633	8.567	10.117	11.651	13.716	15.352	18.338	21.689	23.900	27.204	30.144	33.687	36.191	43.820
20	8.260	9.237	10.851	12.443	14.578	16.266	19.337	22.775	25.038	28.412	31.410	35.020	37.566	45.315
21	8.897	9.915	11.591	13.240	15.445	17.182	20.337	23.858	26.171	29.615	32.671	36.343	38.932	46.797
22	9.542	10.600	12.338	14.041	16.314	18.101	21.337	24.939	27.301	30.813	33.924	37.659	40.289	48.268
23	10.196	11.293	13.091	14.848	17.187	19.021	22.337	26.018	28.429	32.007	35.172	38.968	41.638	49.728
24	10.856	11.992	13.848	15.659	18.062	19.943	23.337	27.096	29.553	33.196	36.415	40.270	42.980	51.179
25	11.524	12.697	14.611	16.473	18.940	20.867	24.337	28.172	30.675	34.382	37.652	41.566	44.314	52.620
26	12.198	13.409	15.379	17.292	19.820	21.792	25.336	29.246	31.795	35.563	38.885	42.856	45.642	54.052
27	12.879	14.125	16.151	18.114	20.703	22.719	26.336	30.319	32.912	36.741	40.113	44.140	46.963	55.476
28	13.565	14.847	16.928	18.939	21.588	23.647	27.336	31.391	34.027	37.916	41.337	45.419	48.278	56.893
29	14.256	15.574	17.708	19.768	22.475	24.577	28.336	32.461	35.139	39.087	42.557	46.693	49.588	58.302
30	14.953	16.306	18.493	20.599	23.364	25.508	29.336	33.530	36.250	40.256	43.773	47.962	50.892	59.703

Source: Ronald A. Fisher and Frank Yates, *Statistical Tables for Biological, Agricultural and Medical Research*, published by Longman Group Ltd., London (previously published by Oliver & Boyd, Edinburgh). By permission of the authors and publishers. Table V. Reprinted from *Basic Statistical Methods* (2nd ed.), N. M. Downie and R. W. Heath, Harper & Row, 1965.

TABLE A5
Distribution of *t*.

Degrees of freedom (df) are defined as $N - 1$ for a single sample. For two-sample tests, df = $(N_1 - 1) + (N_2 - 1)$, where the N's are the respective sample sizes. When the exact df cannot be located down the left-hand side of the table, use the smaller df for locating significant t values. For example, if the researcher has df = 110, use 60 df for entering the table. This renders the decision somewhat more conservative. Any observed t value that equals or exceeds the value shown in the body of the table for any df is significant statistically at the probability level shown at the top of the table.

df	Level of significance for one-tailed test					
	.10	.05	.025	.01	.005	.0005
	Level of significance for two-tailed test					
	.20	.10	.05	.02	.01	.001
1	3.078	6.314	12.706	31.821	63.657	636.619
2	1.886	2.920	4.303	6.965	9.925	31.598
3	1.638	2.353	3.182	4.541	5.841	12.941
4	1.533	2.132	2.776	3.747	4.604	8.610
5	1.476	2.015	2.571	3.365	4.032	6.859
6	1.440	1.943	2.447	3.143	3.707	5.959
7	1.415	1.895	2.365	2.998	3.499	5.405
8	1.397	1.860	2.306	2.896	3.355	5.041
9	1.383	1.833	2.262	2.821	3.250	4.781
10	1.372	1.812	2.228	2.764	3.169	4.587
11	1.363	1.796	2.201	2.718	3.106	4.437
12	1.356	1.782	2.179	2.681	3.055	4.318
13	1.350	1.771	2.160	2.650	3.012	4.221
14	1.345	1.761	2.145	2.624	2.977	4.140
15	1.341	1.753	2.131	2.602	2.947	4.073
16	1.337	1.746	2.120	2.583	2.921	4.015
17	1.333	1.740	2.110	2.567	2.898	3.965
18	1.330	1.734	2.101	2.552	2.878	3.922
19	1.328	1.729	2.093	2.539	2.861	3.883
20	1.325	1.725	2.086	2.528	2.845	3.850
21	1.323	1.721	2.080	2.518	2.831	3.819
22	1.321	1.717	2.074	2.508	2.819	3.792
23	1.319	1.714	2.069	2.500	2.807	3.767
24	1.318	1.711	2.064	2.492	2.797	3.745
25	1.316	1.708	2.060	2.485	2.787	3.725
26	1.315	1.706	2.056	2.479	2.779	3.707
27	1.314	1.703	2.052	2.473	2.771	3.690
28	1.313	1.701	2.048	2.467	2.763	3.674
29	1.311	1.699	2.045	2.462	2.756	3.659
30	1.310	1.697	2.042	2.457	2.750	3.646
40	1.303	1.684	2.021	2.423	2.704	3.551
60	1.296	1.671	2.000	2.390	2.660	3.460
120	1.289	1.658	1.980	2.358	2.617	3.373
∞	1.282	1.645	1.960	2.326	2.576	3.291

Source: Abridged trom Ronald A. Fisher and Frank Yates, *Statistical Tables for Biological, Agricultural and Medical Research*, published by Longman Group Ltd., London (previously published by Oliver & Boyd, Edinburgh). By permission of the authors and publishers. Table III. Reprinted from Sidney Siegel, *Nonparametric Statistics for the Behavioral Sciences* (McGraw-Hill Book Company, 1956) by permission of the publishers.

TABLE A6

Values of Z for Given Values of r.

For the Fisher Z transformation, locate the respective r values down the left-hand column. Use the Z value shown in the column, .000, for all comparisons of r values.

r	.000	.001	.002	.003	.004	.005	.006	.007	.008	.009
.000	.0000	.0010	.0020	.0030	.0040	.0050	.0060	.0070	.0080	.0090
.010	.0100	.0110	.0120	.0130	.0140	.0150	.0160	.0170	.0180	.0190
.020	.0200	.0210	.0220	.0230	.0240	.0250	.0260	.0270	.0280	.0290
.030	.0300	.0310	.0320	.0330	.0340	.0350	.0360	.0370	.0380	.0390
.040	.0400	.0410	.0420	.0430	.0440	.0450	.0460	.0470	.0480	.0490
.050	.0501	.0511	.0521	.0531	.0541	.0551	.0561	.0571	.0581	.0591
.060	.0601	.0611	.0621	.0631	.0641	.0651	.0661	.0671	.0681	.0691
.070	.0701	.0711	.0721	.0731	.0741	.0751	.0761	.0771	.0782	.0792
.080	.0802	.0812	.0822	.0832	.0842	.0852	.0862	.0872	.0882	.0892
.090	.0902	.0912	.0922	.0933	.0943	.0953	.0963	.0973	.0983	.0993
.100	.1003	.1013	.1024	.1034	.1044	.1054	.1064	.1074	.1084	.1094
.110	.1105	.1115	.1125	.1135	.1145	.1155	.1165	.1175	.1185	.1195
.120	.1206	.1216	.1226	.1236	.1246	.1257	.1267	.1277	.1287	.1297
.130	.1308	.1318	.1328	.1338	.1348	.1358	.1368	.1379	.1389	.1399
.140	.1409	.1419	.1430	.1440	.1450	.1460	.1470	.1481	.1491	.1501
.150	.1511	.1522	.1532	.1542	.1552	.1563	.1573	.1583	.1593	.1604
.160	.1614	.1624	.1634	.1644	.1655	.1665	.1676	.1686	.1696	.1706
.170	.1717	.1727	.1737	.1748	.1758	.1768	.1779	.1789	.1799	.1810
.180	.1820	.1830	.1841	.1851	.1861	.1872	.1882	.1892	.1903	.1913
.190	.1923	.1934	.1944	.1954	.1965	.1975	.1986	.1996	.2007	.2017
.200	.2027	.2038	.2048	.2059	.2069	.2079	.2090	.2100	.2111	.2121
.210	.2132	.2142	.2153	.2163	.2174	.2184	.2194	.2205	.2215	.2226
.220	.2237	.2247	.2258	.2268	.2279	.2289	.2300	.2310	.2321	.2331
.230	.2342	.2353	.2363	.2374	.2384	.2395	.2405	.2416	.2427	.2437
.240	.2448	.2458	.2469	.2480	.2490	.2501	.2511	.2522	.2533	.2543
.250	.2554	.2565	.2575	.2586	.2597	.2608	.2618	.2629	.2640	.2650
.260	.2661	.2672	.2682	.2693	.2704	.2715	.2726	.2736	.2747	.2758
.370	.2769	.2779	.2790	.2801	.2812	.2823	.2833	.2844	.2855	.2866
.280	.2877	.2888	.2898	.2909	.2920	.2931	.2942	.2953	.2964	.2975
.290	.2986	.2997	.3008	.3019	.3029	.3040	.3051	.3062	.3073	.3084
.300	.3095	.3106	.3117	.3128	.3139	.3150	.3161	.3172	.3183	.3195
.310	.3206	.3217	.3228	.3239	.3250	.3261	.3272	.3283	.3294	.3305
.320	.3317	.3328	.3339	.3350	.3361	.3372	.3384	.3395	.3406	.3417
.330	.3428	.3439	.3451	.3462	.3473	.3484	.3496	.3507	.3518	.3530
.340	.3541	.3552	.3564	.3575	.3586	.3597	.3609	.3620	.3632	.3643
.350	.3654	.3666	.3677	.3689	.3700	.3712	.3723	.3734	.3746	.3757
.360	.3769	.3780	.3792	.3803	.3815	.3826	.3838	.3850	.3861	.3873
.370	.3884	.3896	.3907	.3919	.3931	.3942	.3954	.3966	.3977	.3989
.380	.4001	.4012	.4024	.4036	.4047	.4059	.4071	.4083	.4094	.4106
.390	.4118	.4130	.4142	.4153	.4165	.4177	.4189	.4201	.4213	.4225
.400	.4236	.4248	.4260	.4272	.4284	.4296	.4308	.4320	.4332	.4344
.410	.4356	.4368	.4380	.4392	.4404	.4416	.4429	.4441	.4453	.4465
.420	.4477	.4489	.4501	.4513	.4526	.4538	.4550	.4562	.4574	.4587
.430	.4599	.4611	.4623	.4636	.4648	.4660	.4673	.4685	.4697	.4710
.440	.4722	.4735	.4747	.4760	.4772	.4784	.4797	.4809	.4822	.4835
.450	.4847	.4860	.4872	.4885	.4897	.4910	.4923	.4935	.4948	.4961
.460	.4973	.4986	.4999	.5011	.5024	.5037	.5049	.5062	.5075	.5088
.470	.5101	.5114	.5126	.5139	.5152	.5165	.5178	.5191	.5204	.5217
.480	.5230	.5243	.5256	.5279	.5282	.5295	.5308	.5321	.5334	.5347
.490	.5361	.5374	.5387	.5400	.5413	.5427	.5440	.5453	.5466	.5480

Source: From *Statistical Tables and Problems* by Albert E. Waugh. Copyright © 1952 by McGraw-Hill Book Company. Used with the permission of McGraw-Hill Book Company.

TABLE A6 *(continued)*

r	.000	.001	.002	.003	.004	.005	.006	.007	.008	.009
.500	.5493	.5506	.5520	.5533	.5547	.5560	.5573	.5587	.5600	.5614
.510	.5627	.5641	.5654	.5668	.5681	.5695	.5709	.5722	.5736	.5750
.520	.5763	.5777	.5791	.5805	.5818	.5832	.5846	.5860	.5874	.5888
.530	.5901	.5915	.5929	.5943	.5957	.5971	.5985	.5999	.6013	.6027
.540	.6042	.6056	.6070	.6084	.6098	.6112	.6127	.6141	.6155	.6170
.550	.6184	.6198	.6213	.6227	.6241	.6256	.6270	.6285	.6299	.6314
.560	.6328	.6343	.6358	.6372	.6387	.6401	.6416	.6431	.6446	.6460
.570	.6475	.6490	.6505	.6520	.6535	.6550	.6565	.6579	.6594	.6610
.580	.6625	.6640	.6655	.6670	.6685	.6700	.6715	.6731	.6746	.6761
.590	.6777	.6792	.6807	.6823	.6838	.6854	.6869	.6885	.6900	.6916
.600	.6931	.6947	.6963	.6978	.6994	.7010	.7026	.7042	.7057	.7073
.610	.7089	.7105	.7121	.7137	.7153	.7169	.7185	.7201	.7218	.7234
.620	.7250	.7266	.7283	.7299	.7315	.7332	.7348	.7364	.7381	.7398
.630	.7414	.7431	.7447	.7464	.7481	.7497	.7514	.7531	.7548	.7565
.640	.7582	.7599	.7616	.7633	.7650	.7667	.7684	.7701	.7718	.7736
.650	.7753	.7770	.7788	.7805	.7823	.7840	.7858	.7875	.7893	.7910
.660	.7928	.7946	.7964	.7981	.7999	.8017	.8035	.8053	.8071	.8089
.670	.8107	.8126	.8144	.8162	.8180	.8199	.8217	.8236	.8254	.8273
.680	.8291	.8310	.8328	.8347	.8366	.8385	.8404	.8423	.8442	.8461
.690	.8480	.8499	.8518	.8537	.8556	.8576	.8595	.8614	.8634	.8653
.700	.8673	.8693	.8712	.8732	.8752	.8772	.8792	.8812	.8832	.8852
.710	.8872	.8892	.8912	.8933	.8953	.8973	.8994	.9014	.9035	.9056
.720	.9076	.9097	.9118	.9139	.9160	.9181	.9202	.9223	.9245	.9266
.730	.9287	.9309	.9330	.9352	.9373	.9395	.9417	.9439	.9461	.9483
.740	.9505	.9527	.9549	.9571	.9594	.9616	.9639	.9661	.9684	.9707
.750	.9730	.9752	.9775	.9799	.9822	.9845	.9868	.9892	.9915	.9939
.760	.9962	.9986	1.0010	1.0034	1.0058	1.0082	1.0106	1.0130	1.0154	1.0179
.770	1.0203	1.0228	1.0253	1.0277	1.0302	1.0327	1.0352	1.0378	1.0403	1.0428
.780	1.0454	1.0479	1.0505	1.0531	1.0557	1.0583	1.0609	1.0635	1.0661	1.0688
.790	1.0714	1.0741	1.0768	1.0795	1.0822	1.0849	1.0876	1.0903	1.0931	1.0958
.800	1.0986	1.1014	1.1041	1.1070	1.1098	1.1127	1.1155	1.1184	1.1212	1.1241
.810	1.1270	1.1299	1.1329	1.1358	1.1388	1.1417	1.1447	1.1477	1.1507	1.1538
.820	1.1568	1.1599	1.1630	1.1660	1.1692	1.1723	1.1754	1.1786	1.1817	1.1849
.830	1.1870	1.1913	1.1946	1.1979	1.2011	1.2044	1.2077	1.2111	1.2144	1.2178
.840	1.2212	1.2246	1.2280	1.2315	1.2349	1.2384	1.2419	1.2454	1.2490	1.2526
.850	1.2561	1.2598	1.2634	1.2670	1.2708	1.2744	1.2782	1.2819	1.2857	1.2895
.860	1.2934	1.2972	1.3011	1.3050	1.3089	1.3129	1.3168	1.3209	1.3249	1.3290
.870	1.3331	1.3372	1.3414	1.3456	1.3498	1.3540	1.3583	1.3626	1.3670	1.3714
.880	1.3758	1.3802	1.3847	1.3892	1.3938	1.3984	1.4030	1.4077	1.4124	1.4171
.890	1.4219	1.4268	1.4316	1.4366	1.4415	1.4465	1.4516	1.4566	1.4618	1.4670
.900	1.4722	1.4775	1.4828	1.4883	1.4937	1.4992	1.5047	1.5103	1.5160	1.5217
.910	1.5275	1.5334	1.5393	1.5453	1.5513	1.5574	1.5636	1.5698	1.5762	1.5825
.920	1.5890	1.5956	1.6022	1.6089	1.6157	1.6226	1.6296	1.6366	1.6438	1.6510
.930	1.6584	1.6659	1.6734	1.6811	1.6888	1.6967	1.7047	1.7129	1.7211	1.7295
.940	1.7380	1.7467	1.7555	1.7645	1.7736	1.7828	1.7923	1.8019	1.8117	1.8216
.950	1.8318	1.8421	1.8527	1.8635	1.8745	1.8857	1.8972	1.9090	1.9210	1.9333
.960	1.9459	1.9588	1.9721	1.9857	1.9996	2.0140	2.0287	2.0439	2.0595	2.0756
.970	2.0923	2.1095	2.1273	2.1457	2.1649	2.1847	2.2054	2.2269	2.2494	2.2729
.980	2.2976	2.3223	2.3507	2.3796	2.4101	2.4426	2.4774	2.5147	2.5550	2.5988
.990	2.6467	2.6996	2.7587	2.8257	2.9031	2.9945	3.1063	3.2504	3.4534	3.8002

r	z
.9999	4.95172
.99999	6.10303

TABLE A7

Values of r for Different Levels of Significance.

Degrees of freedom are defined as $N - 2$ for entering the table. If the exact df cannot be located down the left-hand side of the table, use the smaller df for all table entries. Any observed r value that equals or exceeds r values shown in the body of the table is significant at the probabilities shown across the top of the table. If a researcher enters the table with 60 df, .3248 or .32 is the critical r value for the .01 level of significance. Any observed r value that equals or exceeds .32 is significant at .01.

df	.1	.05	.02	.01	.001
1	.98769	.99692	.999507	.999877	.9999988
2	.90000	.95000	.98000	.990000	.99900
3	.8054	.8783	.93433	.95873	.99116
4	.7293	.8114	.8822	.91720	.97406
5	.6694	.7545	.8329	.8745	.95074
6	.6215	.7067	.7887	.8343	.92493
7	.5822	.6664	.7498	.7977	.8982
8	.5494	.6319	.7155	.7646	.8721
9	.5214	.6021	.6851	.7348	.8471
10	.4973	.5760	.6581	.7079	.8233
11	.4762	.5529	.6339	.6835	.8010
12	.4575	.5324	.6120	.6614	.7800
13	.4409	.5139	.5923	.6411	.7603
14	.4259	.4973	.5742	.6226	.7420
15	.4124	.4821	.5577	.6055	.7246
16	.4000	.4683	.5425	.5897	.7084
17	.3887	.4555	.5285	.5751	.6932
18	.3783	.4438	.5155	.5614	.6787
19	.3687	.4329	.5034	.5487	.6652
20	.3598	.4227	.4921	.5368	.6524
25	.3233	.3809	.4451	.4869	.5974
30	.2960	.3494	.4093	.4487	.5541
35	.2746	.3246	.3810	.4182	.5189
40	.2573	.3044	.3578	.3932	.4896
45	.2428	.2875	.3384	.3721	.4648
50	.2306	.2732	.3218	.3541	.4433
60	.2108	.2500	.2948	.3248	.4078
70	.1954	.2319	.2737	.3017	.3799
80	.1829	.2172	.2565	.2830	.3568
90	.1726	.2050	.2422	.2673	.3375
100	.1638	.1946	.2301	.2540	.3211

Source: Ronald A. Fisher and Frank Yates, ***Statistical Tables for Biological, Agricultural and Medical Research***, published by Longman Group Ltd., London (previously published by Oliver & Boyd, Edinburgh). By permission of the authors and publishers. Table VI. Reprinted from N. M. Downie and R. W. Heath, ***Basic Statistical Methods***, 2nd ed. (New York: Harper & Row, Publishers, 1965).

TABLE A8

Probabilities Associated with Values as Small as Observed Values of U in the Mann-Whitney Test.

(1 through 6) These tables are used for two-sample situations, where the larger of the two samples does not exceed 8. Adjacent to each table heading is N_1, which is always defined as the larger of the two samples. Across the top of the table is N_2, which is the smaller of the two samples. The body of the table contains probabilities associated with the smaller observed U value. These probabilities are compared directly with probabilities used in hypothesis tests. For example, if $N_1 = 5$ and $N_2 = 4$, we would turn to Table A8.3. If we observed a smaller U value of 2, the probability associated with this would be .032.

TABLE A8.1

$n_1 = 3$ (M and W).

U \ n_2	1	2	3
0	.250	.100	.050
1	.500	.200	.100
2	.750	.400	.200
3		.600	.350
4			.500
5			.650

TABLE A8.2

$n_1 = 4$ (M and W).

U \ n_2	1	2	3	4
0	.200	.067	.028	.014
1	.400	.133	.057	.029
2	.600	.267	.114	.057
3		.400	.200	.100
4		.600	.314	.171
5			.429	.243
6			.571	.343
7				.443
8				.557

Source: (M and W; subtables A8.1 to A8.6) E. B. Mann and D. R. Whitney, "On a Test of Whether One of Two Random Variables Is Stochastically Larger Than the Other," *Annals of Mathematical Statistics*, 18:52–54, 1947. With permission of the editor; notation modified for this book. (Auble; subtables A8.7 to A8.10) D. Auble, "Extended Tables for the Mann–Whitney Statistic," *Bulletin of the Institute of Educational Research at Indiana University*, 1, No. 2. Adapted and abridged; with permission of the editor. Reprinted from Sidney Siegel, *Nonparametric Statistics for the Behavioral Sciences* (New York: McGraw-Hill Book Company, 1956), by permission of the publishers; notation modified for this book.

TABLE A8 *(continued)*

TABLE A8.3
$n_1 = 5$ (M and W).

U \ n_2	1	2	3	4	5
0	.167	.047	.018	.008	.004
1	.333	.095	.036	.016	.008
2	.500	.190	.071	.032	.016
3	.667	.286	.125	.056	.028
4		.429	.196	.095	.048
5		.571	.286	.143	.075
6			.393	.206	.111
7			.500	.278	.155
8			.607	.365	.210
9				.452	.274
10				.548	.345
11					.421
12					.500
13					.579

TABLE A8.4
$n_1 = 6$ (M and W).

U \ n_2	1	2	3	4	5	6
0	.143	.036	.012	.005	.002	.001
1	.286	.071	.024	.010	.004	.002
2	.428	.143	.048	.019	.009	.004
3	.571	.214	.083	.033	.015	.008
4		.321	.131	.057	.026	.013
5		.429	.190	.086	.041	.021
6		.571	.274	.129	.063	.032
7			.357	.176	.089	.047
8			.452	.238	.123	.066
9			.548	.305	.165	.090
10				.381	.214	.120
11				.457	.268	.155
12				.545	.331	.197
13					.396	.242
14					.465	.294
15					.535	.350
16						.409
17						.469
18						.531

TABLE A8 *(continued)*

TABLE A8.5

$n_1 = 7$ (M and W).

U \ n_2	1	2	3	4	5	6	7
0	.125	.028	.008	.003	.001	.001	.000
1	.250	.056	.017	.006	.003	.001	.001
2	.375	.111	.033	.012	.005	.002	.001
3	.500	.167	.058	.021	.009	.004	.002
4	.625	.250	.092	.036	.015	.007	.003
5		.333	.133	.055	.024	.011	.006
6		.444	.192	.082	.037	.017	.009
7		.556	.258	.115	.053	.026	.013
8			.333	.158	.074	.037	.019
9			.417	.206	.101	.051	.027
10			.500	.264	.134	.069	.036
11			.583	.324	.172	.090	.049
12				.394	.216	.117	.064
13				.464	.265	.147	.082
14				.538	.319	.183	.104
15					.378	.223	.130
16					.438	.267	.159
17					.500	.314	.191
18					.562	.365	.228
19						.418	.267
20						.473	.310
21						.527	.355
22							.402
23							.451
24							.500
25							.549

TABLE A8 *(continued)*

TABLE A8.6

$n_1 = 8$ (M and W).

U \ n_2	1	2	3	4	5	6	7	8	t	Normal
0	.111	.022	.006	.002	.001	.000	.000	.000	3.308	.001
1	.222	.044	.012	.004	.002	.001	.000	.000	3.203	.001
2	.333	.089	.024	.008	.003	.001	.001	.000	3.098	.001
3	.444	.133	.042	.014	.005	.002	.001	.001	2.993	.001
4	.556	.200	.067	.024	.009	.004	.002	.001	2.888	.002
5		.267	.097	.036	.015	.006	.003	.001	2.783	.003
6		.356	.139	.055	.023	.010	.005	.002	2.678	.004
7		.444	.188	.077	.033	.015	.007	.003	2.573	.005
8		.556	.248	.107	.047	.021	.010	.005	2.468	.007
9			.315	.141	.064	.030	.014	.007	2.363	.009
10			.387	.184	.085	.041	.020	.010	2.258	.012
11			.461	.230	.111	.054	.027	.014	2.153	.016
12			.539	.285	.142	.071	.036	.019	2.048	.020
13				.341	.177	.091	.047	.025	1.943	.026
14				.404	.217	.114	.060	.032	1.838	.033
15				.467	.262	.141	.076	.041	1.733	.041
16				.533	.311	.172	.095	.052	1.628	.052
17					.362	.207	.116	.065	1.523	.064
18					.416	.245	.140	.080	1.418	.078
19					.472	.286	.168	.097	1.313	.094
20					.528	.331	.198	.117	1.208	.113
21						.377	.232	.139	1.102	.135
22						.426	.268	.164	.998	.159
23						.475	.306	.191	.893	.185
24						.525	.347	.221	.788	.215
25							.389	.253	.683	.247
26							.433	.287	.578	.282
27							.478	.323	.473	.318
28							.522	.360	.368	.356
29								.399	.263	.396
30								.439	.158	.437
31								.480	.052	.481
32								.520		

TABLE A8 *(continued)*

TABLE A8.7

Critical Values of U for a One-Tailed Test at $\alpha = .001$ or for a Two-Tailed Test at $\alpha = .002$ (Auble).

(7 through 10) These tables are for situations in which the investigator has two samples, where the larger sample is from 9 to 20. The appropriate level of significance is selected for either a one- or a two-tailed test. These probabilities are the table headings. The larger N is found across the top of the table, while the smaller N is located down the left-hand side. The smaller of two observed U values is compared with the U value shown in the body of the table. If the observed U value is equal to or smaller than the one shown where N_1 and N_2 intersect, the two groups are considered different statistically at the probability shown at the top of the table.

n_2 \ n_1	9	10	11	12	13	14	15	16	17	18	19	20
1												
2												
3									0	0	0	0
4		0	0	0	1	1	1	2	2	3	3	3
5	1	1	2	2	3	3	4	5	5	6	7	7
6	2	3	4	4	5	6	7	8	9	10	11	12
7	3	5	6	7	8	9	10	11	13	14	15	16
8	5	6	8	9	11	12	14	15	17	18	20	21
9	7	8	10	12	14	15	17	19	21	23	25	26
10	8	10	12	14	17	19	21	23	25	27	29	32
11	10	12	15	17	20	22	24	27	29	32	34	37
12	12	14	17	20	23	25	28	31	34	37	40	42
13	14	17	20	23	26	29	32	35	38	42	45	48
14	15	19	22	25	29	32	36	39	43	46	50	54
15	17	21	24	28	32	36	40	43	47	51	55	59
16	19	23	27	31	35	39	43	48	52	56	60	65
17	21	25	29	34	38	43	47	52	57	61	66	70
18	23	27	32	37	42	46	51	56	61	66	71	76
19	25	29	34	40	45	50	55	60	66	71	77	82
20	26	32	37	42	48	54	59	65	70	76	82	88

TABLE A8.8

Critical Values of U for a One-Tailed Test at $\alpha = .01$ or for a Two-Tailed Test at $\alpha = .02$ (Auble).

n_2 \ n_1	9	10	11	12	13	14	15	16	17	18	19	20
1												
2					0	0	0	0	0	0	1	1
3	1	1	1	2	2	2	3	3	4	4	4	5
4	3	3	4	5	5	6	7	7	8	9	9	10
5	5	6	7	8	9	10	11	12	13	14	15	16
6	7	8	9	11	12	13	15	16	18	19	20	22
7	9	11	12	14	16	17	19	21	23	24	26	28
8	11	13	15	17	20	22	24	26	28	30	32	34
9	14	16	18	21	23	26	28	31	33	36	38	40
10	16	19	22	24	27	30	33	36	38	41	44	47
11	18	22	25	28	31	34	37	41	44	47	50	53
12	21	24	28	31	35	38	42	46	49	53	56	60
13	23	27	31	35	39	43	47	51	55	59	63	67
14	26	30	34	38	43	47	51	56	60	65	69	73
15	28	33	37	42	47	51	56	61	66	70	75	80
16	31	36	41	46	51	56	61	66	71	76	82	87
17	33	38	44	49	55	60	66	71	77	82	88	93
18	36	41	47	53	59	65	70	76	82	88	94	100
19	38	44	50	56	63	69	75	82	88	94	101	107
20	40	47	53	60	67	73	80	87	93	100	107	114

TABLE A8 *(continued)*

TABLE A8.9

Critical Values of U for a One-Tailed Test at $\alpha = .025$ or for a Two-Tailed Test at $\alpha = .05$ (Auble).

n_2 \ n_1	9	10	11	12	13	14	15	16	17	18	19	20
1												
2	0	0	0	1	1	1	1	1	2	2	2	2
3	2	3	3	4	4	5	5	6	6	7	7	8
4	4	5	6	7	8	9	10	11	11	12	13	13
5	7	8	9	11	12	13	14	15	17	18	19	20
6	10	11	13	14	16	17	19	21	22	24	25	27
7	12	14	16	18	20	22	24	26	28	30	32	34
8	15	17	19	22	24	26	29	31	34	36	38	41
9	17	20	23	26	28	31	34	37	39	42	45	48
10	20	23	26	29	33	36	39	42	45	48	52	55
11	23	26	30	33	37	40	44	47	51	55	58	62
12	26	29	33	37	41	45	49	53	57	61	65	69
13	28	33	37	41	45	50	54	59	63	67	72	76
14	31	36	40	45	50	55	59	64	67	74	78	83
15	34	39	44	49	54	59	64	70	75	80	85	90
16	37	42	47	53	59	64	70	75	81	86	92	98
17	39	45	51	57	63	67	75	81	87	93	99	105
18	42	48	55	61	67	74	80	86	93	99	106	112
19	45	52	58	65	72	78	85	92	99	106	113	119
20	48	55	62	69	76	83	90	98	105	112	119	127

TABLE A8.10

Critical Values of U for a One-Tailed Test at $\alpha = .05$ or for a Two-Tailed Test at $\alpha = .10$ (Auble).

n_2 \ n_1	9	10	11	12	13	14	15	16	17	18	19	20
1											0	0
2	1	1	1	2	2	2	3	3	3	4	4	4
3	3	4	5	5	6	7	7	8	9	9	10	11
4	6	7	8	9	10	11	12	14	15	16	17	18
5	9	11	12	13	15	16	18	19	20	22	23	25
6	12	14	16	17	19	21	23	25	26	28	30	32
7	15	17	19	21	24	26	28	30	33	35	37	39
8	18	20	23	26	28	31	33	36	39	41	44	47
9	21	24	27	30	33	36	39	42	45	48	51	54
10	24	27	31	34	37	41	44	48	51	55	58	62
11	27	31	34	38	42	46	50	54	57	61	65	69
12	30	34	38	42	47	51	55	60	64	68	72	77
13	33	37	42	47	51	56	61	65	70	75	80	84
14	36	41	46	51	56	61	66	71	77	82	87	92
15	39	44	50	55	61	66	72	77	83	88	94	100
16	42	48	54	60	65	71	77	83	89	95	101	107
17	45	51	57	64	70	77	83	89	96	102	109	115
18	48	55	61	68	75	82	88	95	102	109	116	123
19	51	58	65	72	80	87	94	101	109	116	123	130
20	54	62	69	77	84	92	100	107	115	123	130	138

TABLE A9

Critical Values of D in the Kolmogorov-Smirnov One-Sample Test.

The body of the table contains critical proportions that must be equaled or exceeded by observed proportion differences for significance at various probabilities shown across the top of the table. The probabilities are two-tailed and may be halved for a one-tailed interpretation. That is, .10 for a two-tailed test becomes .10/2 = .05 for a one-tailed or directional test. If a sample size is encountered that is between two sample size points (i.e., between 25 and 30), always use the smaller sample size line for determining the critical proportion to be used in the hypothesis test. Any observed proportion difference that is equal to or larger than the proportion shown in the body of the table for a given N value is significant at the probability shown at the top of the table.

Sample size (N)	Level of significance for D = maximum $\lvert F_0(X) - S_N(X) \rvert$				
	.20	.15	.10	.05	.01
1	.900	.925	.950	.975	.995
2	.684	.726	.776	.842	.929
3	.565	.597	.642	.708	.828
4	.494	.525	.564	.624	.733
5	.446	.474	.510	.565	.669
6	.410	.436	.470	.521	.618
7	.381	.405	.438	.486	.577
8	.358	.381	.411	.457	.543
9	.339	.360	.388	.432	.514
10	.322	.342	.368	.410	.490
11	.307	.326	.352	.391	.468
12	.295	.313	.338	.375	.450
13	.284	.302	.325	.361	.433
14	.274	.292	.314	.349	.418
15	.266	.283	.304	.338	.404
16	.258	.274	.295	.328	.392
17	.250	.266	.286	.318	.381
18	.244	.259	.278	.309	.371
19	.237	.252	.272	.301	.363
20	.231	.246	.264	.294	.356
25	.21	.22	.24	.27	.32
30	.19	.20	.22	.24	.29
35	.18	.19	.21	.23	.27
Over 35	$\frac{1.07}{\sqrt{N}}$	$\frac{1.14}{\sqrt{N}}$	$\frac{1.22}{\sqrt{N}}$	$\frac{1.36}{\sqrt{N}}$	$\frac{1.63}{\sqrt{N}}$

Source: F. J. Massey, Jr., "The Kolmogorov-Smirnov Test for Goodness of Fit," *Journal of the American Statistical Association*, 46:70, 1951. With permission of the publishers. Reprinted from Sidney Siegel, *Nonparametric Statistics for the Behavioral Sciences* (New York: McGraw-Hill Book Company, 1956) by permission of the publishers.

Note: Two-tailed values.

TABLE A10

Critical Values for Cochran's Test for Homogeneity of Variance. $C = (\text{largest } s^2)/(\Sigma s_j^2)$.

Across the top of the table are k, the number of variances. The far left-hand side contains degrees of freedom, df, which are defined as $N - 1$, where N = any sample size if sample sizes are equal. If sample sizes are not equal, the largest sample size should be used. If the exact df cannot be found, then the larger df value should be used for purposes of entering the table. The second column from the left defines 1 − alpha values of .95 and .99 respectively. These are equivalent to the .05 and .01 levels of significance. For any given k and df, critical values of C are shown in the body of the table. If an observed C equals or exceeds the critical value of C where k and df intersect, homogeneity of variance does not exist.

df for s_j^2	$1 - \alpha$	k = number of variances										
		2	3	4	5	6	7	8	9	10	15	20
1	.95	.9985	.9669	.9065	.8412	.7808	.7271	.6798	.6385	.6020	.4709	.3894
	.99	.9999	.9933	.9676	.9279	.8828	.8376	.7945	.7544	.7175	.5747	.4799
2	.95	.9750	.8709	.7679	.6838	.6161	.5612	.5157	.4775	.4450	.3346	.2705
	.99	.9950	.9423	.8643	.7885	.7218	.6644	.6152	.5727	.5358	.4069	.3297
3	.95	.9392	.7977	.6841	.5981	.5321	.4800	.4377	.4027	.3733	.2758	.2205
	.99	.9794	.8831	.7814	.6957	.6258	.5685	.5209	.4810	.4469	.3317	.2654
4	.95	.9057	.7457	.6287	.5441	.4803	.4307	.3910	.3584	.3311	.2419	.1921
	.99	.9586	.8335	.7212	.6329	.5635	.5080	.4627	.4251	.3934	.2882	.2288
5	.95	.8772	.7071	.5895	.5065	.4447	.3974	.3595	.3286	.3029	.2195	.1735
	.99	.9373	.7933	.6761	.5875	.5195	.4659	.4226	.3870	.3572	.2593	.2048
6	.95	.8534	.6771	.5598	.4783	.4184	.3726	.3362	.3067	.2823	.2034	.1602
	.99	.9172	.7606	.6410	.5531	.4866	.4347	.3932	.3592	.3308	.2386	.1877
7	.95	.8332	.6530	.5365	.4564	.3980	.3535	.3185	.2901	.2666	.1911	.1501
	.99	.8988	.7335	.6129	.5259	.4608	.4105	.3704	.3378	.3106	.2228	.1748
8	.95	.8159	.6333	.5175	.4387	.3817	.3384	.3043	.2768	.2541	.1815	.1422
	.99	.8823	.7107	.5897	.5037	.4401	.3911	.3522	.3207	.2945	.2104	.1646
9	.95	.8010	.6167	.5017	.4241	.3682	.3259	.2926	.2659	.2439	.1736	.1357
	.99	.8674	.6912	.5702	.4854	.4229	.3751	.3373	.3067	.2813	.2002	.1567
16	.95	.7341	.5466	.4366	.3645	.3135	.2756	.2462	.2226	.2032	.1429	.1108
	.99	.7949	.6059	.4884	.4094	.3529	.3105	.2779	.2514	.2297	.1612	.1248
36	.95	.6602	.4748	.3720	.3066	.2612	.2278	.2022	.1820	.1655	.1144	.0879
	.99	.7067	.5153	.4057	.3351	.2858	.2494	.2214	.1992	.1811	.1251	.0960
144	.95	.5813	.4031	.3093	.2513	.2119	.1833	.1616	.1446	.1308	.0889	.0675
	.99	.6062	.4230	.3251	.2644	.2229	.1929	.1700	.1521	.1376	.0934	.0709

Source: B. J. Winer, ***Statistical Principles and Experimental Design***, 2nd ed. (New York: McGraw-Hill Book Company, 1971).

TABLE A11

Critical Values of D in the Kolmogorov–Smirnov Two-Sample Test (Large Samples; Two-Tailed Test).

The first column contains two-tailed probabilities. These probabilities may be halved for one-tailed or directional interpretations. The second column is a constant formula for each probability level which yields a critical proportion that must be equaled or exceeded by the observed proportion difference for statistical significance. N_1 and N_2 are the respective sample sizes.

Level of significance	Value of D so large as to call for rejection of H_0 at the indicated level of significance, where D = maximum $\lvert S_{n_1}(X) - S_{n_2}(X) \rvert$
.10	$1.22 \sqrt{\frac{n_1 + n_2}{n_1 n_2}}$
.05	$1.36 \sqrt{\frac{n_1 + n_2}{n_1 n_2}}$
.025	$1.48 \sqrt{\frac{n_1 + n_2}{n_1 n_2}}$
.01	$1.63 \sqrt{\frac{n_1 + n_2}{n_1 n_2}}$
.005	$1.73 \sqrt{\frac{n_1 + n_2}{n_1 n_2}}$
.001	$1.95 \sqrt{\frac{n_1 + n_2}{n_1 n_2}}$

Source: N. Smirnov, "Tables for Estimating the Goodness of Fit of Empirical Distributions," *Annals of Mathematical Statistics,* 19:280–281, 1948. Used with permission of the Institute of Mathematical Statistics. Reprinted from Sidney Siegel, *Nonparametric Statistics for the Behavioral Sciences* (New York: McGraw-Hill Book Company, 1956) by permission of the publishers.

TABLE A12
Critical Values of Gamma for .05 and .01 One- and Two-Tailed Tests.

This table contains critical values of gamma for various sample sizes ranging from 4 to 40. Any observed gamma value that equals or exceeds the critical value shown in the body of the table is significant at the level of probability shown at the top of the table.

		Two-Tailed Test		*One-Tailed Test*	
N	α	*.05*	*.01*	*.05*	*.01*
4				1.000	
5		1.000		0.800	1.000
6		0.867	1.000	0.733	0.867
7		0.714	0.905	0.619	0.810
8		0.643	0.786	0.571	0.714
9		0.556	0.722	0.500	0.667
10		0.511	0.644	0.467	0.600
11		0.491	0.600	0.418	0.564
12		0.455	0.576	0.394	0.545
13		0.436	0.564	0.359	0.513
14		0.407	0.516	0.363	0.473
15		0.390	0.505	0.333	0.467
16		0.383	0.483	0.317	0.433
17		0.368	0.471	0.309	0.426
18		0.346	0.451	0.294	0.412
19		0.333	0.439	0.287	0.392
20		0.326	0.421	0.274	0.379
21		0.314	0.410	0.267	0.371
22		0.307	0.394	0.264	0.359
23		0.296	0.391	0.257	0.352
24		0.290	0.377	0.246	0.341
25		0.287	0.367	0.240	0.333
26		0.280	0.360	0.237	0.329
27		0.271	0.356	0.231	0.322
28		0.265	0.344	0.228	0.312
29		0.261	0.340	0.222	0.310
30		0.255	0.333	0.218	0.301
31		0.252	0.325	0.213	0.295
32		0.246	0.323	0.210	0.290
33		0.242	0.314	0.205	0.288
34		0.237	0.312	0.201	0.280
35		0.234	0.304	0.197	0.277
36		0.232	0.302	0.194	0.273
37		0.228	0.297	0.192	0.267
38		0.223	0.292	0.189	0.263
39		0.220	0.287	0.188	0.260
40		0.218	0.285	0.185	0.256
z		1.960	2.576	1.645	2.326
		.000	.000	.000	.000

Source: Linton C. Freeman, *Elementary Applied Statistics: for Students in Behavioral Science* (New York: John Wiley & Sons, Inc., 1965).

TABLE A13

Critical Values of R in the Runs Test.

In the body of the table are given various critical values of R for various values of N_1 and N_2. For the one-sample runs test, any value of R that is equal to or smaller than that shown in the table is significant at the .05 level. For the Wàld–Wolfowitz two-sample runs test, any value of R that is equal to or smaller than that shown in the table is significant at the .05 level.

N_1 \ N_2	2	3	4	5	6	7	8	9	10	11	12	13	14	15	16	17	18	19	20
2											2	2	2	2	2	2	2	2	2
3					2	2	2	2	2	2	2	2	2	3	3	3	3	3	3
4				2	2	2	3	3	3	3	3	3	3	3	4	4	4	4	4
5			2	2	3	3	3	3	3	4	4	4	4	4	4	4	5	5	5
6		2	2	3	3	3	3	4	4	4	4	5	5	5	5	5	5	6	6
7		2	2	3	3	3	4	4	5	5	5	5	5	6	6	6	6	6	6
8		2	3	3	3	4	4	5	5	5	6	6	6	6	6	7	7	7	7
9		2	3	3	4	4	5	5	5	6	6	6	7	7	7	7	8	8	8
10		2	3	3	4	5	5	5	6	6	7	7	7	7	8	8	8	8	9
11		2	3	4	4	5	5	6	6	7	7	7	8	8	8	9	9	9	9
12	2	2	3	4	4	5	6	6	7	7	7	8	8	8	9	9	9	10	10
13	2	2	3	4	5	5	6	6	7	7	8	8	9	9	9	10	10	10	10
14	2	2	3	4	5	5	6	7	7	8	8	9	9	9	10	10	10	11	11
15	2	3	3	4	5	6	6	7	7	8	8	9	9	10	10	11	11	11	12
16	2	3	4	4	5	6	6	7	8	8	9	9	10	10	11	11	11	12	12
17	2	3	4	4	5	6	7	7	8	9	9	10	10	11	11	11	12	12	13
18	2	3	4	5	5	6	7	8	8	9	9	10	10	11	11	12	12	13	13
19	2	3	4	5	6	6	7	8	8	9	10	10	11	11	12	12	13	13	13
20	2	3	4	5	6	6	7	8	9	9	10	10	11	12	12	13	13	13	14

Source: Frieda S. Swed and C. Eisenhart, "Tables for Testing Randomness of Grouping in a Sequence of Alternatives," *Annals of Mathematical Statistics*, 14:83–86, 1943. Used with permission of the Institute of Mathematical Statistics. Reprinted from Sidney Siegel, *Nonparametric Statistics for the Behavioral Sciences* (New York: McGraw-Hill Book Company, 1956) by permission of the publisher; slightly modified for this book.

TABLE A14

Critical Values of r_s, the Spearman Rank Correlation Coefficient.

This table contains critical values of rho where N ranges from 4 to 30. If an N does not match up precisely with one shown in the left-hand column, use the smaller N for entering the table. The probabilities are for one-tailed tests, although the researcher may double these probabilities for two-tailed test interpretations. Any observed rho value that equals or exceeds the one shown in the body of the table for a given N is significant at the probability shown at the top of the table.

N	Significance level (one-tailed test)	
	.05	.01
4	1.000	
5	.900	1.000
6	.829	.943
7	.714	.893
8	.643	.833
9	.600	.783
10	.564	.746
12	.506	.712
14	.456	.645
16	.425	.601
18	.399	.564
20	.377	.534
22	.359	.508
24	.343	.485
26	.329	.465
28	.317	.448
30	.306	.432

Sources: E. G. Olds, "Distributions of Sums of Rank Differences for Small Numbers of Individuals," *Annals of Mathematical Statistics*, 9:133–148, 1943; and "The 5% Significance Levels for Sums of Squares of Rank Differences and a Correction," *Annals of Mathematical Statistics*, 20:117–118, 1949. Used with permission of the Institute of Mathematical Statistics. Reprinted from Signey Siegel, *Nonparametric Statistics for the Behavioral Sciences* (New York: McGraw-Hill Book Company, 1956) by permission of the publishers.

TABLE A15

Standard Scores (or Deviates) and Ordinates Corresponding to Divisions of the Area Under the Normal Curve into a Larger Proportion (B) and a Smaller Proportion (C); Also the Value $\sqrt{BC}$*.

B The larger area	z Standard score	f Ordinate	$\sqrt{BC}$	C The smaller area
.500	.0000	.3989	.5000	.500
.505	.0125	.3989	.5000	.495
.510	.0251	.3988	.4999	.490
.515	.0376	.3987	.4998	.485
.520	.0502	.3984	.4996	.480
.525	.0627	.3982	.4994	.475
.530	.0753	.3978	.4991	.470
.535	.0878	.3974	.4988	.465
.540	.1004	.3969	.4984	.460
.545	.1130	.3964	.4980	.455
.550	.1257	.3958	.4975	.450
.555	.1383	.3951	.4970	.445
.560	.1510	.3944	.4964	.440
.565	.1637	.3936	.4958	.435
.570	.1764	.3928	.4951	.430
.575	.1891	.3919	.4943	.425
.580	.2019	.3909	.4936	.420
.585	.2147	.3899	.4927	.415
.590	.2275	.3887	.4918	.410
.595	.2404	.3876	.4909	.405
.600	.2533	.3863	.4899	.400
.605	.2663	.3850	.4889	.395
.610	.2793	.3837	.4877	.390
.615	.2924	.3822	.4867	.385
.620	.3055	.3808	.4854	.380
.625	.3186	.3792	.4841	.375
.630	.3319	.3776	.4828	.370
.635	.3451	.3759	.4814	.365
.640	.3585	.3741	.4800	.360
.645	.3719	.3723	.4785	.355
.650	.3853	.3704	.4770	.350
.655	.3989	.3684	.4754	.345
.660	.4125	.3664	.4737	.340
.665	.4261	.3643	.4720	.335
.670	.4399	.3621	.4702	.330
.675	.4538	.3599	.4684	.325
.680	.4677	.3576	.4665	.320
.685	.4817	.3552	.4645	.315
.690	.4959	.3528	.4625	.310
.695	.5101	.3503	.4604	.305
.700	.5244	.3477	.4583	.300
.705	.5388	.3450	.4560	.295
.710	.5534	.3423	.4538	.290
.715	.5681	.3395	.4514	.285
.720	.5828	.3366	.4490	.280

TABLE A15 *(continued)*

B *The larger area*	z *Standard score*	f *Ordinate*	$\sqrt{BC}$	C *The smaller area*
.725	.5978	.3337	.4465	.275
.730	.6128	.3306	.4440	.270
.735	.6280	.3275	.4413	.265
.740	.6433	.3244	.4386	.260
.745	.6588	.3211	.4359	.255
.750	.6745	.3178	.4330	.250
.755	.6903	.3144	.4301	.245
.760	.7063	.3109	.4271	.240
.765	.7225	.3073	.4240	.235
.770	.7388	.3036	.4208	.230
.775	.7554	.2999	.4176	.225
.780	.7722	.2961	.4142	.220
.785	.7892	.2922	.4108	.215
.790	.8064	.2882	.4073	.210
.795	.8239	.2841	.4037	.205
.800	.8416	.2800	.4000	.200
.805	.8596	.2757	.3962	.195
.810	.8779	.2714	.3923	.190
.815	.8965	.2669	.3883	.185
.820	.9154	.2624	.3842	.180
.825	.9346	.2578	.3800	.175
.830	.9542	.2531	.3756	.170
.835	.9741	.2482	.3712	.165
.840	.9945	.2433	.3666	.160
.845	1.0152	.2383	.3619	.155
.850	1.0364	.2332	.3571	.150
.855	1.0581	.2279	.3521	.145
.860	1.0803	.2226	.3470	.140
.865	1.1031	.2171	.3417	.135
.870	1.1264	.2115	.3363	.130
.875	1.1503	.2059	.3307	.125
.880	1.1750	.2000	.3250	.120
.885	1.2004	.1941	.3190	.115
.890	1.2265	.1880	.3129	.110
.895	1.2536	.1818	.3066	.105
.900	1.2816	.1755	.3000	.100
.905	1.3106	.1690	.2932	.095
.910	1.3408	.1624	.2862	.090
.915	1.3722	.1556	.2789	.085
.920	1.4051	.1487	.2713	.080
.925	1.4395	.1416	.2634	.075
.930	1.4757	.1343	.2551	.070
.935	1.5141	.1268	.2465	.065
.940	1.5548	.1191	.2375	.060
.945	1.5982	.1112	.2280	.055

TABLE A15 *(continued)*

B The larger area	*z* Standard score	*f* Ordinate	$\sqrt{BC}$	*C* The smaller area
.950	1.6449	.1031	.2179	.050
.955	1.6954	.0948	.2073	.045
.960	1.7507	.0862	.1960	.040
.965	1.8119	.0773	.1838	.035
.970	1.8808	.0680	.1706	.030
.975	1.9600	.0584	.1561	.025
.980	2.0537	.0484	.1400	.020
.985	2.1701	.0379	.1226	.015
.990	2.3263	.0267	.0995	.010
.995	2.5758	.0145	.0705	.005
.996	2.6521	.0118	.0631	.004
.997	2.7478	.0091	.0547	.003
.998	2.8782	.0063	.0447	.002
.999	3.0902	.0034	.0316	.001
.9995	3.2905	.0018	.0224	.0005

TABLE A16

5 Percent (Lightface Type) and 1 Percent (Boldface Type) Points for the Distribution of *F*.

Across the top of the table are degrees of freedom (df) for "Between Group" variation. The far left- and far right-hand columns contain df for "Within Group" variation. Where these values intersect in the body of the table define critical values of F that must be equaled or exceeded for statistical significance at the .05 or .01 levels. The lightface type are .05 critical values, while the boldface type are .01 critical values. If the exact df for either "Between Group" variation or "Within Group" variation cannot be found, the smaller df points should be used for a conservative hypothesis test. For example, if "Within Group" df = 280, we would use the df = 200 for entering the table.

f_2	f_1 Degrees of Freedom (for greater mean square)																								f_2
	1	2	3	4	5	6	7	8	9	10	11	12	14	16	20	24	30	40	50	75	100	200	500	∞	
1	161	200	216	225	230	234	237	239	241	242	243	244	245	246	248	249	250	251	252	253	253	254	254	254	1
	4,052	**4,999**	**5,403**	**5,625**	**5,764**	**5,859**	**5,928**	**5,981**	**6,022**	**6,056**	**6,082**	**6,106**	**6,142**	**6,169**	**6,208**	**6,234**	**6,261**	**6,286**	**6,302**	**6,323**	**6,334**	**6,352**	**6,361**	**6,366**	
2	18.51	19.00	19.16	19.25	19.30	19.33	19.36	19.37	19.38	19.39	19.40	19.41	19.42	19.43	19.44	19.45	19.46	19.47	19.47	19.48	19.49	19.49	19.50	19.50	2
	98.49	**99.00**	**99.17**	**99.25**	**99.30**	**99.33**	**99.36**	**99.37**	**99.39**	**99.40**	**99.41**	**99.42**	**99.43**	**99.44**	**99.45**	**99.46**	**99.47**	**99.48**	**99.48**	**99.49**	**99.49**	**99.49**	**99.50**	**99.50**	
3	10.13	9.55	9.28	9.12	9.01	8.94	8.88	8.84	8.81	8.78	8.76	8.74	8.71	8.69	8.66	8.64	8.62	8.60	8.58	8.57	8.56	8.54	8.54	8.53	3
	34.12	**30.82**	**29.46**	**28.71**	**28.24**	**27.91**	**27.67**	**27.49**	**27.34**	**27.23**	**27.13**	**27.05**	**26.92**	**26.83**	**26.69**	**26.60**	**26.50**	**26.41**	**26.35**	**26.27**	**26.23**	**26.18**	**26.14**	**26.12**	
4	7.71	6.94	6.59	6.39	6.26	6.16	6.09	6.04	6.00	5.96	5.93	5.91	5.87	5.84	5.80	5.77	5.74	5.71	5.70	5.68	5.66	5.65	5.64	5.63	4
	21.20	**18.00**	**16.69**	**15.98**	**15.52**	**15.21**	**14.98**	**14.80**	**14.66**	**14.54**	**14.45**	**14.37**	**14.24**	**14.15**	**14.02**	**13.93**	**13.83**	**13.74**	**13.69**	**13.61**	**13.57**	**13.52**	**13.48**	**13.46**	
5	6.61	5.79	5.41	5.19	5.05	4.95	4.88	4.82	4.78	4.74	4.70	4.68	4.64	4.60	4.56	4.53	4.50	4.46	4.44	4.42	4.40	4.38	4.37	4.36	5
	16.26	**13.27**	**12.06**	**11.39**	**10.97**	**10.67**	**10.45**	**10.29**	**10.15**	**10.05**	**9.96**	**9.89**	**9.77**	**9.68**	**9.55**	**9.47**	**9.38**	**9.29**	**9.24**	**9.17**	**9.13**	**9.07**	**9.04**	**9.02**	
6	5.99	5.14	4.76	4.53	4.39	4.28	4.21	4.15	4.10	4.06	4.03	4.00	3.96	3.92	3.87	3.84	3.81	3.77	3.75	3.72	3.71	3.69	3.68	3.67	6
	13.74	**10.92**	**9.78**	**9.15**	**8.75**	**8.47**	**8.26**	**8.10**	**7.98**	**7.87**	**7.79**	**7.72**	**7.60**	**7.52**	**7.39**	**7.31**	**7.23**	**7.14**	**7.09**	**7.02**	**6.99**	**6.94**	**6.90**	**6.88**	
7	5.59	4.74	4.35	4.12	3.97	3.87	3.79	3.73	3.68	3.63	3.60	3.57	3.52	3.49	3.44	3.41	3.38	3.34	3.32	3.29	3.28	3.25	3.24	3.23	7
	12.25	**9.55**	**8.45**	**7.85**	**7.46**	**7.19**	**7.00**	**6.84**	**6.71**	**6.62**	**6.54**	**6.47**	**6.35**	**6.27**	**6.15**	**6.07**	**5.98**	**5.90**	**5.85**	**5.78**	**5.75**	**5.70**	**5.67**	**5.65**	
8	5.32	4.46	4.07	3.84	3.69	3.58	3.50	3.44	3.39	3.34	3.31	3.28	3.23	3.20	3.15	3.12	3.08	3.05	3.03	3.00	2.98	2.96	2.94	2.93	8
	11.26	**8.65**	**7.59**	**7.01**	**6.63**	**6.37**	**6.19**	**6.03**	**5.91**	**5.82**	**5.74**	**5.67**	**5.56**	**5.48**	**5.36**	**5.28**	**5.20**	**5.11**	**5.06**	**5.00**	**4.96**	**4.91**	**4.88**	**4.86**	
9	5.12	4.26	3.86	3.63	3.48	3.37	3.29	3.23	3.18	3.13	3.10	3.07	3.02	2.98	2.93	2.90	2.86	2.82	2.80	2.77	2.76	2.73	2.72	2.71	9
	10.56	**8.02**	**6.99**	**6.42**	**6.06**	**5.80**	**5.62**	**5.47**	**5.35**	**5.26**	**5.18**	**5.11**	**5.00**	**4.92**	**4.80**	**4.73**	**4.64**	**4.56**	**4.51**	**4.45**	**4.41**	**4.36**	**4.33**	**4.31**	
10	4.96	4.10	3.71	3.48	3.33	3.22	3.14	3.07	3.02	2.97	2.94	2.91	2.86	2.82	2.77	2.74	2.70	2.67	2.64	2.61	2.59	2.56	2.55	2.54	10
	10.04	**7.56**	**6.55**	**5.99**	**5.64**	**5.39**	**5.21**	**5.06**	**4.95**	**4.85**	**4.78**	**4.71**	**4.60**	**4.52**	**4.41**	**4.33**	**4.25**	**4.17**	**4.12**	**4.05**	**4.01**	**3.96**	**3.93**	**3.91**	
11	4.84	3.98	3.59	3.36	3.20	3.09	3.01	2.95	2.90	2.86	2.82	2.79	2.74	2.70	2.65	2.61	2.57	2.53	2.50	2.47	2.45	2.42	2.41	2.40	11
	9.65	**7.20**	**6.22**	**5.67**	**5.32**	**5.07**	**4.88**	**4.74**	**4.63**	**4.54**	**4.46**	**4.40**	**4.29**	**4.21**	**4.10**	**4.02**	**3.94**	**3.86**	**3.80**	**3.74**	**3.70**	**3.66**	**3.62**	**3.60**	
12	4.75	3.88	3.49	3.26	3.11	3.00	2.92	2.85	2.80	2.76	2.72	2.69	2.64	2.60	2.54	2.50	2.46	2.42	2.40	2.36	2.35	2.32	2.31	2.30	12
	9.33	**6.93**	**5.95**	**5.41**	**5.06**	**4.82**	**4.65**	**4.50**	**4.39**	**4.30**	**4.22**	**4.16**	**4.05**	**3.98**	**3.86**	**3.78**	**3.70**	**3.61**	**3.56**	**3.49**	**3.46**	**3.41**	**3.38**	**3.36**	
13	4.67	3.80	3.41	3.18	3.02	2.92	2.84	2.77	2.72	2.67	2.63	2.60	2.55	2.51	2.46	2.42	2.38	2.34	2.32	2.28	2.26	2.24	2.22	2.21	13
	9.07	**6.70**	**5.74**	**5.20**	**4.86**	**4.62**	**4.44**	**4.30**	**4.19**	**4.10**	**4.02**	**3.96**	**3.85**	**3.78**	**3.67**	**3.59**	**3.51**	**3.42**	**3.37**	**3.30**	**3.27**	**3.21**	**3.18**	**3.16**	

Source: By permission from *Statistical Methods*, 6th Edition, by George W. Snedecor and William G. Cochran. © 1967 by the Iowa State University Press, Ames, Iowa. The function, $F = e$ with exponent $2z$, is computed in part from Fisher's Table VI. Additional entries are by interpolation, mostly graphical.

TABLE A16 (continued)

f_2	f_1 Degrees of Freedom (for greater mean square)																								f_2
	1	2	3	4	5	6	7	8	9	10	11	12	14	16	20	24	30	40	50	75	100	200	500	∞	
14	4.60	3.74	3.34	3.11	2.96	2.85	2.77	2.70	2.65	2.60	2.56	2.53	2.48	2.44	2.39	2.35	2.31	2.27	2.24	2.21	2.19	2.16	2.14	2.13	14
	8.86	**6.51**	**5.56**	**5.03**	**4.69**	**4.46**	**4.28**	**4.14**	**4.03**	**3.94**	**3.86**	**3.80**	**3.70**	**3.62**	**3.51**	**3.43**	**3.34**	**3.26**	**3.21**	**3.14**	**3.11**	**3.06**	**3.02**	**3.00**	
15	4.54	3.68	3.29	3.06	2.90	2.79	2.70	2.64	2.59	2.55	2.51	2.48	2.43	2.39	2.33	2.29	2.25	2.21	2.18	2.15	2.12	2.10	2.08	2.07	15
	8.68	**6.36**	**5.42**	**4.89**	**4.56**	**4.32**	**4.14**	**4.00**	**3.89**	**3.80**	**3.73**	**3.67**	**3.56**	**3.48**	**3.36**	**3.29**	**3.20**	**3.12**	**3.07**	**3.00**	**2.97**	**2.92**	**2.89**	**2.87**	
16	4.49	3.63	3.24	3.01	2.85	2.74	2.66	2.59	2.54	2.49	2.45	2.42	2.37	2.33	2.28	2.24	2.20	2.16	2.13	2.09	2.07	2.04	2.02	2.01	16
	8.53	**6.23**	**5.29**	**4.77**	**4.44**	**4.20**	**4.03**	**3.89**	**3.78**	**3.69**	**3.61**	**3.55**	**3.45**	**3.37**	**3.25**	**3.18**	**3.10**	**3.01**	**2.96**	**2.98**	**2.86**	**2.80**	**2.77**	**2.75**	
17	4.45	3.59	3.20	2.96	2.81	2.70	2.62	2.55	2.50	2.45	2.41	2.38	2.33	2.29	2.23	2.19	2.15	2.11	2.08	2.04	2.02	1.99	1.97	1.96	17
	8.40	**6.11**	**5.18**	**4.67**	**4.34**	**4.10**	**3.93**	**3.79**	**3.68**	**3.59**	**3.52**	**3.45**	**3.35**	**3.27**	**3.16**	**3.08**	**3.00**	**2.92**	**2.86**	**2.79**	**2.76**	**2.70**	**2.67**	**2.65**	
18	4.41	3.55	3.16	2.93	2.77	3.66	2.58	2.51	2.46	2.41	2.37	2.34	2.29	2.25	2.19	2.15	2.11	2.07	2.04	2.00	1.98	1.95	1.93	1.92	18
	8.28	**6.01**	**5.09**	**4.58**	**4.25**	**4.01**	**3.85**	**3.71**	**3.60**	**3.51**	**3.44**	**3.37**	**3.27**	**3.19**	**3.07**	**3.00**	**2.91**	**2.83**	**2.78**	**2.71**	**2.68**	**2.62**	**2.59**	**2.57**	
19	4.38	3.52	3.13	2.90	2.74	2.63	2.55	2.48	2.43	2.38	2.34	2.31	2.26	2.21	2.15	2.11	2.07	2.02	2.00	1.96	1.94	1.91	1.90	1.88	19
	8.18	**5.93**	**5.01**	**4.50**	**4.17**	**3.94**	**3.77**	**3.63**	**3.52**	**3.43**	**3.36**	**3.30**	**3.19**	**3.12**	**3.00**	**2.92**	**2.84**	**2.76**	**2.70**	**2.63**	**2.60**	**2.54**	**2.51**	**2.49**	
20	4.35	3.49	3.10	2.87	2.71	2.60	2.52	2.45	2.40	2.35	2.31	2.28	2.23	2.18	2.12	2.08	2.04	1.99	1.96	1.92	1.90	1.87	1.85	1.84	20
	8.10	**5.85**	**4.94**	**4.43**	**4.10**	**3.87**	**3.71**	**3.56**	**3.45**	**3.37**	**3.30**	**3.23**	**3.13**	**3.05**	**2.94**	**2.86**	**2.77**	**2.69**	**2.63**	**2.56**	**2.53**	**2.47**	**2.44**	**2.42**	
21	4.32	3.47	3.07	2.84	2.68	2.57	2.49	2.42	2.37	2.32	2.28	2.25	2.20	2.15	2.09	2.05	2.00	1.96	1.93	1.89	1.87	1.84	1.82	1.81	21
	8.02	**5.78**	**4.87**	**4.37**	**4.04**	**3.81**	**3.65**	**3.51**	**3.40**	**3.31**	**3.24**	**3.17**	**3.07**	**2.99**	**2.88**	**2.80**	**2.72**	**2.63**	**2.58**	**2.51**	**2.47**	**2.42**	**2.38**	**2.36**	
22	4.30	3.44	3.05	2.82	2.66	2.55	2.47	2.40	2.35	2.30	2.26	2.23	2.18	2.13	2.07	2.03	1.98	1.93	1.91	1.87	1.84	1.81	1.80	1.78	22
	7.94	**5.72**	**4.82**	**4.31**	**3.99**	**3.76**	**3.59**	**3.45**	**3.35**	**3.26**	**3.18**	**3.12**	**3.02**	**2.94**	**2.83**	**2.75**	**2.67**	**2.58**	**2.53**	**2.46**	**2.42**	**2.37**	**2.33**	**2.31**	
23	4.28	3.42	3.03	2.80	2.64	2.53	2.45	2.38	2.32	2.28	2.24	2.20	2.14	2.10	2.04	2.00	1.96	1.91	1.88	1.84	1.82	1.79	1.77	1.76	23
	7.88	**5.66**	**4.76**	**4.26**	**3.94**	**3.71**	**3.54**	**3.41**	**3.30**	**3.21**	**3.14**	**3.07**	**2.97**	**2.89**	**2.78**	**2.70**	**2.62**	**2.53**	**2.48**	**2.41**	**2.37**	**2.32**	**2.28**	**2.26**	
24	4.26	3.40	3.01	2.78	2.62	2.51	2.43	2.36	2.30	2.26	2.22	2.18	2.13	2.09	2.02	1.98	1.94	1.89	1.86	1.82	1.80	1.76	1.74	1.73	24
	7.82	**5.61**	**4.72**	**4.22**	**3.90**	**3.67**	**3.50**	**3.36**	**3.25**	**3.17**	**3.09**	**3.03**	**2.93**	**2.85**	**2.74**	**2.66**	**2.58**	**2.49**	**2.44**	**2.36**	**2.33**	**2.27**	**2.23**	**2.21**	
25	4.24	3.38	2.99	2.76	2.60	2.49	2.41	2.34	2.28	2.24	2.20	2.16	2.11	2.06	2.00	1.96	1.92	1.87	1.84	1.80	1.77	1.74	1.72	1.71	25
	7.77	**5.57**	**4.68**	**4.18**	**3.86**	**3.63**	**3.46**	**3.32**	**3.21**	**3.13**	**3.05**	**2.99**	**2.89**	**2.81**	**2.70**	**2.62**	**2.54**	**2.45**	**2.40**	**2.32**	**2.29**	**2.23**	**2.19**	**2.17**	
26	4.22	3.37	2.98	2.74	2.59	2.47	2.39	2.32	2.27	2.22	2.18	2.15	2.10	2.05	1.99	1.95	1.90	1.85	1.82	1.78	1.76	1.72	1.70	1.69	26
	7.72	**5.53**	**4.64**	**4.14**	**3.82**	**3.59**	**3.42**	**3.29**	**3.17**	**3.09**	**3.02**	**2.96**	**2.86**	**2.77**	**2.66**	**2.58**	**2.50**	**2.41**	**2.36**	**2.28**	**2.25**	**2.19**	**2.15**	**2.13**	

TABLE A16 (continued)

f_2	f_1 Degrees of Freedom (for greater mean square)																								f_2
	1	2	3	4	5	6	7	8	9	10	11	12	14	16	20	24	30	40	50	75	100	200	500	∞	
27	4.21	3.35	2.96	2.73	2.57	2.46	2.37	2.30	2.25	2.20	2.16	2.13	2.08	2.03	1.97	1.93	1.88	1.84	1.80	1.76	1.74	1.71	1.68	1.67	27
	7.68	**5.49**	**4.60**	**4.11**	**3.79**	**3.56**	**3.39**	**3.26**	**3.14**	**3.06**	**2.98**	**2.93**	**2.83**	**2.74**	**2.63**	**2.55**	**2.47**	**2.38**	**2.33**	**2.25**	**2.21**	**2.16**	**2.12**	**2.10**	
28	4.20	3.34	2.95	2.71	2.56	2.44	2.36	2.29	2.24	2.19	2.15	2.12	2.06	2.02	1.96	1.91	1.87	1.81	1.78	1.75	1.72	1.69	1.67	1.65	28
	7.64	**5.45**	**4.57**	**4.07**	**3.76**	**3.53**	**3.36**	**3.23**	**3.11**	**3.03**	**2.95**	**2.90**	**2.80**	**2.71**	**2.60**	**2.52**	**2.44**	**2.35**	**2.30**	**2.22**	**2.18**	**2.13**	**2.09**	**2.06**	
29	4.18	3.33	2.93	2.70	2.54	2.43	2.35	2.28	2.22	2.18	2.14	2.10	2.05	2.00	1.94	1.90	1.85	1.80	1.77	1.73	1.71	1.68	1.65	1.64	29
	7.60	**5.42**	**4.54**	**4.04**	**3.73**	**3.50**	**3.33**	**3.20**	**3.08**	**3.00**	**2.92**	**2.87**	**2.77**	**2.68**	**2.57**	**2.49**	**2.41**	**2.32**	**2.27**	**2.19**	**2.15**	**2.10**	**2.06**	**2.03**	
30	4.17	3.32	2.92	2.69	2.53	2.42	2.34	2.27	2.21	2.16	2.12	2.09	2.04	1.99	1.93	1.89	1.84	1.79	1.76	1.72	1.69	1.66	1.64	1.62	30
	7.56	**5.39**	**4.51**	**4.02**	**3.70**	**3.47**	**3.30**	**3.17**	**3.06**	**2.98**	**2.90**	**2.84**	**2.74**	**2.66**	**2.55**	**2.47**	**2.38**	**2.29**	**2.24**	**2.16**	**2.13**	**2.07**	**2.03**	**2.01**	
32	4.15	3.30	2.90	2.67	2.51	2.40	2.32	2.25	2.19	2.14	2.10	2.07	2.02	1.97	1.91	1.86	1.82	1.76	1.74	1.69	1.67	1.64	1.61	1.59	32
	7.50	**5.34**	**4.46**	**3.97**	**3.66**	**3.42**	**3.25**	**3.12**	**3.01**	**2.94**	**2.86**	**2.80**	**2.70**	**2.62**	**2.51**	**2.42**	**2.34**	**2.25**	**2.20**	**2.12**	**2.08**	**2.02**	**1.98**	**1.96**	
34	4.13	3.28	2.88	2.65	2.49	2.38	2.30	2.23	2.17	2.12	2.08	2.05	2.00	1.95	1.89	1.84	1.80	1.74	1.71	1.67	1.64	1.61	1.59	1.57	34
	7.44	**5.29**	**4.42**	**3.93**	**3.61**	**3.38**	**3.21**	**3.08**	**2.97**	**2.89**	**2.82**	**2.76**	**2.66**	**2.58**	**2.47**	**2.38**	**2.30**	**2.21**	**2.15**	**2.08**	**2.04**	**1.98**	**1.94**	**1.91**	
36	4.11	3.26	2.86	2.63	2.48	2.36	2.28	2.21	2.15	2.10	2.06	2.03	1.98	1.93	1.87	1.82	1.78	1.72	1.69	1.65	1.62	1.59	1.56	1.55	36
	7.39	**5.25**	**4.38**	**3.89**	**3.58**	**3.35**	**3.18**	**3.04**	**2.94**	**2.86**	**2.78**	**2.72**	**2.62**	**2.54**	**2.43**	**2.35**	**2.26**	**2.17**	**2.12**	**2.04**	**2.00**	**1.94**	**1.90**	**1.87**	
38	4.10	3.25	2.85	2.62	2.46	2.35	2.26	2.19	2.14	2.09	2.05	2.02	1.96	1.92	1.85	1.80	1.76	1.71	1.67	1.63	1.60	1.57	1.54	1.53	38
	7.35	**5.21**	**4.34**	**3.86**	**3.54**	**3.32**	**3.15**	**3.02**	**2.91**	**2.82**	**2.75**	**2.69**	**2.59**	**2.51**	**2.40**	**2.32**	**2.22**	**2.14**	**2.08**	**2.00**	**1.97**	**1.90**	**1.86**	**1.84**	
40	4.08	3.23	2.84	2.61	2.45	2.34	2.25	2.18	2.12	2.07	2.04	2.00	1.95	1.90	1.84	1.79	1.74	1.69	1.66	1.61	1.59	1.55	1.53	1.51	40
	7.31	**5.18**	**4.31**	**3.83**	**3.51**	**3.29**	**3.12**	**2.99**	**2.88**	**2.80**	**2.73**	**2.66**	**2.56**	**2.49**	**2.37**	**2.29**	**2.20**	**2.11**	**2.05**	**1.97**	**1.94**	**1.88**	**1.84**	**1.81**	
42	4.07	3.22	2.83	2.59	2.44	2.32	2.24	2.17	2.11	2.06	2.02	1.99	1.94	1.89	1.82	1.78	1.73	1.68	1.64	1.60	1.57	1.54	1.51	1.49	42
	7.27	**5.15**	**4.29**	**3.80**	**3.49**	**3.26**	**3.10**	**2.96**	**2.86**	**2.77**	**2.70**	**2.64**	**2.54**	**2.46**	**2.35**	**2.26**	**2.17**	**2.08**	**2.02**	**1.94**	**1.91**	**1.85**	**1.80**	**1.78**	
44	4.06	3.21	2.82	2.58	2.43	2.31	2.23	2.16	2.10	2.05	2.01	1.98	1.92	1.88	1.81	1.76	1.72	1.66	1.63	1.58	1.56	1.52	1.50	1.48	44
	7.24	**5.12**	**4.26**	**3.78**	**3.46**	**3.24**	**3.07**	**2.94**	**2.84**	**2.75**	**2.68**	**2.62**	**2.52**	**2.44**	**2.32**	**2.24**	**2.15**	**2.06**	**2.00**	**1.92**	**1.88**	**1.82**	**1.78**	**1.75**	
46	4.05	3.20	2.81	2.57	2.42	2.30	2.22	2.14	2.09	2.04	2.00	1.97	1.91	1.87	1.80	1.75	1.71	1.65	1.62	1.57	1.54	1.51	1.48	1.46	46
	7.21	**5.10**	**4.24**	**3.76**	**3.44**	**3.22**	**3.05**	**2.92**	**2.82**	**2.73**	**2.66**	**2.60**	**2.50**	**2.42**	**2.30**	**2.22**	**2.13**	**2.04**	**1.98**	**1.90**	**1.86**	**1.80**	**1.76**	**1.72**	
48	4.04	3.19	2.80	2.56	2.41	2.30	2.21	2.14	2.08	2.03	1.99	1.96	1.90	1.86	1.79	1.74	1.70	1.64	1.61	1.56	1.53	1.50	1.47	1.45	48
	7.19	**5.08**	**4.22**	**3.74**	**3.42**	**3.20**	**3.04**	**2.90**	**2.80**	**2.71**	**2.64**	**2.58**	**2.48**	**2.40**	**2.28**	**2.20**	**2.11**	**2.02**	**1.96**	**1.88**	**1.84**	**1.78**	**1.73**	**1.70**	

TABLE A16 *(continued)*

f_2	f_1 Degrees of Freedom (for greater mean square)																								f_2
	1	2	3	4	5	6	7	8	9	10	11	12	14	16	20	24	30	40	50	75	100	200	500	∞	
50	4.03	3.18	2.79	2.56	2.40	2.29	2.20	2.13	2.07	2.02	1.98	1.95	1.90	1.85	1.78	1.74	1.69	1.63	1.60	1.55	1.52	1.48	1.46	1.44	50
	7.17	**5.06**	**4.20**	**3.72**	**3.41**	**3.18**	**3.02**	**2.88**	**2.78**	**2.70**	**2.62**	**2.56**	**2.46**	**2.39**	**2.26**	**2.18**	**2.10**	**2.00**	**1.94**	**1.86**	**1.82**	**1.76**	**1.71**	**1.68**	
55	4.02	3.17	2.78	2.54	2.38	2.27	2.18	2.11	2.05	2.00	1.97	1.93	1.88	1.83	1.76	1.72	1.67	1.61	1.58	1.52	1.50	1.46	1.43	1.41	55
	7.12	**5.01**	**4.16**	**3.68**	**3.37**	**3.15**	**2.98**	**2.85**	**2.75**	**2.66**	**2.59**	**2.53**	**2.43**	**2.35**	**2.23**	**2.15**	**2.06**	**1.96**	**1.90**	**1.82**	**1.78**	**1.71**	**1.66**	**1.64**	
60	4.00	3.15	2.76	2.52	2.37	2.25	2.17	2.10	2.04	1.99	1.95	1.92	1.86	1.81	1.75	1.70	1.65	1.59	1.56	1.50	1.48	1.44	1.41	1.39	60
	7.08	**4.98**	**4.13**	**3.65**	**3.34**	**3.12**	**2.95**	**2.82**	**2.72**	**2.63**	**2.56**	**2.50**	**2.40**	**2.32**	**2.20**	**2.12**	**2.03**	**1.93**	**1.87**	**1.79**	**1.74**	**1.68**	**1.63**	**1.60**	
65	3.99	3.14	2.75	2.51	2.36	2.24	2.15	2.08	2.02	1.98	1.94	1.90	1.85	1.80	1.73	1.68	1.63	1.57	1.54	1.49	1.46	1.42	1.39	1.37	65
	7.04	**4.95**	**4.10**	**3.62**	**3.31**	**3.09**	**2.93**	**2.79**	**2.70**	**2.61**	**2.54**	**2.47**	**2.37**	**2.30**	**2.18**	**2.09**	**2.00**	**1.90**	**1.84**	**1.76**	**1.71**	**1.64**	**1.60**	**1.56**	
70	3.98	3.13	2.74	2.50	2.35	2.23	2.14	2.07	2.01	1.97	1.93	1.89	1.84	1.79	1.72	1.67	1.62	1.56	1.53	1.47	1.45	1.40	1.37	1.35	70
	7.01	**4.92**	**4.08**	**3.60**	**3.29**	**3.07**	**2.91**	**2.77**	**2.67**	**2.59**	**2.51**	**2.45**	**2.35**	**2.28**	**2.15**	**2.07**	**1.98**	**1.88**	**1.82**	**1.74**	**1.69**	**1.62**	**1.56**	**1.53**	
80	3.96	3.11	2.72	2.48	2.33	2.21	2.12	2.05	1.99	1.95	1.91	1.88	1.82	1.77	1.70	1.65	1.60	1.54	1.51	1.45	1.42	1.38	1.35	1.32	80
	6.96	**4.88**	**4.04**	**3.56**	**3.25**	**3.04**	**2.87**	**2.74**	**2.64**	**2.55**	**2.48**	**2.41**	**2.32**	**2.24**	**2.11**	**2.03**	**1.94**	**1.84**	**1.78**	**1.70**	**1.65**	**1.57**	**1.52**	**1.49**	
100	3.94	3.09	2.70	2.46	2.30	2.19	2.10	2.03	1.97	1.92	1.88	1.85	1.79	1.75	1.68	1.63	1.57	1.51	1.48	1.42	1.39	1.34	1.30	1.28	100
	6.90	**4.82**	**3.98**	**3.51**	**3.20**	**2.99**	**2.82**	**2.69**	**2.59**	**2.51**	**2.43**	**2.36**	**2.26**	**2.19**	**2.06**	**1.98**	**1.89**	**1.79**	**1.73**	**1.64**	**1.59**	**1.51**	**1.46**	**1.43**	
125	3.92	3.07	2.68	2.44	2.29	2.17	2.08	2.01	1.95	1.90	1.86	1.83	1.77	1.72	1.65	1.60	1.55	1.49	1.45	1.39	1.36	1.31	1.27	1.25	125
	6.84	**4.78**	**3.94**	**3.47**	**3.17**	**2.95**	**2.79**	**2.65**	**2.56**	**2.47**	**2.40**	**2.33**	**2.23**	**2.15**	**2.03**	**1.94**	**1.85**	**1.75**	**1.68**	**1.59**	**1.54**	**1.46**	**1.40**	**1.37**	
150	3.91	3.06	2.67	2.43	2.27	2.16	2.07	2.00	1.94	1.89	1.85	1.82	1.76	1.71	1.64	1.59	1.54	1.47	1.44	1.37	1.34	1.29	1.25	1.22	150
	6.81	**4.75**	**3.91**	**3.44**	**3.14**	**2.92**	**2.76**	**2.62**	**2.53**	**2.44**	**2.37**	**2.30**	**2.20**	**2.12**	**2.00**	**1.91**	**1.83**	**1.72**	**1.66**	**1.56**	**1.51**	**1.43**	**1.37**	**1.33**	
200	3.89	3.04	2.65	2.41	2.26	2.14	2.05	1.98	1.92	1.87	1.83	1.80	1.74	1.69	1.62	1.57	1.52	1.45	1.42	1.35	1.32	1.26	1.22	1.19	200
	6.76	**4.71**	**3.88**	**3.41**	**3.11**	**2.90**	**2.73**	**2.60**	**2.50**	**2.41**	**2.34**	**2.28**	**2.17**	**2.09**	**1.97**	**1.88**	**1.79**	**1.69**	**1.62**	**1.53**	**1.48**	**1.39**	**1.33**	**1.28**	
400	3.86	3.02	2.62	2.39	2.23	2.12	2.03	1.96	1.90	1.85	1.81	1.78	1.72	1.67	1.60	1.54	1.49	1.42	1.38	1.32	1.28	1.22	1.16	1.13	400
	6.70	**4.66**	**3.83**	**3.36**	**3.06**	**2.85**	**2.69**	**2.55**	**2.46**	**2.37**	**2.29**	**2.23**	**2.12**	**2.04**	**1.92**	**1.84**	**1.74**	**1.64**	**1.57**	**1.47**	**1.42**	**1.32**	**1.24**	**1.19**	
1000	3.85	3.00	2.61	2.38	2.22	2.10	2.02	1.95	1.89	1.84	1.80	1.76	1.70	1.65	1.58	1.53	1.47	1.41	1.36	1.30	1.26	1.19	1.13	1.08	1000
	6.66	**4.62**	**3.80**	**3.34**	**3.04**	**2.82**	**2.66**	**2.53**	**2.43**	**2.34**	**2.26**	**2.20**	**2.09**	**2.01**	**1.89**	**1.81**	**1.71**	**1.61**	**1.54**	**1.44**	**1.38**	**1.28**	**1.19**	**1.11**	
∞	3.84	2.99	2.60	2.37	2.21	2.09	2.01	1.94	1.88	1.83	1.79	1.75	1.69	1.64	1.57	1.52	1.46	1.40	1.35	1.28	1.24	1.17	1.11	1.00	∞
	6.64	**4.60**	**3.78**	**3.32**	**3.02**	**2.80**	**2.64**	**2.51**	**2.41**	**2.32**	**2.24**	**2.18**	**2.07**	**1.99**	**1.87**	**1.79**	**1.69**	**1.59**	**1.52**	**1.41**	**1.36**	**1.25**	**1.15**	**1.00**	

Distribution of the Studentized Range Statistic.

The values across the top of the table define the number of means being investigated. Down the far left-hand column are degrees of freedom (df) for "Within-Group" variation. These df are taken directly from the ANOVA Summary Table. The 1 – alpha column contains .95 and .99 values, which are equivalent to levels of significance of .05 and .01, respectively. If the exact df cannot be found down the left-hand column, the smaller df should be used. For instance, if we have 90 df for within-group variation, we would use 60 df for purposes of entering the table. Where r, the number of means, intersects with df defines the first q value to be used in the Table of Ordered Means for the Newman–Keuls procedure. All values on the same line and to the left of the first q value will also be used in the Table of Ordered Means.

df for $s_{\bar{X}}$	$1 - \alpha$	r = number of steps between ordered means													
		2	3	4	5	6	7	8	9	10	11	12	13	14	15
1	.95	18.0	27.0	32.8	37.1	40.4	43.1	45.4	47.4	49.1	50.6	52.0	53.2	54.3	55.4
	.99	90.0	135	164	186	202	216	227	237	246	253	260	266	272	277
2	.95	6.09	8.3	9.8	10.9	11.7	12.4	13.0	13.5	14.0	14.4	14.7	15.1	15.4	15.7
	.99	14.0	19.0	22.3	24.7	26.6	28.2	29.5	30.7	31.7	32.6	33.4	34.1	34.8	35.4
3	.95	4.50	5.91	6.82	7.50	8.04	8.48	8.85	9.18	9.46	9.72	9.95	10.2	10.4	10.5
	.99	8.26	10.6	12.2	13.3	14.2	15.0	15.6	16.2	16.7	17.1	17.5	17.9	18.2	18.5
4	.95	3.93	5.04	5.76	6.29	6.71	7.05	7.35	7.60	7.83	8.03	8.21	8.37	8.52	8.66
	.99	6.51	8.12	9.17	9.96	10.6	11.1	11.5	11.9	12.3	12.6	12.8	13.1	13.3	13.5
5	.95	3.64	4.60	5.22	5.67	6.03	6.33	6.58	6.80	6.99	7.17	7.32	7.47	7.60	7.72
	.99	5.70	6.97	7.80	8.42	8.91	9.32	9.67	9.97	10.2	10.5	10.7	10.9	11.1	11.2
6	.95	3.46	4.34	4.90	5.31	5.63	5.89	6.12	6.32	6.49	6.65	6.79	6.92	7.03	7.14
	.99	5.24	6.33	7.03	7.56	7.97	8.32	8.61	8.87	9.10	9.30	9.49	9.65	9.81	9.95
7	.95	3.34	4.16	4.69	5.06	5.36	5.61	5.82	6.00	6.16	6.30	6.43	6.55	6.66	6.76
	.99	4.95	5.92	6.54	7.01	7.37	7.68	7.94	8.17	8.37	8.55	8.71	8.86	9.00	9.12
8	.95	3.26	4.04	4.53	4.89	5.17	5.40	5.60	5.77	5.92	6.05	6.18	6.29	6.39	6.48
	.99	4.74	5.63	6.20	6.63	6.96	7.24	7.47	7.68	7.87	8.03	8.18	8.31	8.44	8.55
9	.95	3.20	3.95	4.42	4.76	5.02	5.24	5.43	5.60	5.74	5.87	5.98	6.09	6.19	6.28
	.99	4.60	5.43	5.96	6.35	6.66	6.91	7.13	7.32	7.49	7.65	7.78	7.91	8.03	8.13
10	.95	3.15	3.88	4.33	4.65	4.91	5.12	5.30	5.46	5.60	5.72	5.83	5.93	6.03	6.11
	.99	4.48	5.27	5.77	6.14	6.43	6.67	6.87	7.05	7.21	7.36	7.48	7.60	7.71	7.81

Source: Abridged from Table II.2 in *The Probability Integrals of the Range and of the Studentized Range*, prepared by H. Leon Harter, Donald S. Klemm, and Robert H. Guthrie. These tables are published in WADC Technical Report 58-484, vol. 2, 1959, Wright Air Development Center. Reprinted from B. J. Winer, *Statistical Principles in Experimental Design* (New York: McGraw-Hill Book Company, 1962) by permission of the publishers.

TABLE A17 *(continued)*

11	.95	3.11	3.82	4.26	4.57	4.82	5.03	5.20	5.35	5.49	5.61	5.71	5.81	5.90	5.99
	.99	4.39	5.14	5.62	5.97	6.25	6.48	6.67	6.84	6.99	7.13	7.26	7.36	7.46	7.56
12	.95	3.08	3.77	4.20	4.51	4.75	4.95	5.12	5.27	5.40	5.51	5.62	5.71	5.80	5.88
	.99	4.32	5.04	5.50	5.84	6.10	6.32	6.51	6.67	6.81	6.94	7.06	7.17	7.26	7.36
13	.95	3.06	3.73	4.15	4.45	4.69	4.88	5.05	5.19	5.32	5.43	5.53	5.63	5.71	5.79
	.99	4.26	4.96	5.40	5.73	5.98	6.19	6.37	6.53	6.67	6.79	6.90	7.01	7.10	7.19
14	.95	3.03	3.70	4.11	4.41	4.64	4.83	4.99	5.13	5.25	5.36	5.46	5.55	6.64	5.72
	.99	4.21	4.89	5.32	5.63	5.88	6.08	6.26	6.41	6.54	6.66	6.77	6.87	6.96	7.05
16	.95	3.00	3.65	4.05	4.33	4.56	4.74	4.90	5.03	5.15	5.26	5.35	5.44	5.52	5.59
	.99	4.13	4.78	5.19	5.49	5.72	5.92	6.08	6.22	6.35	6.46	6.56	6.66	6.74	6.82
18	.95	2.97	3.61	4.00	4.28	4.49	4.67	4.82	4.96	5.07	5.17	5.27	5.35	5.43	5.50
	.99	4.07	4.70	5.09	5.38	5.60	5.79	5.94	6.08	6.20	6.31	6.41	6.50	6.58	6.65
20	.95	2.95	3.58	3.96	4.23	4.45	4.62	4.77	4.90	5.01	5.11	5.20	5.28	5.36	5.43
	.99	4.02	4.64	5.02	5.29	5.51	5.69	5.84	5.97	6.09	6.19	6.29	6.37	6.45	6.52
24	.95	2.92	3.53	3.90	4.17	4.37	4.54	4.68	4.81	4.92	5.01	5.10	5.18	5.25	5.32
	.99	3.96	4.54	4.91	5.17	5.37	5.54	5.69	5.81	5.92	6.02	6.11	6.19	6.26	6.33
30	.95	2.89	3.49	3.84	4.10	4.30	4.46	4.60	4.72	4.83	4.92	5.00	5.08	5.15	5.21
	.99	3.89	4.45	4.80	5.05	5.24	5.40	5.54	5.56	5.76	5.85	5.93	6.01	6.08	6.14
40	.95	2.86	3.44	3.79	4.04	4.23	4.39	4.52	4.63	4.74	4.82	4.91	4.98	5.05	5.11
	.99	3.82	4.37	4.70	4.93	5.11	5.27	5.39	5.50	5.60	5.69	5.77	5.84	5.90	5.96
60	.95	2.83	3.40	3.74	3.98	4.16	4.31	4.44	4.55	4.65	4.73	4.81	4.88	4.94	5.00
	.99	3.76	4.28	4.60	4.82	4.99	5.13	5.25	5.36	5.45	5.53	5.60	5.67	5.73	5.79
120	.95	2.80	3.36	3.69	3.92	4.10	4.24	4.36	4.48	4.56	4.64	4.72	4.78	4.84	4.90
	.99	3.70	4.20	4.50	4.71	4.87	5.01	5.12	5.21	5.30	5.38	5.44	5.51	5.56	5.61
∞	.95	2.77	3.31	3.63	3.86	4.03	4.17	4.29	4.39	4.47	4.55	4.62	4.68	4.74	4.80
	.99	3.64	4.12	4.40	4.60	4.76	4.88	4.99	5.08	5.16	5.23	5.29	5.35	5.40	5.45

TABLE A18

Cumulative Binomial Probabilities: $P = .5$.

This table contains one-tailed probabilities that must be doubled for a two-tailed interpretation. In the Sign Test, N = the total number of pluses and minuses, while m = the sign that occurs less frequently. Where these values intersect in the body of the table defines the one-tailed probability (or doubled, the two-tailed probability) of the plus-minus split. Although decimal points are not included, it is assumed that all three-digit probabilities are preceded by a decimal point. For example, 031 is .031, and so on.

N \ m	0	1	2	3	4	5	6	7	8	9	10	11	12	13	14	15
5	031	188	500	812	969	*										
6	016	109	344	656	891	984	*									
7	008	062	227	500	773	938	992	*								
8	004	035	145	363	637	855	965	996	*							
9	002	020	090	254	500	746	910	980	998	*						
10	001	011	055	172	377	623	828	945	989	999	*					
11		006	033	113	274	500	726	887	967	994	*	*				
12		003	019	073	194	387	613	806	927	981	997	*	*			
13		002	011	046	133	291	500	709	867	954	989	998	*	*		
14		001	006	029	090	212	395	605	788	910	971	994	999	*	*	
15			004	018	059	151	304	500	696	849	941	982	996	*	*	*
16			002	011	038	105	227	402	598	773	895	962	989	998	*	*
17			001	006	025	072	166	315	500	685	834	928	975	994	999	*
18			001	004	015	048	119	240	407	593	760	881	952	985	996	999
19				002	010	032	084	180	324	500	676	820	916	968	990	998
20				001	006	021	058	132	252	412	588	748	868	942	979	994
21				001	004	013	039	095	192	332	500	668	808	905	961	987
22					002	008	026	067	143	262	416	584	738	857	933	974
23					001	005	017	047	105	202	339	500	661	798	895	953
24					001	003	011	032	076	154	271	419	581	729	846	924
25						002	007	022	054	115	212	345	500	655	788	885

Source: Helen M. Walker and Joseph Lev, *Statistical Inference* (New York: Henry Holt and Company, 1953). Copyright 1953 by Holt, Rinehart and Winston. With permission of the publishers and Miss Helen M. Walker.

TABLE A19

Distribution of the F_{max} Statistic.

Across the top of the table defines k, the number of sample variances. Down the far left-hand side are degrees of freedom (df), where df $= N - 1$ if all sample sizes are equal. If the sample sizes are not equal, the largest sample size should be used. The second column contains 1 – alpha values for .95 and .99, respectively. These are equivalent to the .05 and .01 levels of significance. If the researcher has df between two df points, the larger df value should be used for entering the table. For example, 58 df would mean that the 60 df line would be used. The body of the table contains critical values of F_{max}. Any observed F_{max} value that equals or exceeds the value shown in the body of the table means that homogeneity of variance or "equal variances" does not exist.

df for s_X^2	$1-\alpha$	k = number of variances								
		2	3	4	5	6	7	8	9	10
4	.95	9.60	15.5	20.6	25.2	29.5	33.6	37.5	41.4	44.6
	.99	23.2	37.	49.	59.	69.	79.	89.	97.	106.
5	.95	7.15	10.8	13.7	16.3	18.7	20.8	22.9	24.7	26.5
	.99	14.9	22.	28.	33.	38.	42.	46.	50.	54.
6	.95	5.82	8.38	10.4	12.1	13.7	15.0	16.3	17.5	18.6
	.99	11.1	15.5	19.1	22.	25.	27.	30.	32.	34.
7	.95	4.99	6.94	8.44	9.70	10.8	11.8	12.7	13.5	14.3
	.99	8.89	12.1	14.5	16.5	18.4	20.	22.	23.	24.
8	.95	4.43	6.00	7.18	8.12	9.03	9.78	10.5	11.1	11.7
	.99	7.50	9.9	11.7	13.2	14.5	15.8	16.9	17.9	18.9
9	.95	4.03	5.34	6.31	7.11	7.80	8.41	8.95	9.45	9.91
	.99	6.54	8.5	9.9	11.1	12.1	13.1	13.9	14.7	15.3
10	.95	3.72	4.85	5.67	6.34	6.92	7.42	7.87	8.28	8.66
	.99	5.85	7.4	8.6	9.6	10.4	11.1	11.8	12.4	12.9
12	.95	3.28	4.16	4.79	5.30	5.72	6.09	6.42	6.72	7.00
	.99	4.91	6.1	6.9	7.6	8.2	8.7	9.1	9.5	9.9
15	.95	2.86	3.54	4.01	4.37	4.68	4.95	5.19	5.40	5.59
	.99	4.07	4.9	5.5	6.0	6.4	6.7	7.1	7.3	7.5
20	.95	2.46	2.95	3.29	3.54	3.76	3.94	4.10	4.24	4.37
	.99	3.32	3.8	4.3	4.6	4.9	5.1	5.3	5.5	5.6
30	.95	2.07	2.40	2.61	2.78	2.91	3.02	3.12	3.21	3.29
	.99	2.63	3.0	3.3	3.4	3.6	3.7	3.8	3.9	4.0
60	.95	1.67	1.85	1.96	2.04	2.11	2.17	2.22	2.26	2.30
	.99	1.96	2.2	2.3	2.4	2.4	2.5	2.5	2.6	2.6
∞	.95	1.00	1.00	1.00	1.00	1.00	1.00	1.00	1.00	1.00
	.99	1.00	1.00	1.00	1.00	1.00	1.00	1.00	1.00	1.00

Source: Abridged from Table 31 in *Biometrika Tables for Statisticians*, vol. 1, 2nd ed. New York: Cambridge University Press, 1958, edited by E. S. Pearson and H. O. Hartley. With permission of E. S. Pearson and the trustees of Biometrika. Reprinted from B. J. Winer, *Statistical Principles in Experimental Design* (New York: McGraw-Hill Book Company, 1962) by permission of the publishers.

TABLE A20

Critical Values of ΣT in the Wilcoxon Matched Pairs-Signed Ranks Test.

This table contains one- and two-tailed probabilities for N's ranging from 6 to 50. Where any given N intersects with a designated level of significance defines a critical value of ΣT. We must observe a ΣT equal to or smaller than that shown in the table in order to conclude that two groups differ significantly at the probability shown at the top of the table.

	Level of significance for one-tailed test		
	.025	.01	.005
N	*Level of significance for two-tailed test*		
	.05	.02	.01
6	0	–	–
7	2	0	–
8	4	2	0
9	6	3	2
10	8	5	3
11	11	7	5
12	14	10	7
13	17	13	10
14	21	16	13
15	25	20	16
16	30	24	19
17	35	28	23
18	40	33	28
19	46	38	32
20	52	43	37
21	59	49	43
22	66	56	49
23	73	62	55
24	81	69	61
25	90	77	68
26	98	85	76
27	107	93	84
28	117	102	92
29	127	111	100
30	137	120	109
31	148	130	118
32	159	141	128
33	171	151	138
34	183	162	149
35	195	174	160
36	208	186	171

Source: Frank Wilcoxon, and Roberta A. Wilcox, *Some Rapid Approximate Statistical Procedures*, revised 1964 (Pearl River, N.Y.: Lederle Laboratories) p. 28. With the permission of the American Cyanamid Company.

TABLE A20 *(continued)*

N	*Level of significance for one-tailed test*		
	.025	.01	.005
	Level of significance for two-tailed test		
	.05	.02	.01
37	222	198	183
38	235	211	195
39	250	224	208
40	264	238	221
41	279	252	234
42	295	267	248
43	311	281	262
44	327	297	277
45	344	313	292
46	361	329	307
47	379	345	323
48	397	362	339
49	415	380	398
50	434	398	373

TABLE A21

Values of Estimated r_t, Based on Pearson's "Cosine Method," for Various Values of bc/ad.

This table contains equivalent values of r_{tet} for various values of bc/ad, where a, b, c, and d are observed cell frequencies in a 2 X 2 table.

r_{tet}	ad/bc	r_{tet}	ad/bc	r_{tet}	ad/bc
.00	0–1.00	.35	2.49–2.55	.70	8.50–8.90
.01	1.01–1.03	.36	2.56–2.63	.71	8.91–9.35
.02	1.04–1.06	.37	2.64–2.71	.72	9.36–9.82
.03	1.07–1.08	.38	2.72–2.79	.73	9.83–10.33
.04	1.09–1.11	.39	2.80–2.87	.74	10.34–10.90
.05	1.12–1.14	.40	2.88–2.96	.75	10.91–11.51
.06	1.15–1.17	.41	2.97–3.05	.76	11.52–12.16
.07	1.18–1.20	.42	3.06–3.14	.77	12.17–12.89
.08	1.21–1.23	.43	3.15–3.24	.78	12.90–13.70
.09	1.24–1.27	.44	3.25–3.34	.79	13.71–14.58
.10	1.28–1.30	.45	3.35–3.45	.80	14.59–15.57
.11	1.31–1.33	.46	3.46–3.56	.81	15.58–16.65
.12	1.34–1.37	.47	3.57–3.68	.82	16.66–17.88
.13	1.38–1.40	.48	3.69–3.80	.83	17.89–19.28
.14	1.41–1.44	.49	3.81–3.92	.84	19.29–20.85
.15	1.45–1.48	.50	3.93–4.06	.85	20.86–22.68
.16	1.49–1.52	.51	4.07–4.20	.86	22.69–24.76
.17	1.53–1.56	.52	4.21–4.34	.87	24.77–27.22
.18	1.57–1.60	.53	4.35–4.49	.88	27.23–30.09
.19	1.61–1.64	.54	4.50–4.66	.89	30.10–33.60
.20	1.65–1.69	.55	4.67–4.82	.90	33.61–37.79
.21	1.70–1.73	.56	4.83–4.99	.91	37.80–43.06
.22	1.74–1.78	.57	5.00–5.18	.92	43.07–49.83
.23	1.79–1.83	.58	5.19–5.38	.93	49.84–58.79
.24	1.84–1.88	.59	5.39–5.59	.94	58.80–70.95
.25	1.89–1.93	.60	5.60–5.80	.95	70.96–89.01
.26	1.94–1.98	.61	5.81–6.03	.96	89.02–117.54
.27	1.99–2.04	.62	6.04–6.28	.97	117.55–169.67
.28	2.05–2.10	.63	6.29–6.54	.98	169.68–293.12
.29	2.11–2.15	.64	6.55–6.81	.99	293.13–923.97
.30	2.16–2.22	.65	6.82–7.10	1.00	923.98 . . .
.31	2.23–2.28	.66	7.11–7.42		
.32	2.29–2.34	.67	7.43–7.75		
.33	2.35–2.41	.68	7.76–8.11		
.34	2.42–2.48	.69	8.12–8.49		

Source: M. D. Davidoff and H. W. Goheen, "A Table for the Rapid Determination of the Tetrachoric Correlation Coefficient," *Psychometrika*, 18:115–121, 1953, by permission of the authors and editors.

Answers to Exercises

Chapter 3

4. (a) 89.5 and 109.5 (b) 1499.5 and 1599.5
   (c) .195 to .295 (d) .00545 to .00595
   (e) 135.5 to 139.5 (f) 199.5 to 249.5

   Midpoints:

   (a) 99.5 (b) 1549.5 (c) .245
   (d) .0057 (e) 137.5 (f) 224.5

6. (a) 65.3 (b) 138.8 (c) 152.5
   (d) 35.9 (e) 100.3 (f) 61.9
   (g) 169.3 (h) 70.5

   Proportion below points:

   (a) .27 (b) .75 (c) .80
   (d) .04 (e) .50 (f) .25
   (g) .90 (h) .30

9. (a) .36% (b) 15.6% (c) 97%
   (d) 11.58% (e) 55.5% (f) .04%
10. Midpoints = 322, 327, 332, 337, 342, 347, 352, 357, 362, 367, 372, 377, 382, 387, 392.

    Upper and lower limits = 319.5 to 324.5, 324.5 to 329.5, 329.5 to 334.5, 334.5 to 339.5, 339.5 to 344.5, 344.5 to 349.5, 349.5 to 354.5, 354.5 to 359.5, 359.5 to 364.5, 364.5 to 369.5, 369.5 to 374.5, 374.5 to 379.5, 379.5 to 384.5, 384.5 to 389.5, 389.5 to 394.5.

Chapter 4

1. Mode = 522; median = 524.9, mean = 527
2. Mode = 14; median = 12.5; mean = 12.6
3. Mode = 114.5; median = 96.5; mean = 94.7
4. Mode = 15; median = 24; mean = 35.8
6. $\overline{X}_T = 42.5$
7. $\overline{X}_T = 48.2$; disproportionate weight given to smaller sample sizes, thereby inflating the grand mean value
8. Mode = 55 and 75; median = 55; mean = 56.4
10. Mode = 132; median = 142; mean = 143.8

Chapter 5

1. (a) $s = 13.9; s^2 = 193.21$
   (b) 39.7
   (c) 10.2
2. (a) 85.3 (b) 31.3
   (c) 27.4 (d) 52.4
3. $\text{IQV}_1 = 97.9\%$
   $\text{IQV}_2 = 96\%$
   $\text{IQV}_3 = 95.7\%$
   $\text{IQV}_4 = 84.2\%$
5. (a) 58 (b) 17.3
6. (a) 75 or 70 (b) 470.9
   (c) 21.7 (d) 17.9
7. (a) 15 (b) 3.9 (c) 3.6
8. (a) 13.7 (b) 56
9. $\text{IQV}_1 = 82.8\%$
   $\text{IQV}_2 = 90.4\%$
   $\text{IQV}_3 = 85.2\%$
10. $\overline{X} = 16.5$
11. (a) 20 or 18 (b) 5.5 (c) 30.3
    (d) 5 (e) 5

Chapter 6

1. (a) .0735 (b) .9901 (c) .5000
   (d) .6554 (e) .0233 (f) .1587
2. (a) .0782 (b) .9030
   (c) .4666 (d) .0026
3. (a) 4.10 (b) 0
   (c) −1.50 (d) −3.00
4. (a) 137 (b) 242
   (c) 267 (d) 220
5. (a) 550 (b) 412
   (c) 750 (d) 500
6. (a) .6255 (b) .0146 (c) .8389
   (d) .4880 (e) .8665 (f) .9871
   (g) .2090 (h) .8413
7. (a) 35 (b) 40 (c) 55
   (d) 15 (e) 40 (f) 31
8. (a) .2843 (b) .8475 (c) .3413
   (d) .7726 (e) .0003 (f) .8790
   (g) .8593 (h) .3284
9. (a) 1.31 (b) 3.00 (c) 1.50
   (d) .34 (e) 2.03 (f) 2.50
10. (a) 1513 (b) 1300 (c) 742
    (d) 1771 (e) 1987 (f) 229
11. (a) .1587 (b) .9970
    (c) .9998 (d) .8944
12. (a) .5998 (b) .0347 (c) .0022
    (d) .0795 (e) .9577 (f) .5205
13. (a) .0009 (b) .4880 (c) .9382
    (d) .0116 (e) .9946 (f) .5279
14. (a) .4514 (b) .9030 (c) .0007
    (d) .0723 (e) .4984 (f) .0619
15. (a) 0 (b) −1.00 (c) −3.17
    (d) .75 (e) 1.00 (f) 2.00
16. (a) 32 (b) 11
    (c) 19 (d) 52

Chapter 7

1. (a) 95.82 to 104.18 (b) 96.74 to 103.26
   (c) 93.43 to 106.57
2. (a) 69.26 to 80.74 (b) 68.14 to 81.86
   (c) 69.96 to 80.04 (d) 70.98 to 79.02
3. (a) $r_{xy} \leqslant 105$ (b) $\mu_1 \neq \mu_2$
   (c) $\overline{X} > 55$ (d) $r_{xy_1} = r_{xy_2}$
4. (a) 94.12 to 105.88 (b) 96.16 to 103.84
   (c) 95.68 to 104.32

5. (a) 5% (b) .1% (c) 1%
6. (a) 480.32 to 519.68 (b) 484.64 to 515.36
8. (a) 97.06 to 102.94 (b) 97.54 to 102.46
   (c) 96.13 to 103.87
9. (a) 326.76 to 333.24 (b) 325.92 to 334.08
   (c) 327.84 to 332.16
10. (a) 69.16 to 70.84 (b) 69.56 to 70.44
    (c) 69.72 to 70.28 (d) 69.01 to 70.99
11. (1a) 1.64 (1b) 1.28 (1c) 2.58
    (2a) 1.64 (2b) 1.96 (2c) 1.44
    (2d) 1.15
12. + or - 2.58
14. (a) 120.55 to 123.45 (b) 120.02 to 123.98
    (c) 121.06 to 122.94

Chapter 8

1. Not significantly different at the .05 level
2. $F = 3.854$; no significance at the .01 level
3. $s_{\bar{t}} = .99$
5. Homogeneity of variance does not exist ($F_{max} = 3.9$); F observed = 7.9, significant at the .05 level; $s_{\bar{t}} = .57$
6. $t = 6.23$; critical value of $t = 2.660$
7. $F_{max} = 2.78$; F observed = 3.81; $s_{\bar{t}} = 1.414$
8. Significant at .05 (two-tailed test); $\Sigma T = 37.5$
9. No significant difference
10. Observed $t = 3.125$; critical $t = 2.660$
11. $F = 4.50$; critical F value = 2.33; there is a significant difference between means; $s_{\bar{t}} = .83$
12. $t = 4.31$; critical value of $t = 1.671$; reject H_0

Chapter 9

1. (b) 14.416 (c) df = 1
   (d) 3.841 (e) Reject H_0
2. (a) 11.281
   (b) 6.635
   (c) df = 1
   (d) There is a significant attitude change.
3. (a) No significant difference between groups
   (b) Critical Z = + or - 2.58; Z observed = -.35
4. (a) 42.38 (approximately)
   (b) 12.592
   (c) Reject H_0
   (d) No; cannot be applied to tables larger than 2×2
   (e) df = 6
   (f) k-sample chi-square test

5. (a) $Q = 5.67$
   (b) No significant difference at .01
   (c) 11.345
   (d) df = 3
   (e) Chi-square distribution
7. (a) Chi square observed = 5.714; critical value = 6.635; not significant
   (b) 1 df
8. (a) The chi-square value becomes smaller.
   (b) 25 to 75
9. (a) $P_c = .012$ (one-tailed); .024 (two tailed)
   (b) Three probabilities

Chapter 10

1. (a) $P = .095$ (not significant)
2. (a) Groups are not significantly different at .05.
3. (a) There are significant differences between the observed and expected distributions at the .05 level.
4. (a) Not significantly different; smaller $U = 34$
5. (a) $k = 4$; $N = 9$; df = 3; chi-square distribution; the $\chi_r^2 = 20.6$, the critical value = 7.815
6. (a) Significant difference exists at .05.
   (b) .235
7. (a) H observed = 25.701; critical H value = 9.210
   (c) df = 2
   (d) Chi-square distribution
8. (a) Significant difference at the .05 level
   (b) df = 3
9. $Z = -3.67$ (significant at .05)

Chapter 11

1. (a) Gamma = .59
2. (a) $r_s = .54$
3. (a) $d_{yx} = .26; d_{xy} = .25$
4. (a) $r = -.34$
5. (a) Phi = .63
   (b) $C = .55$
   (d) Lambda = .61
6. (a) Theta = .33
7. (a) Eta = .18
8. (a) Tau = .36
9. (a) Phi = .11
   (b) $r_{tet} = .21$

Chapter 12

1. $r_{12.3} = .40$
2. (a) $W = .44$
3. $R_{1.23} = .48$
4. $W = .09$

Author Index

Subject Index